Macmillan Professional Masters

Torts

MACMILLAN LAW MASTERS

Series Editor: Marise Cremona

Business Law (2nd edn) Stephen Judge
Company Law (3rd edn) Janet Dine
Constitutional and Administrative Law (3rd edn) John Alder
Contract Law (3rd edn) Ewan McKendrick
Conveyancing (3rd edn) Priscilla Sarton
Criminal Law (2nd edn) Jonathan Herring and Marise Cremona
Employment Law (3rd edn) Deborah J. Lockton
Environmental Law and Ethics John Alder and David Wilkinson
Evidence Raymond Emson
Family Law (2nd edn) Kate Standley
Housing Law and Policy David Cowan
Intellectual Property Law Tina Hart and Linda Fazzani
Land Law (3rd edn) Kate Green
Landlord and Tenant Law (3rd edn) Margaret Wilkie and Godfrey Cole
Law of the European Union (2nd edn) Jo Shaw
Law of Succession Catherine Rendell
Law of Trusts Patrick McLoughlin and Catherine Rendell
Legal Method (3rd edn) Ian McLeod
Legal Theory Ian McLeod
Social Security Law Robert East
Torts (2nd edn) Alastair Mullis and Ken Oliphant

Torts

Alastair Mullis
Lecturer in Law at King's College
University of London

and

Ken Oliphant
Lecturer in Law at King's College
University of London

Law series editor: Marise Cremona
Senior Fellow, Centre for Commercial Law Studies
Queen Mary and Westfield College, University of London

First edition 1993
Reprinted twice
Second edition 1997
Published by
MACMILLAN PRESS LTD
Houndmills, Basingstoke, Hampshire RG21 6XS
and London
Companies and representatives
throughout the world

ISBN 0-333-71903-4

A catalogue record for this book is available
from the British Library.

Copy-edited and typeset by Povey-Edmondson
Tavistock and Rochdale, England

10   9   8   7   6   5   4
06   05   04   03   02   01   00   99

Printed in Malaysia

Contents

Preface

Torts make headline news. From mass disasters like Hillsborough and King's Cross to scandal-mongering in the popular press, torts are seldom far from the front pages. Yet, despite its human interest, the law of torts is notoriously difficult for students.

We aim in this book to provide an accessible introduction to the law of torts. We cover the basic principles of the law and examine them in the context of those torts which most commonly feature in degree courses. In doing so, we hope to stimulate thought about the complexities of the subject and about the law's role in society.

In this second edition, we have extensively revised the section on negligence in order to take account of crucial recent decisions in relation to nervous shock, economic loss and the liability of local authorities; important caselaw developments elsewhere have also been incorporated. New legislation considered includes the Damages Act 1996, the Defamation Act 1996 and the Prevention of Harassment Act 1997.

In preparing the new edition, we have benefitted greatly from discussions with many of our colleagues at King's and we thank them for their help and encouragement. We are also indebted to our external reader for his constructive criticisms. Others to whom we are grateful include Keith Povey and John Winckler. Alastair Mullis's special thanks are due to Camilla, Lara and Max for their love and support.

As in the first edition, 'he' and 'she' are used in alternating parts of the book to indicate persons of both genders.

We have endeavoured to state the law on the material available to us on 1 July 1997.

ALASTAIR MULLIS
KEN OLIPHANT

Table of Cases

Table of Statutes

1 Introduction

1.1 **What Is a Tort?**

'Tort' is the French word for wrong. (Other terms derived from this root are the adjective 'tortious', the adverb 'tortiously' and 'tortfeasor', the name for one who commits a tort.) Yet, just as all dogs are animals but not all animals are dogs, so all torts are wrongs but not all wrongs are torts. To make sense of this conundrum, we must distinguish (a) civil wrongs from criminal wrongs; (b) equitable civil wrongs from common law civil wrongs; and (c) the different varieties of common law civil wrongs, some of them known as 'torts', some going under different names.

Criminal and Civil Wrongs

If I punch you in the face, that is both a crime and a civil wrong (both the crime and the tort of battery). The one event gives rise to two legal responses. First, I may be prosecuted by the state for committing the criminal offence and, if found guilty by the court, made to pay a fine to the state, or sent to prison or punished in some other way. Secondly, I may be sued by you in the civil courts (the County Courts or the High Court) and, if found liable, ordered to pay you a sum of money (damages) or to change my behaviour in the future (by an injunction). Unlike criminal proceedings, civil actions are brought by individuals, not (generally) the state. Furthermore, it is those individuals, again not the state, who stand to benefit directly from a court judgment against the defendant. Because of this, and because the defendant who is held liable is not exposed to the stigma of a criminal conviction, civil actions are possible in many circumstances in which no criminal liability arises. It should be noted, however, that not all crimes give rise to concurrent tortious liability: this is true especially of so-called victimless crimes (e.g. possession of drugs) which have no effect upon other people.

Some would press the distinction between criminal and civil law further and say that the criminal law is designed to punish the defendant while the civil law aims only to vindicate the plaintiff's rights, but we should not pursue doctrinal purity at the expense of practical convenience. Medieval English law certainly knew no such purity. Criminal proceedings were originally instituted by individuals, for the law enforcement arm of the state did not develop until much later. Furthermore, many proceedings we would now recognise as civil were at least semi-criminal in character: the unsuccessful defendant would be punished as well as being obliged to pay damages, while the defendant who failed to appear in court would not only lose her case but would also be liable to arrest and imprisonment (see Maitland, 1936, pp. 39–40). In view of these beginnings, and of the pragmatic nature of English lawyers throughout history, it is no surprise that the modern criminal and civil law borrow elements from each other. Thus a criminal court may order the guilty party to pay compensation to the victim under s. 35 of the Powers of Criminal Courts Act 1973 as well as passing a criminal sentence. Conversely, the damages awarded by a civil court may include a punitive element designed not to vindicate the plaintiff's rights but to punish the defendant for her wrongdoing (see 22.2).

Equitable and Common Law Wrongs

Within the category of civil wrongs, history obliges us to make a fundamental distinction between wrongs at common law and wrongs in equity (see Baker, 1990, ch. 6). Before 1875, two distinct court systems existed side by side. The first to evolve had been the common law courts of the King's Bench and Common Pleas. The law applied in these courts was embodied in the 'forms of action', the verbal formulas written on the 'writs' purchased from the Chancellor's office (the Chancery) which authorised citizens to commence an action. In order to mount successful proceedings, litigants of the period had to ensure that the form of words inscribed on the writ matched the substance of their complaint. In the case of the writ of trespass to the person, for example, this required them to establish that, in the florid language of the writ, they had been beaten, wounded and maltreated by force and arms, against the King's peace. With the passage of time, the forms of action became more or less set in stone. Such rigidity in the law led to injustice because litigants were denied the remedy they deserved simply because none of the existing forms of action covered their case.

It was to remedy this injustice that the equitable jurisdiction was developed. (The common law's response to the same problem was to recognise the flexible 'action on the case'; even this did not go far enough and the writ system was finally abolished by the Judicature Act 1873.) Some of the victims of such injustice took to petitioning the King for help, and in time these petitions came to be passed on to the Chancellor who proved willing in some cases to grant relief when the common law provided no remedy. The grant of this relief was at first purely discretionary, but after a while a body of established rules and principles evolved. A primary concern of these rules was to lay down the circumstances under which property, whose official 'legal' title was held by one person, should be held on trust for another. They thus laid the foundation for our modern law of trusts. For present purposes, the rules are significant for their recognition of a class of equitable wrongs. Examples of equitable wrongs might include an employee 'stealing' a trade secret from her employer in the hope of selling it to a rival, or a company director accepting a bribe to ensure that the company enters into contracts with a particular supplier. The remedies that equity gave in respect of these wrongs differed from the normal common law remedy of damages: the employee might be subjected to an injunction forbidding her to pass on the trade secret to anyone else, while the company director might be required to 'account for' (hand over) the value of the bribe she received.

This equitable jurisdiction, and these equitable remedies, grew up outside the common law courts; however, the Judicature Act 1875 'fused' the two separate systems so that, from that time on, both common law and equitable principles were applied by the same courts. Nevertheless, and despite the views of many judges who – like Lord Diplock in *United Scientific Holdings Ltd v. Burnley Borough Council* [1978] AC 904 – believe that 'the waters of the confluent streams of law and equity have surely mingled now', most commentators continue to regard breach of equitable duty as entirely distinct from the civil wrongs at common law (cf. North, 1972). The result is not only that the subjects are treated in different textbooks (breach of equitable duty being consigned to books on equity and trusts), but also that certain equitable remedies, particularly the account of profits made by a wrongdoer, are generally held not to be available in respect of common law wrongs (cf. Birks, 1991).

Torts and Other Common Law Wrongs

Common law wrongs themselves come in different varieties, breach of contract, tort and unjust enrichment being the most familiar. This subdivision of the common law wrongs was unknown to the early common law and only took shape closer in time to the modern era when lawyers looked to impose some order on the many disparate forms of action that history had bequeathed them (see Baker, 1990, pp. 454–5). Their first move was to seize upon a body of law dealing with undertakings or promises and, sharply differentiating breach of promise from other forms of wrong, to develop a set of rules that we recognise today as our law of contract. A comparable, and ongoing, endeavour has been the attempt to formulate a law of unjust enrichment by drawing together a variety of causes of action, many of which had previously been considered to be rather anomalous appendages to the law of contract, torts or equity (see Birks, 1985). The common element of such cases is that the defendant has acquired a benefit which the law requires her to surrender to the plaintiff. The law of tort is what is left behind after cases of breach of contract and unjust enrichment have been withdrawn from the list of common law wrongs and may be accurately described as 'our residual category of civil liability' (Gilmore, 1974, p. 87).

1.2 The Classification of Torts

The status of the law of tort as our residual category of civil liability means that it consists of a 'rag-bag' of disparate cases which very often have little connection with one another. This fact makes efforts to elaborate general principles of the law of tort, in order to match the general principles of the law of contract which have been developed over the years, fraught with difficulty. The considerations raised by a road traffic accident are very different from those raised by a smear campaign of a public figure conducted in the popular press, which in turn are very different from those raised by industrial action taken by disgruntled employees. All these incidents might lead to liability in the law of tort, but it would be impossible to apply the same principles in relation to each. So when we turn to modern works on the law of tort, we find chapters dealing with principles said to be common to all torts intermixed with discussions of the divergent rules applicable to different kinds of case. These rules are generally listed under the name of a particular tort, but they may come under a heading under which a number of different torts are grouped together. These groupings may be justified on the grounds that the torts are all relevant in a particular context (e.g. 'Liability for Land and Structures'), that they all serve to protect a particular interest (e.g. 'Interests in Reputation'), that they can all be traced back to one of the early common law's forms of action (e.g. 'Trespass'), or that they share a common mental element (e.g. 'Intentional Wrongs').

The different torts that we can identify today often overlap with one another in their application. They are a mixture of 'hand-me-downs' from the age of the forms of action, abolished by the Judicature Act 1873, whose names recall the names of the original writs (e.g. trespass), and later creations, both judicial and legislative. These later judicial creations were attempts to draw together different instances of liability recognised under the old forms of action. The most notable of these is the tort of negligence, which united a variety of instances of liability for damage caused by negligence and was recognised as a fully-fledged tort in its own right in 1932 (see 2.1). Since that time it has done the work of a number of the older torts and has become the favoured head of claim for many plaintiffs, being the purest expression recognised by the law of the moral notion that wrongdoers should pay for their wrongs.

1.3 The Organisation of This Book

This book conforms to type in giving separate treatment to the general principles of tortious liability (Part V) and to the various discrete torts (Parts I–IV). In dealing with the latter, we start with the tort of negligence (Part I) which merits this prime position by virtue of its present practical importance and its tendency with the passage of time to subsume the other torts under its mantle. When we come to dealing with the remaining torts, we make no pretence of completeness: this is a student book and the torts covered in depth are those that typically feature in tort courses in university. We have omitted detailed coverage of areas of the law that are generally found in the syllabuses of other subjects (thus conversion has been left to the commercial lawyers and intimidation, conspiracy, etc., to courses on labour law). Despite these exclusions, we have been left with a wide-ranging though ramshackle body of law, as befits tort law's status as the great dustbin of civil liability.

To impose some order on this expanse of materials, we have looked at the various torts in terms of the interests they may be said primarily to protect, dealing in turn with interests in the person and personal property (Part II), interests in land (Part III) and interests in reputation and privacy (Part IV). We preface our discussion of the torts selected under each heading with a few words on the extent to which negligence provides protection in each area, and on the continuing importance of the other torts in furnishing additional relief. One major interest has been largely omitted: that in financial well-being. As financial well-being is largely dependent on one's ability to exploit one's labour, goods and land, it is protected by those torts that provide relief in respect of physical interference with the person and personal property (Part II) and with land (Part III). Other torts provide relief even where there has been no physical interference with these interests, as where *I pass off* my goods as yours so that I can sell at a better price or where *I conspire* with militant workers to picket your factory and cause you to cease trading by *intimidating* you with threats of personal violence. The torts of passing off, conspiracy, intimidation and the like are omitted for the reason given above, namely that they are best left to be considered in depth in other, more specialised works. Liability in respect of pure economic loss sustained as a result of another's negligence is, however, dealt with in the chapters on negligence (see ch. 5).

Summary

1.1 A tort is a civil, as opposed to criminal, wrong. The category of civil wrongs contains breaches of contract and equitable wrongs as well as torts.
1.2 Different torts deal with different types of wrongful conduct and developed, often haphazardly, over the course of time. This makes it difficult, if not impossible, to identify general principles about the law of tort.
1.3 In this book, we look at (a) the tort of negligence, the most important tort in both theory and practice; (b) a selection of other torts arranged according to the interest they primarily protect; and (c) such general principles as do exist.

Part I

The Tort of Negligence

2 Negligence: Introduction

2.1 **Origins**

It all began in August 1928. The scene was Minchella's cafe in Paisley, near Glasgow. A certain Mrs Donoghue had gone in for a drink. This is her story: a friend bought her a bottle of ginger beer; she began to drink it; then, as her friend topped up her tumbler, she watched in horror as the decomposed remnants of a snail floated out with the ginger beer; she suffered shock and an upset stomach. Now Mrs Donoghue's injuries may seem of less than earth-shattering importance to us today, but it is to these unlikely beginnings that the modern law of negligence owes its existence. Mrs Donoghue, unable to sue Minchella in the law of contract because she had not bought the bottle herself (there was no 'privity of contract'), brought an action in tort against the manufacturer, Stevenson. She alleged that he had been negligent in producing the drink. In response, Stevenson denied that those injured by a negligently manufactured product had any right to recover damages outside certain exceptional categories (e.g. inherently or patently dangerous products like firearms). The case reached the House of Lords, which found in favour of Mrs Donoghue. It was not a unanimous decision: two powerful dissents were registered. Neither was the decision of the majority clear and unambiguous in every respect: was it to be a rule confined to defective products or was it to have wider effect? Today, however, its status is unquestioned and its effect plain for all to see, for *Donoghue* v. *Stevenson* [1932] AC 562 is the case that changed the face of the law of negligence.

Up to that time, liability for negligent conduct had been recognised only in certain carefully defined circumstances, for example where innkeepers were careless in looking after property in guests' rooms or where fire damage resulted from negligence. The courts allowed actions for damages in these cases because – they said – the special circumstances gave rise to a 'duty of care'. The significance of *Donoghue* v. *Stevenson*, and of Lord Atkin's speech in particular, was that it sought to unify these disparate duties of care in a single general theory. Lord Atkin noted (pp. 579–80) that the courts had previously been 'engaged upon an elaborate classification of duties' as they existed in various fact situations, and urged them to recognise that 'the duty which is common to all the cases where liability is established must logically be based upon some element common to the cases where it is found to exist'. He continued:

'[I]n English law there must be and is some general conception of relations giving rise to a duty of care, of which the particular cases found in the books are but instances. The liability for negligence . . . is no doubt based upon a general public sentiment of moral wrongdoing for which the offender must pay. But acts or omissions which any moral code would censure cannot in a practical world be treated so as to give a right to every person injured by them to demand relief. In this way rules of law arise which limit the range of complainants and the extent of their remedy. The rule that you are to love your neighbour becomes in law: You must not injure your neighbour, and the lawyer's question: Who is my neighbour? receives a restricted reply. You must take reasonable care to avoid acts or omissions which you can reasonably foresee would be likely to injure your neighbour. Who then, in law, is my neighbour? The answer seems to be persons who are so closely and directly affected by my act that I ought reasonably to have them in contemplation as being so affected when I am directing my mind to the acts or omissions which are called in question.'

2.2 **The Elements of the Tort of Negligence**

Negligence is a common word, used to refer to a species of fault, and it is often treated as synonymous with 'carelessness'. But since *Donoghue* v. *Stevenson* it has also become the name of a self-contained tort with its own internal framework of rules. The elements of liability in the tort of negligence can be outlined as follows:

(a) the defendant must owe the plaintiff a *duty of care*;
(b) the defendant must be in *breach* of that duty (i.e. she must be careless or negligent);
(c) this must *cause* the plaintiff loss;
(d) that loss must not be too *remote* (i.e. it must be foreseeable);
(e) the defendant must not be able to raise any *defence* to the plaintiff's claim.

This list of requirements makes it plain that it can be misleading simply to talk of liability for negligence. In the first place, in negligence (which is descended from the action on the case and is not a form of trespass) damage is the gist of the action; there is no liability for negligence 'in the air', only for negligently causing harm. Secondly, *factual responsibility* for negligently causing harm cannot be equated with *legal responsibility*: it is not every harmful result of one's negligence for which one must pay damages. Although Lord Atkin appealed in his 'neighbour principle' to our moral intuitions which suggest that there should be general recognition of tortious liability for harm caused by negligence, he himself stressed the need for 'rules of law . . . which limit the range of complainants and the extent of their remedy'. Legal responsibility is thus determined by the concepts of the duty of care and remoteness of damage (and to a certain extent also causation), and by the law relating to defences. Because they have the function of limiting legal responsibility for negligently inflicting injury, those concepts and the various defences can be thought of as limitation mechanisms or control devices in the tort of negligence, keeping liability for (factual) negligence within acceptable bounds.

The distinction between questions of factual and legal responsibility is not clear-cut – even the factual questions of negligence, i.e. breach of duty, and causation are determined within a framework of legal principle, while the 'duty' question raises factual issues of foreseeability and not just issues of law – but it is nevertheless useful for pedagogical purposes. It also has great practical importance, even in a modern system in which questions of fact are determined by a judge rather than a jury. First, questions of law may be dealt with in preliminary proceedings in advance of trial of the factual issues, thereby saving unnecessary expense in calling witnesses, compiling expert reports, etc. (especially where it transpires that the plaintiff has no case in law). A very common example of this is the striking-out application, in which the defendant makes a pre-emptive attack against the plaintiff's claim, contending that it would reveal no arguable case in law even if the plaintiff were to make out all the factual allegations; typically the assertion is that there was no duty of care. Secondly, rights of appeal are more extensive in relation to questions of law than questions of fact. Although many of the key questions of what we have been calling 'factual' responsibility in reality relate to *inferences* from primary facts (e.g. as to whether the case exercised by the defendant was reasonable), and can hence be attacked on grounds other than that they were 'plainly wrong', the judge's conclusions on such questions are entitled to respect and should not be rejected simply because the appellate court might itself have rule differently. Conversely, in relations to questions of law, the appellate court must impose its own view. The treatment of certain preconditions of liability, especially that of 'duty', as questions of law rather than fact enables appellate courts to keep the scope of liability within acceptable bounds, not only by overruling errant decisions but also and more importantly by setting down binding guidelines for use in subsequent cases.

2.3 Negligence: A Developing Tort

In terms of legal history, the tort of negligence is of comparatively recent birth and it remains in its adolescence. It lacks many of the characteristics of a mature system of law, most notably a settled conceptual apparatus and a set of reasonably clear boundaries. In many areas, the question whether liability may arise has yet to be determined. Courts encountering unprecedented claims must grapple with concepts (of duty, causation, remoteness, etc.) which all too often lack any fixed meaning and all too rarely provide a clear answer as to whether a claim should be allowed. This has produced a certain scepticism about the way judges decide cases in the tort of negligence. Some feel that conceptual language is used inconsistently and instrumentally, in order to give an aura of legal respectability to decisions reached on non-legal (policy) grounds. The following, typically bold expression of this view comes from a judgment of that leading judicial sceptic, Lord Denning:

> 'The truth is that all these three, duty, remoteness and causation, are all devices by which the courts limit the range of liability for negligence . . . As I said recently . . . "it is not every consequence of a wrongful act which is the subject of compensation." The law has to draw a line somewhere. Sometimes it is done by limiting the range of persons to whom a duty is owed. Sometimes it is done by saying that there is a break in the chain of causation. At other times it is done by saying that the consequence is too remote to be a head of damage. All these devices are useful in their way. But ultimately it is a question of policy for the judges to decide.' (*Lamb* v. *Camden LBC* [1981] QB 625, 636)

Lord Denning perhaps puts his case too strongly, for it would be wrong to suggest that judges feel free to disregard rules laid down in previous cases and to impose whatever solution they feel is warranted in terms of public policy. Nevertheless, his words stand as a useful indication of the imprecision that surrounds the use of the key concepts in the tort of neligence and of the scope that this imprecision allows for judges to give effect to policy choices.

We should not ignore, however, the extent to which there exists a bedrock of settled principle in the modern law of negligence. The typical cases of everyday legal practice – cases of accidents on the roads or at the workplace – give rise to few legal difficulties: the issue between the parties is more likely to concern questions of fact than questions of law. In this, the 'core' area of negligence, the law is simplicity itself: the person who carelessly injures the person or property of another is liable to compensate for that loss. *Factual* responsibility is equated with *legal* responsibility. Only when we move from the core to peripheral areas of the tort – to cases involving more problematic forms of loss, or omissions rather than positive acts, etc. – do the principles become more complex as the courts struggle to contain liability within acceptable bounds, to limit the scope of *legal* responsibility for *factually* causing harm through a lack of care. Here the language of the law reports becomes more abstract and conceptual, and it is difficult to discriminate between the technical-legal employment of certain terms and their purely rhetorical use. In some cases technical-legal definitions of some precision do in fact exist, or may at least be posited, albeit that they can only be identified after stripping away several layers of unnecessary and unrevealing abstraction (see especially the discussion of 'proximity' at 3.5). Elsewhere, however, especially where a case presents novel features, the analysis may amount to no more than a vague appeal to what is reasonable in the circumstances (see 3.6). This perhaps is inevitable in an area of law that is still relatively young and that continues to develop rapidly, and, far from being cause for exasperation or despair, accounts in large measure for the fascination of the subject, for study of the modern law of negligence inevitably entails a creative engagement with the principles of justice and the concerns of public policy that shape the law in the light of changing social conditions.

2.4 The Objectives of Negligence Law

Negligence law may be seen as embodying the principle of corrective justice, i.e. that one who wrongfully causes another harm should correct that injustice by the payment of compensation (see especially Weinrib, 1995). But, although the 'righting of wrongs' must be regarded as the central tenet of the tort of negligence (and perhaps of all liability in private law), it is possible to identify certain secondary objectives which serve to temper the law's pursuit of its goal of corrective justice; to see the modern law of negligence as concerned purely with corrective justice is to pay scant regard to its vibrant complexity. The law is shaped not only by 'principle' but also by considerations of public policy which fluctuate in the light of changing social conditions.

A number of secondary objectives may be posited for the tort of negligence: vindication of the plaintiff's rights, denunciation of the defendant's wrong, education of people generally as to proper standards of safety, the peaceful settlement of disputes arising from the accidental infliction of injury, etc. (for a review, see Williams, 1951). But the two most often cited objectives of negligence law are compensation and deterrence, and it is these that we now proceed to consider in more detail.

Compensation

The provision of compensation is so central to the tort of negligence that it is often regarded as *the* objective of the tort, rather than just as one of its policies. Yet it is helpful to view it as one of many policies pursued in the tort of negligence, for this emphasises that in some circumstances the goal of compensation may be outweighed by other, competing considerations.

It is important to be clear what we mean when we talk of compensation. 'Compensation' is the goal both of the tort of negligence and of the social security system, but the meaning of the term varies according to the context. In the former, it is part of a regime of corrective justice; in the latter, part of a regime of distributive justice. This is reflected in two ways. First, the payment of compensation in negligence depends on a finding that the plaintiff's loss was caused by fault. In the context of social security, fault is generally irrelevant. Thus we can say that, whereas tort damages are awarded as a matter of individual responsibility, social security benefits are paid as a matter of social responsibility. Secondly, the amount of compensation paid differs according to the context. Damages are designed to compensate for *loss*: the sum awarded is that needed to restore the plaintiff, as nearly as possible, to the position she would have been in but for the defendant's negligence. Social security benefits, in contrast, aim to compensate for *need*, and benefits are generally limited to the amount necessary to sustain the recipient at an acceptable standard of living.

This is not to say that there has been no cross-fertilisation between the notions of compensation adopted in negligence and social security respectively. Entitlement to social security payments may depend on proof that the claimant's injuries were caused by someone else's fault. This is the case under the Criminal Injuries Compensation Scheme, which provides for the payment of compensation in respect of personal injury attributable to a criminal offence, the arrest of a suspect or the prevention of crime. Awards, formerly assessed in the same way as common law damages, are now made according to a scale of tariffs but remain broadly comparable to damages in terms of size and can be seen as compensating for loss rather than need (see Criminal Justice Act 1995). It is also conceivable that social security benefits should be earnings-related rather than flat-rate (as has in the past been the case), and to that extent should compensate for loss rather than need, but the current political desire to constrain public expenditure and encourage private provision against the misfortunes of life has resulted in the abolition of the earnings-related components of such benefits (see Ogus *et al.*, 1995, pp. 20–21).

Conversely, concerns of social responsibility that underpin the compensation objectives of the social security system have also had an influence on the development of the law of tort, both in the tort of negligence and elsewhere. Certain tort doctrines (the vicarious liability of employers for the torts of their employees, see ch. 21; liability for the breach of strict statutory duties imposed in the workplace, ch. 15) serve to direct losses away from individuals towards defendants whose 'deep pockets' can easily bear the cost, irrespective of whether they were personally at fault. The influence of such considerations is evident within the tort of negligence itself, notably in the observed tendency of the courts to characterise blameless and inevitable slips as negligence in contexts in which liability insurance is widespread (see 8.3). It is also evident in relation to many recent attempts to expand the scope of the duty of care into areas in which popular sentiment has it that the 'victim' should take responsibility for what has occurred. Thus the so-called 'socks' school of psychiatry expresses scepticism about the expansion of liability for psychiatric illness, relying upon its defining tenet that sufferers are best left to 'pull their socks up' (cf. ch. 4). The recognition of duties to protect plaintiffs from third parties, or even from themselves, has also led to claims that we are undermining individual responsibility and inculcating a 'pass the buck' mentality in a 'something for nothing' society (cf. ch. 6). All in all, according to some commentators, we have developed 'a culture of complaintiffs' (Weir, 1996, p. vi).

This popular backlash against the increasing modern tendency to 'pass the buck' and 'chase the bucks' should not, however, divert attention away from society's need to develop a humane, efficient and coherent system of compensating those whose suffering and needs warrant redress. We may doubt whether principles of tort law, in which negligence plays the central role, properly merit a place in such a system. Tort may be seen adrift in the 'high Cs' – costly, cumbersome, confrontational and capricious. It is too expensive, takes too long, concerns itself with 'winning' rather than 'justice', and limits compensation to those injured by another's fault (denying it to the victims of 'pure' accidents regardless of the severity of their condition or the extent of their needs). Perhaps compensation should be regarded as a matter exclusively of social responsibility, and the relevant principles of tort law swept away to make space for the introduction of a 'no-fault' compensation scheme offering real compensation to all those suffering from disability. We return to such questions, and consider them in more detail, in ch. 12.

Deterrence

Doubts as to negligence's success as a mechanism of compensation has prompted some to seek an alternative justification for it in the goal of deterrence (see Cane, 1993, pp. 361–94). They argue that negligence has a major role to play in the prevention of accidents as actual and potential liability costs encourage people to take care in what they do and drive them away from activities that are fraught with unnecessary danger. Thus, if a manufacturer of fizzy drinks thinks that the installation of an Acme Patent Snailguard on her bottling line will reduce the risk of consumers suffering food poisoning, and hence reduce her liability costs, she will have an incentive to go ahead and have one fitted. And if she finds that she still cannot produce the drink without an unacceptable risk of food poisoning, the liabilities she incurs may force her to raise her prices to an extent that she is no longer be able to compete in the market ('market deterrence': see Calabresi, 1970, ch. 5). Nowadays, these arguments are most often made by lawyer-economists, who view the law as a series of incentives designed to promote a state of economic efficiency in which the wealth of society is maximised; the function of negligence thus becomes 'the deterrence of *inefficient* accidents' (Posner, 1992, p. 202; emphasis added). Looking at the law exclusively in these terms is regarded by many as morally disreputable, because it pays no heed to individual rights, which ought not to be sacrificed in the public interest (see Dworkin, 1986, ch. 8). In any case, attempts to evaluate the law of negligence in terms of economic efficiency tend to rely on too many unproven assumptions for them to be of significant practical value (albeit that occasional references to the economic analysis literature will be made in the course of this book).

Again the key question is whether negligence law, and tort law as a whole, performs a deterrent function better than its alternatives. It seems odd at first sight that the threat of liability, which operates indirectly and materialises only where a lack of care results in injury, should be more effective than the 'direct' or 'specific' deterrence achieved by regulation backed up with criminal sanctions; the latter not only allows for liability even where the carelessness fortuitously causes no harm but also enables standards of safe conduct to be specified with a measure of precision quite beyond negligence, where the injunction is simply to take such care as is reasonable in the circumstances. Against this, it may be said that government regulation cannot deal with the complexity and constantly fluctuating circumstances of life and attaches insufficient importance to individual views as to what risks are worth running (see Calabresi, 1970, ch. 6). No conclusive view can be drawn from the evidence on this question (for an excellent survey, see Dewees and Trebilcock, 1992), but it may perhaps be accepted that such evidence as there is at least puts the burden of proof on those who would replace negligence liability for personal injury with a no-fault compensation scheme to show that other mechanisms are in fact apt to maintain the standards of safety that modern society demands.

Summary

2.1   In *Donoghue* v. *Stevenson*, the House of Lords recognised for the first time a general rule of liability for harm caused by negligence. As a result, it became possible to talk of a tort of negligence.

2.2   Notwithstanding this general rule, liability for the consequences of carelessness is limited by the requirements of the duty of care, causation and remoteness, and by the various defences that the defendant might raise.

2.3   The tort of negligence is of comparatively recent birth and it is still developing; the precise scope of liability for negligence is still uncertain in a number of key respects.

2.4   Negligence law reflects the principle of corrective justice, but it has been shaped by a variety of competing social policies (e.g. deterrence of accidents, compensation of the victims of accidents).

Exercises

2.1   What was the significance of *Donoghue* v. *Stevenson*?

2.2   In addition to showing that the defendant was in fact negligent, what else must the plaintiff in a negligence action establish?

2.3   What is the difference between 'policy' and 'principle'? Should judges be concerned with both?

2.4   What impact has the desire to compensate the needy had on the development of the tort of negligence? Why should the courts ever want to deny the claim to compensation of someone injured by another's negligence?

2.5   What role might the tort of negligence have in accident prevention? Is there a danger of going too far?.

3 The Duty of Care Concept

3.1 The Nature of the Duty of Care Concept

Not every instance of carelessness resulting in harm will lead to liability in the tort of negligence. Liability is limited by reference to various 'control devices' (see 2.2) of which the most significant is the duty of care. The existence of a duty of care is a precondition of liability in negligence; it is what transforms *factual* responsibility for carelessly causing harm into *legal* responsibility.

In most cases encountered in practice – e.g. cases of foreseeable physical injury suffered in accidents at work or on the roads – the existence of a duty of care is clearly established by the authorities (see *Alcock* v. *Chief Constable of South Yorkshire Police* [1992] 1 AC 310, 396). The only question will be whether the defendant was *in fact* negligent (in breach of duty). In such cases, the moral imperative expressed by Lord Atkin in his 'neighbour principle' points towards liability on the part of the person at fault. But other cases are not so simple. Deviation from the 'typical' case of physical injury caused by positive act, by one private individual to another, may necessitate a more cautious approach to the imposition of liability and bring the duty of care issue 'into play'. There may be doubts as to whether the loss of which the plaintiff complains should be recoverable (especially in cases of nervous shock or pure economic loss). Alternatively, the doubts might concern the way in which the plaintiff's loss was caused (especially where it was caused by the defendant's statement or omission). Or they might be associated with the identity of the plaintiff or the defendant.

The duty of case concept marks out these cases – the 'atypical' cases – in which it cannot be taken for granted that the defendant should pay compensation for carelessly caused harm. And it determines whether the special circumstances of these cases are sufficient to outweigh the plaintiff's moral claim to compensation. Hence the concept's role is essentially negative. As Lord Goff stated in *Smith* v. *Littlewoods Organisation Ltd* [1987] 1 AC 241, 270, 'nowadays . . . the broad general principle of liability for foreseeable damage is so widely applicable that the function of the duty of care is not so much to identify cases where liability is imposed as to identify those where it is not.' The duty of care question is raised in order to deny liability even where the defendant was at fault, and even if that fault caused the plaintiff harm. To deny the existence of a duty of care is to afford an immunity from liability no matter how culpable the defendant's carelessness and no matter how severe the plaintiff's injury.

3.2 **Testing the Existence of a Duty of Care**

How do we know when a duty of care will be recognised? The courts have wavered between different approaches to this question. In *Caparo Industries* v. *Dickman* [1990] 2 AC 605, 616, Lord Bridge described the 'traditional' approach as follows:

> 'Traditionally the law find the existence of the duty in different specific situations each exhibiting its own particular characteristics. In this way the law has identified a wide variety of duty situations, all falling within the ambit of the tort of negligence, but sufficiently distinct to require separate definition of the essential ingredients by which the existence of the duty is to be recognised.'

From the time of *Donoghue* v. *Stevenson* onwards, however, the courts began to find the traditional approach wanting. It lacked any basis in principle for determining whether the frontiers of liability should be pushed forward or the *status quo* maintained. So judges sought to identify the principles by which the existence of a duty of care could be determined.

The most celebrated of such attempts was made by Lord Wilberforce in delivering the opinion of the House of Lords in *Anns* v. *London Borough of Merton* [1978] 1 AC 728, 751–2. He laid down a two-stage test of the existence of a duty of care:

> 'First one has to ask whether, as between the alleged wrongdoer and the person who has suffered damage, there is a sufficient relationship of proximity or neighbourhood such that, in the reasonable contemplation of the former, carelessness on his part may be likely to cause damage to the latter, in which case a prima facie duty of care arises. Secondly, if the first question is answered affirmatively, it is necessary to consider whether there are any considerations which ought to negative, or to reduce or limit, the scope of the duty or the class of person to whom it is owed or the damages to which a breach of it may give rise.'

The most natural interpretation of this passage is that it lays down a presumption of liability where the defendant, in the circumstances in which she found herself, *ought to have foreseen* injury to the plaintiff. This will be a question of fact to be determined by the judge in every case. The judge then has to decide whether to decline to allow recovery on grounds of public policy. This interpretation of Lord Wilberforce's words found favour for some time and judges soon began to adopt them enthusiastically as a simple test of liability in negligence. More recently, however, the courts have expressed dissatisfaction with this way of proceeding and have sought to return to the more traditional approach (see 3.3).

So what was wrong with Lord Wilberforce's two-stage test? Essentially, the problem was that it provided the springboard for a massive expansion of liability in the late 1970s and early 1980s. The first stage of Lord

Wilberforce's test presented no hurdle to litigants at all: almost everything in life is foreseeable if you have a vivid enough imagination. This meant that the courts were left to restrict the scope of negligence liability by reference to the policy considerations that come in at the second stage of Lord Wilberforce's test. In fact, judges proved unwilling to let matters of public policy stand in the way of their understandable sympathy for the injured plaintiffs in court before them. As Lord Keith subsequently observed:

'[A] too literal application of the well-known observation of Lord Wilberforce in *Anns* . . . may be productive of a failure to have regard to, and to analyse and weigh, all the relevant considerations in considering whether it is appropriate that a duty of care should be imposed' (*Rowling* v. *Takaro Properties Ltd* [1988] 1 AC 473, 501).

In key cases such as *McLoughlin* v. *O'Brian* [1983] 1 AC 410 and *Junior Books* v. *Veitchi Co Ltd* [1983] 1 AC 520 (see 4.2 and 5.3), judges roundly condemned the policy arguments which were said to justify restrictions on liability. The 'floodgates' argument (see 2.5), in particular, was dismissed in cavalier fashion ('I believe that the "floodgates" argument . . . is, as it always has been, greatly exaggerated': *McLoughlin* v. *O'Brian* [1983] 1 AC 410, 442 per Lord Bridge). The results were twofold. First, the courts recognised duties of care in a wide variety of situations that had not previously come before the courts (e.g. in respect of 'wrongful birth': see 7.3). Secondly, and more controversially, judges used the two-stage test as a justification for recognising duties of care whose existence had previously been denied, thereby casting aside restrictions on liability that had been recognised in older cases (particularly in the context of economic loss and omissions). It was this tendency that raised judicial concerns and prompted a 'retreat from *Anns*'. As Lord Brandon commented in *Leigh & Sillivan Ltd* v. *Aliakmon Shipping Co Ltd* [1986] AC 785, 816, it was an error to use the test 'as a means of re-opening issues relating to the existence of a duty of care long settled by past decisions.'

3.3 *Caparo* and the Retreat from *Anns*

Unhappy with the way things were shaping up, the courts have recently sought to reverse many of the developments of the last 20 or so years. This has led to a so-called 'retreat from *Anns*'. In a series of decisions (beginning perhaps with *Peabody Donation Fund* v. *Parkinson* [1985] AC 210), appellate courts have warned against the lazy reliance upon too simple a test of liability, and have sought to reassert limits on the scope of liability that had traditionally been recognised in the caselaw (e.g. in the areas of pure economic loss, nervous shock and omissions). These decisions insist that the questions of 'foreseeability' and 'proximity', apparently run together by Lord Wilberforce, be clearly separated out, and that the concept of 'proximity' be dissected to reveal 'the narrower but still identifiable principles . . . [on the basis of which] . . . liability can properly be imposed' (*Smith* v. *Littlewoods Organisation Ltd* [1987] 1 AC 241, 280 per Lord Goff.

The decisive moment in this trend is the speech of Lord Bridge in *Caparo Industries* v. *Dickman.* He suggested that the courts should abandon 'the modern approach' of looking for a single general principle underlying the tort of negligence and revert to 'the more traditional categorisation of different specific situations as guides to the existence, the scope and limits of the varied duties of care which the law imposes.' His approach depended upon a 'pragmatic' evaluation of the exact circumstances of every individual case, but certain general observations could be made. In a passage of great influence and importance, he explained (pp. 617–18):

'[I]n addition to the foreseeability of damage, necessary ingredients in any situation giving rise to a duty of care are that there should exist between the party owing the duty and the party to whom it is owed a relationship characterised by the law as one of 'proximity' or 'neighbourhood' and that the situation should be one in which the court considers it fair, just and reasonable that the law should impose a duty of a given scope on the one party for the benefit of the other. But . . . the concepts of proximity and fairness embodied in these additional ingredients are not susceptible of any such precise definition as would be necessary to give them utility as practical tests but amount in effect to little more than convenient labels to attach to the features of different specific situations which, on a detailed consideration of all the circumstances, the law recognises pragmatically as giving rise to a duty of care of a given scope.'

Although it appears that Lord Bridge intended in this passage to rule out any simple recourse to a universal formula for determining the existence of a duty of care, subsequent decisions have seen him as laying down a three-stage test for recognition of the duty under which the questions of 'foreseeability', 'proximity' and 'fairness, justice and reason-ableness' replace the two stages of the discredited *Anns* inquiry. This trend is probably too well-established to buck at the present time, but it should be remembered that the so-called '*Caparo* principles' represent no more than useful shorthand in indicating the *types* of factors which determine whether a duty of care will arise. The principles provide a *framework* for inquiry into the existence of the duty by identifying the principal *stages* of that inquiry, but they do not in themselves provide a practical test of the duty; treating them as such is likely to produce the same liability 'beanfeast' as was alleged to follow from *Anns.* The following explanations are an attempt to rationalise the role of the key elements of the *Caparo* principles, although it must be admitted that judicial expressions of opinion on this issue are often inconsistent and that this attempt therefore has elements of prescription as well as mere description.

3.4 Foreseeability

The plaintiff must fall within the class foreseeably put at risk by the defendant's failure to exercise due care and skill. The same requirement is expressed by the principle that the defendant must be in breach of a duty of care owed to the plaintiff rather than to the world at large: what singles the plaintiff out is that she is the foreseeable victim of the defendant's wrong. The rule serves to weed out claims by those whose injury is regarded as far-fetched in much the same way as the *Wagon Mound* rule of remoteness of damage weeds out heads of damage that are unforeseeable consequences of the defendant's negligence (see ch. 10). Like the remoteness rule, the issue it raises is primarily one of fact, and this stage of the duty inquiry may therefore be termed the question of 'factual duty' (cf. Clerk and Lindsell, 1995, para. 7–07).

The most famous elaboration of the principle that only the foreseeable plaintiff can recover damages in negligence is that attempted by Cardozo J in the New York Court of Appeals in *Palsgraf* v. *Long Island Rail Road* 248 NY 339 (1928). The case also provides a memorable example of the principle at work. Mrs Palsgraf was injured while standing on a railway platform. Some distance away, commotion had broken out as a man, running to catch a train that was beginning to move out of the station, was pushed on board by railway employees. The man dropped an innocuous-looking paper package. It contained fireworks and exploded on contact with the ground. The shock waves caused heavy metal scales near to Mrs Palsgraf to topple over and strike her, causing her injury (or were scales merely knocked over in the commotion? See Prosser, 1953.) The majority of the court held that the railway employees owed her no duty of care as she was not a foreseeable victim of their negligence; it was not enough that their negligence exposed others to risk. Cardozo J explained:

'One who seeks redress at law does not make out a cause of action by showing without more that there has been damage to his person. If the harm was not willful [*sic*], he must show that the act as to him had possibilities of danger so many and so apparent as to entitle him to be protected against the doing of it though the harm was unintended. The victim does not sue derivatively, or by right of subrogation, to vindicate an interest invaded in the person of another. He sues for a breach of a duty owing to himself.'

In England, the same sort of analysis was soon to appeal to the House of Lords in the case of *Bourhill* v. *Young* [1943] AC 92. The case arose out of a motorcycle accident. The motorcyclist, John Young, who was killed, had been travelling too fast and had collided with a car a short distance away from where Mrs Bourhill was standing. She was eight months pregnant at the time of the accident and she alleged, in a suit against Young's estate, that hearing the impact and seeing the pool of blood afterwards had caused her to miscarry and to suffer nervous shock. The House of Lords found that Young could not have been expected to foresee that anyone in the position of Mrs Bourhill could be affected. The following words of Lord Wright call to mind the reasoning of Cardozo J (p. 108):

'John Young was certainly negligent in an issue between himself and the owner of the car which he ran into, but it is a different issue whether he was negligent *vis-à-vis* the appellant. She cannot build upon a wrong to someone else. Her interest, which was in her own bodily security, was of a different order from the interest of the owner of the car.'

The requirement of the foreseeable plaintiff has attracted criticism on the grounds that, as between innocent victim and careless injurer, the equities favour the former (see Fleming, 1992, p. 143). It may also be criticised in that the test of foreseeability is easily manipulated and may serve merely to obscure the policy considerations that have caused the courts to develop the law as they have. One learned overseas observer, a former President of the New Zealand Court of Appeal, has detected signs that 'the English Courts are coming to speak of reasonable foresight in a deliberately artificial sense' and has warned of the need to take care lest the concept be 'employed to conceal the fact that the decision is one of policy rather than one as to what was reasonably foreseeable in fact' (*South Pacific Manufacturing Co* v. *New Zealand Security Consultants & Investigations Ltd* [1992] 2 NZLR 282, 295 per Cooke P). This temptation most frequently arises in cases involving so-called 'secondary' victims. Even the most typical of tort cases may involve losses that extend beyond the immediate victim of the tortfeasor. Those who suffer as a result of a car accident may include those injured in rescue attempts, the bystanders who suffer psychiatric illness as a result of witnessing the scenes of carnage, the relatives who have to spend time and money to care for their disabled family members and the taxpayer whose contributions fund the emergency services and the National Health Service (NHS). None of these 'ripple effect' losses can be regarded as far-fetched. Nevertheless, some types of secondary victims (e.g. rescuers) habitually gain compensation in the courts on the grounds that they are foreseeable plaintiffs, while others (e.g. bystanders, like Mrs Bourhill, who suffer nervous shock) are regarded as unforeseeable and have to go without. In fact, this has nothing to do with the probability of loss to the various parties; rather it reflects the law's view of the desert of each and of the consequences of recognising liability. This was seen clearly by Andrews J when, in his dissenting judgment in *Palsgraf*, he derided the manipulation of the foreseeability device in such cases as 'merely an attempt to fit facts to theory'.

The better approach, evident in many recent decisions, is to distinguish such issues of legal policy from the factual duty question, i.e. the question of foreseeability. These issues relate to the question of 'legal' or 'notional' duty (cf. Clerk and Lindsell, 1995, para. 7–07), whose existence determines whether liability is *in principle* capable of arising on facts analogous to those in the present case (given for instance the nature of the plaintiff's loss, the means by which it was caused and the identity of the parties). The legal duty question has two components – 'proximity' and 'fairness, justice and reasonableness' – to which we now turn our attention.

3.5 **Proximity**

The requirement that the plaintiff stand in a relationship of proximity with the defendant is now of central importance in the tort of negligence. Although 'proximity' was once equated with 'reasonable foreseeability' (such that a relationship was presumed to be proximate wherever it was reasonably foreseeable that negligence by one party might cause harm to another: see the discussion of *Anns* above at 3.3), it has now assumed an independent existence, and acts in many cases as the primary determinant of whether a duty of care will arise. Its meaning, however, must be considered elusive. It is not to be interpreted literally as referring to 'closeness' either in time or space; its use is as a legal term of art, but even understood as such it may conceal more than it reveals, for there is a tendency to affirm the presence or absence of proximity on the facts of an individual case without adequate explanation. Accordingly, we may have some sympathy with Weir's wry observation (1991) that 'Proximity is now the key word, though it doesn't open many doors.'

Yet the meaning of proximity need not remain obscure. It is no more than what Lord Bridge described in *Caparo* as a 'convenient label' identifying 'the features of different specific situations which . . . the law reecognises pragmatically as giving rise to a duty of care . . .' (see 3.3). It is an error to regard it as having an immutable core meaning such as to give it utility as a practical test of whether a duty arises; rather it is the generic name for *all* the more specific – and practically useful – tests for the existence of the duty which have been established in different types of case. Different 'proximity principles' will apply in different duty situations. In what we have been calling the 'typical' or 'core' cases of negligence – cases of personal injury caused by the positive act of a private individual – the proximity rules generally add nothing to the requirement of foreseeability (albeit that the question of proximity remains theoretically distinct: see *Marc Rich and Co AG* v. *Bishop Rock Marine Co Ltd, The Nicholas H* [1996] AC 211): it may be said that it is the reasonable foreseeability of injury that establishes the necessary proximity. But as we move towards the problematic peripheral area of the tort – towards cases involving different forms of loss, or an omission rather than a positive act, or some other 'atypical' feature – 'proximity' imposes a more substantial hurdle. For example, where the plaintiff complains of 'nervous shock' as a result of witnessing an accident, a number of new proximity requirements arise: the plaintiff must show a proximate relationship (i.e. a close tie of love and affection) with the 'primary victim' of the accident; she must have been 'proximate' to the accident (literally, this time) in time and space, etc. (see further ch. 4). Equally, in cases where the plaintiff's loss is purely economic, the authorities hold that there can be no proximity between the parties unless the defendant has 'voluntarily assumed responsibility' for the performance of a particular task (see further ch. 5). Here, it is the voluntary assumption of the responsibility that establishes the necessary proximity.

The concept of proximity thus refers to the established legal rules – varying from one duty situation to another – that determine whether liability is *in principle* capable of arising. These rules can only be found in the caselaw, so the first injunction to a negligence lawyer is: 'see how far the authorities have gone' (*Hedley Byrne & Co* v. *Heller and Partners* [1964] AC 465, 526 per Lord Devlin). Analysis of the caselaw need not, of course, reveal a clear answer, for there may be disagreement as to the precise scope of a rule in a particular case (did it depend on factors (a), (b) *and* (c), or just (a) and (b)?). Nevertheless, the court must ultimately take a view on this question, and determine whether or not the authorities conclusively establish the presence or absence of proximity in the case at hand. If the matter is as yet unresolved (e.g. if the case is a novel one), the court must decide whether or not to extend the scope of negligence liability to the new situation. Such an expansion should be allowed only when warranted by considerations of public policy, i.e. of 'fairness, justice and reasonableness', and should be effected only, to quote a much-cited dictum, 'incrementally and by analogy with established categories [sc. of liability]' (*Sutherland Shire Council* v. *Heyman* (1985) 157 CLR 424, 481 per Brennan J).

So enthusiastically have the courts embraced the language of Brennan J's dictum that some commentators have used the term 'incrementalism' to describe the current judicial approach to the duty question. This accurately reflects the judiciary's currently cautious approach to the expansion of negligence liability, but two caveats are nevertheless warranted. First, to say that extensions of the scope of the duty of care should be allowed only incrementally is not to indicate the principles which determine *whether* such extensions should be allowed: it merely prescribes that those principles should be narrowly defined. The need to identify the relevant principles remains. As the leading practitioners' work states, incrementalism should be seen to 'support rather than supplant the development of principles as the basis for determining the existence and scope of the duty of care' (Clerk and Lindsell, 1995, para. 7–16). Secondly, there is a danger that the principles by which step-by-step expansions of the duty are permitted will reflect arbitrary features of the decided cases rather than the essential merits of the plaintiff's claim against the defendant; liability may turn upon history rather than justice. In short, as an Irish judge has astutely noted, 'the verbally attractive proposition of incremental growth . . . suffers from a temporal defect – that rights should be determined by the accident of birth' (*Ward* v. *McMaster* [1988] IR 337, 347 per McCarthy J). This concern may however be alleviated if judges are prepared to allow a measure of flexibility – and sensitivity to the underlying merits of the claim – in the development of rules at the proximity stage.

3.6 **Fairness, Justice and Reasonableness**

A duty will only be recognised where it is fair, just and reasonable to hold the defendant liable to the plaintiff. Like the question of proximity, the question of fairness reflects matters of legal policy. Where proximity deals with principles already developed in the decided cases, consideration of the fairness of the plaintiff's case allows the court to raise matters of policy on an *ad hoc* basis . Fairness is 'raw' policy; proximity is policy 'crystallised' into legal principle.

The courts have not always been prepared openly to acknowledge the extent to which policy choices influence their decisions. Understandably, many judges have been keen to play down their political role by emphasising that their task is merely to apply principles developed over the course of time in case after case. They recognise that they have no special training or democratic mandate to determine issues of social or economic policy and that a trial involving only two parties may deny a hearing to many with a legitimate interest in its outcome. The best-known elaboration of this position is found in Lord Scarman's speech in *McLoughlin* v. *O'Brian* [1983] 1 AC 410, 430:

> 'By concentrating on principle the judges can keep the common law alive, flexible and consistent, and can keep the legal system clear of policy problems which neither they, nor the forensic process which it is their duty to operate, are equipped to resolve. If principle leads to results which are thought to be socially unacceptable, Parliament can legislate to draw a line or map out a new path.'

This approach may be criticised for trusting too much in Parliament's willingness to intervene where the common law produces injustice and Lord Scarman's speech attracted a sharp rebuke from Lord Edmund Davies in the very same case. The latter asserted that 'public policy issues *are* "justiciable"' (p. 428) and it seems that the current House of Lords would agree. Indeed, in a series of recent decisions, their Lordships have embarked upon an open and full discussion of policy considerations relevant to the question whether it was fair, just and reasonable to impose a duty of care (e.g. in *White* v. *Jones* [1995] 2 AC 207 (see 5.6), *X (Minors)* v. *Bedfordshire County Council* [1995] 2 AC 633 (see 7.3), and *Marc Rich and Co AG* v. *Bishop Rock Marine Co Ltd, The Nicholas H* [1996] AC 211).

Such issues of fairness arise in two types of case. First, they must be invoked where the proximity issue is unresolved by binding precedent (as where the situation before the court is novel). Here it is up to plaintiff to demonstrate the fairness of recognising a duty. A typical strategy is to reinforce the plaintiff's basic claim to corrective justice by reference to the 'secondary purposes' of negligence liability (see 2.4), e.g. by alleging that denial of duty would deprive a certain class of people of all prospect of compensation, there being no 'alternative avenue of protection' (see *White* v. *Jones*; Stapleton, 199), or would remove the primary mechanism for deterring a certain type of wrongdoing. Secondly, where the court accepts that there is proximity between the parties, considerations of whether it is fair, just and reasonable to allow a claim may serve to rebut the prima facie inference of a duty of care. Here attention is often directed at the so-called 'floodgates' and 'overkill' arguments, which we now turn to consider in more detail.

'Floodgates'

The so-called floodgates argument has often been deployed as a justification for the refusal to recognise alleged liabilities in negligence. However, despite the frequent judicial recourse to the argument, there is considerable confusion as to what it stands for and what weight should be attached to it (see 3.2). The argument takes many different forms (see Bell, 1983, ch. 3) and it is not always clear in which sense a court means to use it. Sometimes it focuses attention on the administration of the courts and points to the risk that the courts, were they to allow a particular type of claim, might be swamped with more claims than they could handle. This form of the argument seems rather weak, for the more people that suffer a particular wrong, the more reason there is for the courts to redress it. Another variation of the floodgates argument commands greater respect. This focuses on the defendant and asks whether it is fair to expose her to liability. A court may find that it is not where the extent of the liability would be too great ('excessively burdensome') or too indeterminate: as the American judge Cardozo J remarked, in a phrase that has often been adopted in English decisions, the courts should be wary of imposing 'liability in an indeterminate amount for an indeterminate time to an indeterminate class' (*Ultramares Corpn* v. *Touche* 174 NE 441, 444 (1931)).

The floodgates argument is becoming increasingly linked with fears about the ability of the liability insurance industry to cope with the demands placed on it. Such fears warrant serious attention, for the ability of the tort of negligence to furnish the victims of accidents with compensation depends on the efficient operation of the liability insurance market. Without insurance, the process of compensation through the tort of negligence would effectively grind to a halt. The principal fear is that the continuing expansion of the tort of negligence threatens to 'overload' the liability insurance system. Insurers are now exposed to potential liabilities of such an extent that they have become wary of undertaking new business (see Alexander, 1992) The are also concerned for their continued existence, because their liabilities under policies they have already issued may considerably exceed their estimates, which may not have taken account of recent developments in the law. Furthermore, the liabilities that insurers face have become increasingly indeterminate in size, especially as a result of the recent judicial willingness to allow claims for so-called 'ripple effect' losses suffered by an unpredictable number of 'secondary victims' of accidents (see Stapleton, 1991). This indeterminacy inhibits insurers in the necessary task of adjusting their premiums in line with the risks they take on, with the result that insureds who are better able to forecast their own liabilities may opt to self-insure; if they do so in sufficient numbers, the insurance market will simply 'unravel' (see Priest, 1987).

Although the courts have repeatedly held that the existence of liability insurance is in itself no reason for upholding a damages claim against the insured (see *Davie* v. *New Merton Board Mills Ltd* [1959] AC 604; *Morgans* v. *Launchberry* [1973] AC 127), the above analysis suggests that the difficulty of insuring against excessive and indeterminate liabilities may make it unfair to recognise a duty of care. Admittedly, insurance-based arguments are rarely deployed explicitly by the courts. But such arguments do seem to have a certain force and have on occasion been invoked, e.g. in *Caparo Industries plc* v. *Dickman* [1990] 2 AC 605, 643 where Lord Oliver warned against the imposition of a duty of care on company auditors for fear of opening up 'a limitless vista of uninsurable risk.' In the light of continuing concerns about the health of the Lloyd's of London insurance market, we may expect courts increasingly to make the link between the floodgates argument and the so-called 'insurance crisis'.

The Danger of Overkill

Just as the floodgates arguments warns of the risk of pursuing a policy of *compensation* too single-mindedly, the overkill argument points out the deleterious consequences that arise if the *deterrent* effect of negligence liability is too great. The argument was considered in some depth by Lord Keith in *Rowling* v. *Takaro Properties Ltd* [1988] AC 473, 502. His Lordship explained:

'It is to be hoped that, as a general rule, imposition of liability in negligence will lead to a higher standard of care in the performance of the relevant type of act; but sometimes not only may this not be so, but the imposition of liability may even lead to harmful consequences. In other words, the cure may be worse than the disease.'

In 'the overkill scenario', those threatened with liability respond by taking unnecessary safety precautions or by giving up a socially beneficial activity altogether. Impressed by the risk of such detrimentally defensive conduct, the House of Lords has ruled that it is not fair, just and reasonable to impose a duty on local authorities in discharging their functions *vis-à-vis* the prevention of child abuse and the allocation of special schooling for those with learning difficulties (*X* v. *Bedfordshire County Council* [1995] 2 AC 633) or on the police in their investigation of crime (*Hill* v. *Chief Constable rf West Yorkshire* [1989] AC 53. And, in a different context, their Lordships have recently ruled that considerations of fairness also precluded any claim in negligence by cargo owners after the loss at sea of a vessel that had recently been surveyed and certified as fit to sail by an international maritime classification society (*The Nicholas H* [1996] AC 211). According to Lord Steyn, who spoke for the majority of the House

of Lords, the classification society's performance of its public role, as a
'non-profit-making entity, created and operating for the sole purpose of
promoting the collective welfare, namely the safety of lives and ships at
sea', might be jeopardised by the threat of liability. Classification societies
might be induced to adopt 'a more defensive position', e.g. by declining to
take on high-risk business, where their services were most necessary, or by
diverting their resources away from their primary task of saving lives and
ships. This risk (among others) outweighed the countervailing argument,
advanced by Lord Lloyd (dissenting), that the recognition of a duty would
induce classification societies to take due care in surveying vessels,
promoting safety at sea and thereby addressing concerns within the
shipping community about declining standards.

Yet, although there is sometimes a sound basis for the overkill
argument (this is one area in which economic analysis has produced
interesting insights into the law: see Bishop, 1980 and 1982; 5.5), all too
often it seems to rely less on hard facts than on speculation and
secondhand knowledge of the alleged 'liability crisis' in the USA (on
which, see Huber, 1988). The following statement, taken from the
judgment of Purchas LJ in *Greater Nottingham Co-operative Society Ltd* v.
Cementation Piling and Foundations Ltd [1989] QB 71, 95 may be
construed as exhibiting this shortcoming:

> 'That this is a field in which the law has properly applied policy
> restrictions [on the scope of liability] is justified by a glance at the
> position reached on the other side of the Atlantic where damages
> awarded in respect of medical and surgical negligence is, it is believed,
> affecting the proper execution by surgeons of their professional tasks to
> the detriment of the patients.'

In the absence of real evidence of such questions, the courts' approach is
inevitably speculative and intuitive, and the risk of inconsistency is high.
Although the House of Lords in *Hill* was swayed by the danger that the
risk of liability might induce police officers to adopt a detrimentally
defensive frame of mind in investigating crime, it had previously rejected
such arguments in respect of officers at a training camp for young
offenders (*Home Office* v. *Dorset Yacht Co Ltd* [1970] AC 1004).
Memorably dismissing any analogy with US authority where the overkill
argument had succeeded, Lord Reid stated (p. 1033):

> 'It may be that the public servants of the State of New York are so
> apprehensive, easily dissuaded from doing their duty, and intent of
> preserving public funds from costly claims, that they could be
> influenced in this way. But my experience leads me to believe that
> Her Majesty's servants are made of sterner stuff.'

There must, accordingly, be doubts about the strength of the overkill
argument in some of the situations in which it is employed. Courts should
be reluctant to dismiss otherwise deserving claims for damages on the

basis of grounds as flimsy as a mere 'glance at . . . the other side of the Atlantic' and should bear in mind Lord Browne-Wilkinson's prescription that 'the public policy consideration which has first claim on the loyalty of the law is that wrongs should be remedied and that *very potent* counter-considerations are required to override that policy' (*X (Minors)* v. *Bedfordshire County Council* [1995] 2 AC 633, 749; emphasis added).

Summary

3.1 The existence of a duty of care is a precondition of liability in the tort of negligence. In cases where the positive acts of a private individual cause physical damage, the existence of such a duty can be presumed, but in other cases the question whether a duty of care exists may be problematic.

3.2 The courts have wavered between different approaches to the question when a duty of care will be recognised. In *Anns*, Lord Wilberforce advanced a presumption of a duty of care where the parties were in a relationship of proximity such that it was reasonably foreseeable the defendant's negligence would injure the plaintiff. This approach led to a rapid expansion of the scope of liability in negligence.

3.3 The last few years have seen a retreat from *Anns* in an attempt to restrict the scope of liability for negligence. Rather than seeking a single general principle of liability, the courts have reverted to the traditional approach of identifying different specific situations in which a duty of care arises. The situations share a number of common features.

3.4 First, the plaintiff must have been a foreseeable victim of the defendant's negligence (the question of 'duty in fact').

3.5 Secondly, the plaintiff must stand in a relationship of proximity with the defendant (the first aspect of the 'legal' duty question). The requirement of 'proximity' has no fixed and immutable content, and is merely a convenient label for identifying the features of those situations which give rise to a duty of care.

3.6 Lastly, it must be fair, just and reasonable to hold the defendant liable to the plaintiff (the second aspect of the 'legal' duty question). The courts have restricted liability under this heading by reference to a number of policy considerations (e.g. the floodgates and overkill arguments).

Exercises

3.1 What purpose does the duty of care concept serve?

3.2 What considerations do you think Lord Keith had in mind when he said that 'a too literal application of the well-known observation of Lord Wilberforce in *Anns* . . . may be productive of a failure to have regard to, and to analyse and weigh, all the relevant considerations in considering whether it is appropriate that a duty of care should be imposed' (*Rowling* v. *Takaro Properties Ltd*)?

3.3 What differences are there between the approach of the courts to the duty of care concept at the beginning of the 1980s and their approach at the beginning of the 1990s.

4   Nervous Shock

4.1 What is Nervous Shock?

Cases of what lawyers call 'nervous shock' have given rise to significant difficulties in the modern law of negligence and the courts have adopted a cautious and restrictive approach to the imposition of liability. A persistent failure on the part of the courts to value psychiatric illness as highly as physical injury, coupled with the fear of a flood of – perhaps unfalsifiable – claims, has resulted in the imposition of a number of proximity requirements limiting the circumstance in which a duty of care is owed.

Before considering the precise scope of the duty, an initial question of definition must be addressed: what precisely are we to understand by the phrase 'nervous shock'? In *Attia* v. *British Gas plc* [1988] QB 304, 317 Sir Thomas Bingham MR suggested that it could be equated with 'psychiatric damage' and that, for the sake of precision, the latter label should be used from that time forward. Yet, as Hoffman LJ pointed out in *Page* v. *Smith* [1994] 4 All ER 522, 549 (CA), not all nervous shock cases involve harm of a psychiatric nature: the label is just as appropriately applied when the plaintiff suffers non-psychiatric personal injury ('physical injury') as the result of a 'shock'. In the view of the learned judge, what was special about this type of case was the means by which the plaintiff's injury was caused – 'its distinguishing feature is its causation rather than its symptoms' – namely its resulting from mental trauma.

It is possible to identify two types of case in which the plaintiff's injury is caused by mental trauma and which therefore fall within the general category of nervous shock. First, there are cases in which the injury is indeed of a psychiatric nature. To claim damages in tort, a plaintiff must prove that she is suffering from what Lord Bridge has described as a 'positive psychiatric illness' (*McLoughlin* v. *O'Brian* [1983] AC 410, 431). By contrast, the normal human emotions that ordinary people experience after particularly traumatic events – 'mere' grief, anxiety and depression – give rise to no liability in the absence of physical injury. Whether the plaintiff's mental condition amounts to a positive (i.e. recognised) condition is a matter for the court after hearing expert evidence from psychiatrists. As the medical profession's understanding of psychiatric conditions develops, so the law may recognise new varieties of nervous shock. Recently, attention has focused upon post-traumatic stress disorder (PTSD), the condition at the centre of many high-profile law suits in recent years (the actions arising from the sinking of the ferry *Herald of Free Enterprise* in Zeebrugge harbour and the fire at King's Cross Underground station are prominent examples). The condition is provoked by an event of an exceptionally threatening or catastrophic nature and may manifest itself in a variety of symptoms, including sleeping disorders, tension and depression. PTSD for the first time received judicial recognition in the litigation following the Hillsborough football stadium tragedy in which 95 fans were crushed to death as a result of overcrowding (*Alcock* v. *Chief Constable of South Yorkshire* [1992] 1 AC 310).

Secondly, there are cases in which the plaintiff suffers physical damage, as where a traumatic event triggers a heart attack. In *Bourhill* v. *Young* [1943] AC 92, the plaintiff (a pregnant woman) suffered a miscarriage after coming upon the scene of a fatal road accident in which the defendant motor cyclist was killed. The House of Lords held that she was owed no duty of care. The court's reasoning is perhaps not as transparent at that to be found in the more recent nervous shock cases, but undeniably it was important that the plaintiff was put in no danger of physical impact by the accident, had no prior relationship with the deceased, and was considered – on account of her pregnancy – to be unusually vulnerable to mental trauma. These factors would no doubt dictate the same result if the case were to be decided again today, and it is submitted that the restrictive approach adopted by the courts in cases of psychiatric illness is equally applicable to cases where mental trauma produces a physical injury. This outcome is especially desirable given uncertainty within the medical profession as to whether certain conditions arising from mental trauma are more appropriately regarded as physical or psychiatric in nature (see especially *Page* v. *Smith* [1996] 1 AC 155 in which doubts as to the exact nature of the condition known as myalgic encephalomyelitis (ME) or chronic fatigue syndrome (CFS) were noted but considered irrelevant to the outcome of the case).

4.2 Competing Judicial Approaches

In asking whether a duty of care arises in cases of nervous shock, the courts wavered for some time between the two broad types of approach identified by Lord Bridge in *Caparo* (see 3.2). This equivocation was readily apparent in a significant House of Lords decision of the early 1980s, *McLoughlin* v. *O'Brian* [1983] AC 410. Mrs McLoughlin suffered nervous shock after a car crash involving her husband and three children. One child was killed; the others were badly injured. Mrs McLoughlin had been at home at the time the accident happened. She was told the grim news an hour or so afterwards by a friend who drove her to the hospital. There, Mrs McLoughlin saw the surviving members of her family – bruised and battered, covered in mud and oil – and heard their sobs and screams. Subsequently, she suffered the condition of which she complained.

Her claim for damages was unanimously allowed by the House of Lords although the approach of the different members of the House differed markedly. Somewhat surprisingly (given the approach he had previously taken in *Anns*), Lord Wilberforce adopted a very traditional approach, focusing narrowly on the facts of previous cases (p. 419). In these cases, he perceived a gradual expansion of liability for nervous shock but noted that nevertheless '[t]hroughout these developments. . . the courts have proceeded in the traditional manner of the common law from case to case, upon a basis of logical necessity.' He explained that '[t]o argue from one factual situation to another and to decide by analogy is a natural tendency of the human and legal mind'. In this way, he noted, the common law was developed incrementally from case to case. Hence, for example, the class of plaintiff able to recover for nervous shock had been enlarged beyond those who were themselves at risk of physical harm to include those fearful for the safety of close relatives: 'If a mother . . . could recover on account of fear for herself, how can she be denied recovery on account of fear for her accompanying children?'

Looking at the past caselaw in the round, Lord Wilberforce identified three key limitations on the scope of the duty of care. These concerned 'the class of persons whose claims should be recognised; the proximity of such persons to the accident; and the means by which the shock was caused' (p. 422). It would be necessary for a court to determine whether, in these respects, Mrs McLoughlin's claim was sufficiently analogous to those in which the courts had already allowed recovery to allow her claim to succeed. As by that time it was clearly established that a mother could recover in respect of psychiatric illness occasioned by the sight of injury to her daughter, the first and third limitation identified by Lord Wilberforce (class of plaintiff and means of perception) posed no obstacle. The difficulty arose in relation to Mrs McLoughlin's 'proximity' to the accident (here 'proximity' is employed in something like its literal sense, referring to closeness in time and space). Mrs McLoughlin had not been present at the scene of the accident: her trauma arose from the distressing scenes she witnessed on arrival at the hospital some two hours later. Lord Wilberforce recognised that to allow her claim would be to effect an expansion in the scope of liability. Nevertheless, he thought that an incremental expansion was appropriate in the present case. Previous cases had recognised liability to those who, though not witnessing the accident itself, had come upon its 'immediate aftermath', and it was only a small step to recognise that the aftermath of an accident might encompass not only the location at which it occurred but also the location to which the survivors were taken for emergency treatment.

In contrast with Lord Wilberforce's incremental approach, the other judges in *McLoughlin* disavowed the arbitrary and rigid limitations on recovery adopted in previous cases. They preferred to start from the presumption that, if nervous shock was the foreseeable consequence of the defendant's carelessness, then the victim was entitled to damages. It was possible, however, to rebut this presumption if arguments of policy militated against recovery in the present case. (Lord Scarman dissented on this point, pursuing his rather idiosyncratic argument that concerns of public policy have no place in private law adjudication: see 3.6). Paradoxically, it was precisely this way of proceeding that Lord Wilberforce had seemed to advocate in *Anns*.

The case for the majority's approach was put most powerfully by Lord Bridge. He stated his opposition to the incrementalism of Lord Wilberforce in the clearest of terms: 'we should resist the temptation to try yet once more to freeze the law in a rigid posture which would deny justice to some who . . . ought to succeed'. Illustrating the injustice that might follow from this, Lord Bridge gave an example that seems to go much further than Lord Wilberforce would have allowed (p. 442). Suppose a mother suffers nervous shock after learning of the death of the rest of her family in a hotel fire and seeing a newspaper photograph of unidentifiable victims trapped on the top floor waving for help from the windows: can she recover for her psychiatric injury? Lord Bridge thought that she could. In his view, it should make no difference whether her condition was brought about 'by her imagination of the agonies of mind and body in which her family died, rather than direct perception of the event': the mother should not be denied damages by the operation of hard and fast legal rules.

Persuasive as Lord Bridge's argument is, it is now apparent that Lord Wilberforce's approach now prevails. In *Alcock*, the House of Lords unanimously preferred Lord Wilberforce's cautious incrementalism to Lord Bridge's reduction of the duty of care question to the single general principle of foreseeability. Liability for nervous shock is now kept within narrow confines by various limitations on the scope of the duty of care (encapsulated in a number of 'proximity requirements'). These proximity requirements do not apply in all cases, and it is necessary to distinguish three different sub-categories of case before proceeding further. These are cases in which (a) the plaintiff was personally exposed to physical danger by the defendant's negligence; (b) the plaintiff merely witnessed the exposure of a third party to such danger; and (c) the plaintiff falls within some other category of claimant (e.g. when the plaintiff is a rescuer). We shall now consider these cases in turn.

4.3 **Personal Exposure to the Risk of Physical Harm**

Where the plaintiff is personally exposed to the risk of physical harm it is sufficient that some form of personal injury – whether occasioned by physical or psychiatric means – be foreseeable. It is not necessary to show that injury *by shock* was itself foreseeable. This was determined by the House of Lords in the recent decision of *Page* v. *Smith* [1996] 1 AC 155, disapproving a dictum of Lord Denning in *King* v. *Phillips* [1953] 1 QB 429, 441 that 'the test for liability for shock is foreseeability of injury by shock.' Lord Denning's approach held good in the witness or 'secondary victim' cases to be considered below, but had no place in relation to claims brought by 'primary victims'.

Page v. *Smith* concerned a car crash described as 'of moderate severity'. The plaintiff was driving with due care when, suddenly and without warning, the defendant, coming in the opposite direction, turned into his path. The impact caused some physical damage to the cars but none to the occupants. Three hours later, however, the plaintiff felt exhausted and took to his bed. The exhaustion continued and the plaintiff never fully recovered. At the time of appeal, and despite the lapse of almost eight years, the plaintiff had not yet returned to work. The diagnosis was the recrudescence of the condition known as myalgic encephalomyelitis or chronic fatigue syndrome; the plaintiff had suffered from a mild form of this sporadically in the past, but it now became an illness of chronic intensity and permanency. The principal defence was that it was not reasonably foreseeable that a person of normal fortitude would have suffered psychiatric injury in such circumstances. The House of Lords, by a bare majority (Lord Keith and Lord Jauncey dissented), held that this was irrelevant. Lord Lloyd, who delivered the leading speech, held that where *injury by physical means* was foreseeable the plaintiff could be regarded as a 'primary victim' of the accident and it was not necessary to show that *injury by psychiatric means* was also foreseeable; it made no difference that the plaintiff might have been abnormally susceptible to the onset of ME/CFS, for this affected only the foreseeability of injury by psychiatric means, not the foreseeability of injury *howsoever caused*. Lord Lloyd added that in these primary victim cases there was no need for the plaintiff to satisfy the various proximity requirements laid down by the House of Lords in *McLoughlin* and *Alcock*; these applied only to claims brought by witnesses.

Page v. *Smith* is a subtle case that requires careful attention. It has a twofold significance. First, it makes clear the importance of the distinction between the person within the 'area of impact' (i.e. at risk of injury by physical means) and the witness: the requirements of proximity of relationship, proximity in time and space, and proximity of perception only apply to the latter. It leaves open the question whether the requirement that psychiatric illness be caused by 'a shock', which (as we shall see) is applied in the case of the witness, also applies to the action brought by a person exposed to the risk of physical harm; the issue becomes particularly important in the context of stress-related psychiatric illness, considered below (see 4.6). Secondly, the decision elaborates the nature of the harm that must be foreseeable in order to satisfy the test of remoteness of damage; in laying down that the plaintiff need generally show only the foreseeability of some personal injury, whether by physical or psychiatric means, the case seems to put forward a rule applicable to all personal injury, not just to nervous shock (see further ch. 10).

A final aspect of the case warrants consideration. In distinguishing the person who is physically endangered from the mere witness, Lord Lloyd described the former as the 'primary victim' of the accident and the latter as the 'secondary victim'. The terminology is useful shorthand provided that it is used with care. A difficult, however, arises when other classes of plaintiff are considered, especially in the case of the rescuer and the so-called 'unwitting agent of misfortune' (see 4.5); the two latter types of plaintiff do not fit easily into the primary/secondary plaintiff dichotomy. In *Alcock*, Lord Oliver had treated the rescuer and the unwitting agent as analogous to the person who is physically endangered on the basis that they were 'involved, either mediately or immediately, as a participant'; in such cases, he thought that it was the foreseeability of the plaintiff's being involved and suffering injury that 'establishes of itself a sufficiently proximate relationship'. Yet it is unclear from Lord Oliver's formulation whether it remains for the rescuer and the unwitting agent to satisfy other proximity requirements, over and above that of 'proximity of relationship', which are applied in relation to claims brought by witnesses (e.g. 'proximity in time and space' and 'proximity of perception'). They cannot therefore be assumed without more to be in the same position as the person who is physically endangered, and for this reason we have resisted the temptation to label them as 'primary victims'; to label them thus might be thought to beg the question of the nature of the proximity hurdle in such cases. Accordingly, we shall return to these 'other categories' of plaintiff, after discussing first the position of the witness.

4.4 Witnesses

As has been indicated, a much more restrictive approach is adopted towards those who merely witness the exposure of others to physical danger ('secondary victims'). In such cases, it is necessary to satisfy a number of proximity requirements, most notably those identified by Lord Wilberforce in *McLoughlin* v. *O'Brian* and approved, with further elaboration, by a unanimous House of Lords in *Alcock*. They are here addressed under the heading of proximity of relationship, proximity in time and space, and proximity of perception.

Before turning to these, however, it is appropriate to deal briefly with three additional matters arising in relation to claims for nervous shock brought by witnesses of traumatic events. First, it appears that the psychiatric injury or illness suffered by the plaintiff must be occasioned *by shock*. It is not enough that the harm be caused by a series of events that result in the gradual accumulation of pressures on the nervous system. This at least was the view expressed in *Alcock* by Lord Ackner and Lord Oliver. The former illustrated the sort of case he had in mind by instancing the spouse who has been worn down by caring for a tortiously injured husband or wife, and the parent made distraught by the wayward conduct of a tortiously brain-damaged child; he thought that the absence of a 'shock' precluded liability in such cases (cf. 4.6). Secondly, it must be reasonably foreseeable that a person of normal fortitude (or 'customary phlegm', as Lord Porter put it in *Bourhill* v. *Young*) would suffer harm as a result of mental trauma. Where the plaintiff suffers nervous shock only by reason of an abnormal susceptibility (i.e. in circumstances in which a normal person would not be affected), then no liability will arise. It was for this reason, amongst others, that the plaintiff's claim failed in *Bourhill* itself: the court considered (on evidence that may be considered less than convincing by some) that her pregnancy made her abnormally vulnerable to nervous shock and that other passers-by would have had the fortitude to withstand the traumatic scenes. Once *some* psychiatric harm is foreseeable to a person of normal fortitude, however, a person whose abnormal susceptibility aggravates the injury sustained is entitled to recover to the full extent of her loss (*Brice* v. *Brown* [1984] 1 WLR 997). In *Page* v. *Smith*, the House of Lords recognised that the customary phlegm rule was warranted in relation to claims by secondary victims in order to limit the number of claims, but emphasised that it had no application to primary victims. Thirdly, it may be that a defendant who imperils or injures herself owes no duty to those who suffer shock as a result. This was the view expressed in *Alcock* by Lord Oliver, who considered that there would be no liability on the part of the son who, watched by his mother, negligently walks in front of an oncoming motor car. The rule proposed may result in injustice where a third party shares responsibility of the shocking event with the person imperilled or injured: if the latter is exempted from liability, the burden of compensating the plaintiff in full would fall on the third party, even if her fault was comparatively minor.

Let us now turn to the three principal restrictions on nervous shock liability to witnesses: proximity of relationship, of time and space, and of perception.

Proximity of Relationship

The witness of a traumatic event must establish a 'close tie of love and affection' with a person injured or endangered by the event in order to satisfy the requirement of proximity of relationship. The most detailed analysis of this issue is to be found in the decision of the House of Lords in *Alcock* v. *Chief Constable of South Yorkshire Police* [1992] 1 AC 310, one of the cases that arose out of the Hillsborough football stadium tragedy. This was a test case, consolidating a number of separate appeals that exemplified the different legal issues raised by hundreds of actions brought in the aftermath of the tragedy by friends and relatives of those caught in the crush at the Leppings Lane end of the ground. The diagnosis in each case was of post-traumatic stress disorder. Various relationships with those in the Leppings Lane pen were represented, including those between children, grandchildren, brothers and fiancés. The House of Lords held that they all had to be subjected to the requirement of a close tie of love and affection.

Precisely how one measures love and affection is an issue on which their Lordships were silent. It appears that the courts are entitled to presume the existence of the requisite ties in certain relationships, such as those of parent and child, spouses and – going beyond the relationships specified by Lord Wilberforce in *McLoughlin* – fiancés (p. 398, per Lord Keith). Their Lordships denied, however, that the relationship between brothers is such as to allow the same presumption to be made, for the quality of relationship between siblings is recognised to vary enormously, and it was for this reason that the claim of one of the Hillsborough plaintiffs was dismissed. In these and other relationships, the plaintiff must lead evidence to prove a special bond of affection existed between her and the victim. (Is the judiciary ready to hear our courtrooms swell with the sounds of wailing and gnashing of teeth on the part of plaintiffs seeking to establish their love for the deceased?) Conversely, in the case of relationships in which a special bond is to be presumed, it is open to the defendant to seek to rebut the presumption of liability', for example by showing that a married couple had fallen out several years ago and were virtual strangers. As Weir (1992) has pointed out, 'this will be very messy in practice', and risks causing 'perplexity to advisers and embarrassment to litigants' (p. vi).

Although in the majority of cases the plaintiff will have to prove the existence of a special bond of affection between herself and the victim, the House of Lords was not prepared to rule out the possibility that a mere bystander might recover if the circumstances of a catastrophe occurring close to the bystander were especially horrific. As an example of circumstances under which a mere bystander might recover, Lord Ackner envisaged the case of a passer-by witnessing a petrol tanker careering out of control into a school in session and bursting into flames. He failed to explain, however, why this would be regarded as more horrific than the terrible events at Hillsborough. Subsequently, the Court of Appeal has indicated that it is not prepared to recognise a duty to a mere bystander even in the case of an exceptionally horrific accident. In *McFarlane* v. *EE Caledonia Ltd* [1994] 1 Lloyd's Rep 16, the plaintiff brought an action alleging PTSD arising out of the Piper Alpha disaster in which a blazing inferno engulfed an oil platform in the North Sea, killing 164 people. The plaintiff had witnessed the scenes from a support vessel which was engaged in the effort to fight the fire and came within 100 metres of the rig. One of the grounds on which he submitted he was owed a duty of care by the owners of the rig, who accepted responsibility for the fire, was that the fire was exceptionally horrific. He relied upon the dictum of Lord Ackner noted above. The Court of Appeal declined to follow the learned Lord of Appeal, citing objections both practical and principled. In the first place, there was no scale against which could be measured the horror generated by any particular accident. Furthermore, Lord Ackner's unexpressed premise – that recovery should be allowed in particularly horrific cases because it was more foreseeable that psychiatric damage would result – effectively reduced the duty of care issue to the single general principle of foreseeability, an approach that was now discredited.

Can a plaintiff establish a close tie of love and affection with an item of property? Some support for an affirmative answer to this question can be derived from the decision in *Attia* v. *British Gas* [1988] QB 304. Mrs Attia, having earlier in the day let the gasman in to install central heating, returned home to find her house in flames. She alleged that she suffered a serious psychological reaction as a result. The Court of Appeal accepted that liability for psychiatric damage might arise in such circumstances. It considered that, as the gas company undeniably owed a duty not to cause physical damage to the house, the question of whether the plaintiff could claim also for psychiatric damage was simply one of remoteness, in relation to which the only relevant consideration was the foreseeability of the plaintiff's injury. This analysis may be criticised in that the question of whether a duty is owed must be addressed in relation to each of the different types of loss suffered by the plaintiff. The fact that the plaintiff can recover for *some* loss (e.g. property damage or personal injury) does not entail that she can recover for *all* her losses purely on satisfying the court of their foreseeability. A more satisfactory basis for the decision is that a person's home is of such emotional significance that its loss is comparable with, though not to be equated to, the loss of a loved relative (cf. Law Commission, 1995, para. 2.44). Focusing on the emotional attachment to the property rather than on its mere ownership would also obviate the need for unfortunate discriminations between the owners of property and others (e.g. their children) who might suffer equal shock and loss but lack any legal interest in the family home.

Proximity in Time and Space

The plaintiff need not suffer nervous shock as a result of experiencing the traumatic event unfold: it is sufficient that she comes upon its 'immediate aftermath'. The issue of what counts as the immediate aftermath of such an event remains problematic despite attempts to clarify it in the leading cases. It seems destined to be approached in an intuitive and impressionistic fashion. In *McLoughlin*, Lord Wilberforce had been content to treat Mrs McLoughlin as coming on the immediate aftermath even though she did not go to the scene of the crash but only went to the hospital. He stressed, however, that the scenes at the hospital were particularly horrific: Mrs McLoughlin's relatives 'were in the same condition [as they had been immediately after the accident], covered with oil and mud, and distraught with pain' (p. 419). By contrast, in *Alcock*, the House of Lords held that the immediate aftermath did not extend to cover those who had attended at temporary mortuaries some nine hours or more after the disaster in order to identify bodies. Lord Jauncey distinguished *McLoughlin* v. *O'Brian* on the basis that the lapse of time in the Hillsborough case was much greater and that the visits were made not for the purpose of rescuing or giving comfort to a victim, but purely for the purposes of identification (pp. 423–4). His Lordship warned, however, against attempting to draw up any exhaustive catalogue of examples that would fall within the immediate aftermath and his words should not be treated as precluding claims by those who do not come upon the aftermath in order to make a rescue or give comfort. Thus the woman who returns home to find the charred body of her husband, electrocuted by a defectively wired product, should be able to argue she had come upon the immediate aftermath of the accident. Unlike the plaintiffs in *Alcock*, she would have had no chance to steel herself in advance of exposing herself to the tragic scenes.

Proximity of Perception

The basic rule is that the plaintiff must personally perceive the shocking event or its immediate aftermath. In *McLoughlin*, Lord Wilberforce contrasted cases where an accident, or its immediate aftermath, was witnessed in person with those in which the victim was told of the accident by a third party. Only in the former type of case did he consider that liability would arise (see further *Ravenscroft* v. *Rederiaktiebølaget Transatlantic* [1992] 2 All ER 470 (note); query whether an action might lie against the communicant in some circumstances: see *Barnes* v. *Commonwealth* (1937) SR (NSW) 511). He reserved his judgment on the question whether watching live television coverage of an accident, or employing any other 'equivalent of sight or hearing', would suffice. The issue subsequently came before the House of Lords in *Alcock*. On the facts, the House concluded that those plaintiffs who had only viewed the disaster on television or listened on the radio, or who had merely been told about it, were barred from recovering for that reason. Their Lordships urged that the interpolation of television coverage between event and observer robbed the scenes of their sudden impact upon the senses. All their Lordships, however, confined their decision to the facts in front of them and Lord Ackner was prepared to accept that there might be occasions on which television pictures would have at least as great an impact on observers as actual presence at the scene. An example of such a case would, he said, be where parents viewed live television pictures of a special event of children travelling in a hot-air balloon in which the balloon suddenly burst into flames and plummeted to the ground (p. 405). Perhaps the crucial distinguishing factor in this case is that the parents knew their children would be injured whereas in the Hillsborough case the television viewers, unable to make out recognisable individuals in the crowd, merely feared that their friends and relatives would be caught up in the crush.

4.5 Other Categories of Claimant

In some cases, the plaintiff – although not physically threatened – is more intimately involved in the traumatic events than a mere witness, as would be the case with the bystander who attempts to rescue the injured, or the person who unwittingly (and without fault) contributes to the accident (e.g. the train driver who is misdirected at the points and ploughs into workers busy on the tracks: *Galt* v. *British Railways Board* (1983) 133 NLJ 870; cf. *Dooley* v. *Cammel Laird & Co* [1951] 1 Lloyd's Rep 271). In *Alcock*, Lord Oliver distinguished the rescuer and the unwitting agent of misfortune from the mere witness on account of their involvement in the shocking events. He classified them alongside the person who was personally threatened as participants in the accident and exempted them from the need to establish a close tie of love and affection with the primary victim (pp. 407–8); it is unclear whether they must satisfy the other requirements of proximity that are applicable in relation to witnesses (e.g. proximity in time and space and proximity of perception), but these requirements are unlikely to represent a substantial obstacle in many cases, given that the plaintiff's intimate involvement in the accident must ex hypothesi be presupposed.

'Whether a particular plaintiff is a rescuer is, in each case, a question of fact' (*Frost* v. *Chief Constable of the South Yorkshire Police* [1997] 1 All ER 540, 550 per Rose LJ). Among the factors to be taken into account in assessing the plaintiff's status are the following (none decisive in itself): 'the character and extent of the initial accident caused by the tortfeasor; whether that incident has finished or is continuing; whether there is any danger, continuing or otherwise, to the victim or to the plaintiff; the character of the plaintiff's conduct, in itself and in relation to the victim; and how proximate, in time and space, the plaintiff's conduct is to the incident' (ibid.). Hence, in *Chadwick* v. *British Railways Board* [1967] 1 WLR 912, there could be no doubt that the deceased Mr Chadwick was a rescuer when, after the Lewisham railway disaster of 1957 (in which 90 people died), he assisted in the rescue operation for a period of some 12 hours; his assistance involved him climbing into the wreckage to give first aid to the injured and to help them to extricate themselves from the wreckage. Waller J held that in such circumstances he was owed a duty of care by those responsible for the accident and was entitled to damages for the psychoneurotic condition he developed as a result of his experiences. Yet it is not every minor act of aid or assistance in the aftermath of an accident that entitles the actor to claim as a rescuer. In *McFarlane* (considered above: see 4.3), the plaintiff had helped to move blankets on board the support vessel on which he was stationed with a view to preparing a heli-hangar to receive casualties from the burning Piper Alpha oil rig; he claimed also to have assisted two of the walking-wounded as they arrived on the vessel. The Court of Appeal held that this 'very limited degree of involvement' had not exposed him to a reasonably foreseeable risk of psychiatric injury; the case could easily be distinguished from *Chadwick* where the plaintiff had been involved at close quarters and for an extended period of time.

The Court of Appeal again considered the issue in the recent case of *Frost* v. *Chief Constable of the South Yorkshire Police* [1997] 1 All ER 540. In this case, the court was faced with actions by a number of police officers who were on duty at the time of the Hillsborough football stadium disaster (for which the Chief Constable accepted responsibility) and who alleged they had suffered PTSD as a consequence of their experiences; in a separate case heard at the same time, the claim was by a pit deputy who for a period of two hours had attempted mouth to mouth resuscitation on a colleague crushed to death by the admitted negligence of their employer (*Duncan* v. *British Coal Corp*). Applying the basic approach outlined above, Rose LJ (with whom Henry LJ agreed) considered which of the plaintiffs in the cases before him were rescuers. In relation to the Hillsborough actions, he held that the officers who did not actually give aid and assistance at the Leppings Lane end of the ground, but only (for example) at the opposite end of the stadium or in the gymnasium used as a temporary mortuary, 'were not rescuers because they were not sufficiently closely involved in the crushing incident or its immediate aftermath' (p. 551). Other officers who carried the bodies of the dead or injured from the pens or who gave first aid on the pitch in the area in front of the pens did, however, count as rescuers; this was so even where the officers only arrived at the ground after the incident, provided that they attended in its immediate aftermath. As regards *Duncan* v. *British Coal Corp*, Rose LJ held that the first aid given by the plaintiff pit deputy did not make him a rescuer: although what he did was proximate in time to the accident, when he arrived at the scene there was no danger to him or to the deceased; '[f]urthermore, the first aid which he rendered was plainly within the normal scope of his employment and was not attended by any unusually distressing features' (p. 554; there was no sign of any injury or blood). It appears therefore that it was the unusually distressing nature of the scenes at Hillsborough that was crucial in making rescuers of the officers who arrived at the ground after the incident but gave assistance in the vicinity of the pens in the immediate aftermath. This seems a somewhat imprecise criterion to apply in such cases (could one not argue that the prolonged but ultimately futile effort to breathe life into the deceased's limp body might be 'unusually distressing' even for a hardened pit deputy?).

The Court of Appeal in *Frost* also identified an additional category of plaintiff to be accorded special treatment in determining liability for nervous shock, namely the employee. According to Rose LJ, 'the court has long recognised a duty of care to guard employees and rescuers against all kinds of injury, whereas, in deciding whether any duty of care exists towards plaintiffs who are not employees, rescuers, or primary victims, the courts have, in recent years, imposed specific criteria in relation to claims for psychiatric injury' (p. 551). The duty does not extend to all psychiatric injury sustained in the course of employment, but only to such injury as results from the plaintiff's being exposed in the course of duty to 'exceptionally horrific events' (p. 552, per Rose LJ) or, in accordance with the apparently narrower approach of Henry LJ, from the plaintiff's 'participation' in the course of duty in an incident caused by the negligence of her employer (p. 560). This apparent divergence of approach made no difference on the facts of this case, as Henry LJ agreed with Rose LJ's conclusions with respect to the individual cases. The effect of recognising this new category of privileged claimant was that certain of the Hillsborough officers who had not been recognised as rescuers were held to have been owed a duty of care by the Chief Constable: even those officers who had been on duty elsewhere in the stadium at the time of the incident, and had at no time approached closed to the Leppings Lane pens, were exposed to scenes of an exceptionally horrific nature. However, an officer who was asked to strip bodies in the hospital mortuary 'did no more than could properly be asked of any police officer in the ordinary carrying out of her duties following a serious incident' (p. 551, per Rose LJ). The argument that the plaintiff in *Duncan* was owed a duty of care as an employee failed for the same reason, namely that the incident was such that the plaintiff could expect to come across in the ordinary course of employment.

Frost is undoubtedly an important decision, but it goes beyond existing authority in ways that may have unexpected consequences. The privileging, of employees relative to other witnesses is novel and not warranted by the reasoning given by Rose LJ, for the fact that a duty is owed by the employer in respect of injury caused *by physical means* does not of itself entail that a duty should be owed where the injury is caused *by psychiatric means*; the Court of Appeal seems to have begged the question whether the employer's duty *should* extend to injury by psychiatric means. If the House of Lords grants leave to appeal, it will be interesting to see whether this aspect of the decision is upheld.

4.6 Liability for Stress

In the cases thus far discussed, the plaintiff's condition has resulted from a single shocking event rather than from an accumulation of mental pressures over a period of time. In *Alcock*, as we have seen, Lord Ackner and Lord Oliver expressed their opinion that the element of shock was necessary to establishing a duty of care (at least as far as secondary victims were concerned). But it has recently been accepted that liability for stress may, in appropriate circumstances, arise in the tort of negligence.

In *Walker* v. *Northumberland County Council* [1995] 1 All ER 737, the plaintiff, a person of ordinary robustness, was an officer in the social services department of a local authority. His work was of an intrinsically stressful character: a large proportion of it involved investigating and responding to reports of child abuse. In addition to the inherent stresses of the job, the department in which he was employed was under-staffed and over-worked. As a result of the combined operation of these factors, he suffered a nervous breakdown and was off work for some three months; he returned only after assurances that he would be given assistance in performing his duties in order to reduce the pressures of his job. Yet the burden of his work remained excessive: he received only very limited assistance, while his caseload in fact increased. Six months after his return to work he experienced a second nervous breakdown and was obliged to stop work permanently on grounds of ill health. On these facts, Colman J found that the second breakdown (but not the first) arose from a breach of the duty of care by the defendant employer, the local authority, which ought to have taken protective steps to ensure the mental health of an employee whose nervous exhaustion was already known. The learned judge held that there was 'no logical reason' why the well-established duty of an employer to ensure the safety of employees should not address the risk of injury to mental health as well as physical injury.

How is this decision to be reconciled with the insistence of Lord Ackner and Lord Oliver in *Alcock* that there should be a 'shock'? One response is that this requirement arises only in the witness cases and not where the plaintiff is a 'primary victim' (see *Sion* v. *Hampstead Health Authority*, 27 May 1994, unreported). This is not unproblematic, however, as the distinction between 'primary' and 'secondary' victims has yet to be fully thought through. The very terminology is potentially confusing as it suggests that the liability to the latter is derivative from that to the former, whereas it is clear that there need not in fact be any liability to the primary victim (e.g. where the witness reasonably fears for the safety of another who in fact avoids injury: see *Hambrook* v. *Stokes Bros* [1925] 1 KB 141) and that the duty to the witness is an independent duty, owed to the witness in her own right. Furthermore, the substance of the distinction is unclear. It is tempting to define the primary victim as one who is personally at risk of harm and the secondary victim as one who is traumatised by seeing another being put at risk of harm, but this begs the question of what constitutes 'harm'. To accept the risk of *psychiatric* harm as the touchstone is clearly incoherent, because it is well established that the secondary victim must be exposed to a reasonably foreseeable risk of psychiatric harm. Yet if the class of primary victims is limited to those who are *physically* endangered, then *Walker* is not a primary victim case at all.

Perhaps the duty recognised in the case is best justified as a special feature of the employer's duty to provide employees with a safe place and system of work, with no significance outside the employment context (cf. *Frost* v. *Chief Constable of the South Yorkshire Police* [1997] 1 All ER 540: see 4.5). Nevertheless, it cannot be regarded as finally settled that there can be no liability for stress-related psychiatric illness outside the employment context, e.g. on the part of a father who watches at the hospital bedside while his son deteriorates in health and eventually dies, allegedly as a result of negligent treatment, or on the part of a child who is separated from her mother as a result of a psychiatrist's erroneous diagnosis of abuse by the mother's boyfriend (see respectively *Sion*, above (against liability) and *X (Minors)* v. *Bedfordshire County Council* [1995] 2 AC 633, 665–7 (CA), where Sir Thomas Bingham MR thought that liability might arise; the matter was not addressed by the other members of the court or by the House of Lords in the subsequent appeal).

4.7 Reform

Many of the original fears accounting for judicial reluctance to accept claims for nervous shock have now been dispelled. The nature of psychiatric illness is now more fully understood, and the medical profession more confident of its ability to provide accurate and consistent diagnoses. Consequently, the danger of fraudulent and exaggerated claims has receded. This in turn has allowed a proper recognition of the seriousness of psychiatric illness, and it is no longer thought appropriate to denigrate the moral fibre of sufferers and to urge them simply to 'pull themselves together'. Nevertheless the floodgates argument continues to exert a significant influence on the development of the law relating to nervous shock. In *McLoughlin*, for instance, Lord Wilberforce (while accepting that the fears aroused by the floodgates argument were often exaggerated) thought it necessary to impose proximity restrictions on liability for nervous shock 'just because 'shock' in its nature is capable of affecting so wide a range of people' (pp. 421–2). These sentiments were echoed by the House of Lords in *Alcock* and used as a justification for the restrictive approach adopted.

The Law Commission (1995), in a thorough review of liability for psychiatric illness, has recognised the diminishing force in an age of increasing medical sophistication of policy arguments that rest upon the risk of fraudulent and exaggerated claims or conflicting medical opinions. It notes that medical and legal experts working in the field now give due recognition to 'how life-shattering psychiatric illness can be and how, in many cases, it can be more debilitating than physical injuries' (para. 1.9). Such arguments were of insufficient weight to warrant serious contemplation of any proposal that liability for psychiatric illness be abandoned, or – less drastically – denied to mere witnesses. Yet the Law Commission accepted that the floodgates argument retained considerable force, above all in the witness cases: 'One thinks, for example, of all those who may suffer psychiatric illness from watching a particularly gruesome news broadcast or from being present at a disaster at a sports event' (para. 5.11). For this reason, the Law Commission by and large endorsed the current state of the law, while suggesting slight refinements in particular areas.

The main recommendations put out for consultation by the Law Commission were the following. First, liability for nervous shock should continue to be restricted in order to prevent a mass of claims arising from a single event (which the Law Commission saw as the major concern underlying the floodgates argument). The reasonable foreseeability of psychiatric illness should not be sufficient to give rise to a duty of care. Secondly, witnesses establishing a close tie of love and affection with a primary victim of the accident would no longer have to satisfy the requirements of proximity in time and space and proximity of perception. In the Law Commission's view, these requirements were 'unnecessarily restrictive' because the need to establish a close tie of love and affection was itself sufficient to undermine the floodgates objection. Furthermore, they 'might justly give rise to accusations of arbitrary and insensitive line-drawing', especially given medical recognition 'that, for those with a close tie to the primary victim, merely learning about unexpected death or injury is a triggering event for PTSD' (paras. 5.23–24). Thirdly, the list of qualifying relationships might be put on a statutory footing and extended beyond parents, children and spouses to encompass brothers and sisters as well as unmarried partners, including those in a stable homosexual relationship. The list could be either fixed or rebuttable; the latter option would allow those not on the list (e.g. close friends) to claim provided they could prove the necessary tie of love and affection with someone who was actually within the zone of impact (paras. 5.14–14). Lastly, the position of mere bystanders was left open. The Law Commission accepted that liability in such cases could not be based upon foreseeability alone, but invited views as to whether a duty might be recognised to bystanders who are close in time and space to the accident or its aftermath and perceive it through their own unaided senses. The Commission considered that the retention of the requirements of proximity in time and space and proximity of perception might arguably be sufficient to prevent any opening of the floodgates of liability, although it recognised that in some cases (e.g. a tragedy at an air-show or sporting event) the number of bystanders might be huge (paras. 5.29–30).

At the time of writing, the Commission's final report on the above consultation issues is still awaited. One might, however, question whether such a restrictive approach is in fact called for. The Law Commission presents no convincing argument that psychiatric illness raises the floodgates objection – that a single event might result in a mass of claims – to any greater degree than does physical injury. It should be noted, for instance, that some 500 people were killed or suffered physical injury in the Hillsborough football stadium tragedy, yet it has never been suggested that they should be denied compensation in order to prevent a flood of claims. Although the Commission cites medical evidence that a very sizeable proportion of those *involved* in catastrophic events suffer PTSD, this does not address the key question of whether significant numbers of *witnesses* – the category of plaintiff whose claims to compensation the Commission wishes to restrict – suffer such a reaction. In any case, it has received judicial notice that awards for psychiatric illness are 'surprisingly low' compared with those for physical injury (*R* v. *Liverpool City Council*, 23 November 1988, unreported, per Hodgson J) and many claims are scarcely worth pursuing at all (the Judicial Studies Board's official guidelines, 1994, suggest a figure of only £500 for very minor psychiatric illness). But in the severe cases – e.g. where the victim is forced to forego paid employment – the losses may be very substantial indeed and surely demand compensation.

In conclusion, it may be asked whether the Law Commission has satisfied the challenge – thrown down by Lord Browne-Wilkinson in *X (Minors)* v. *Bedfordshire County Council* [1995] 2 AC 633, 749 – of identifying 'very potent considerations' that justify restricting the scope of liability in negligence. Only on the basis of the most persuasive evidence and argument ought the law to deny the moral claim to compensation for negligently-inflicted injury. It is submitted that the considerations relied upon by the Commission fall short of satisfying that prescription, and that the resulting proposal is as open to charges of arbitariness and anomaly as is the existing law.

Summary

4.1 Cases of what lawyers call 'nervous shock', i.e. psychiatric illness and other personal injury caused by mental trauma, have given rise to significant difficulties in the modern law of negligence and the courts have adopted a cautious and restrictive approach to the recognition of a duty of care.

4.2 Despite earlier indications that a more expansive approach might be taken, the courts now limit the scope of the duty of care by reference to a number of proximity requirements (at least in relation to claims brought by witnesses of a traumatic event).

4.3 To be distinguished from the witness cases are cases brought by the 'primary victim' of the defendant's negligence, i.e. the person subjected to the risk of physical harm. Where injury by physical means is reasonably foreseeable, it is not necessary to show that injury by psychiatric means was also foreseeable, nor to satisfy the various proximity requirements imposed in the 'witness' cases.

4.4   The witness to a traumatic event who brings an action in respect of nervous shock must satisfy the requirements of proximity of relationship, proximity in time and space, and proximity of perception.

4.5   Other categories of claimant (namely the rescuer, the unwitting agent of misfortune, and the employee) warrant separate attention.

4.6   Liability for stress may, in appropriate circumstances, arise in the tort of negligence but the precise scope of such liability has yet to be determined.

4.7   The Law Commission (1995), in a thorough review of liability for psychiatric illness, has by and large endorsed the current state of the law, while suggesting slight refinements in particular areas.

Exercises

4.1   Is psychiatric illness to be treated as an unexceptional type of personal injury in respect of which the sole criterion of liability is foreseeability or is it a type of injury that requires the scope of the duty of care to be limited? If the latter, what is it about psychiatric illness that calls for a restrictive approach?

4.2   What is the importance of the distinction between the 'primary victim' of a traumatic event and mere witnesses to it?

4.3   In what circumstances might brothers and sisters of a deceased claim damages for nervous shock after witnessing her death? What evidence about their relationship with the deceased would they have to produce in court?

4.4   Must the plaintiff in a nervous shock action always actually see the traumatic event in person? What if the plaintiff is blind?

4.5   Two years ago a fatal train crash occurred at Thames Junction. The 7.20 a.m. from Fleet was directed down the wrong tracks through the negligence of a railway employee and ploughed into a group of workers laying new track. Three of the workers were killed; two were seriously injured. Only G escaped being caught in the impact, though she had felt sure that she was doomed. None of the passengers in the train, driven by H, was hurt. J, the station supervisor and the twin sister of one of those killed, had watched the accident as it happened on closed circuit television; she proceeded bravely to coordinate the rescue attempts from her office with the aid of the television cameras. It took several hours to recover the bodies of the dead and wounded from the wreck. As they were laid by the side of the track, relatives were allowed to approach. K saw her daughter wracked with pain and attempted to give her comfort; L saw the lifeless body of her son and kissed him farewell. Railway staff refrained from telling K that her daughter, having been designated look-out, was partly responsible for the injuries suffered. The whole proceedings, from the moment of the crash on, were observed by M, a five-year-old child. G, H, J, K L and M all suffered post-traumatic stress disorder as a consequence of their experiences. N, the lover of one of those injured in the crash, nursed her loved one slowly back to health but herself suffered a nervous breakdown as a result of the strain which this caused. Advise the parties as to their rights and liabilities in tort.

5   Economic Loss

5.1 What Is 'Pure Economic Loss'?

The tort of negligence provides compensation for all sorts of losses that are financial in nature. If you were to be run over by a negligent car driver, you would get damages not only for your physical injuries (your pain and suffering, etc.) but also for the financial consequences of those injuries. Hence you would be able to recover in respect of any medical costs incurred and any wages lost. However, when the courts are faced with loss that is *purely* economic in nature – that is, which does not stem from any physical damage to the plaintiff or her property – their approach is very different. The courts have so restricted liability for pure economic loss that it is possible to state as a general rule that it is not recoverable in the tort of negligence.

The crucial distinction is between (recoverable) *consequential* economic loss and *pure* economic loss (not generally recoverable), as is illustrated by the instructive case of *Spartan Steel and Alloys Ltd* v. *Martin & Co Ltd* [1973] QB 27. Martin & Co were building contractors carrying out road works near Spartan Steel's metal-processing plant. Their men were careless in digging up the road and damaged the electricity cable running to the plant. The power was cut off for several hours. Spartan Steel sued Martin & Co for their lost profits. The Court of Appeal allowed the claim only in part. The majority of the court made the following distinction. The profits lost on the metal that was being processed at the time the electricity was cut off were recoverable. This metal was actually damaged by the power cut and so these profits could be regarded as consequential economic loss stemming from physical damage to the plaintiff's property. The rest of Spartan Steel's loss, however, was purely economic. This loss arose from the fact that Spartan Steel was not able to process other lots of metal in the time the power was off: it did not stem from damage to any of these lots. Admittedly, the electricity cable had been damaged, but the cable belonged to the electricity board, not to Spartan Steel: to recover financial loss you have to establish that it was caused by physical damage to your own person or property (see further *Leigh & Sillivan Ltd* v. *Aliakmon Shipping Co Ltd* [1986] AC 785, but note the Carriage of Goods by Sea Act 1992, s. 2).

The courts' adoption of a general 'no recovery' or 'exclusionary' rule for pure economic loss is explained by a number of underlying policy considerations. The floodgates argument has perhaps been most influential: the principal fear is that liability might extend to an indeterminate class of plaintiffs, in an indeterminate amount, thereby imposing an undue burden upon the defendant. In *Hedley Byrne & Co.* v. *Heller & Partners Ltd* [1964] AC 465, 536–7, Lord Pearce explicitly acknowledged that the risk of indeterminate liability justified restrictions on the scope of the duty of care:

> 'How wide the sphere of the duty of care in negligence is to be laid depends ultimately upon the courts' assessment of the demands of society for protection from the carelessness of others. Economic protection has lagged behind protection in physical matters where there is injury to person and property. It may be that the size and the width of the range of possible claims has acted as a deterrent to extension of economic protection.'

The same concern was identified and developed by Lord Denning in *Spartan Steel* itself (p. 38):

> 'If claims for economic loss were permitted for this particular hazard there would be no end of claims.. Some might be genuine, but many might be inflated or even false.'

In Lord Denning's view, it was best to leave the losses to lie where they fell rather than concentrating them on the defendant: if the losses were small, they might without hardship be absorbed by the victims themselves; if they were serious, then the victims ought themselves to have taken out insurance by way of protection against that risk.

5.2 Defective Product Economic Loss

We must now elaborate our definition of pure economic loss to take into account the question of defective products. The courts insist that the manufacturer of a defective product will be liable only in respect of damage that the product causes to another's person or property. If a product is simply no good, or merely physically deteriorates, even if it blows up and destroys itself, any financial loss that results is purely economic. In short, a defect does not constitute 'damage'. So, while Mrs Donoghue's claim for compensation for being ill after drinking that fabled bottle of ginger beer would today be unanswerable, she would not be entitled to recover the cost of a replacement bottle of ginger beer, that cost arising solely from the bottle's defective nature.

Three decisions of the House of Lords stand out as of first rate importance: *Anns* v. *Merton LBC* [1978] AC 728, *D & F Estates* v. *Church Commissioners* [1989] AC 177 and *Murphy* v. *Brentwood DC* [1991] 1 AC 398; all three cases raised the question of defective product economic loss in relation to the construction of buildings (for application of the same principles to defective goods rather than buildings, see, e.g., *Muirhead* v. *International Tank Specialities Ltd* [1986] QB 507). In *Anns*, the House of Lords had held that, where the defective nature of the building's foundations had caused subsidence, then cracks that consequently appeared in the walls of the building might be regarded as 'material, physical damage' (p. 759, per Lord Wilberforce); the plaintiff, who had proceeded against the local authority which had the power to supervise the building work, was allowed to recover the cost of remedying the damage so as to avoid a 'present or imminent danger to the health or safety of the persons occupying it' (p. 760, per Lord Wilberforce; for analysis of other aspects of the decision, see 6.7). In *D & F Estates*, however, the House of Lords disputed Lord Wilberforce's categorisation of the loss in such cases as arising from 'material physical damage' and held that the loss was purely economic because it was attributable solely to the defective condition of the building. In *D & F Estates*, the action was brought against the builder who was directly responsible for the defective work, and so it was not necessary for the House of Lords to rule on the correctness of its earlier decision in *Anns*; nevertheless, the decision in *D & F Estates* effectively undermined the reasoning in *Anns*, and it was perhaps inevitable that the House of Lords would exercise its power to overrule that decision when the opportunity presented itself. That opportunity arose in *Murphy* v. *Brentwood DC* [1991] AC 398, which like *Anns* concerned the liability of a local authority in respect of alleged negligence in supervising the construction of a dwelling; the property was eventually acquired by the plaintiff, who suffered loss on its subsequent sale after defects in the foundations had been discovered following the appearance of cracks in the walls of the house. The House of Lords followed its decision in *D & F Estates* and treated the cracks and subsidence as merely the manifestation of a defect in the building, not as damage; accordingly, the money Mr Murphy lost on the subsequent sale of his house was purely economic and fell within the scope of the general 'no recovery' rule.

The decisions of the House of Lords in *D & F Estates* and *Murphy* leave a number of loose ends to be tied together. In the following paragraphs, we look at two – the availability of preventative damages and the complex structures argument – before considering the question of reform. But we should also draw attention to a further matter, to be discussed further below, namely the extent to which the recognition of liability under the rule in *Hedley Byrne & Co.* v. *Heller & Partners Ltd* [1964] AC 465 may serve to undermine the general 'no recovery' rule adopted in those decisions (see 5.3).

Preventative Damages

An alternative explanation of *Anns*, which did not depend upon the classification of the loss in that case as arising from 'material physical damage', was that there should be a limited exception to the general 'no recovery' rule applicable to pure economic loss where it was necessary to incur the cost of repair work in order to prevent the occurrence of anticipated physical damage. Under this approach (recently adopted by the Supreme Court of Canade in *Winnipeg Condominium Corp No. 36* v. *Bird Construction Co* (1995) 121 DLR (4th) 193), liability might arise in respect of 'dangerous' defects, but not in respect of pure defects of quality. The award of 'preventative damages' in such cases might be thought to have intuitive appeal in so far as it allows a property owner to claim damages in order to avert personal injury or damage to *other* property without having to wait until the loss is sustained; it reflects the commonsense maxim that prevention is better than cure.

In *Murphy*, however, the House of Lords rejected an argument that the decision in *Anns* should be upheld on this limited basis. Their Lordships appear to have taken the view that damages in respect of the cost of preventative repair work were not warranted because, if the property owner had decided to wait until physical damage was sustained, it would not have been appropriate to compensate for the cost of remedying that damage. In such a case, the owner's knowledge of the defect was enough to neutralise the danger because she would have the option of repairing the defect or abandoning the building as unfit for habitation; in either case, the loss sustained was in essence a purely economic loss. As Lord Bridge explained, 'because the danger is now known . . . the defect becomes merely a defect in quality' (p. 475). His Lordship continued:

> 'If a builder erects a structure containing a latent defect which renders it dangerous to persons or property, he will be liable in tort for any injury to persons or damage to property resulting from that dangerous defect. But, if the defect becomes apparent before any injury or damage has been caused, the loss sustained by the building owner is purely economic.'

Their Lordships' analysis is difficult to follow and appears to be somewhat questionable. In so far as it rests on an assumption that the occupier who knows the full extent of the defect yet continues to occupy the building is the author of her own misfortune, the analysis seems to rest on principles of causation and voluntary assumption of risk; yet these principles only bar claims by those who voluntarily and unreasonably run the risk of injury, and we may doubt whether these conditions are truly satisfied here (see 9.4 and 11.3). Is the homeowner who, lacking the financial means to effect a repair or to move to alternative accommodation, continues in occupation after discovery of a dangerous defect really to have no recourse against the builder? The Court of Appeal has apparently found this prospect unpalatable and in *Targett* v. *Torfaen Borough Council* [1992] 3 All ER 27 declined to treat *Murphy* as barring a claim by an occupier who was injured by a known defect on the premises. Sir Donald Nicholls V-C noted (p. 37) that

> 'knowledge of the existence of a danger does not always enable a person to avoid the danger. In simple cases it does. In other cases, especially where buildings are concerned, it would be absurdly unrealistic to suggest that a person can always take steps to avoid a danger once he knows of its existence, and that if he does not do so he is the author of his own misfortune'.

In his view, the real question was whether 'it is reasonable for the plaintiff to remove or avoid the danger, and unreasonable for him to run the risk of being injured by the danger' (ibid). It is submitted that the Vice-

Chancellor's approach is entirely convincing and that it substantially undermines the reasons for the House of Lords' rejection of a doctrine of preventative damages in *Murphy*: if homeowners might in appropriate cases recover compensation for damage suffered as a consequence of a known defect, then there should also be a remedy for those homeowners who have both the prudence and the means to effect repairs before damage is sustained.

In any case, there are indications that the House of Lords' rejection of a doctrine of preventative damages was somewhat equivocal. Lord Bridge was apparently prepared to contemplate an exception to the general rule if a dangerous defect in a building should threaten to injure those in neighbouring houses or on the street; in such circumstances, he thought that the owner might be able to recover the cost of demolition or repair work effected to remove the danger to third parties. Although Lord Oliver expressed doubts whether it was right to admit such an exception, Lord Bridge's suggestion has since been followed by the High Court in *Morse* v. *Barratt (Leeds) Ltd* [1992] Const. L.J. 158. In that case, the defendant property developers were held liable for the cost of repairing a stone retaining wall at the rear of their development which had become liable to collapse as a result of their negligence. The wall had become a danger to users of the highway, and the plaintiff residents of the development were entitled to recover the cost of making the wall safe and thereby protecting them against liability to highway users. This leaves the law in a puzzling state for it seems that, while a property owner may be expected to abandon her property to save herself from physical harm, she is not expected to bear the costs of demolition work to protect those on adjacent land from such a risk.

The complex structures argument

The decisions in *D & F Estates* and *Murphy* leave a potential loophole for plaintiffs to exploit. This centres upon the 'complex structures' argument first advanced by Lord Bridge in *D & F Estates* v. *Church Commissioners* [1989] AC 177 and developed by Lord Bridge and other members of the House of Lords in *Murphy* v. *Brentwood District Council* [1991] 1 AC 398, esp. 470, 476–9 and 497. The argument suggests a qualification to the general rule preventing recovery in respect of any physical deterioration of a product which arises out of a mere defect: certain products might be analysed as 'complex structures' made up of several separate and distinct component items of property, such that the owner would be able to sue in respect of *damage* to one component part caused by a *defect* in another. Such damage would not be considered pure economic loss and would be recoverable under normal *Donoghue* v. *Stevenson* principles. Doubts exist as to the circumstances in which the complex structures analysis might operate. Lord Bridge in *Murphy* suggested that it might apply if a defective central heating boiler in a house were to cause a fire damaging the house and that the owner might therefore recover damages from the boiler manufacturer. However, the House of Lords in *Murphy* was adamant that the complex structures argument had no place in the case before it: it could not be said that the cracks in the walls of Mr Murphy's house were damage to a part of the building separate from the defective foundations which were the root of the problem. It seems that the argument depends upon a number of factors, among them whether the component causing the damage came from a supplier different from that of the rest of the product and whether the component might be replaced without doing structural damage to the rest of the product. But whether the argument will find favour with the courts, and (if so) precisely how it will be applied, is as yet uncertain (see Fleming 1989b; Grubb and Mullis, 1991).

Reform

What is the justification for applying the 'no recovery' rule to defective product economic loss? In the context of pure economic loss generally, the principal fear seems to be that recognition of a duty of care would open up a 'liability in an indeterminate amount for an indeterminate time to an indeterminate class' (*Ultramares Corpn* v *Touche* 174 NE 441, 444 (1931), per Cardozo J). Yet the fear of indeterminate liability loses its force in the context of defective products, for the amount of the loss attributable to the defect is limited by the value of the product itself, while the class of potential plaintiffs is limited to the owner of the product for the time being. In fact, an entirely distinct consideration of public policy is raised in relation to defective products, namely the danger of subverting key doctrines of the law of contract and hence of upsetting the settled expectations of those engaged in business dealings. Allowing the purchaser of a defective product to sue the producer in tort in respect of a merely qualitative (as opposed to dangerous) defect would effectively expose the producer to 'the obligations of an indefinitely transmissible warranty of quality' ([1991] 1 AC 398, 480 per Lord Bridge). The scope of the producer's liability would no longer be limited by the contractual doctrine of privity. Perhaps we should pause for thought before urging the courts to take such a dramatic step. As Lord Keith observed in *Murphy*, 'in what is essentially a consumer protection field . . . the precise extent and limits of the liabilities which in the public interest are imposed on builders and local authorities are best left to the legislature' (p. 472).

In fact, the legislature has already acted to address the plight of homeowners in Mr Murphy's situation (although the material facts of his case arose before the legislation came into effect). By s. 1 of the Defective Premises Act 1972, architects, builders and others 'taking on work for or in connection with the provision of a dwelling-house' may be held liable to owners of those dwellings if they fail to carry out their work in a workmanlike or professional manner and this failure results in the building being unfit for habitation (query whether this extends to local authorities who approve the plans of a proposed development). The Act only applies to 'dwellings'; commercial properties are excluded. Also excluded are houses erected under schemes approved by the Secretary of State. Such schemes, notably the 'Buildmark' scheme run by the National

House Building Council, for a long time covered virtually all newly built homes, and the effect of this exclusion in practice was therefore to limit the operation of the Act to renovations and improvements. It now seems, however, that the NHBC no longer seeks ministerial approval for its schemes, with the result that purchasers under the schemes retain their statutory remedy (see Clerk and Lindsell, 1995, para. 7–93). The Act imposes a limitation period of six years from the completion of the relevant work, which contrasts unfavourably with the position at common law where the six-year limitation period only begins to run from the date at which the loss is sustained. (In so far as defective product economic loss is recoverable, the loss is deemed to arise when the defect becomes evident and thereby affects the value of the property: see *Invercargill City Council* v. *Hamlin* [1996] AC 624.) The Law Commission in its report (1970b) which formed the basis for the Act had stated that the new legislation it proposed was not intended to prevent further development of the common law, but the House of Lords in *Murphy* thought it unwise to add at common law to the statutory obligations. Lord Bridge's view was typical:

'It would be remarkable to find that similar obligations in the nature of a transmissible warranty of quality, applicable to buildings of every kind and subject to no such limitations or exclusions as are imposed by the 1972 Act, could be derived from the builder's common law duty of care. . .'

The existence of the statutory remedy may well be enough to deflate further pressure for recognition of a common law action against the builder, and enables the English courts to justify their approach in an area in which many Commonwealth jurisdictions have taken a contrary view. Indeed, in *Invercargill City Council* v. *Hamlin* [1996] AC 624, the Privy Council accepted that the New Zealand courts might legitimately decline to follow *Murphy* given the absence of any legislation equivalent to the 1972 Act in that country: the decision whether or not to recognise a duty of care reflected policy considerations that might be expected to vary from one country to another, in the light *inter alia* of the legislative background (see also *Bryan* v. *Maloney* (1995) 128 ALR 163 (Australia); *Winnipeg Condominium Corp No. 36* v. *Bird Construction Co* (1995) 121 DLR (4th) 193 (Canada; liability for dangerous defects only)).

5.3 Exceptional Liability for Pure Economic Loss

Over the years, the courts have recognised a number of exceptions to the rule against recovery for the negligent infliction of pure economic loss, but the only exceptions of lasting and general significance derive from the decision of the House of Lords in *Hedley Byrne & Co.* v. *Heller & Partners Ltd* [1964] AC 465. The case considered the liability of a bank in respect of an inaccurate credit-reference. Hedley Byrne, a firm of advertising agents, was engaged to conduct an advertising campaign by a certain company, Easipower Ltd. In the course of this engagement, Hedley Byrne became personally liable under a number of contracts for advertising time and space. As a precautionary measure, the firm had its bank check Easipower's creditworthiness by writing to Heller & Partners, Easipower's bankers. Heller & Partners replied, in a letter marked 'without responsibility', that Easipower was in a sound business position. This turned out to be false and Hedley Byrne lost several thousands of pounds under the contracts when Easipower went into liquidation. Hedley Byrne sued Easipower's bankers to try to recover this money. Its claim was rejected by the House of Lords on the grounds that Heller & Partners had successfully excluded any liability to Hedley Byrne by making it clear that they supplied the information requested 'without responsibility'. The House of Lords did, however, accept (by a bare majority) that the bankers would have been liable for Hedley Byrne's pure economic loss had they not made this disclaimer of responsibility. Furthermore, their Lordships were unanimous that there would be cases outside the banker–creditor context in which liability for pure economic loss would be imposed.

This was a major breakthrough. Although the courts had previously recognised liability for pure economic loss resulting from misrepresentation in the tort of deceit, negligence is not sufficient to make out liability in deceit (*Derry* v. *Peek* (1889) 14 App Cas 337) and the Court of Appeal (Denning LJ dissenting) had ruled in *Candler* v. *Crane, Christmas & Co* [1959] 2 QB 164 that no liability would arise in the tort of negligence. The latter decision was overturned by *Hedley Byrne* and the dissent of Denning LJ approved. The House of Lords did not, however, found itself directly upon the duty of care of broad scope recognised in *Donoghue* v. *Stevenson*. Instead it sought to develop a narrow exception to the 'no liability' rule by building incrementally upon an existing principle by which liability for carelessness might arise. This principle was one of equity rather than tort law: the principle that in a fiduciary relationship the fiduciary must take reasonable care of the interests of the beneficiary (*Nocton* v. *Lord Ashburton* [1914] AC 932; this obligation is in fact only one of the incidents of the fiduciary duty, which also entails, e.g., the obligation to account for profits: see *Boardman* v. *Phipps* [1967] 2 AC 46). The House of Lords took the view that there were other analogous 'special relationships' in which a duty to take care at common law – a duty, in this context, to speak carefully and not merely honestly – might arise.

This landmark decision paved the way for judicial recognition of liability for pure economic loss in a variety of situations. A surveyor employed to value a house for a building society to determine whether it is adequate security for a prospective mortgage may owe a duty of care not only to the building society but also to the prospective mortgagor who proceeds with the purchase in reliance upon the valuation (*Smith* v. *Eric S Bush* [1990] AC 831). An accountant may be may be held liable to a takeover bidder who effects a takeover in reliance upon a specially prepared audit statement (*Morgan Crucible Co* v. *Hill Samuel Bank* [1991] Ch. 259), but not, it seems, to shareholders who are simply sent a copy of the annual audit required by statute (*Caparo Industries* v. *Dickman* [1990] 2 AC 605). When acting as a referee for a former employee or agent, an employer owes the latter a duty of care (*Spring* v. *Guardian Assurance* [1995] 2 AC 296). Of all these and similar applications of the rule in *Hedley Byrne* v. *Heller*, however, perhaps the most significant has been its application to acts as well as representations. In *Henderson* v. *Merrett Syndicates Ltd* [1995] 2 AC 145, the House of Lords held that 'the principle extends beyond the provision of information and advice to include the performance of other services' (p. 180, per Lord Goff); applying the principle in *Hedley Byrne*, the House of Lords held that managing agents in the Lloyd's of London insurance market owe a duty of care to the 'names' who subscribe to their syndicate.

Not all the subsequent cases which allowed recovery for pure economic loss were brought under the *Hedley Byrne* umbrella. In the rapid expansion of liability for negligence that occurred in the 1970s and early 1980s, some courts took a more radical approach and claimed to base liability on normal *Donoghue* v. *Stevenson* principles, rather than on the narrower rule in *Hedley Byrne* (see *Ministry of Housing and Local Government* v. *Sharp* [1970] 2 QB 223; *Ross* v. *Caunters* [1980] Ch 297). The high-water mark came with the problematic case of *Junior Books Ltd* v. *Veitchi Co. Ltd* [1983] AC 520, in which a majority of the House of Lords imposed liability in respect of defective product economic loss representing the cost of replacing a negligently laid floor. The action was brought by the owner of premises, who had engaged contractors to do construction work, against the defendant subcontractor, whom the owner had nominated to lay the floor. It subsequently transpired that the plaintiff had already settled a contractual claim against the main contractors, subject to an agreed limitation of liability (Atiyah, 1989, p. 397; this evidence was not before the House of Lords); the case therefore raised in stark form the question of whether it was right to allow the tort remedy to bypass limitations of liability and other protections built into the contractual structure. Reaction to *Junior Books* was largely hostile and since that time there has been a marked retrenchment of liability in this area; in a series of cases, the Court of Appeal declined to apply the decision, finding it distinguishable on the facts (see *Muirhead* v. *International Tank Specialities Ltd* [1986] QB 507; *Simaan General Contracting Co* v. *Pilkington Glass Ltd* (No. 2) [1988] QB 758; *Greater Nottingham Co-operative Society Ltd* v. *Cementation Piling and Foundations Ltd* [1989] QB 71). Consigning the case to what appeared to be early oblivion, Lord Bridge described it (in *D & F Estates*) as depending upon a 'unique' relationship between the parties and asserted that 'the decision cannot be regarded as laying down any principle of general application in the law of tort' (p. 202). Nevertheless, his Lordship has more recently suggested that *Junior Books* might now be regarded as falling within the scope of *Hedley Byrne* (see *Murphy* v. *Brentwood District Council* [1991] AC 398, 481) and it may well be that the case warrants renewed attention on that account (see 5.7).

We must now turn to the important question of the ingredients of the *Hedley Byrne* liability. These cannot be identified by reference to *Hedley Byrne* alone, as their Lordships in that case were initiating a major departure in the law and were able to predict its subsequent development to only a limited extent. It is only through practical experience of the application of the rule in *Hedley Byrne* that a complete and coherent view of the law can be derived. The position adopted here is that there is in fact *a set* of principles based upon the central notion of a special relationship – rather than a single general principle – that give rise to a duty to take care in protecting another's purely economic interests. In addition to (a) the type of relationship exemplified by *Hedley Byrne*, in which there is direct reliance upon a voluntary assumption of responsibility by the defendant to the plaintiff, there are cases of (b) *indirect reliance*, i.e. reliance upon the defendant's assumption of responsibility to a third party, and (c) *indirect loss without reliance*, where the defendant's failure to fulfill a responsibility assumed towards a third party causes loss to the plaintiff without the plaintiff's having acted in reliance upon the assumption of responsibility at all. It can be seen that the latter two categories are derived from and parasitic upon the first in that they depend upon the existence of a special relationship in which responsibility is assumed by the defendant, albeit to a third party and not to the plaintiff.

5.4 Direct Assumption of Responsibility

A duty of care may arise in respect of pure economic loss on the basis of the defendant's voluntary assumption of responsibility to the plaintiff. The basic principle is that the defendant is taken to assume responsibility to the plaintiff by their jointly entering into a special relationship (sometimes said to be one which is 'equivalent to contract') in which the plaintiff reasonably relies upon the defendant's careful exercise of special skill, knowledge or authority. The concepts here are not, however, used entirely consistently, and it is necessary to spend some time elaborating the meaning and interrelationship of the concepts of voluntary assumption of responsibility, special relationship, special skill, and reasonable reliance.

Voluntary Assumption of Responsibility

The concept of voluntary assumption of responsibility was apparently invoked by the House of Lords in *Hedley Byrne* in order to pre-empt the argument that, given that the defendant bankers had no duty to answer the credit inquiry, they could have no duty to exercise due care if they chose to respond. This reasoning was exposed as fallacious by the House of Lords. Recognition of a duty to exercise due care where an answer was in fact given was quite consistent with there being no legal compulsion to respond at all. The point was put clearly by Lord Reid in a well-known passage (p. 486):

'A reasonable man, knowing that he was being trusted or that his skill and judgment were being relied upon, would, I think, have three courses open to him. He could keep silent or decline to give the information or advice sought: or he could give an answer with a clear qualification that he accepted no responsibility for it or that it was given without that reflection or inquiry which a careful answer would require: or he could simply answer without any such qualification. If he chooses to adopt the last course he must, I think, be held to have accepted some responsibility for his answer being given carefully, or to have accepted a relationship with the inquirer which requires him to exercise such care as the circumstances require.'

The original purpose of the concept of a voluntary assumption of responsibility was therefore to explain how liability might arise in relation to a gratuitous undertaking, and it was not originally intended to function as a means of limiting the situations in which the duty might arise or the parties to whom the duty might be owed. Now that it seems to have acquired the latter purpose, the circumstances in which responsibility will be treated as assumed must be specified. It has been said that the words should be 'understood . . . as referring to a conscious assumption of responsibility for the task rather than a conscious assumption of legal liability to the plaintiff for its careful performance' (*White* v. *Jones* [1995] 2 AC 207, 274 per Lord Browne-Wilkinson; see also Lord Nolan at p. 293). This formulation has the merit of emphasising that the responsibility is imposed by law and is therefore not precluded by the defendant's failure consciously to advert to it (or even by the defendant's purported refusal to accept any responsibility at all: see further *Smith* v. *Eric S Bush* [1990] AC 831, considered below at 5.4). But it fails to account for the special position – relative to the world at large – of *the person to whom the responsibility is assumed* and thus runs the risk of opening the floodgates to a multitude of claims from an indeterminate number of plaintiffs. It is better to regard the responsibility as assumed to the plaintiff by the voluntary act of entering into a special relationship with the plaintiff, and as a legal incident of that relationship, in which the plaintiff is distinguished from the world at large by virtue of her reciprocal dealings with the defendant (i.e. by an element of 'mutuality').

A Special Relationship ('Equivalence to Contract')

The voluntary assumption of responsibility arises 'internally from the relationship in which the parties [have] chosen to place themselves' and is 'a reflection of the relationship in question' (*White* v. *Jones* [1995] 2 AC 207, 287 per Lord Mustill; his Lordship dissented from the final decision, but his analysis of the authorities is still most convincing). It cannot arise purely out of *the situation* in which the plaintiff and defendant found themselves, e.g. whereby the plaintiff was foreseeably affected by the defendant's acts or the plaintiff foreseeably relied upon the defendant's words. Lord Devlin placed considerable emphasis on this point in the course of his exemplary analysis in *Hedley Byrne* itself of the 'sort of relationship which gives rise to a responsibility' (p. 529):

'I do not understand any of your Lordships to hold that it is a responsibility imposed by law upon certain types of persons or in certain sorts of situations. It is a responsibility that is voluntarily accepted or undertaken, either generally where a general relationship, such as that of solicitors and client or banker and customer, is created, or specifically in relation to a particular transaction.'

The relationship, as Lord Devlin makes clear, may be either general or specific. In addition to the examples he gives of the former, we may add the relationships (among others) between employer and employee (in which the former is under a duty – continuing even after employment has been terminated – to take reasonable care while acting as the latter's referee: *Spring* v. *Guardian Assurance* [1995] 2 AC 296) and between underwriters managing an insurance syndicate and the members of (i.e. investors in) that syndicate (see *Henderson* v. *Merrett Syndicates Ltd*, below). Whether a relationship will arise in the absence of such a continuing relationship, i.e. in relation to a specific transaction, depends upon whether the parties engage in dealings of a bilateral and reciprocal character. It is this element of 'mutuality' (as it was termed by Lord Mustill in *White*, p. 283) that creates the special relationship between the parties and makes their relationship different from that between the defendant and others who might foreseeably suffer economic loss as a result of the defendant's carelessness. Lord Mustill explained how such mutuality had formed the basis for the special relationship, arising in relation to a specific transaction, in *Hedley Byrne* (p. 287):

'this relationship was bilateral, being created on the one hand by the acts of the plaintiffs in first asking for a reference in circumstances which showed that the bankers' skill and care would be relied upon and then subsequently relying upon it; and on the other hand by the bankers' compliance with the request.'

In Lord Mustill's analysis, the plaintiff company's request was particularly important in demonstrating the 'active role' the plaintiff had played in the transaction and indeed in 'initiating' the relationship. Without such a request, there would have been no mutuality and (we may add) no simple mechanism for limiting the class of those to whom the responsibility was undertaken.

The relationship between the parties 'may or may not be contractual in nature' (*Henderson* v. *Merret Syndicates Ltd* [1995] 2 AC 145, 180 per Lord Goff). It may arise in relation to pre-contractual negotiations (see *Esso Petroleum Co Ltd* v. *Mardon* [1976] QB 801; and note the concurrent liability under Misrepresentation Act 1967, s. 2) or even, as in *Hedley Byrne* itself, in relation to dealings which do not have a contract as their object. But the relationship must be at least 'equivalent to contract'. This notion was propounded by Lord Devlin in *Hedley Byrne* itself (p. 529); he indicated that there would be the necessary equivalence 'where there is an assumption of responsibility in circumstances, in which, but for the absence of consideration, there would be a contract.' Although consideration need not, therefore, pass from plaintiff to defendant, this is not to say that in cases outside contract the law entirely ignores what the defendant stands to gain from the transaction. This may be relevant to the court's determination of whether the reciprocal dealings are apt to give rise to legal responsibility or are purely social in character, a point to which Lord Devlin also adverted (p. 529):

> 'It may often be a material factor to consider whether the adviser is acting purely out of good nature or whether he is getting his reward in some indirect form. The service that a bank performs in giving a reference is not done simply out of a desire to assist commerce. It would discourage the customers of the bank if their deals fell through because the bank had refused to testify to their credit when it was good.'

The requirement of a contractual or equivalent relationship has the merit of emphasising the need for dealings of a bilateral and reciprocal character and of thereby serving to limit the scope of the liability owed. But it also highlights a possible tension between the principles of contract and those of tort. Two issues are raised. First, if there is a contract between the plaintiff and the defendant, is it necessary and desirable for the law to recognise a tort claim as well? If concurrent liability were to arise, it may be that the plaintiff would be able to pick and chose according to which cause of action – tortious or contractual – were more beneficial (e.g. in relation to the question of remoteness where tort is more generous than contract, allowing liability even for 'extremely unlikely results' on the basis of their reasonable foreseeability where contract requires 'a very substantial degree of probability': *Koufos* v. *C. Czarnikow Ltd.* [1969] 1 AC 350, 388–9 per Lord Reid). Secondly, if there is *no* contract between the parties, is it right that the law of tort should impose liability in respect of what may be a gratuitous undertaking, or an obligation undertaken contractually *vis-à-vis* a third party? These questions are considered further below (see 5.7).

Special Skill, Knowledge or Authority

The requirement that the defendant exercise a special skill (or employ special knowledge or authority) serves to limit the extent to which the liability arising under *Hedley Byrne* v. *Heller* might subvert central doctrines of the law of contract. It restricts the scope of the remedy in tort and channels liability to professionals and the like who might be expected to have insurance to protect themselves against possible liabilities.

The general principle was first formulated by Lord Morris in *Hedley Byrne* (pp. 502–3):

> '[I]f someone possessed of a special skill undertakes, quite irrespective of contract, to apply that skill for the assistance of another person who relies upon such, a duty of care will arise.'

A restrictive interpretation of this principle was given by the Privy Council in *Mutual Life and Citizens Assurance Co* v. *Evatt* [1971] AC 793. The opinion of the majority was that liability should be restricted to those who give advice in a professional capacity: architects, surveyors, accountants and the like. Applying that rule, the Privy Council held that the plaintiff was not entitled to damages from his insurance company who had carelessly given him false information about the financial stability of an associated company in which he invested: the defendant was not in the business of giving advice about investments. A dissenting opinion was offered by Lord Reid and Lord Morris. In their view, it was sufficient that considered advice was sought from a businessman in the course of his business, which was clearly the case on the facts before them. This more expansive conception of *Hedley Byrne* liability has been preferred in the English courts to the narrow view of the majority. It was applied in *Esso Petroleum Co Ltd* v. *Mardon* [1976] QB 801 in which Esso was held liable under the *Hedley Byrne* doctrine, as well as under contract, to the owner of a petrol-filling station whom it had negligently advised about the likely profitability of his investment in the station.

This broader view of *Hedley Byrne* liability was effectively confirmed in the House of Lords in *Spring* v. *Guardian Assurance* in which an employer was held to owe a duty of care in writing a reference about a former employee or equivalent. The plaintiff had recently been engaged as a 'company representative', acting in a self-employed capacity, for Guardian Assurance. Seeking to go into business as an insurance agent on his own, he applied to become a company representative of another insurance firm, which requested a reference from Guardian Assurance. The latter was bound to provide this under the relevant regulatory regime (governed by LAUTRO). The reply (which the trial judge found to have been carelessly compiled) amounted to a 'kiss of death' as it called the plaintiff's honesty into question. The plaintiff's job application was rejected, as were two further applications made to other companies who received the same reference. A majority of the House of Lords (Lord Keith dissenting) held that the former employer owed a duty of care on the facts of this case and that the case should be remitted to the Court of Appeal to determine whether the plaintiff had suffered loss as a result of the established breach of duty (Lord Lowry dissented on this last point). Their Lordships held that there were no reasons of public policy that precluded the imposition of liability. They could not imagine that this would have a significantly adverse effect upon the willingness of employers to give references, or upon the frankness of disclosure in those references; nor did the fact that employers have a defence against liability in defamation prevent liability in negligence, for liability in defamation is in crucial respects more stringent than that in negligence (see ch. 20).

Although Lord Slynn and Lord Woolf held that liability arose without express reliance upon *Hedley Byrne* principles, those principles formed the basis of the decision of Lord Goff, with whom Lord Lowry agreed on this point. Lord Goff carefully refrained from approving the approach of the majority in *Mutual Life*, noting the 'formidable' dissent of Lord Reid and

Lord Morris and that the case had attracted 'serious criticism'. Nevertheless he stated that the result in the case before him was consistent with the majority's reasoning: 'the skill in preparing a reference in respect of an employee falls as much within the expertise of an employer as the skill of preparing a bank reference fell within the expertise of the defendant bank in *Hedley Byrne* itself.' It seems that Lord Goff regarded the defendant's 'special skill' as crucial to the imposition of liability, provided that the phrase was understood in a broad sense to include special knowledge or the ability to acquire knowledge (p. 318). In fact, even this may not be broad enough. In *Spring*, the defendant undoubtedly possessed knowledge that was 'special' relative to the enquirer, but it is difficult to see how that can be the basis of a duty owed to the subject of the reference. In relation to that person, what is special about the position of the former employer is that the latter provides the reference with special *authority*, namely as a former employer, and the subject of the reference has no opportunity to challenge any inaccuracy. There is an imbalance of power between them. The notion of 'special skill' must therefore be broad enough to encompass not only special knowledge but also special authority in the sense described.

One issue yet to be resolved satisfactorily is whether *Hedley Byrne* liability might arise outside the commercial context where a mere social acquaintance possesses or claims special skill. This question was raised in *Chaudhry* v. *Prabhakar* [1988] 3 All ER 718. A young woman sought the advice of a friend in buying a second-hand motor car. He recommended a car he had seen in the garage of a panel-beater, notwithstanding obvious signs that it had been involved in an accident. She took his advice and gave him money to make an initial payment for the car; she paid the balance directly to the seller. The case concerned the standard of care owed by the friend giving the advice; it was conceded that the friend did owe a duty of care, under the law of principal and agent, as he was acting as a gratuitous agent. As the existence of the duty was conceded, the case is at best of limited authority, although two out of three members of the Court of Appeal accepted that the concession was correctly made and that the rule in *Hedley Byrne* v. *Heller* represented an alternative basis for the duty. May LJ doubted this, and the issue cannot be taken to have been finally resolved.

Reasonable Reliance

Reliance is a problematic concept: there is a sense in which all negligence cases involve reliance, 'as every motorist relies upon every other motorist in the vicinity to drive carefully' (*Muirhead* v. *International Tank Specialities Ltd* [1986] QB 507, 527 per Robert Goff LJ). Here, however, the concept of reliance bears a narrower meaning: it refers to the plaintiff's reliance upon the defendant's exercising special skill, knowledge or authority which the defendant has undertaken to apply to the plaintiff's benefit. In other words, there must be *specific* reliance upon the defendant's voluntary assumption of responsibility, not merely the *general* reliance exhibited in Robert Goff LJ's motorist example. In the case of the negligent provision of information or advice, the plaintiff must act upon the information or advice in question; in the case of the negligent provision of services, the plaintiff must entrust the conduct of her affairs to the defendant. Such reliance serves to 'consummate' the reciprocal relationship between plaintiff and defendant that has previously been initiated by the plaintiff (*White* v. *Jones* [1995] 2 AC 145, 288 per Lord Mustill). It also provides the necessary causal link between the defendant's negligence and the plaintiff's loss. In cases where the plaintiff's reliance is unreasonable, this may negate the causal connection (or alternatively provide the basis for a defence of *volenti* or contributory negligence).

5.5 Indirect Reliance

In the cases to which we now turn, the plaintiff suffers loss through reliance upon the defendant's assumption of responsibility to another person with whom the defendant is in a direct relationship. Although it is possible that the defendant might assume responsibility to both that other and the plaintiff, it seems that liability can arise when the responsibility is assumed only to the former, i.e. when there is no course of reciprocal dealings and hence no relationship between plaintiff and defendant. This may be regarded as problematic, as it deprives the courts of a ready mechanism for limiting the range of claims (hence raising the fear of indeterminate liability). Furthermore, it may be thought to distort the economic incentives on service providers (including advisers) who are held liable without having any opportunity to negotiate payment for their services or, in appropriate cases, exemption from liability. This raises fears of overkill as service providers resort to unduly defensive practice, or even withdraw from certain fields of activity altogether (see Bishop, 1980). Indeed, a government inquiry has recently warned that professionals faced with increasing liabilities might carry out unnecessary checks on their work, which serve no purpose other than to protect themselves in the event of a claim, or reject categories of clients who seem to raise particular risks, or even leave the profession altogether, to the detriment of the British business community which depends on having highly qualified professional advisers (Likierman, 1989).

Given the dual fears of indeterminate liability and overkill, it should be no surprise that the courts have proceeded cautiously in this type of case. Yet, although the results of cases have so far kept the scope of liability in check, the leading cases in this area have tended to employ tests of the necessary proximity between plaintiff and defendant that are too vague to provide a workable test of when a duty of care will arise, that promote *ad hoc* decision-making, that keep alive the possibility of an expansion in the sphere of liability, and that thereby result in unnecessary litigation and concomitant uncertainty in the insurance markets.

The crucial case is *Caparo Industries* v. *Dickman* [1990] 2 AC 605, in which the issue before the House of Lords was whether accountants performing their statutory task of auditing company accounts at the end of each business year could be held liable to those who invest in the company in reliance upon those accounts and suffer losses as a consequence. Their Lordships held that no liability arose on the facts, saying that the purpose of the statutory audit was to enable shareholders to monitor the performance of the board of directors, not to enable them – or members of the investing public generally – to purchase shares with confidence (in fact, the government which introduced the statutory requirement had precisely the latter purpose in mind: see Mullis and Oliphant, 1991). They declined to follow the Court of Appeal in drawing a distinction between the first purchase of shares by the plaintiffs, who were then simply members of the investing world generally, and the purchase of subsequent tranches of shares at a time when the plaintiffs had of course become shareholders. But their Lordships accepted that liability might arise in exceptional circumstances, e.g. where the auditor made specific representations to a particular investor in anticipation of a proposed takeover.

The actual decision in *Caparo* was undoubtedly cautious, and indeed was criticised as excessively cautious by those worried by the absence of any alternative legal incentive on auditors diligently to pursue their role as company 'watchdogs' (Mullis and Oliphant, 1991). But their Lordships based their decision on an interpretation of *Hedley Byrne* v. *Heller* that might be regarded as rather vague. According to Lord Bridge, for instance, the necessary proximity resided in the following requirements (p. 621; the other members of the House of Lords adopted very similar tests):

'that the defendant knew that his statement would be communicated to the plaintiff, either as an individual or as a member of an identifiable class, specifically in connection with a particular transaction or transactions of a particular kind . . . and that the plaintiff would be very likely to rely on it for the purpose of deciding whether or not to enter on that transaction or on a transaction of that kind.'

This language is so imprecise as to make us ask why the test was not satisfied in *Caparo*. The auditors undoubtedly knew that their statements would be communicated to a 'class' of individuals, namely shareholders, and they undoubtedly knew that some members of that class would rely upon the information in relation to 'transactions of a particular kind' (further share purchases). The suspicion is that the House of Lords was guilty of somewhat manipulative reasoning in deciding that the group of shareholders was too wide to constitute 'a class' and that the purchase of shares was not a matter of sufficient specificity to count as 'a particular kind' of transaction.

Aside from its imprecision, the principal difficulty with the test employed is its liability to collapse into a test of mere foreseeability. Their Lordships clearly allowed that the duty might arise from the *inferential* knowledge of the defendant, i.e. what the defendant *ought to know*, and it is easy to slip from this into an acceptance that one *ought to know* things which are foreseeable with a certain degree of probability. If the liability of auditors is to be kept within reasonable bounds, it is necessary to test the existence of the duty by reference to factors which are more concrete than the notions of foreseeability and probability. It is submitted that the concept of voluntary assumption of responsibility, arising out of a reciprocal relationship between the parties, provides a more precise mechanism with which to determine the existence and extent of liability. The result in *Caparo* might itself be justified on this basis, in that there was no reciprocal relationship between auditor and investor: the auditor was engaged by the company and undertook responsibility only to the company. This reasoning would also allow the exceptional imposition of liability upon auditors who have direct dealings with a prospective take-over bidder, as was countenanced in *Caparo* (cf. *JEB Fasteners Ltd* v. *Marks, Bloom & Co* [1981] 3 All ER 289). More problematic is the case where a corporate 'predator', having already made one offer to the shareholders of the target company, makes a further, higher offer in reliance upon representations by financial advisers contained in the 'defence documents' prepared by the directors of the target company. The existence of a reciprocal relationship might perhaps be inferred from such facts, in that the course of events was initiated by the plaintiff's first bid for the company and that, although the defence documents are addressed to shareholders of the target company, it is well known that one of their purposes is to induce the bidder to raise its offer (cf. *Morgan Crucible Co* v. *Hill Samuel Bank* [1991] Ch. 259).

Another recent House of Lords decision gives rise to problems of analysis similar to those in *Caparo*. In *Smith* v. *Eric S Bush* [1990] AC 831 (heard with *Harris* v. *Wyre District Council*), surveyors valued a house at the request of a lending institution which passed the information on to its customer, Mrs Smith. The latter purchased the property in reliance upon the valuer's report which had erroneously stated that the property needed no essential repairs. Shortly afterwards, a chimney flue collapsed and crashed through the bedroom ceiling and floor. Mrs Smith sought damages from the valuer, notwithstanding that she had declined to commission a full structural survey of the property and that the report contained a purported disclaimer of liability. In *Harris* v. *Wyre District Council*, the plaintiffs, Mr and Mrs Harris, obtained a loan from their local authority in order to make a house purchase; the house was valued by the authority's own employee who failed to report that the house suffered from serious settlement necessitating major repairs. The Harrises did not see this report, but took the authority's offer of a loan to indicate that the house suffered from no significant defects; like Mrs Smith, they did not commission an independent survey. In each case, the plaintiffs were charged a valuation fee by their lending institution.

The House of Lords held that, in the circumstances of these cases (both of which involved a modest residential property), the valuer owed a duty of care to the potential purchaser (conceded in *Smith* v. *Bush*) and that the attempted disclaimer of liability did not satisfy the requirement of reasonableness imposed by the Unfair Contract Terms Act 1977 (see further 11.4). In looking for the necessary relationship of proximity, their Lordships focused upon two factors: 'The necessary proximity arises from the surveyor's knowledge that the overwhelming probability is that the purchaser will rely on his valuation . . . and the fact that the surveyor only obtains the work because the purchaser is willing to pay his fee' (p. 865, per Lord Griffiths). It did not matter that the property valuation was designed to reassure the lending institution that the property in question represented adequate security because it has become common practice for house purchasers to treat such valuations as evidence of the structural soundness of the property and very few go to the additional expense of commissioning a full structural survey. Lord Griffiths added that '[t]here is no question here of creating a liability of indeterminate amount to an indeterminate class', emphasising that '[t]he extent of the liability is limited to the purchaser of the house' and that '[t]he amount of the liability cannot be very great because it relates to a modest house' (p. 865).

Although these cases are sometimes seen as 'three party' cases equivalent to *Caparo*, they are better differentiated from *Caparo* on the basis that each involved a direct assumption of responsibility by the valuer to the house purchaser, cutting across the indirect contractual relationship between the parties (see also the case of the indirect names in *Henderson* v. *Merrett*: 5.7). Although Lord Griffiths expressly doubted the utility of the concept of voluntary assumption of responsibility, it seems that he erroneously thought that it required the defendant's conscious assumption of legal responsibility rather than merely the voluntary entering into a relationship of reciprocal character (see 5.4, 'Voluntary Assumption of Responsibility'). In both *Smith* and *Harris*, the element of 'mutuality' which is necessary to create such a relationship seems to have been present: in each case, the plaintiffs *initiated* the reciprocal relationship between the parties by their request for a mortgage and payment of valuation fee, and *consummated* it by relying upon the valuer's (express or implied) representation as to the property's soundness. Seen in this light, the most controversial aspect of these cases is that the House of Lords implicitly regarded the assumption of responsibility as consistent with a contractual framework within which the plaintiffs were given, but declined, the option of entering into a direct relationship with the valuer by commissioning a full structural survey (carrying with it full guarantees). It is, one might think, unusual for the courts to impose a policy of consumer protection where consumers have the ready means of purchasing such protection for themselves.

5.6 Indirect Loss Without Reliance

Another exceptional type of case is where the defendant's conduct, for which the defendant has assumed a responsibility towards a third party, causes loss to the plaintiff without reliance on the part of the latter. Once again, if liability is to be recognised in such circumstances it becomes difficult to limit the scope of the duty, and the fear arises of a flood of claims placing an excessive burden on the defendant. So the courts have proceeded cautiously but have nevertheless recognised a duty in certain exceptional circumstances.

In *White* v. *Jones* [1995] 2 AC 145, the House of Lords had to consider the correctness of the decision in *Ross* v. *Caunters* (a firm) [1980] Ch 297 that solicitors who undertake the task of drawing up a will owe a duty of care to intended beneficiaries left unable to inherit as a result of the solicitors' negligence. As a result of a family quarrel, the elderly testator, Mr Barratt, had excluded his two daughters (the plaintiffs) from his will. Shortly afterwards, there was a reconciliation and Mr Barratt instructed his solicitors to draw up a new will in which his daughters would be named as beneficiaries. His instructions were accepted but the solicitors unreasonably delayed in acting upon them, and had failed to draw up the new will at the time of Mr Barratt's sudden death a couple of months later. Under established principles of the law of succession, the estate could only be divided in accordance with the terms of the existent will: the subsequent instructions to the solicitors were not witnessed and could not take effect as a will. The daughters were therefore deprived of their intended inheritance, and brought an action for damages in negligence. By a majority of 3–2, the House of Lords held that the solicitors owed the intended beneficiaries a duty of care and could be held liable to indemnify the plaintiffs for their loss of expectation.

The primary significance of this case is that it allows liability for the negligent provision of a service which was undertaken at the request of a third party and caused loss without any specific act of reliance by the plaintiff (but note Lord Nolan's reservations on this last point, below). As Lord Goff stated, the case did not fall within the standard *Hedley Byrne* v. *Heller* special relationship (p. 262):

> '[T]here is great difficulty in holding, on ordinary principles, that the solicitor has assumed any responsibility towards an intended bene-ficiary under a will which he has undertaken to prepare on behalf of his client but which, through his negligence, has failed to take effect in accordance with his client's instructions. The relevant work is plainly performed by the solicitor for his client; but, in the absence of special circumstances, it cannot be said to have been undertaken for the intended beneficiary. . . [T]here will have been no reliance by the intended beneficiary on the exercise by the solicitor of due care and skill; indeed the intended beneficiary may not even have been aware that the solicitor was engaged on such a task, or that his position might be affected.'

Nevertheless, the majority of the House of Lords was prepared to allow an incremental expansion on the existing categories of liability for pure economic loss and to fashion a remedy to meet the special circumstances of the case.

What most impressed the majority of their Lordships' House was the practical justice of the plaintiffs' case. In the absence of a tort remedy, there was, as Lord Goff noted, an asymmetry as between loss and remedy (pp. 259–60):

> 'if such a duty is not recognised, the only person who might have a valid claim (i.e. the testator and his estate) has suffered no loss, and the only person who has suffered a loss (i.e. the disappointed beneficiary) has no claim. . . It can therefore be said that, if the solicitor owes no duty to the intended beneficiaries, there is a lacuna in the law which needs to be filled.'

To their Lordships, it was immaterial that recognition of the duty would result in a windfall benefit to the estate, which would still distribute the bequest in accordance with the terms of the actual will.

Their Lordships agreed that the duty of care arose from the defendant's voluntary assumption of responsibility for the task of preparing the will, but their speeches reveal small yet significant variations of approach. Lord Goff held that responsibility was *in fact* assumed only to the testator. Nevertheless, in view of the need to fill the lacuna in the law, he was prepared to *deem* the assumption of responsibility to have wider effect: 'the assumption of responsibility by the solicitor towards his client should be held in law to extend to the intended beneficiary' (p. 268). By means of this legal fiction, he was able to disregard the need for any reliance by the plaintiff upon the defendant's care and skill.

In contrast, both Lord Browne-Wilkinson and Lord Nolan found that the solicitors had voluntarily assumed responsibility by accepting Mr Barratt's instructions: it was up to the law to specify the scope of that responsibility and, in particular, to determine whether it extended to the plaintiffs. Both decided that it did indeed extend to them, Lord Nolan on the narrow ground that there were (on the facts of this case) specific acts of reliance by the plaintiffs who had been 'intimately concerned' in instructing the solicitors to revise the will (they had been in direct contact with the solicitors: p. 295); Lord Nolan appears therefore to have regarded the course of dealings between the parties as crucial in this case and to have treated the case as falling within the straightforward *Hedley Byrne* type of special relationship. Lord Browne-Wilkinson (like Lord Goff), however, preferred not to leave the result dependant upon the actual dealings between the parties on the facts of the case, as in many cases the intended beneficiaries might not even know of the proposed bequest. His approach was to identify a new class of special relationship – by incremental expansion upon the existing classes of relationship, namely the fiduciary relationship and the *Hedley Byrne* special relationship – in which liability depended upon the defendant's voluntary assumption of responsibility in agreeing to perform a task but not upon any specific acts of reliance by the plaintiff.

The decision cannot be regarded as satisfactory. First, the divergence of approach as between the members of the majority makes it impossible to state the *ratio decidendi* of the case and makes further litigation inevitable; indeed, the narrowness of the ground on which Lord Nolan, the 'swing judge', found for the plaintiffs means that another visit to the Lords will be required just to resolve the case of the intended beneficiaries who are ignorant of the proposed bequest. Secondly, the interpretation given to the concept of voluntary assumption of responsibility by Lord Browne-Wilkinson and Lord Nolan is so broad as to deprive it of all meaning and utility. Responsibility is assumed in the sense described by their Lordships in the performance of any potentially harmful activity: 'If the defendant drives his car on the highway, he implicitly assumes a responsibility towards other road users' (p. 293, per Lord Nolan). Yet such an interpretation negates the concept's role in specifying the scope of liability in the particular sphere of pure economic loss because it provides no way to limit the class of those to whom responsibility is assumed. The more precise conception of Lord Goff, which requires evidence of a course of dealings between the parties, is to be preferred (see 5.4, 'Voluntary Assumption of Responsibility').

It is submitted, therefore, that the rule in *White* v. *Jones* should be interpreted as applying where the defendant assumes responsibility to one person with a view to conferring a benefit upon another, in circumstances where the latter will be without a remedy should the defendant fail to discharge that responsibility. (The principle should have no application where the arrangements between the parties are designed to exclude or restrict any remedy: cf. *Leigh & Sillivan Ltd* v. *Aliakmon Shipping Co Ltd* [1986] AC 785.) As the duty to the plaintiff is derivative from the initial assumption of responsibility, it follows that the scope of that duty will reflect the extent of the responsibility assumed, and that the defendant's disclaimer of responsibility may defeat the plaintiff's claim irrespective of whether the plaintiff had notice of it (p. 268, per Lord Goff); conversely, where responsibility is directly assumed to the plaintiff under normal *Hedley Byrne* principles, it would seem that the plaintiff must have notice of the disclaimer if it is to have effect. The duty is designed to fill a lacuna in the law, and hence will not be imposed where the intending benefactor retains the means to perfect the transaction or provide some equivalent benefit, as in the case of a typical *inter vivos* gift (see *Clarke* v. *Bruce Lance & Co* (a firm) [1988] 1 WLR 881). But there may be exceptional cases of *inter vivos* transactions in which the ability to perfect the transaction has been irretrievably lost, and it has been suggested that the rule might apply in such circumstances, e.g. where a solicitor's negligence results in a settlor conferring benefits under an irrevocable deed of settlement to someone other than the intended beneficiary, or where solicitors retained by an employer in order to draft an effective tax avoidance scheme for the benefit of employee are negligent with the result that the scheme is ineffective and the tax payable (*Hemmens* v. *Wilson Browne (a firm)* [1995] Ch 223, per Judge Moseley QC).

5.7 Hedley Byrne and the Contract–Tort Boundary

Having surveyed the principal headings under which liability for pure economic loss may exceptionally arise, we now turn to the difficult questions which result from the interplay of principles of contract and tort in this area. Questions of the contract–tort boundary – of that area of law termed 'contorts' by one commentator (Hedley, 1995) – arise in cases of concurrent liability and in other cases in which an action in tort might be thought to 'short-circuit' a set of contractual arrangements. This might be the case where to recognise a tort liability would give the plaintiff the benefit of a gratuitous undertaking, or a contractual undertaking contained in a contract to which the plaintiff was not privy. We here consider these issues in turn.

The question of concurrent liability was authoritatively addressed by the House of Lords in *Henderson* v. *Merrett Syndicates Ltd* [1995] 2 AC 145. The case involved a multiplicity of claims arising out of the near-collapse of the Lloyd's of London insurance market in the early 1990s. At this time, many Lloyd's syndicates sustained heavy losses, partly as a result of unprecedented liabilities for storm damage following hurricanes in the USA, and called upon their members (known as 'names') to make good the losses. The names alleged negligence on the part of the managing agents who organised the affairs of the syndicates. Their claims fell into two groups: those brought by the so-called 'direct names', i.e. those who were in a direct contractual relationship with the managing agents, and those brought by the 'indirect names', i.e. those who were linked with the managing agents indirectly through a contractual chain (the names had contracted with 'members' agents', who had in turn contracted with the managing agents). The House of Lords held that in both types of case the managing agents had assumed a direct responsibility to the names. Lord Goff, who delivered the leading speech, emphasised the reciprocal nature of the relationship between names and managing agents (p. 182):

'The managing agents have accepted the names as members of a syndicate under their management. . . The names . . . gave authority to the managing agents to bind them to contracts of insurance and reinsurance and to the settlement of claims.'

In such circumstances, a prima facie duty of care arose.

This conclusion was, however, subject to consideration of the relevance of the contractual context. The case of the direct names required the House of Lords to decide whether the plaintiffs should be limited to their claim under the contract or free as an alternative to pursue a concurrent remedy in tort. This was in the interest of some of the plaintiffs because of the more favourable limitation period applying to the claim in tort (six years from the date of loss, rather than three years from the date of the breach of contract). The defendants relied upon a well-known statement of Lord Scarman in the decision of the Privy Council in *Tai Hing Cotton Mill Ltd* v. *Liu Chong Hing Bank Ltd* [1986] AC 80, 107 where he said:

'Their Lordships do not believe that there is anything to the advantage of the law's development in searching for a liability in tort where the parties are in a contractual relationship.'

The House of Lords rejected the implicit premiss of this view, which saw 'the law of tort as supplementary to the law of contract, i.e. as providing for a tortious liability in cases in which there is no contract', holding that it was the law of tort that was fundamental ('the general law': p. 193, per Lord Goff). Although 'the contract can modify and shape the tortious duties which, in the absence of contract, would be applicable' (p. 206, per Lord Browne-Wilkinson, who delivered a short concurring speech), the tortious liability is presumed to survive unless 'so inconsistent with the applicable contract that . . . the parties must be taken to have agreed that the tortious remedy is to be limited or excluded' (p. 194, per Lord Goff). Such agreement might be inferred where the contract specifies duties which are less extensive than those in tort, but this was not the case in *Henderson*, and the plaintiffs were therefore to be left to chose whichever remedy was more advantageous to them (e.g. in relation to limitation periods).

If the relationship between plaintiff and defendant is not contractual, is it desirable for the law to recognise a tort claim on the basis that the relationship is nevertheless 'equivalent to contract'? In the classic example of a such a relationship identified by Lord Devlin in *Hedley Byrne* – namely 'where there is an assumption of responsibility in circumstances, in which, but for the absence of consideration, there would be a contract' – it might be thought that recognition of a tort liability would effectively undermine the requirement of consideration in contract. Other central doctrines of contract law might be under similar threat. The case of the indirect names in *Henderson* provides an example, for, notwithstanding the reciprocal nature of their relationship with the managing agents, the contractual link between them was so structured as to give the names contractual rights only against their agents (the members' agents) and to limit the contractual liability of the managing agents to their sub-agency agreement with the members' agents. In short, there was no privity of contract: the plaintiffs' contractual rights arose under one contract; the defendants' contractual duties arose under another.

Lord Goff's approach to this problem in *Henderson* was to start with the propositions identified above, namely that the law of tort is the general law but that tortious duties may be displaced by the contrary agreement of the parties. He suggested that the existence of a contractual chain structured so as to avoid privity between plaintiff and defendant would often enable such agreement to be inferred, e.g. in the case of subcontracting under an ordinary building contract:

> 'in many cases in which a contractual chain comparable to that in the present case is constructed it may well prove to be inconsistent with an assumption of responsibility which has the effect of, so to speak, short circuiting the contractual structure so put in place by the parties.' (p. 195; cf. *Simaan General Contracting Co* v. *Pilkington Glass Ltd (No. 2)* [1988] QB 758)

But he denied that the agreements in the present case were inconsistent with the defendant's prima facie assumption of responsibility to the plaintiffs, commenting only that, in this respect, the facts of the present case were 'most unusual'.

Lord Goff provides little guidance as to the factors that are relevant in determining when an assumption of responsibility will be permitted to 'short-circuit' a contractual chain. He declined to pass substantive comment upon the problematic case of *Junior Books Ltd* v. *Veitchi Co Ltd* [1983] 1 AC 520 (considered above, 5.3) in which specialist subcontractors were held to have assumed responsibility directly to the owners of premises then under development, despite the fact that their contractual rights and liabilities arose only in respect of the main contractor. Nevertheless, and despite Lord Goff's opinion that there might be inferred an agreement to exclude tort liability in the ordinary case of subcontracting under a building contract, the decision may be justified on the basis that there was a mutuality of relationship between the building owner and the subcontractor (the former having nominated the latter to perform the work) and that the latter was a specialist, exercising a special skill, who might be expected to have insurance against such loss. The extent to which this analysis might serve to undermine the basic 'no recovery' rule in *Murphy* v. *Brentwood District Council* [1991] 1 AC 398 remains to be seen. This is perhaps the most crucial of the questions left unresolved by the House of Lords in its recent attempts to define the scope of the exceptional liability for pure economic loss under *Hedley Byrne* v. *Heller* and other similar principles.

Summary

5.1 Pure economic loss is financial loss not consequent upon damage to the plaintiff or her property.

5.2 Any harm that a defective product causes to itself is pure economic loss: a claim can generally only be made in respect of a defective product if it damages *other* property. Parliament has, however, created a statutory liability in respect of defective dwellings (Defective Premises Act 1972).

5.3 Exceptionally, liability for pure economic loss is recognised under the principle in *Hedley Byrne* v. *Heller* and related principles.

5.4 The basic principle of *Hedley Byrne* v. *Heller* provides that a person may assume a legal responsibility to another when they enter into a special relationship in which the latter reasonably relies upon the former's careful exercise of special skill, knowledge or capacities.

5.5 By an analogous principle, it appears that a duty may be owed to a person who suffers loss through reliance upon the defendant's assumption of responsibility to a third party.

5.6 By another analogous principle, the defendant's assumption of responsibility to one person, with a view to conferring a benefit upon another who would otherwise be without a remedy, may be deemed to extend to the latter.

5.7 Questions of the contract–tort boundary arise in cases of concurrent liability and in other cases in which an action in tort might be thought to 'short-circuit' a set of contractual arrangements.

Exercises

5.1 Is the loss suffered in the following examples to be counted as pure economic loss:

(a) A's hotel is damaged by fire. It has to close for repairs. A suffers a loss of profits as a consequence.

(b) B's hotel has to close for repairs after the plaster on the dining room ceiling collapses, damaging furniture underneath. It takes one week to replace the furniture and two further weeks to have the room replastered. B suffers a loss of profits as a consequence.

(c) C, a newsagent, is injured in a car crash and has to close the shop for two months while she recuperates. She suffers a loss of profits as a consequence. D, who delivers newspapers for C, suffers a loss of earnings while the shop is closed.

5.2 Lord Wilberforce in *Anns* classified the loss suffered by the plaintiff in that case as 'material, physical damage'. Discuss.

5.3 In *Spartan Steel*, Edmund Davies LJ (dissenting) stated that 'an action lies in negligence for damages in respect of pure economic loss, provided that it was a reasonably foreseeable and direct consequence of failure in a duty of care.' In *Junior Books*, Lord Roskill suggested that Edmund Davies's reasoning might be preferred to that of the majority of the Court of Appeal in *Spartan Steel*. Do you think it would?

5.4 In what circumstances (a) was pure economic loss recoverable in 1983 and (b) is it recoverable now?

5.5 How is the concept of a 'voluntary assumption of responsibility' understood by (a) Lord Griffiths in *Smith* v. *Eric S Bush*, (b) Lord Goff in *Henderson* v. *Merrett*, and (c) Lord Browne-Wilkinson in *White* v. *Jones*? Does the concept have any utility?

5.6 Why should the courts adopt a restrictive approach to the recovery of damages for negligently inflicted pure economic loss? Would the argument in favour of liability be stronger or weaker if the loss were *intentionally* inflicted?

5.7 P is a keen wine collector who used to seek advice from Q, a wine consultant, who gave her advice without payment as P was a friend. Q negligently advised P to keep cases of Woolloomooloo White, an Australian wine which she already possessed, far too long. When P opened the first bottle, she found that the wine had turned to vinegar. Her tasting of other bottles confirmed that all of them were spoiled. She was doubly dismayed as she had arranged to sell a couple of cases of the wine at a large profit. Q had also advised P to put in a bid at auction for some very old wine labelled Château Mutton. P succeeded in buying the wine for £500 but later discovered that Q had confused the name of the wine at the auction for that of a far superior producer, Château Mouton. The wine turned out to be undrinkable. P also had in her cellar two cases of English table wine, Chateau Strand and Chateau Aldwych, which she had received as a gift. These also turn out to be spoiled. This time the cause is a mould which was present in the corks of the bottles. The corks in the bottles of Chateau Strand had been produced for the winery by R Ltd. Those in the bottles of Chateau Aldwych, also produced by R Ltd, had been inserted by Q by way of replacement of the original corks after the bottles had come into P's possession. Advise the parties as to their rights and liabilities in tort.

6   Omissions

6.1 **Introduction**

In formulating his general statement of principle in *Donoghue* v. *Stevenson*, Lord Atkin took as his starting point the biblical command that you are to love your neighbour, a reference to the parable of the good Samaritan. Some 40 years or so later, Lord Diplock returned to that parable to illustrate the limits of the 'neighbour' principle, particularly in the context of omissions. According to Lord Diplock, although the priest and the Levite who passed by on the other side of the road might attract moral censure, they would have incurred no civil liability in English law (*Home Office* v. *Dorset Yacht Co* [1970] AC 1004, 1060).

The traditional approach of the common law has been to adopt the general rule that there is no liability for omissions or, to put it another way, that there is no duty to act to prevent harm. This approach is premised upon a highly individualist political theory which holds that people should be concerned purely and simply with their own self-advancement and should not be subject to legal liability for failing to intervene for the benefit of others. This, the theory suggests, is the most effective way of maximising individuals' freedom of action (see Smith and Burns, 1983). In addition to the fear of unduly burdening individuals, another justification for the general rule of no liability for omissions is the pragmatic concern that there may be no reason for holding any particular defendant liable for harm she could have prevented rather than all the others who were just as able to intervene. Why pick on the priest and the Levite when countless others might have passed by on the road to Jericho that celebrated afternoon?

With the advance of community values, evident in particular in the institution of the welfare state, a categorical denial of liability for omissions looks out of touch with reality. Conscious of this, judges have begun to admit exceptions to the general rule. The exceptions have arisen where the two responses identified above – 'Don't burden me' and 'Why pick on me?' – are weakest. Thus, for instance, it does not seem unfair to burden an employer with the duty actively to take precautions for the safety of her workforce as it was for her benefit that they were exposed to danger in the first place. Furthermore, this provides a clear reason for picking on the employer rather than, say, those passing by in the street who see that the working practices are unsafe yet do nothing about it. Yet, despite the growing number of cases of liability for omission, the general rule of no liability remains. In cases which fall outside the exceptions, often labelled cases of 'pure' omissions, people can ignore their moral responsibilities towards others without legal sanction. It is, for instance, quite unthinkable that there should be 'liability in negligence on the part of one who sees another about to walk over a cliff with his head in the air and forbears to shout a warning' (*Yuen Kun Yeu* v. *A-G of Hong Kong* [1988] AC 175, 192 per Lord Keith).

The exceptional cases in which the courts have imposed liability for omission defy easy categorisation. It is nevertheless possible to identify a number of factors which trigger the imposition of a duty of affirmative action in different types of case, and which may indeed overlap on the facts of an individual case. It is these factors which, together or in isolation, may provide the element of proximity necessary for the recognition of a duty of care. We now proceed to consider a number of these factors in turn.

6.2 **Voluntary Assumption of Responsibility**

In stark contrast to the law of tort, the law of contract is all about imposing duties of affirmative action. Accordingly, it is no surprise that the courts are most willing to hold people liable in tort for their negligent omissions in cases where they have agreed, expressly or impliedly, to take on a responsibility for the benefit of others. Hence, where a decorator agrees to lock the premises on leaving but neglects to do so, this may amount to a breach of a duty of affirmative action owed to the occupier who may recover as damages the value of any goods stolen by thieves during the decorator's absence (see *Stansbie* v. *Troman* [1948] 2 KB 48). In such circumstances, the fact that the defendant has freely undertaken the responsibility can be taken to indicate that she regards her conduct as advancing her own interests, and the 'Don't burden me' objection is therefore weakened. Furthermore, where the defendant induces reliance upon her conduct by others, it may be said that she has actually made their position worse, not merely failed to render a benefit.

Responsibility may be assumed by acceptance of a particular office or position, or simply on an *ad hoc* basis. Where a swimmer encounters trouble at sea and is in peril of drowning, the lifeguard has a duty to intervene which arises by virtue of her accepting her position of responsibility; ordinary bystanders, under no such obligation (irrespective of their swimming ability), might nevertheless assume responsibility on that particular occasion if they were to embark on a rescue or go in search of assistance. At what point in time does the rescuer assume a responsibility towards the person in danger? There is a divergence of opinion on this issue in other jurisdictions (see Fleming, 1992, p. 148), but no real English authority. At one extreme is the view that only if the rescuer should carelessly inflict fresh injury on the person in danger would liability arise. At the other extreme is the opinion that the duty arises at the moment the rescue is commenced or at least when the rescuer takes charge of the situation (e.g. by pulling the drowning person from the water). Perhaps the strongest view, however, is that the rescuer assumes responsibility for the rescue as soon as her intervention induces reliance by others which is detrimental to the interests of the person in danger (e.g. by discouraging others from coming to her aid). It is the adverse impact of the rescuer upon the position of the person in danger that justifies the imposition of the duty.

6.3 **Protection of the vulnerable**

The premise of individualistic political theory – that people are best off if left to their own devices – is clearly false when applied to particular groups of vulnerable people. In such cases, a social or moral responsibility will often fall upon certain others who stand in a continuing relationship with the vulnerable person (close family, health care practitioners, etc.). And the law of tort may regard this as sufficient warrant for the imposition of a concurrent *legal* responsibility.

The most obvious example of such a responsibility is that owed to very young children. Infants are manifestly vulnerable in that they are incapable of looking after themselves. Thus, parents and those *in loco parentis* must take steps to ensure that children in their care are reasonably safe, and a teacher who after class lets a small schoolchild wander off onto a busy main road, without adult supervision, may be held liable if the child is run over (*Barnes* v. *Hampshire County Council* [1969] 1 WLR 1563). Those with mental disabilities have an equal claim to special consideration and it is clear that nurses at mental hospitals owe a duty to prevent the patients harming themselves. A case of a similar type is *Kirkham* v. *Chief Constable of Greater Manchester Police* [1990] 2 QB 283. In that case, the Court of Appeal was faced by a claim brought by the widow of a man who had committed suicide while remanded in custody. The widow alleged that the police who had arrested her husband, and who knew he had mental problems and associated suicidal tendencies, should have informed the remand authorities of this. If the authorities had known Mr Kirkham was a special risk, they would have put him under close supervision and prevented his suicide attempt. The court agreed that the police had a duty to relay this information and awarded Mrs Kirkham damages for loss of dependency. Cases like this will be rare, because the court will normally find that those committing suicide are the cause of their own death. However, the causal difficulty may be overcome where the very reason for regarding the victim as vulnerable and as recognising a positive duty of care was her propensity to do an act of that sort (as in *Kirkham*).

6.4 **Acts of Third Parties and Relationships of Control**

Just as the basic rule is that I have no duty to protect others from harm, so too I generally have no responsibility for the actions of others. A third party's intervention is normally sufficient to break the chain of causation between the defendant's negligent conduct and the plaintiff's injury. Exceptionally, however, the law recognises a positive duty to control the actions of another person arising out of a relationship with that person. In some of these exceptional cases, the third party lacks the capacity to count as a new intervening cause of the plaintiffs injury. Cases involving very young children again provide the best example: as very young children lack the capacity to take full responsibility for their actions, those looking after them cannot justifiably abandon them to their own devices. Thus, in *Carmarthenshire County Council* v. *Lewis* [1955] AC 549, the House of Lords held a local authority liable for its failure to secure a school playground which allowed a small child to wander onto the road, causing a lorry to swerve and crash; the driver was injured.

Other exceptional cases involve liabilities arising in respect of harm caused by third parties who are fully responsible for their own actions. Such actions are normally sufficient to break the chain of causation, but the law meets this difficulty by recognising an exceptional duty to control the third party in question. Where such a duty is imposed, the liability is based upon a weaker form of causal connection than is usually required, namely the provision of the means or opportunity for a third party to bring about the harm. The defendant's liability is not, strictly speaking, for *causing* the harm, but for *occasioning* it (see Hart and Honoré, 1985, pp. 194–204).

Liabilities of this description – where a special duty of care allows the defendant to be held liable merely for occasioning, rather than causing, harm – are currently very restricted in scope. One of the few unequivocal instances of such liability is where the defendant is charged with the task, as a matter of public safety, of holding the third party in lawful custody. Hence, prison authorities may be held responsible for harm caused by one inmate to her fellows while in custody, and even for harm caused to those in the vicinity in the course of an escape from custody. In *Home Office* v. *Dorset Yacht Co* [1970] AC 1004, Borstal officers had, in breach of instructions, left their charges unsupervised while on a training exercise. A number of young offenders made good their escape; in the course of this they damaged a yacht. The House of Lords held the Home Office vicariously liable for this damage. It would, however, have been excessive to have burdened the custodians with responsibility for all the harm subsequently done by the escapees and Lord Diplock, whose speech seems the one most in tune with current judicial attitudes, made it clear that he would impose liability only in respect of harm caused in the course of the escape, at roughly the same time and in the vicinity. Thus it seems that the Home Office would not have been liable if the complaint had been that the escapees had some weeks later robbed a post office in another part of the country.

In the course of the decision, Lord Pearson advanced the proposition that 'control imports responsibility'. This should not be taken to mean that the defendants mere *ability* to control the activities of a third party is sufficient foundation for a duty of care. The *obligation* to control is limited to a narrow set of control relationships (e.g. that between prisoner and custodian). For instance, although it may be said that the police – through their powers of arrest – may exercise a degree of control over those suspected of criminal activities, they do not stand in any relationship of control with those suspects (except for any period in which the latter are actually in police custody). So the police are not responsible for injuries inflicted by suspects whom they unreasonably fail to arrest. In *Hill* v. *Chief Constable of West Yorkshire* [1989] AC 53, an action was brought against the police by the estate of one of the victims of the so-called 'Yorkshire Ripper', Peter Sutcliffe. The House of Lords held that the police owed no duty of care on the facts of the case, distinguishing the *Dorset Yacht* case on the grounds that Sutcliffe had never been taken into police custody (see further 7.4).

6.5 Creation of a Source of Danger

A more general consideration giving rise to a duty of affirmative action is the defendant's creation of a special source of danger. This is the basis of the driver's obligation, after being involved in an accident, to stop and render assistance to the injured, even if blameless, and of the manufacturer's duty to recall or warn of dangerous products (*Rivtow Marine Ltd* v. *Washington Iron Works* [1974] SCR 1189). In such cases, it can be said that the defendant has not merely failed to render a benefit to the plaintiff but has actually, albeit over an expanded 'time-frame', made the plaintiff worse off by creating the risk of harm.

This principle may also apply where the danger is sparked off by a third party. The classic example is *Haynes* v. *Harwood* [1935] 1 KB 146: the defendant's employee, the driver of a horse-drawn cart, left the horses unattended in the street. The horses bolted when an unknown third party threw a stone at them. The plaintiff policeman saw the horses galloping down the street and grabbed them to bring them to a halt and thereby protect the general public from danger; in doing so, he suffered injuries. The Court of Appeal held the defendant liable, notwithstanding the intervention of the third party. In the language we have adopted, the defendant had *occasioned* injury to the plaintiff by creating a special danger which was foreseeably sparked off by the third party.

It is not enough that foreseeable intervention by a third party might create a danger. the circumstances of the case must give rise to a *special* risk. In *Topp* v. *London Country Buses (South West) Ltd* [1993] 1 WLR 976, the Court of Appeal declined to accept that vehicles left unattended in the street would meet this requirement, even in the extreme circumstances of the case. During licensing hours one evening, a minibus used for public transport was left unattended outside the White Horse public house in Epsom, its keys still in the ignition. At around closing time, persons unknown (possibly from the pub, although the trial judge stated that there was 'no evidence' of this) commandeered the bus and drove off down the street, erratically and without headlights. Shortly afterwards, it careered out of control and fatally collided with the deceased. The Court of Appeal upheld the decision of the trial judge, May J, that a parked minibus was no more a source of danger than any other vehicle on the road and was clearly distinguishable from such obvious sources of danger as '[a] startled horse or a spilt paraffin lamp or a substantial quantity of fireworks stored in an unlocked garden shed'. Further, the learned judge submitted that to treat the defendant's minibus as, in the circumstances, especially alluring would require the courts to make impossible distinctions in the future, e.g. as to 'the relative allurements of (say) a blue Volvo estate, a Ford GTi, . . . or a pink VW beetle, to mention but a few.' What then is the difference between an unattended vehicle and unattended horses? Perhaps it is that horses, if left unattended, might present a danger even without the involvement of an independent third party, whereas a car will usually be harmless until driven away.

Liability might well arise, however, where a vehicle owner hands over the car to a person who is plainly drunk, and the latter then runs over the plaintiff (*P Perl (Exporters)* v. *Camden London Borough Council* [1984] QB 342, 359 per Robert Goff LJ). In such a case, the use of the car by the drunken driver, entailing an obvious danger to other road users, is actually authorised by the owner. Would the drunken driver have an action against the owner if injured in the same collision? It is submitted that the owner should bear some portion of the responsibility, subject of course to a deduction for the driver's contributory negligence, at least where the driver's intoxication is so extreme as to blind her to her inability to drive safely.

To be distinguished from such cases where a drunk is encharged with a dangerous thing are cases where the plaintiff is exposed to the dangers of drink. As alcohol may be consumed safely within certain limits, which are best ascertained by each drinker personally, the scope of the duty here is more restricted than where a special danger arises from the conjunction of drink with an independent factor; the person responsible for a bar owes no duty to intoxicated customers in respect of self-inflicted injury, but may have to assume a responsibility for their care if they lapse into unconsciousness (*Barrett* v. *Ministry of Defence* [1995] 1 WLR 1217).

6.6   Owners and Occupiers of Land

The privilege of owning or occupying land carries with it certain obligations and may warrant the imposition of a duty of care in respect of those foreseeably injured by events or activities on the land. As Lord Nicholls has stated, 'In cases involving the use of land, proximity is found in the fact of occupation. The right to occupy can reasonably be regarded as carrying obligations as well as rights' (see *Stovin* v. *Wise* [1996] 3 All ER 801, 807). Whether or not the occupation of land serves *in all cases* to satisfy the requirement of proximity is, however, a disputed question, as the following discussion will reveal.

A number of different types of case must be distinguished as the scope of the duty – and indeed its source – may vary from one to another. We should note immediately that the liability of landowners to those who come onto their land and are injured by the state of the land is governed by statute (see Ch. 13), though it seems probable that the tort of negligence would have developed to impose similar liabilities. Liability towards those on neighbouring property or on the public highway arises at common law but is governed by a variety of legal principles. In so far as the injury arises out of the action of natural forces on the defendant's land, liability is well established in the torts of both negligence and nuisance, and it seems that little turns upon the plaintiff's choice of cause of action (see *Goldman* v. *Hargrave* [1967] AC 645). Cases where the harm is caused by the actions of third parties on the defendant's land have, however, caused more problems, for they elicit the individualistic response that one ought not be held responsible for the actions of others.

A distinction may be drawn between cases in which harm to those on adjoining land is caused by visitors on the defendant's property and those involving trespassers. In the former type of case, the choice to allow the visitors onto the land can be taken as evidence of a benefit derived from their presence, and it may be regarded as appropriate to impose a corresponding burden in the form of an obligation to supervise their activities. Consider the case of a football club that allows known hooligans into its ground for a match, appreciating that there is a risk that they will tear up lumps of concrete for use as missiles as the terracing is in a state of disrepair. If the hooligans were to throw the lumps of concrete at police gathered in the street beside the ground, injuring some of them, it is probable that the club would be held liable for their actions. The club after all derived the benefit of the admission fees paid by the hooligans (see *Cunningham* v. *Reading FC Ltd* (1991) *The Times*, 22 March).

Different considerations apply where the harm is caused by trespassers. Here, the case for liability is much weaker, but a duty of care may nevertheless arise in exceptional circumstances. This was accepted by the House of Lords in *Smith* v. *Littlewoods Organisation Ltd* [1987] AC 241. In that case, a fire was started by vandals on the site of a disused cinema bought by Littlewoods, who wanted to locate a supermarket there. The fire spread to neighbouring properties, causing serious damage, and the owners of those properties sued the supermarket chain. All members of the House of Lords agreed that liability could be imposed for the acts of trespassers on one's land only in exceptional circumstances, and that those circumstances were not present on the facts of the case. However, the approach of the various judges differed significantly.

Lord Goff adopted the traditional approach favoured by Lord Bridge in *Caparo* (see 3.3). First of all, he denied that there was any general duty placed on owners or occupiers of property to take reasonable precautions against the wrongdoing of third parties. This seems tantamount to a denial that the mere occupation of land supplies the necessary element of proximity between the parties (cf. the view of Lord Nicholls in *Stovin* v. *Wise*, cited above). His Lordship then explained how to identify the exceptional cases in which liability might arise (p. 280): 'having rejected the generalised principle, we have to search for special cases in which, upon narrower but still identifiable principles, liability can properly be imposed'. In his view, the case law identified two such principles. In the first place, where a landowner has knowledge, or means of knowledge, that intruders have created the risk of fire on her property, she may be liable for failing to take reasonable steps to prevent any such fire damaging neighbouring property. On the facts before him, he could see no reason why Littlewoods should have known that vandals were creating a fire risk; it was not enough to point to a foreseeable possibility that this might have been the case. The second principle applied where a landowner creates, or allows to be created, an unusual source of danger on her land. Lord Goff illustrated this principle by considering the case of a villager deputed to buy the fireworks for the village Guy Fawkes night display who stores the fireworks in an unlocked garden shed. He suggested that the villager might be liable if mischievous children from the village were to sneak into the shed and, playing with the fireworks, start a fire which burns down the neighbouring house. However, he concluded that an empty cinema was not an unusual danger in the nature of a stock of fireworks.

Whereas Lord Goff made an effort to isolate a number of rules governing the liability of landowners for the acts of third parties, the other members of the House of Lords spoke in much more generalised terms. The common theme of these other speeches was that the outbreak of fire was not sufficiently likely to justify holding Littlewoods liable, particularly in view of the burdensome nature of the precautions necessary to stop the vandals: only a 24-hour guard would have been likely to prevent the fire. As Markesinis (1989) points out, it is not clear whether these other Law Lords dismissed the claim for damages because Littlewoods owed its neighbours no duty of care or because, although there was a duty of care, Littlewoods' behaviour could not have been regarded as unreasonable. Markesinis claims the latter is the better interpretation of the speeches (consistently with Lord Nicholls' view that proximity is found in the fact of occupation: see *Stovin* v. *Wise*, above) and suggests that, where the burden of precautions is less, the courts might well hold a landowner liable. More ambitiously, Markesinis claims that the majority opinion heralds 'an unnoticed revolution'. In his view, the case is a significant forward step towards a generalised liability for omissions and 'may mark a new beginning for the law of negligence'. However, it is unlikely that the case will be regarded as authority outside the area of the liability of landowners and the categorical denial of liability for 'pure' omissions seems no less insistent now than ever before.

6.7 Statuory Powers and Duties

Finally, it may be argued that the fact that a governmental agency is by statute empowered or obligated to perform a particular task, and given funds for that purpose, is reason enough to hold it accountable to individuals who suffer through its failure to act (see Fleming, 1990); it might be said that the existence of the statutory power or duty itself provides the necessary element of 'proximity'. But the courts currently adopt a most cautious approach to such questions, and have largely resiled from the more relaxed stance evident in the notorious case of *Anns* where a local authority's statutory power to inspect building work was held to give rise to a common law duty to take reasonable care to ensure that the building would be safe. The actual decision in *Anns* has been overruled, but only on the basis that the cost of repairing the defective building in such a case was pure economic loss; the question of whether a local authority might owe a duty in respect of physical damage was left open (*Murphy* v. *Brentwood District Council* [1991] AC 391, esp. pp. 457, 463, 492). Nevertheless, it is clear that the mere existence of the power is insufficient to satisfy the proximity requirement; something more is required.

In seeking to identify this additional element we may first dispose of those cases which involve one or other of the factors already highlighted as giving rise to a duty of affirmative action, e.g. the existence of a control relationship or the defendant's creation of a source of danger (both factors were arguably present in *Home Office* v. *Dorset Yacht Co* [1970] AC 1004). Similar for present purposes is the case where the defendant's acceptance of responsibility for a particular task induces reliance on the part of the plaintiff, e.g. in the case of a lighthouse authority's implied representation that it will warn mariners away from dangers in the vicinity of the lighthouse (see *Stovin* v. *Wise* [1996] 3 All ER 801, 828 per Lord Hoffmann). But in such cases the imposition of the duty is not dependent upon the public nature of the defendant's powers, as the considerations listed – control, creation of a source of danger, and assumption of responsibility – are equally capable of giving rise to a duty of affirmative action on the part of a private individual.

In *Stovin* v. *Wise* [1996] 3 All ER 801, the House of Lords considered whether this public aspect of a régime of statutory powers or duties might give rise to a duty of affirmative action in the tort of negligence, even in the absence of the factors identified above. Lord Hoffmann, who delivered the leading speech, stated that for liability in negligence to arise the court must be satisfied that 'there are exceptional grounds for holding that the policy of the statute requires compensation to be paid to persons who suffer loss because the power was not exercised' (*Stovin* v. *Wise* [1996] 3 All ER 801, 828).

When will it be legitimate to infer that the policy of a statute was to require the compensation of those suffering loss through the failure to perform a duty or to exercise a power? It seems at the very least that the statute must be construed as designed to protect a determinate class of person against a particular type of loss. Hence, the power of local authorities to inspect building work arising under the public health legislation does not give rise to a cause of action on the part of property developers in relation to pure economic loss, whatever the position with regard to residents whose personal safety is at risk (*Governors of the Peabody Donation Fund* v. *Sir Lindsay Parkinson & Co* [1985] AC 210); similarly, a 'regulator' established to maintain a register of deposit-taking companies owes no duty to those suffering loss through the fraudulent mismanagement of registered companies, for the regulator exercises only a 'quasi-judicial' power to determine whether the company should be allowed to trade and this can only be construed as for the benefit of the public generally, not of any particular class (*Yuen Kun Yeu* v. *Attorney-General of Hong Kong* [1988] AC 175).

Even more than this may be required in the case of a statutory power rather than duty. In *Stovin* v. *Wise*, Lord Hoffmann accepted that liability for failure to exercise a statutory power could only be rare, as the element of discretion in the exercise of a power 'must be some indication that the policy of the Act conferring the power was not to create a right to compensation (p. 828). But he declined to affirm the proposition that 'a statutory "may" can never give rise to a common law duty of care', preferring to leave this question open for the time being. He proceeded to consider the possible bases for such a duty of care, among which he highlighted the principle of 'general reliance'. This principle, which had 'little in common with the ordinary doctrine of reliance' (p. 829), depended upon there being a general expectation in the community, not necessarily shared by the plaintiff, that the power would be exercised, and upon this expectation's affecting the general pattern of economic and social behaviour, e.g. in the setting of insurance premiums. For the doctrine to apply, it was 'essential . . . that the benefit or service provided under statutory powers should be of a uniform and routine nature, so that one can describe exactly what the public authority was supposed to do' (p. 829).

It is unclear precisely when this doctrine might apply, for the House of Lords rejected its application on the facts of the case in front of it. The principal question was whether a highway authority's statutory power to remove dangerous visual obstructions on land adjacent to the highway gave rise to a duty of care by virtue of which the authority could be held liable for an accident caused by its negligent failure to exercise its power. By a bare majority, the House of Lords held that the highway authority owed no duty of care because there were no exceptional grounds to indicate that the policy of the relevant statute entailed the provision of compensation to those injured by such a failure. It could not be said that the doctrine of general reliance applied because, as each hazardous junction is different and requires individual consideration on the part of the relevant highway authority, the plaintiff was not arbitrarily denied a benefit which was routinely provided to others (p. 832). In addition, the decision not only whether to proceed with the work but also when and how it should be done raised budgetary questions and fell within the authority's unreviewable 'policy' discretion ('the court is not in a position to say what an appropriate standard of improvement would be. This must be a matter for the discretion of the authority': see further 7.2).

Notwithstanding the rejection of the general reliance doctrine on the particular facts of *Stovin*, its operation is not precluded in different situations (cf. *Invercargill City Council* v. *Hamlin* [1994] 3 NZLR 513, New Zealand Court of Appeal; [1996] AC 624, Privy Council). But it may be questioned whether the doctrine has as yet been elaborated with sufficient clarity to enable it to operate as a workable test of whether liability should be imposed for the simple failure to exercise statutory powers.

Summary

6.1 The courts have been wary of imposing liability for omissions because they fear unduly burdening individuals and recognise the pragmatic difficulty of determining which of those who could have intervened should be held liable. Nevertheless, liability has been recognised in exceptional cases.
6.2 A duty to protect another person may arise by virtue of one's voluntary assumption of responsibility to the other (either in the course of a particular office or position or on an *ad hoc* basis).
6.3 A duty to protect another person may arise by virtue of a relationship (e.g. a family relationship) with a vulnerable person (e.g. an infant).
6.4 Although a third party's intervention will normally break the chain of causation between the defendant's negligent conduct and the plaintiff's injury, the law exceptionally recognises a positive duty to control the actions of another person (e.g. where there is a 'control' relationship) and thereby accepts a liability for 'occasioning' harm (a weaker form of causal responsibility).
6.5 The defendant's creation of a special source of danger may also create a duty of affirmative action, and the defendant may be liable for the acts of a third party who sparks off the danger.
6.6 The defendant's occupation of land may warrant the imposition of a duty of care in respect of those foreseeably injured by events or activities on the land. The precise scope of this duty is disputed.
6.7 Exceptionally, liability may arise in respect of the negligent failure to exercise a statutory power, on the basis that there are exceptional grounds for holding that the policy of the statute requires compensation to be paid to persons who suffer loss because the power was not exercised.

Exercises

6.1 Is this an area of the law where the courts have adopted, in the words of Lord Bridge in *Caparo*, the 'modern approach' of looking for a single general principle that can be applied in all cases, or is it one in which they have preferred the 'traditional approach' of developing the law incrementally and by analogy with established heads of liability?
6.2 Will the law, in any circumstances, impose liability for failing to shout a warning at someone who is about to walk over the edge of a cliff?
6.3 What is the significance of the decision of the House of Lords in *Smith* v. *Littlewoods Organisation Ltd*?
6.4 Might liability in negligence arise in the following circumstances?
  (a) A fails to brake as she approaches an intersection in her car and crashes into B.
  (b) C receives a telephone call to say that her daughter, who ought to have been at school, is standing in the middle of a busy road. C does nothing. D is injured when she swerves to avoid the girl. (Would it make any difference whether the girl was aged 5 or 15?)
  (c) E sells F a pistol. Before F leaves the premises, she tells E that she plans to shoot her mother. E does nothing. F is in fact mentally ill and she shoots her mother later that day.

7   Special Duty Problems: Particular Parties

Special duty problems arise not only out of the nature of the loss and the way it was caused but also out of the identity of the parties. We deal here first with two classes of plaintiff that call for special consideration: rescuers, whose cases raise questions of foreseeability, of the fairness justice and reasonableness of recognising a duty, and of defences; and unborn children, in respect of whom it was unclear for some time whether any duty was owed at all. Then we turn to look at certain classes of defendant who for reasons of public policy are granted a degree of immunity from negligence liability, namely public bodies, the police and the legal profession. This is not a complete list of those with immunities from suit: others have been, or may yet be, added to the list. It has been decided, for instance, that it would not be fair, just and reasonable to expose members of the armed forces to the threat of liability towards colleagues injured in 'friendly fire' incidents (*Mulcahy* v. *Ministry of Defence* [1996] 2 All ER 758) and, as the authors are relieved to note, that the examiners of the University of London LLB owe no duty of care to candidates who allege that their examination scripts are marked without due care and attention (*Thorne* v. *University of London* [1966] 2 QB 237). Nevertheless the special types of defendant considered here are the most significant in both practice and principle.

7.1 Rescuers

The courts' sympathy for those who have selflessly exposed themselves to danger for the sake of others, allied with their desire not to deter those who might undertake rescues, has caused them to adopt a generous stance in respect of claims brought by rescuers; it is possible to discern a general leniency in the courts' application of the requirements for liability in the tort of negligence. Thus rescuers responding to an emergency situation are invariably held to be foreseeable victims of the negligence of those who caused the emergency in the first place. As the American judge Cardozo J remarked: 'Danger invites rescue. The cry of distress is the summons to relief. The law does not ignore these reactions of the mind in tracing conduct to its consequences. It recognises them as normal. It places their effects within the range of the natural and probable' (*Wagner* v. *International Railway Co* 232 NY 176, 180 (1921)).

A similar leniency is apparent when it comes to consideration of the defences that might be raised against those injured in a rescue attempt: courts are very loath to say that a rescuer was contributorily negligent or voluntarily assumed the risk of injury, or indeed that her actions negatived any causal connection between her injury and the defendant's negligence (see Ch. 9 and 11). These issues were canvassed in the leading case of *Baker* v. *TE Hopkins & Son Ltd* [1959] 1 WLR 966. Dr Baker had descended into a well containing poisonous fumes in an attempt to rescue two workers who were feared to be in difficulty. The rope by which the doctor was lowered into the well became caught and both he and the workers were fatally overcome by the fumes. An action in respect of the doctor's death was brought against the employers of the dead workers. The Court of Appeal allowed the claim. First, it held that the doctor was owed a duty of care as it was reasonably foreseeable that, if the employees were imperilled, someone would seek to rescue them from their peril. Secondly, it denied that principles of causation or the law relating to defences barred the action. The court emphasised especially that a rescuer will very rarely be found to have been contributorily negligent. Such a finding would only be appropriate where the rescuer's conduct was 'so foolhardy as to amount to a wholly unreasonable disregard for his own safety' (per Willmer LJ; for an example of a case where such a finding was made, see *Harrison* v. *British Railways Board* [1981] 3 All ER 679).

A number of more particular issues arise in relation to the so-called 'rescuer' cases. First, are 'professional rescuers' like members of the fire brigade owed the same duty as that owed to ordinary people who undertake to assist someone in peril? English courts have declined to apply a 'fireman's rule' akin to that adopted in several US states by which liability is denied on the basis that fire officers are trained and paid out of public funds to deal with the very risk that eventuated and that it would therefore be unduly burdensome to charge private individuals with the cost of their injuries (see *Ogwo* v. *Taylor* [1988] AC 431). Nor do they distinguish between the 'ordinary' risks inherent in fire-fighting and 'exceptional' risks, created by some unusual feature of the fire (e.g. one relating to the state of the premises in question), which the defendant is able to eliminate by warning or otherwise; in *Ogwo*, the House of Lords declined to disadvantage the professional rescuer relative to the ordinary member of the public by limiting liability to cases involving exceptional risks of that description. The same approach has also been applied in relation to the police where officers, in the Hillsborough football stadium tragey, were exposed to excessively horrific scenes in the course of the rescue attempt. The Court of Appeal rejected an argument that professional rescuers could be in no better position than mere bystanders and followed the principle in *Ogwo* (*Frost* v. *Chief Constable of South Yorkshire Police* (1997) 1 All ER 540).

Secondly, can a rescuer recover damages from the person imperilled if the latter was negligent in exposing herself to danger? In *Harrison* v. *British Railways Board* [1981] 3 All ER 679, the plaintiff (a train guard) injured himself in his attempt to assist another person who, while trying to board a moving train, found himself in difficulty. Boreham J held that the plaintiff was entitled to recover damages (subject to a reduction for his contributory negligence): there was no reason to deny the existence of a duty of care simply because the defendant was also the person imperilled. Implicit in this conclusion is the premiss that the duty owed to the rescuer is an independent duty, not merely one derived from that owed to the person imperilled (see *Videan* v. *British Transport Commission* [1963] 2 AB 650; cf. 4.6).

Lastly, does a rescuer owes a duty of care to others who intervene when the rescuer's attempts to assist the person imperilled prove unsuccessful? This issue was considered in the Canadian case of *Horsley* v. *Maclaren* (1972) 22 DLR (3d) 545. The case concerned a boating accident: a guest on Maclaren's vessel fell overboard and Maclaren tried to manoeuvre the boat in order to carry out a rescue; this was unsuccessful and another guest, Horsley, dived in to do what he could; both guests died. The Supreme Court of Canada held that on the facts Maclaren had not been negligent; if he had been, however, the court would have been prepared to hold him liable to Horsley provided that his rescue attempts had placed the first guest in a 'new situation of peril' (per Ritchie J) distinct from the peril to which he was originally exposed. While it seems equitable that one rescuer should be liable to another, the 'new situation of peril' requirement imposed by the Supreme Court may be too restrictive. Liability should not be limited only to a case in which the defendant, by increasing the danger to the plaintiff, has made a second rescue attempt more likely; it should also arise in a case where the defendant makes the rescue attempted by the second rescuer more risky than it would otherwise have been, e.g. where the captain of a rescue vessel assisting at an oil rig fire approaches unreasonably close to the blaze and thereby exposes the crew to danger (see *McFarlane* v. *EE Caledonia* [1994] 2 All ER 1, 10 per Stuart-Smith LJ). It should be noted that in such a case the captain's negligence might negate any causal connection between the fault of the party responsible for the fire and the injuries suffered by those on board the vessel (ibid.).

7.2 The Unborn Child

In the case of children born after suffering congenital disabilities, the only requirement is that injury to the mother was foreseeable; there is no need to establish that the unborn child was a foreseeable victim of the defendant's negligence. This rule is set out in the Congenital Disabilities (Civil Liability) Act 1976 which was implemented because of confusion as to the rights of the unborn child at common law. It is now clear, however, that a claim can be brought at common law in respect of births occurring prior to that reform (*Burton* v. *Islington HA* [1993] QB 204); only the statutory claim is possible in respect of births since that time.

The liability under the Act is derivative in that the child's claim is dependent upon the defendant owing a duty of care to the parent; however, there is no need to prove that the parent suffered actionable injury (s. 1(3)). The derivative nature of the action is also evident in the rule that the child's claim may be reduced to reflect the parent's share of responsibility for the disability (s. 1(7)). Similarly, there is no right to recover where either or both the parents (but not just the father if he is the defendant) knew of the risk of the child's disability before she was conceived (s. 1(4)). The child may sue her own father, but she can only recover damages from her mother where the latter's negligence occurred while driving a motor vehicle (s. 2); in such a case, the desire to maintain harmonious relations between mother and child is outweighed by the recognition that the mother will carry compulsory insurance against such an eventuality. It may be doubted whether these restrictions apply to the common law claim recognised in *Burton* in respect of births occurring before the Act came into force in 1976. As the limitation period does not begin to run until the child reaches the age of majority, it is quite possible that cases arising in the next few years will test whether the 'contributory negligence' of a parent will affect the claim brought by the child or whether a child can sue her mother alleging, for example, that her congenital defect resulted from the mother's drinking or smoking during pregnancy.

The Act only applies to those who suffer congenital disabilities as the result of another's tort. It does not cover 'wrongful life' claims by those whose disability is attributable to natural causes but who allege negligence on the part of a doctor who could have prevented the birth in the light of the likely extent of the child's disability. At common law, such claims were held to be contrary to public policy by the Court of Appeal in *McKay* v. *Essex Area Health Authority* [1982] QB 1166. The court in that case rejected an action for damages by an infant who was born disabled after her mother contracted German measles during pregnancy, and who claimed that the mother's doctor should have advised her of the baby's condition and thereby given her an opportunity to seek an abortion. The court also held that the 1976 Act excluded the possibility of such claims in respect of any birth subsequent to its coming into effect.

To be distinguished from a 'wrongful life' claim is one in respect of a 'wrongful birth' (see generally Mullis, 1993). In such an action, it is the parents who sue in respect of the financial, psychological and other consequences of giving birth to a child whom they would rather not have had and whose birth should have been avoided by the defendants. In *Emeh* v. *Kensington and Chelsea and Westminster Area Health Authority* [1985] QB 1012, the Court of Appeal accepted that all foreseeable losses of that nature were recoverable. Accordingly, it awarded damages to a woman who became pregnant after a sterilisation operation, performed negligently by the defendant, proved ineffective. It seems that the doctor's duty in respect of an unwanted birth is only to the patient and the patient's partner for the time being, not to subsequent partners. In *Goodwill* v. *British Pregnancy Advisory Service* [1996] 2 All ER 161, the Court of Appeal struck out an action brought by a woman who had become pregnant in the course of a sexual relationship commenced some three year's after a vasectomy operation on her partner. She alleged negligence on the part of the defendants, who had arranged the operation, in advising her partner that he no longer needed to use any other method of contraception; she had relied upon this 'warranty of permanent infertility' in removing her contraceptive coil, thereby exposing herself to the risk of pregnancy, of which the defendants should have warned, when there was a spontaneous reversal of the vasectomy. The Court of Appeal, raising what might be called the 'Don Juan scenario', held that it could not be the policy of the law to impose a duty towards the indeterminately large class of partners with whom the patient might have a sexual relationship in the future and rejected the plaintiff's claim.

7.3 Public Bodies

Courts are wary of holding public bodies liable in negligence for a number of reasons which, broadly speaking, fall into two categories. First, certain difficulties in establishing a duty of care which we have already encountered in relation to the liability of private persons – questions of proximity and of fairness, justice and reasonableness – are raised with disproportionate frequency, and with a novel slant, in cases brought against public bodies. We consider these under the heading of 'ordinary duty questions'. Secondly, the fact that the defendant is a public body creates problems of a different nature concerning the extent to which it is appropriate for a court to intervene in the workings of a body involved in the political process (the question of 'justiciability').

Ordinary Duty Questions

We begin by considering ordinary duty of care problems as they are raised in actions brought against public bodies. As elsewhere in the tort of negligence, the ordinary requirements of foreseeability, proximity, and fairness, justice and reasonableness must be satisfied if a duty of care is to be recognised. And, as elsewhere, public body cases may present the same special duty problems which make it necessary to restrict the scope of the duty of care. Thus, for example, the *type of loss* suffered by the plaintiff (did it flow from physical damage or was it purely economic?) and the *character of the defendant's conduct* (was it a positive act or a mere omission?) may throw doubt upon the existence of the necessary element of proximity between plaintiff and defendant. (On the question of a public body's liability for omissions, see especially *Stovin* v. *Wise*, 6.7.) Additionally, the particular position and role of the public body may make it unfair, unjust and unreasonable to impose liability, even where proximity can be established. Among the most important concerns in this context are the need to protect limited public funds against the flood of claims that might perhaps be released by the recognition of a duty and the importance of ensuring that public bodies are able to devote themselves to the performance of their public functions without constantly having to look over their shoulders to guard themselves against the risk of liability (the 'overkill' argument).

A wide cross-section of these 'ordinary duty questions' was raised by the case of *X* v. *Bedfordshire County Council* [1995] 2 AC 633. In this case, the House of Lords was presented with five consolidated appeals, all concerned with the liability in negligence of local authorities. The appeals raised questions about two different functions of local authorities: in relation to suspected child abuse and to the provision of special education for children with special needs. In the first of the child abuse cases ('the *Bedfordshire* case'), the five plaintiffs were brothers and sisters who claimed that they had suffered ill treatment and ill health as a result of the defendant local authority's negligent failure to act expeditiously to put them on the child protection register and to take them into care; in the second ('the *Newham* case'), a mother and daughter claimed damages for anxiety neuroses allegedly suffered as a result of the defendant local authority's erroneously taking the child into care. In two of the special educational provision cases ('*Dorset*' and '*Hampshire*'), the alleged negligence was to all intents and purposes the same, namely the unreasonable failure to provide special schooling for a child who was subsequently recognised to have particular needs. The nature of the loss alleged in the two cases, however, differed: in *Dorset*, it was the cost of private special needs schooling; in *Hampshire*, in which the child had remained at an ordinary state school, it was psychological injury, under-achievement and the significant restriction of vocational prospects. In the final case ('*Bromley*'), the local authority was said to have acted in breach of duty in placing a child in special schooling unnecessarily, with consequent impairment of his personal and intellectual development. In each of the five cases, the actions against the local authority concerned were brought both directly and indirectly (in the sense that the authorities were alleged to have been vicariously liable for the negligence of their employees).

It is readily apparent that the claims raised a number of special duty problems. First, the losses alleged posed difficulties, because they included pure economic loss (the cost of private tuition in *Dorset*), psychiatric illness sustained in the absence of 'shock' (in *Newham*; cf. 4.6), and other novel types of harm, such as impaired development (which was the gist of the action in both *Hampshire* and *Bromley*). Secondly, the complaint in a number of cases was not of misfeasance by the local authority but non-feasance (the failure to take the children into care in *Bedfordshire* and to provide special schooling in both *Dorset* and *Hampshire*). These considerations would no doubt make it difficult to establish proximity at trial but they were not in fact analysed in detail in *X* because the case came to the House of Lords on a preliminary striking-out application and their Lordships were content to allow such matters to await the full trial. In any case, their Lordships were able to strike out many of the claims on an entirely separate basis, namely that it would not be fair, just and reasonable to allow the claims to proceed against the local authorities. Their Lordships' paramount concern was overkill: 'if a liability in damages were to be imposed, it might well be that local authorities would adopt a more cautious and defensive approach to their duties. . . [M]oney and human resources will be diverted away from the performance of the social service for which they were provided' (p. 750, per Lord Browne-

Wilkinson). Furthermore, private citizens had alternative means of ensuring that local authorities properly discharged the responsibilities in question (via statutory appeals procedures and the right to petition the local authority ombudsman), although it had to be admitted that none of these provided for a right to compensation. In the light of these and other considerations, the House of Lords struck out the claims in negligence in all the cases, save only the claims alleging vicarious liability for the acts of local authority employees in the special educational provision cases, which their Lordships did not consider to raise the same danger of overkill. (The authors have no knowledge of the subsequent history of these cases.)

It can be seen from the above summary of *X* v. *Bedfordshire County Council* that the issues raised by actions against public bodies may be extraordinarily complex and require the courts to make extremely difficult value judgements (for a fuller analysis, see Oliphant, 1996). Ought public funds to be used to provide compensation in such cases? What impact would this have upon public services in general? Would paying compensation serve to undermine individual responsibility and lead to the development of a 'pass the buck' mentality? The courts have an unenviable task in resolving such matters, but it may perhaps be permissible to suggest that where the positive acts of a local authority cause personal injury by physical means the courts should be reluctant to allow the overkill argument to prevail over the plaintiff's claim for compensation. The combination of the law's paramount purpose of protecting personal safety and its greater willingness to penalise misfeasance than nonfeasance should defeat all save the most potent of countervailing considerations.

The Question of Justiciability

In addition to the above 'ordinary duty questions', actions against public bodies raise a particular problem of their own. This reflects a concern that a private law claim for damages may not be the appropriate means by which to challenge the actions and decisions of a public body. In the first place, the decisions made by a public body may require a more wide-ranging investigation than is possible in the courtroom. No court is equipped, for example, to decide whether the Home Office is right to operate an 'open' borstal policy and, as part of it, to take young offenders away from safe confinement in highly secure institutions on training exercises (cf. *Home Office* v. *Dorset Yacht Co Ltd* [1970] AC 1004). This decision requires the balancing of considerations that the courts are scarcely able to identify never mind weigh: How much does it cost to operate an open borstal system as opposed to a closed one? Should the object of the system be to punish young offenders or to rehabilitate them? What additional risks are imposed on the local community by allowing young offenders more freedom of movement? Such is the diversity of the issues that might be relevant that it is inconceivable that the two parties represented in court would raise them all. Matters like these should be decided only after a public enquiry has given all interested parties an opportunity to air their views. This suggests a second reason why courts should stay clear of cases that raise these matters: the decisions made by public bodies are often the product of the democratic process and it would be unconstitutional for the courts to undermine this by challenging those decisions. This consideration is particularly weighty when the public body in question is an elected one, for example a local authority. Where this is the case, the body is accountable to its electorate and there is a strong argument for saying that the electorate alone should pass judgment on it.

These concerns are all too familiar to public lawyers. As a matter of public law, actions of public bodies under statute are not reviewable by the courts unless *ultra vires* (i.e. in excess of their power or discretion). Is it necessary in a private law action for damages to show that the public body acted in an *ultra vires* fashion? Different judicial answers have been given to this question. According to a well-known dictum of Lord Diplock, '[t]he public law concept of ultra vires has replaced the civil law concept of negligence as the test of the legality, and consequently of the actionability, of acts or omissions of government departments or public authorities done in the exercise of a discretion conferred on them by Parliament. . .' (*Home Office* v. *Dorset Yacht Co Ltd* [1970] AC 1004, 1067). More recently, however, Lord Browne-Wilkinson has doubted the utility of employing concepts of public law in relation to a private law claim: 'I do not believe that it is either helpful or necessary to introduce public law concepts as to the validity of a decision into the question of liability at common law for negligence' (*X (Minors)* v. *Bedfordshire County Council* [1995] 2 AC 633, 736–7). His Lordship pointed out that Lord Diplock's dictum was potentially misleading, for in public law a decision could be ultra vires for reasons which had no relevance to the question of negligence (see further *Rowling* v. *Takaro Properties* [1988] AC 473, where the Privy Council accepted that a government minister had acted without negligence, albeit in excess of his powers, in basing a particular decision on an irrelevant consideration). In Lord Browne-Wilkinson's view, Lord Diplock's words did no more than stipulate that the exercise of a statutory discretion could not be impugned unless it was so unreasonable that it fell altogether outside the ambit of the discretion (i.e. was unreasonable in what public lawyers know as the *Wednesbury* sense). To avoid confusion in such matters, his Lordship preferred in a private action for damages to employ the concepts of *justiciability* and *excess of discretion* rather than that of vires (cf. Craig, 1994, pp. 618–32).

It is submitted that the concepts of justiciability and excess of discretion relied upon by Lord Browne-Wilkinson represent twin legal responses to a single policy consideration, namely the need to protect public bodies against inappropriate judicial scrutiny of their actions. The question of justiciability arises at the duty stage and requires the court to ask whether the subject matter of the case raises 'policy' issues which the court is not competent to determine. This turns upon a distinction, introduced by Lord Wilberforce in *Anns* v. *Merton London Borough Council* [1978] AC 728, between a public body's formulation of a policy and its operation of that policy. According to Lord Wilberforce, the more 'operational' the matter before the court is, the easier it is for the court to regard the public body as owing a common law duty of care (although the ordinary duty requirements of proximity and fairness must also, of course, be satisfied). He considered the difference between policy and operational matters was probably one of degree. Subsequent decisions have made clear that the distinction is not self-executing and that the ultimate question is always whether the subject matter of the case is fit for judicial scrutiny ('justiciable'). As Lord Keith has said:

> '[T]his distinction does not provide a touchstone of liability, but rather is expressive of the need to exclude altogether those cases in which the decision under attack is of such a kind that a question whether it has been made negligently is unsuitable for judicial resolution, of which notable examples are discretionary decisions on the allocation of scarce resources or the distribution of risks.' (*Rowling* v. *Takaro Properties Ltd* [1988] AC 473, 501)

Although there is no simple rule by which 'policy' may be distinguished from 'operational' matters, it is possible to identify a number of conventional heads of 'policy', most notably the allocation of scarce resources and the imposition of risks on sectors of the community for a wider public benefit. Hence, in *Home Office* v. *Dorset Yacht Co Ltd* [1970] AC 1004, to chose an illustrative example, it is clear that the decision of the Home Office to operate an open borstal system was a policy matter and hence unchallengeable in the courts: it involved the deliberate exposure of local residents to the risk of damage in the pursuit of a higher social purpose, the rehabilitation of offenders. By way of contrast, however, the carelessness of the borstal officers in going off to bed and thereby leaving their charges to their own devices, contrary to regulations, was an operational matter and it was appropriate to hold the Home Office liable for that carelessness.

Where the question of justiciability arises at the duty stage, allowing a public body's defence that it was acting in its *policy* sphere to be raised at a preliminary hearing of a case's legal issues (e.g. in a striking out application), the question of whether the body exceeded the scope of its *discretion* seems to be one of breach of duty. Unlike the question of justiciability, the question of discretion addresses the reasonableness of the public body's conduct rather than the reasonableness of imposing liability even given unreasonable conduct (which is the gist of the duty inquiry); in deference to the public body's special position in the democratic process, the usual test of reasonable care is in this context replaced by the test of *Wednesbury* unreasonableness by which the court does not simply substitute its view of what was reasonable for that of the body, and intervenes only on the basis that *no* reasonable body would have acted in such a way (cf. *Associated Provincial Picture Houses Ltd* v. *Wednesbury Corporation* [1948] 1 KB 223). The deferential attitude of the courts here may be compared with that adopted through the mechanism of the *Bolam* test in relation to doctors and other professionals (see 8.4; cf. Bowman and

Bailey, 1986). Because a public body's exercise of its discretion can only be impugned after consideration of its reasonableness in the circumstances of the case, the question of discretion is essentially one of fact. It can therefore only be determined at full trial and, unlike the question of justiciability, is not suitable for resolution in a striking-out application

7.4 The Police

There is no question that a police officer, like anyone else, may be liable in tort where her negligent acts result in injury to another. By s. 48 of the Police Act 1964, the chief constable of the area may be vicariously liable for these acts, in which case damages will be paid out of the police fund (see Chapter 21). In order to avoid undue interference with the exercise of police discretion, the police's liability is restricted to the operational sphere of their activities; as is the case with other public institutions, their activities in the policy sphere are non-justiciable. In *Rigby* v. *Chief Constable of Northamptonshire* [1985] 1 WLR 1242, a building owner claimed against the police after they had used inflammable CS gas to smoke out a gunman holed up in the property, a ploy which achieved its aim but also succeeded in causing serious fire damage to the building. Taylor J relied on Lord Wilberforce's distinction between the policy and operational spheres of activity to hold that he could not impugn the police force for equipping itself with inflammable CS gas even though a non-flammable alternative was available: this was a policy decision. However, he did hold the police liable in negligence for failing to have firefighting equipment in attendance at the time they used the gas: this, evidently, was a matter falling within the operational area.

More difficult than cases like *Rigby* which involve the direct infliction of injury by means of a positive act are cases of police nonfeasance. In principle, a claim against the police in respect of an allegedly negligent omission may succeed if it falls within one of the established categories of proximity (e.g. a care or control relationship). Thus, as we have seen (see 6.2), the police have been held liable for failing to prevent a mentally ill potential suicide from killing himself after he has been taken into custody. Furthermore, by analogy with the *Dorset Yacht* case, they may also be held liable for damage caused in the course of a prisoner's escape from their control. However, the police cannot be held liable to those who simply suffer harm from criminal activities which they allege the police should have prevented. This conclusion was reached by the House of Lords after considering the issue in a case brought by the estate of the last victim of one Peter Sutcliffe, the so-called 'Yorkshire Ripper', a mass-murderer who conducted a campaign of terror against young women in Yorkshire from 1975 to 1980 (*Hill* v. *Chief Constable of West Yorkshire* [1989] AC 53). The claim failed both for want of the necessary ingredient of proximity and also for a variety of policy reasons which made it unfair, unjust and unreasonable to recognise a duty of care. On the question of proximity, Lord Keith distinguished the case before him from the *Dorset*

Yacht case on the basis that Sutcliffe had never been in police custody, while 'Miss Hill [the victim] was one of a vast number of the female general public who might be at risk from his activities but was at no special distinctive risk. . .' By way of contrast, in the *Dorset Yacht* case the Home Office's open Borstal policy had exposed local residents to the additional risk of injury in the course of any escape. On the question of fairness, justice and reasonableness, Lord Keith listed a number of policy reasons for allowing the police substantial immunity from suit. First, the fear of liability might cause the police to carry out their tasks in a detrimentally defensive frame of mind. (It seems that borstal officers are made of sterner stuff: in the *Dorset Yacht* case, Lord Reid expressly dismissed the argument that officers might be dissuaded from doing their duty by the fear of liability.) Secondly, many cases would concern the exercise of discretion as to the way an investigation should proceed: this could not be called into question by the courts. Thirdly, the time, trouble and expense put into the defence of claims, even those that were totally meritless, would represent a significant diversion of police manpower and attention from their task of suppressing crime.

The decision in *Hill* does not entail however that the police have a 'blanket' immunity from suit in relation to the prevention and investigation of crime (see *Swinney* v. *Chief Constable of the Northumbria Police* [1996] 3 All ER 449). In every case, it will be necessary to enquire as to the existence of proximity between the parties and to weigh up the various, perhaps competing considerations of public policy to see whether it is fair, just and reasonable to recognise a duty. In many cases, the lack of any pre-existing relationship between the police and a victim of crime will negate the necessary ingredient of proximity. It is for this reason that the police cannot be held liable for losses sustained in a burglary when, without proper investigation of the scene, they dismiss an emergency 999 call as a false alarm (*Alexandrou* v. *Oxford* [1993] 4 All ER 328). And even when there is sufficient proximity, considerations of policy akin to those recognised in *Hill* may preclude the recognition of a duty. In *Osman* v. *Ferguson* [1993] 4 All ER 344, a majority of the Court of Appeal was prepared to accept that there might be proximity as between a teenage boy (and his family) and police officers investigating his harassment by a former schoolteacher who had developed a dangerous obsession with the boy: after a series of disturbing encounters, the teacher one day followed the boy and his father home and shot them both, severely wounding the boy and killing his father. The court accepted that a 'special relationship' might arguably arise from the fact that the boy and his family were (on the alleged facts) exposed to a risk from the man which was over and above that faced by the public at large. But the court held unanimously that the considerations of public policy relied upon by the House of Lords in *Hill* doomed the action to failure.

Other cases might, however, throw up countervailing policy considerations. In *Swinney*, the first plaintiff provided confidential information to the police about the fatal running-down of an officer by the driver of a vehicle he was trying to stop. The police record of the incident, which revealed the identity of the plaintiff, was left unattended in a parked vehicle and was stolen in the course of a break-in. It was alleged that the documents were subsequently obtained by criminals, that the first plaintiff and her husband (the second plaintiff) were as a result threatened with violence and arson, and that they suffered psychiatric illness which prevented them continuing to run their business, with consequent loss of profits. The Court of Appeal declined to strike out the claim. By her provision of confidential information and the consequent exposure of herself and her husband to danger, the first plaintiff had entered into a relationship of proximity with the police. Furthermore, it was possible to argue that it was fair, just and reasonable to recognise a duty, as the danger of inhibiting police investigations was on this occasion outweighed by the need to encourage members of the public to volunteer information to the police without fear of reprisal.

7.5 The Legal Profession

A lawyer, whether barrister or – in these progressive times – solicitor, cannot be sued by her client for negligence in presenting the latter's case in court. This was decided by the House of Lords in the case of *Rondel* v. *Worsley* [1969] 1 AC 191 in which a man convicted of causing grievous bodily harm complained that his barrister had negligently failed to lead evidence that the accused had caused the injuries with his teeth and hands, rather than with a knife. The House of Lords held that, on grounds of public policy, the case should not be heard. The following reasons for this stance were identified in the speeches.

First, if an advocate were required constantly to look over her shoulder this would hamper the true administration of justice. An advocate owes an overriding duty to the court which, on occasion, may conflict with her duty to her client. She may, for instance, have to clear up a misunderstanding on the part of the judge even though it may be favourable to her client's case. Equally, the judge may rely upon her to pare her client's case down to its bare essentials, rather than allow the client an opportunity to air all her grievances, at the expense of valuable court time, whether they are legally relevant or not. If an advocate were to face the threat of actions for negligence, this might cause her to turn a blind eye to the interests of justice in order to keep her client happy.

Secondly, removing the immunity might have the effect that advocates would begin to pick and choose their clients in order to avoid those whose case is wholly without merit and who seem intent on airing their grievance in whatever forum is open to them. These evasions of the so-called 'cab-rank' rule – that an advocate is bound to provide her services for any client who can pay her fee – would risk injustice, for an unpleasant client with an apparently hopeless case may, after a full and fair hearing, turn out to be in the right.

Lastly, a suit alleging negligent conduct of a court case would inevitably require a retrial of the original case. This, according to Lord Morris, would be contrary to public policy (pp. 250–1). If the action were brought in respect of a criminal conviction, allowing the accused to seek to establish her innocence in a civil court would be to graft onto the criminal appeals system 'a sort of unseemly excrescence.' If it concerned a civil action, the result would be 'litigation upon litigation with the possibility of a recurring chain-like course of litigation'. This would offend against the interest in finality in litigation.

The barrister's immunity extends only to the conduct of litigation and those preliminary matters that are intimately connected with the conduct of the case in court (see *Saif Ali* v. *Sidney Mitchell & Co* [1980] AC 198). An immunity of the same extent also applies to solicitors (Courts and Legal Services Act 1990, s. 62). In cases that fall outside these immunities, it seems that a solicitor or barrister may be liable for carelessly giving negligent advice or otherwise negligently managing her client's affairs, provided that the necessary element of proximity is present. An example of such a liability is where a solicitor negligently fails to draw up a will correctly, with the result that an intended beneficiary loses out on her bequest (see 5.6). Liability to someone other than the lawyer's client is opposed by yet more potent considerations. Even in non-contentious business, e.g. a property transaction, one side's lawyers owe no duty to the other side, for the simple reason that the duty to the other side might conflict with the duty to their client (*Gran Gelato* v. *Richcliff* [1992] 1 All ER 865; *aliter* if the lawyer 'voluntarily assumes responsibility' to the other side: *Al-Kandari* v. *JR Brown & Co* [1988] QB 665). Equally, in the criminal rather than civil sphere, the Crown Prosecution Service and its lawyers owe no duty to persons being prosecuted, e.g. to discontinue prosecution and ensure their release from custody once the evidence against them is revealed to be unsound (*Elguzouli-Daf* v. *Commissioner of Police of the Metropolis* [1995] QB 335).

Summary

7.1   Rescuers are invariably held to be foreseeable plaintiffs and are rarely defeated by claims that they unreasonably exposed themselves to the risk of injury.

7.2   Two types of action are currently available in respect of pre-natal negligence. First, there is the action under the Congenital Disabilities (Civil Liability) Act 1976 brought by a child born with a disability as a result of negligence. Secondly, there is the common law action for 'wrongful birth' brought by the parents of a child who would not have been born but for the defendant's negligence. Neither under the common law nor under the 1976 Act is it possible for a disabled child to bring a 'wrongful life' action claiming she should not have been born.

7.3   Judicial reluctance to recognise liability on the part of public bodies has led to the imposition of a requirement of 'justiciability' in respect of actions brought against public bodies, as well as the frequent invocation of policy considerations (e.g. the overkill argument) to justify the refusal to recognise a duty of care.

7.4   Similar concerns underlie limitations on the scope of liability in negligence on the part of the police. Only in very exceptional circumstances do the police owe potential victims of crime a duty of care to safeguard them from criminal acts.

7.5 Barristers and solicitors owe no duty of care with regard to the conduct of litigation or to preliminary matters which are intimately connected with the conduct of a case in court.

Exercises

7.1 Is the duty of care owed to a rescuer a 'derivative' duty or one owed to her in her own right? What difference does it make?

7.2 In what circumstances will the birth of a child give rise to an action in negligence? In what circumstances will the conception of a child give rise to such an action?

7.3 Should the courts allow an action for 'wrongful life'?

7.4 A local authority is empowered by statute to supervise and control the operations of builders with a view to maintaining proper standards of health and safety and has set up an inspectorate to perform this task. One of the inspectors, A, carelessly fails to spot that a certain house is built on defective foundations. The house subsequently falls down and injures its occupier, B. Advise the parties as to their rights and liabilities in tort. Would it make any difference if B's house had not been inspected because (a) for budgetary reasons, the authority had decided to suspend all inspections, or (b) the authority's lawyers had misinterpreted the relevant statute and advised the authority that it was not in fact entitled to carry out on-site inspections.

7.5 Assess the strength of the 'overkill' argument in relation to lawyers, the police and public bodies generally.

7.6 In what circumstances is the interest in the finality of litigation considered relevant to an action in negligence? Whose interest is it? What weight should the courts attach to it?

---

8 Breach of the Duty of Care

8.1 Introduction

Under the heading of breach of a duty of care the question is not whether the defendant should be held liable for her negligence (which is the question in relation to duty, causation and remoteness), but whether the defendant was in fact negligent in the first place. Negligence consists in falling below the standard of care required in the circumstances to protect others from the unreasonable risk of harm. This is judged in relation to the position in which the defendant found herself: it is easy to be wise after the event, but the court should not let hindsight influence its judgment as to what the defendant ought to have done in the circumstances. It follows that, where knowledge of the risks involved in particular activities has developed over the course of time, the defendant's conduct should be assessed in the light of the state of knowledge at the time she acted, not that at the date of trial. In *Roe* v. *Minister of Health* [1954] 2 QB 66, the plaintiffs had become paralysed after being injected with anaesthetic which had been contaminated by disinfectant. The anaesthetic had been stored in ampoules placed in the disinfectant; the latter had seeped into the ampoules through invisible cracks. At the date of the injuries, 1947, this was not generally considered possible. In the Court of Appeal, Denning LJ stressed that developments in scientific knowledge should be ignored in assessing the culpability of the defendants (p. 84): 'We must not look at the 1947 accident with 1954 spectacles.'

8.2 The Objective Standard of Care

In general, the law requires defendants in negligence actions to measure up to an objective standard of care demanded by the activity in question and declines to accept excuses that are founded on the defendant's inability to measure up to that standard. The question to be asked is, 'What level of care and skill was required by the activity which the defendant was pursuing?' rather than 'What could this particular defendant have done?' As Lord Macmillan put it in the case of *Glasgow Corporation* v. *Muir* [1943] AC 448, 458 the objective standard 'eliminates the personal equation and is independent of the idiosyncrasies of the particular person whose conduct is in question'. The reason for this approach was clearly expressed by the great American judge and jurist, Oliver Wendell Holmes (1881):

'The standards of the law are standards of general application. The law takes no account of the infinite varieties of temperament, intellect and education which make the internal character of a given act so different in different men. It does not attempt to see men as God sees them. . .

[W]hen men live in society, a certain average of conduct, a sacrifice of individual peculiarities going beyond a certain point, is necessary to the general welfare. If, for instance, a man is born hasty and awkward, is always having accidents and hurting himself or his neighbours, no doubt his congenital defects will be allowed for in the courts of Heaven, but his slips are no less troublesome to his neighbours than if they sprang from guilty neglect. His neighbours accordingly require him, at his proper peril, to come up to their standard, and the courts which they establish decline to take his personal equation into account.'

This general rule holds true when we are concerned with those whose lack of skill, experience or intelligence leads them to injure others. In the leading English case, *Nettleship* v. *Weston* [1971] 2 QB 691, a learner-driver failed to straighten the steering-wheel after turning a corner and ran into a street lamp; her driving instructor was injured. The Court of Appeal held her liable to the instructor, finding that she had fallen below the standard expected of a qualified and experienced driver; it was irrelevant that she as a learner might not be able to attain that standard. However, it may be that certain physical characteristics will be taken into account. Though the matter has yet to come before an appellate court, it seems likely that child defendants in negligence actions will not generally be judged as if they were adults and will be required to do no more than live up to the standards expected of a child of their age (see *Staley* v. *Suffolk County Council*, 26 November 1985, unreported). If a child should embark upon an activity (e.g. driving) that she knows demands the skills of an adult, however, then it may be that the child would be required to exercise those skills at her peril.

The position with regard to those whose ability to exercise due care and skill is suddenly and temporarily impaired, e.g. as a result of a physical or mental disability, is less certain. In *Roberts* v. *Ramsbottom* [1980] 1 WLR 823, the question was whether and on what basis liability might be imposed on the defendant driver who, as a result of suffering a stroke while driving, lost control of his vehicle and crashed into the plaintiff. Neill J held that the defendant should be judged by the standards of the ordinary competent driver, without regard to his personal circumstances; only if his actions had been 'wholly beyond his control' would it be appropriate to vary the normal standard to take account of the incapacity. This reasoning has been criticised as liable to lead to injustice, although drivers are of course insulated from the effects of liability by compulsory insurance, and a preference stated for Neill J's alternative reasoning, namely that 'the defendant continued to drive when he was unfit to do so and when he should have been aware of his unfitness' (Clerk and Lindsell, 1995, para. 7–121). It is submitted that the court should properly take into account all circumstances, whether external (e.g. an 'emergency' situation) or internal (e.g. a physical or mental incapacity), that affect the defendant's conduct and do not simply amount to a denial that the defendant possessed the skill or experience necessary to pursue the activity in question.

Where a person holds herself out as possessing a special skill over and above that of reasonable people, then she will of course be expected to live up to the standard she has represented she can attain. It would be no excuse for the surgeon whose piercing of your ears resulted in an infection to say that you were not entitled to demand more in the way of hygiene or competence than you would expect had you visited a jeweller instead. However, a jeweller performing the same service is not to be judged by the standards of a surgeon, because ear-piercing is not an activity that requires surgical skill (see *Philips* v. *Whiteley (William) Ltd* [1938] 1 All ER 566).

8.3 Application of the Objective Standard

Many commentators have discerned a progressive raising of the objective standard in the course of the last century which they attribute to the spread of liability insurance (see Tunc, 1983). The courts are now inclined to treat inevitable lapses of concentration or judgement as deviations from the standard of the reasonable person, though occasionally a judge will stand against the tide by arguing that not every careless slip can give rise to liability (especially in emergencies and other situations demanding split-second judgements: see *Wooldridge* v. *Sumner* [1963] 2 QB 43). In terms of ease of adjudication, cases involving lapses of concentration or judgement present few problems, for the defendant would be almost bound to admit that she had done something wrong and that she could think of no justification for doing what she did. However, as we move away from simple lapses of attention into the area of accidents that might have been avoided with a bit of foresight, things become more complicated. In these cases, it might be that the defendant can argue that she thought she could not be expected to behave differently to guard against possible injury to the plaintiff. Taking risks with our own and others' personal welfare and property is part of everyday existence. Indeed, life would be impossible if we did not do so. The point was put graphically by Asquith LG in Daborn v. *Bath Tramways* [1946] 2 All ER 333: 'if all the trains in this country were restricted to a speed of 5 miles an hour, there would be fewer accidents, but our national life would be intolerably slowed down'. The question the law of negligence must confront then is: 'Just how much is the law to require us to do in order avoid causing harm to others?'

The precautions we should take to guard against injury to others depend on the circumstances of the case. The more likely injury is to result, and the greater the severity of that injury if it does result, the more we should do to eliminate the risk. On the other hand, if the costs of eliminating the risk exceed the benefits to be gained from doing so, then it might be reasonable to do nothing. This has been expressed as a mathematical formula by the American judge, Learned Hand J. Where the probability of injury occurring is P, the extent of the likely loss is L and the burden of taking precautions to eliminate the risk is B, liability will arise if $B < PL$ (in other words, if the seriousness of the risk, assessed by combining the factors on the right-hand side of the equation, outweighs the burden of eliminating it). This is known as the 'Learned Hand formula'.

While English courts might deride such an approach for its veneer of scientific infallibility, the cases show that they attach significance to the same factors as feature in the 'Learned Hand formula', namely (a) probability, (b) the severity of the possible loss, and (c) the burden of eliminating the risk of loss.

All other things being equal, the greater the *probability of harm* resulting from the defendant's conduct (measured from the defendant's standpoint), the more likely it is that the conduct will be judged negligent. It is not possible, of course, to stipulate precisely how probable the harm must be, for the probability of harm is not considered on its own but only in conjunction with the other elements of the Learned Hand equation. Nevertheless it is possible to see that consideration of the probability of harm may exercise a decisive influence on the outcome of a case. Such considerations seem to explain, for example, why the courts have reached superficially conflicting decisions on the issue of whether a cricket club can be held liable for damage caused by balls hit over the boundary fence. In a case where balls were hit out of the ground into neighbouring gardens several times each season, the club might reasonably be expected to erect a taller fence or even to move to another site, and might therefore be held liable for any damage caused (as in *Miller* v. *Jackson* [1977] QB 966). However, if evidence were to show that balls had cleared the fence on only a handful of occasions in the last several years, the club may be said to have done all that it reasonably could to limit the risk of harm (as in *Bolton* v. *Stone* [1951] AC 850).

The *severity of the likely loss or injury* is combined with the probability of its occurring in order to quantify the risk of harm. Again, we can say that (other things being equal) the more serious the likely harm, the stronger the inference of negligence. By way of example we may consider the decision of the House of Lords in *Paris* v. *Stepney Borough Council* [1951] AC 367. In that case, their Lordships found that an employer was negligent in failing to provide safety goggles to a particular employee, who was blind in one eye, even though there was no need to provide them for all employees: the consequences of losing the sight of one's only good eye were far worse than losing the sight of one of two good eyes.

Finally, the risk of harm must be weighed against the *burden or cost of eliminating the risk* in order to determine whether the reasonable person in the defendant's position would have incurred the burden or cost. The mere fact that the defendant had the opportunity to remove or reduce the risk does not point to the conclusion that the defendant should have taken that opportunity, for the burden or cost of precautions might be excessive relative to the degree of risk. In *Latimer* v. *AEC Ltd* [1953] AC 643, for example, the defendant's factory had been flooded and the water, mixed with oil from channels in the floor, left the floor exceedingly slippery. The trial judge held that in these circumstances the factory should have been shut down until the floor was made safe. The House of Lords overturned this ruling on the grounds that the circumstances did not demand that the employer take such a drastic step. In looking at the cost of eliminating the risk of injury, the court's enquiry may go beyond the consequences for the defendant and look at the consequences for society as a whole; the social utility of the defendant's conduct may justify the creation of a risk of harm that would otherwise be unreasonable. Thus, in *Watt* v. *Hertfordshire County Council* [1954] 1 WLR 835, the Court of Appeal accepted that it might be reasonable for firemen responding to an emergency situation to load a heavy jack onto a lorry that was not fitted to carry it when the specially adapted lorry was unavailable. Accordingly, a fireman injured when the jack rolled against him in the back of the lorry was unable to obtain compensation.

8.4 **Common Practice**

The cost–benefit analysis performed by the court in assessing whether defendants have acted unreasonably is not to be regarded as merely an economic calculation: it requires the court to weigh up matters such as the value of human life and limb which cannot be reduced to a simple arithmetical quantity. It is necessary, therefore, for the court to exercise a value judgement in the light of prevailing community standards. For this reason, and also in recognition of the need to defer to expert or more qualified opinion, the courts attach great importance to the common practice of those involved in the activity in question. Where it is common practice to take certain precautions in the course of a particular activity, then failure to take those precautions creates a strong inference of negligence, rebuttable only on presentation of convincing reasons why the precautions were unnecessary. Conversely, where the defendant does take all the precautions commonly adopted by others in her field of activity, then this on its own will often be sufficient evidence that all reasonable care was taken.

Although common practice may be relevant in asking what the defendant might reasonably have done, it is not decisive. The courts reserve the power to set standards for a field of activity and do not limit themselves merely to reflecting the standards of those engaged in that activity. Thus, in the context of industry, the courts have on occasion declared an industry-wide practice to be negligent and have insisted that standards be raised across the board. A progressive judgment in this respect is that of Mustill J in *Thompson* v. *Smith Shiprepairers Ltd* [1984] QB 405, a case concerning industrial deafness suffered by workers in shipyards. Mustill J proceeded on the basis that 'the defendants simply shared in the indifference and inertia which characterised the industry as a whole' (p. 417), and made it clear that one employer was not exonerated merely by proving that other employers were just as negligent. His view was that there were certain cases in which an employer might be penalised for failing to take the initiative in seeking out developing knowledge of possible risks and precautions. He emphasised, however, that the obligation placed on employers should not be too demanding (p. 416):

'The employer must keep up to date, but the court must be slow to blame him for not ploughing a lone furrow.'

Where an action in negligence is brought against a professional (e.g. a doctor, architect or lawyer), the test is whether the defendant complied with a 'responsible body of opinion' in the profession in question. This is known as the *Bolam* test, named after the case in which McNair J explained the issue of a doctor's liability in negligence to a jury in substantially those terms (*Bolam* v. *Friern Hospital Management Committee* [1957] 1 WLR 582). There may, of course, be conflicting views as to the appropriate practice to adopt, but it is enough that the defendant complies with one such view; the fact that a contrary view exists is regarded as irrelevant. Although the test was developed in the particular context of medical negligence, it has now been applied to all professions or callings which require special skill, knowledge or experience.

8.5 **Proof of Negligence**

Plaintiffs may face an uphill struggle in proving that the defendant's negligence was responsible for the harm they have suffered. Often the scale of the task will be immense. In the litigation arising out of the use of the anti-arthritis drug, Opren (see *Davies* v. *Eli Lilly & Co* (1987) 137 NLJ 1183), the plaintiffs had to hire a team of scientific, medical, pharmaceutical and legal experts to plough through literally millions of documents released to them by the manufacturer of the drug. Furthermore, in many cases the plaintiffs will have to rely on the defendant releasing information to them (e.g. as to the tests to which a new pharmaceutical product was subjected); an unscrupulous defendant might attempt to destroy documents unfavourable to her case rather than comply with a court order for the disclosure of such evidence (known as an order for discovery). The plight of plaintiffs in such cases has prompted innovation on the part of Parliament and the courts to ensure just claims are not defeated by evidential difficulties. In the area of substantive law, legislative reform of the law of product liability was motivated in part by this concern (see Chapter 14). At a procedural level, Parliament has made rules of discovery more stringent over the last century. The response of the courts to the same problem can be seen in the doctrine of *res ipsa loquitur* ('the accident tells its own story').

The classic exposition of the doctrine is that of Erle CJ delivering the judgment of the Court of Exchequer Chamber in the case of *Scott* v. *London and St Katherine Docks Co* (1865) 3 H&C 596. The plaintiff had been injured when struck by six bags of sugar which fell on him from above when he walked under a crane. The crane was being used by the defendants' servant to lower the sugar to the ground from the defendants' warehouse. At trial, the plaintiff gave no explanation of how the accident had happened, with the result that the trial judge directed the jury to find for the defendants on the grounds that there was no evidence of negligence on their part. The plaintiff appealed and the case eventually came before the Court of Exchequer Chamber to determine if there should be a new trial. The court held that there should, applying the following proposition of law (p. 601):

> 'There must be reasonable evidence of negligence, but, where the thing is shown to be under the management of the defendant, or his servants, and the accident is such as, in the ordinary course of things, does not happen if those who have the management of the machinery use proper care, it affords reasonable evidence, in the absence of explanation by the defendant, that the accident arose from want of care.'

This passage makes it clear that two requirements must be met before the rule comes into operation. In the first place, the thing causing the accident must be 'shown to be under the management of the defendant or his servants'. This would be the case where you were driving your car when it suddenly swerved across the road, colliding with oncoming traffic. However, if the car had been driven by a friend to whom you had lent it, it could not be said to have been under your management and the doctrine could not be raised against you. Erle CJ's second requirement was that 'the accident is such as, in the ordinary course of things, does not happen if those who have the management of the [thing] use proper care'. Whether this requirement is satisfied will depend on all the circumstances. Thus, for example, the inference of negligence where you slip on yoghurt spilt on someone's floor will be stronger where the accident takes place in a supermarket rather than an office block, for in the former case the owners should have known that spillages would not be infrequent and should have taken precautions to deal with them as soon as they occur (compare *Ward* v. *Tesco Stores Ltd* [1976] 1 WLR 810 with *Bell* v. *Department of Health and Social Security* (1989) *The Times*, 13 June).

Views have differed as to the effect of the doctrine of *res ipsa loquitur* and the law on the subject remains murky. Two diametrically opposed positions have attracted the most support (see Atiyah, 1972). One school of thought holds that the proposition lays down no new rule of law but merely reflects the common-sense view that, in some circumstances, the likelihood that an accident was caused by the defendant's negligence is so great that it is not necessary for the plaintiff to explain exactly how the accident came to occur. Accordingly, if Erle CJ's requirements are met, it is permissible for the court to infer from the occurrence of an accident that it was probably caused by the defendant's negligence. The opposing view is that the doctrine of *res ipsa loquitur* is a distinct legal rule which casts the legal burden of proof on the defendant when certain requirements are met. This burden requires the defendant to do one of two things. One course is for her to explain precisely how the accident happened, for once the facts are known the maxim can have no application: it is simply a matter of deciding whether those facts support the allegation of negligence or not. If she cannot do this, she may take the second course of trying to prove that she took all reasonable care irrespective of the cause of the accident. As, on this view, the burden of proof lies with the defendant, the judge must resolve any doubt she has as to whether the defendant's negligence caused the accident in favour of the plaintiff rather than the defendant. The extent of the hurdle facing the defendant can be gauged from *Henderson* v. *Henry E. Jenkins & Sons* [1970] AC 282. Mr Henderson had been killed after the brakes on the defendant's lorry had failed. The defendant firm produced evidence that the lorry had been inspected in accordance with the manufacturer's instructions; however, the House of Lords held that, in order to prove it had exercised all reasonable care, the firm should have produced evidence that the lorry had not been carrying corrosive loads of any kind.

Despite this House of Lords authority that the effect of the doctrine is to reverse the legal burden of proof, the Privy Council has subsequently expressed a preference for the alternative view in *Ng Chun Pui* v. *Lee Chuen Tat* [1988] RTR 298. This is to be regretted. As Atiyah (1972) has pointed out, there is good reason for allowing an exception to the general rule that it is up to the plaintiff to prove her case on the balance of probabilities in precisely those cases identified by Erle CJ in which the thing causing the accident was under the control or management of the defendant. In such cases, the plaintiff may face grave evidential difficulties as she will have no information as to the precautions the defendant took in using the thing. A shift in the burden of proof would help to redress this imbalance.

Summary

8.1 'Negligence' or 'breach of duty' consists in falling below the standard of care required in the circumstances to protect others from the unreasonable risk of harm.
8.2 Negligence does not connote personal fault but merely the failure to comply with the standard of conduct to be expected of a reasonable person pursuing the activity in question; lack of skill or experience is no defence.
8.3 Breach of duty consists in creating an unreasonable risk of harm. The creation of the risk of harm will be *unreasonable* unless it is outweighed by the cost to the defendant of reducing the risk or by the social utility of the defendant's conduct.
8.4 The existence of a common industrial or professional practice creates a standard against which to judge the defendant. However, deviation from that practice is not conclusive of negligence, and neither is compliance conclusive of lack of negligence.
8.5 Where the plaintiff alleges that the defendant was negligent in causing an accident but does not know how the accident occurred, she may be aided by the doctrine of *res ipsa loquitur*. The way the doctrine operates is disputed.

Exercises

8.1 What does it mean to describe the standard of care as 'objective'? When can the courts take account of factors peculiar to the defendant?
8.2 Is the ratio of *Nettleship* v. *Weston* that, although women drivers are unable to match up to the standards of their male counterparts, they should be judged by

those standards for the purposes of the tort of negligence? If not, what is the ratio of that case? Is it fair?

8.3   What is the 'Learned Hand formula'? Is it employed by the English courts?

8.4   Is it ever legitimate to ignore a very sizeable risk of harming another person? If so, in what sort of case?

8.5   To what extent is the plea 'Well, everybody else does it' sufficient to rebut an allegation of negligence?

8.6   What is the doctrine of res ipsa loquitur? Is it a doctrine at all? If so, what effect does it have?

8.7   A owns a medical supplies business and employs a number of van drivers to deliver the supplies to hospitals throughout the country. In the aftermath of a mining disaster in South Wales, she receives an emergency request for supplies from a local hospital. Unfortunately, all her regular drivers are away making deliveries in France and, rather than arrange for one of them to be flown back, she reluctantly decides to drive the van herself although it is some time since she has driven. On the way, the brakes of A's van fail and it crashes into a car travelling in the opposite direction. B, the driver of that car, is badly hurt; A escapes unharmed. There is some evidence that a van driver who drove regularly would have been able to control the vehicle and avoid the collision. It seems that the brake failure was caused by a hole in an unusually corroded part of the brake pipe which would only have been visible had the pipe been removed from the van. In fact, A, following the practice of other firms, had not done so, though she had complied with the manufacturer's advice that the visible parts of the pipe be inspected regularly. It is not clear whether the van had previously been used to carry any corrosive chemical agents. Advise the parties as to their rights and liabilities in tort.

9 Causation

Causation is a central, but elusive, concept in the law of tort. In the tort of negligence, the plaintiff is required to prove that the defendant's negligence caused her to suffer actionable damage, and there is an equivalent causation requirement for most other torts as well. In the vast majority of cases causation presents no problems. In a small minority, however, the questions raised are ones that have taxed lawyers and philosophers for centuries.

9.1 Causation in Fact and the "But For" Test

If you were to witness a car accident and afterwards note down all the details that you could remember, your list would include some factors that were causally relevant to the accident and some that were not. Among the former, you might count the treacherously icy condition of the road, the fact that the driver of one of the cars had evidently been drinking and the failure of a faulty traffic light to turn to red. Conversely, the registration numbers of the vehicles involved, the colour of the victims' hair and the clothes they were wearing could not be treated as causally relevant. The presence of these factors was in no way *necessary* for the accident to happen.

The notion of a 'necessary condition' is crucial to the issue of causal relevance or, as it is often called, causation in fact. When we stipulate that a factor must be a necessary condition of the harm in question, we mean that it must be a necessary member of a set of conditions which together are sufficient to produce that harm. If you were to throw a lighted match into the waste-paper basket, your action would be treated as the cause of the fire: it is plain that what you did was necessary to complete a set of conditions (which also includes the presence of inflammable material in the basket and oxygen in the atmosphere) jointly sufficient to produce the fire.

In seeking to identify what is a cause in fact and what is simply irrelevant, courts often rely on the so-called 'but for' test. This poses the question: would the plaintiff not have suffered harm but for defendant's negligence (i.e. in the absence of defendant's negligence, would she have avoided the harm)? The case of *Barnett* v. *Chelsea and Kensington Hospital Management* [1969] 1 QB 428 is frequently cited as an example of how the test is applied. In that case, the plaintiff's husband had experienced persistent vomiting after drinking some tea and had gone to the casualty department of a hospital. The duty doctor refused to see him and Mr Barnett subsequently died from arsenical poisoning. The court found that the doctor's refusal to see Mr Barnett, though negligent, was not a cause in fact of his death. It was considered causally irrelevant, for there was little or no chance that effective treatment could have been given in time anyway. To put it another way, Mr Barnett's drinking the poisoned tea would have brought about his death whether or not he was treated in hospital.

The 'but for' test demands, then, a hypothetical inquiry into what would have happened if the defendant had acted without fault. This entails consideration not only of how the *defendant* should have acted but also of how the *plaintiff* would have reacted to the defendant's hypothetical conduct; to be taken into account are both purely physical reactions, e.g. how the plaintiff would have responded to proper medical treatment, and reactions reflecting the plaintiff's deliberate choice. Hence, where the defendant employer's breach of duty consisted in the failure to provide a safety harness to a worker who fell 70 feet to his death from scaffolding, it was necessary for his widow to establish that he would have worn the harness if it had been provided (which she was unable to do on the facts: see *McWilliams* v. *Sir William Arrol & Co* [1962] 1 WLR 295).

It is not enough that the damage results from the defendant's conduct; it must result from *the wrongful aspect* of the defendant's conduct. This general rule was stated by Lord Hoffman in *South Australia Asset Management Corp* v. *York Montague Ltd* [1996] 3 All ER 365, 371: 'the law limits liability to those consequences which are attributable to that which made the act wrongful'. So where, for example, the defendant's alleged negligence consists in driving with faulty brake-lights, this cannot be treated as the factual cause of a head-on collision in which the defendant's vehicle is involved: the accident would have occurred even if the defendant's brake lights had been in full working order (see further *The Empire Jamaica* [1957] AC 386).

In order to determine whether the plaintiff's loss result from the aspect of the defendant's conduct which constitutes a breach of duty, it is necessary to determine precisely the scope of that duty and the risks against which its imposition is designed to guard. In the *South Australia* case, the issue was the extent of a surveyor's liability in respect of the negligent overvaluation of property, in circumstances in which the loss was increased as a result of market falls occurring between the date of the valuation and the date of trial. In three separate actions consolidated before the House of Lords, the plaintiff was the lender who had advanced money to the purchaser on security of the property; on the purchaser's default, the plaintiff sought to recover the money advanced by selling the property but a shortfall remained. On a simple 'but for' approach, it might be said that, if the plaintiffs would not have continued with the transaction had they known the property's true value, they would not have been affected by the market falls at all and should therefore be entitled to recover in respect of the entire amount of the shortfall. The House of Lords rejected this argument, however, on the basis that, as the defendants had only undertaken to provide the plaintiffs with information as to the value of the properties, not advice concerning the contemplated loans, they could only be liable 'for the consequences of the information being inaccurate' (p. 371, per Lord Hoffmann). The defendants' liability was that portion of the loss that was attributable to the inaccuracy of the valuation, and was limited to the difference between the amount of the negligent overvaluation and the actual value of the property at that time; any additional loss was attributable only to the market fall. One of the cases before the House of Lords may be employed to illustrate this principle. The plaintiff lender advanced £1.75 million on security of property negligently overvalued at £2.5 million and actually worth only £1.85 million; after the borrower defaulted, the property realised only £0.95. Although the plaintiff's total loss was the difference between the sum advanced and that recovered (i.e. £0.8 million), only £0.65 million was held to be attributable to the inaccuracy of the valuation, being the difference between the erroneous valuation and the actual value at that time; the rest of the loss was exclusively attributable to the collapse of prices in the property market. This rule will no doubt lead to increased certainty in a difficult area of legal practice, but it must be said that it seems to owe less to strict considerations of legal principle than to a policy that the risk of market fluctuations should be borne primarily by speculators in the marketplace. (For criticism of the decision, see Stapleton, 1997.)

9.2 Multiple Causation

The 'but for' test is generally a good guide as to whether a given factor was a cause in fact. However, it is not a perfect guide. As Hart and Honoré (1985) point out, the test's major defect is that it rests on the assumption that there was, at the moment in question, only one set of conditions sufficient to bring about the plaintiff's injury. Where this is not so – in cases of 'multiple causation' – the test will produce misleading answers. Thus, if two raging fires converge and together burn down your house, applying the 'but for' test would lead to the absurd conclusion that neither fire was the cause provided that each was sufficient to cause the damage: whichever one we imagine not to have happened, we could only conclude that the damage would have resulted anyway. In these cases, it is generally accepted that the law puts aside the 'but for' test and addresses the more fundamental matter of whether the factor in question was necessary to complete a set of conditions together sufficient to produce the result. Looked at this way, it is clear that each fire was a cause of your house burning down, assuming that each fire, together with other conditions such as the way the wind was blowing and the presence of dry leaves on the ground, made a material contribution to the causal process that brought about the damage. Accordingly, if each fire was started through the negligence of different people, each of them would be jointly and severally liable for the harm. If one fire was attributable to natural causes, however, it is far from clear that the person who negligently started the other fire should be liable for the entire loss. Could she not argue that, although her fire was a cause of the harm, the damages that she was liable to pay should be reduced in view of the inevitable destruction of the house by the natural fire? The difficulties arising in this context from the interplay of principles of causation and of the assessment of damages have yet to be satisfactorily resolved by the courts.

Two types of case involving multiple causation can be distinguished. First, there are instances of 'cumulative' causation, as in the example above where two fires converge on a house. The two fires act contribute to a single causal process which results in the destruction of the house. The leading case is *McGhee* v. *National Coal Board* [1973] 1 WLR 1, in which a worker in a brick kiln contracted industrial dermatitis through exposure to brick dust. The defendant employers had negligently failed to provide showering facilities at the workplace and this failure had increased the risk of dermatitis as brick dust was left caked on the bodies of workers until they got home. However, the risk of contracting dermatitis was part of the job of a kiln worker and there was no evidence that the worker would have remained healthy had showers been installed. In a radical response to the evidential difficulties of the plaintiff's case, Lord Wilberforce stated that, in cases where the defendant had negligently increased the risk of injury to the plaintiff but there was no evidence that this had actually affected the plaintiff, the burden of proof should be reversed; the defendant would inevitably be unable to discharge that burden and would therefore have to bear the loss. The other members of the House of Lords did not go so far, but nevertheless held for the plaintiff on the basis that the increase in the risk of dermatitis in this case made a substantial contribution to the injury; it did not have to be the sole cause. In *Wilsher* v. *Essex Area Health Authority* [1988] AC 1074, the House of Lords declared that Lord Wilberforce's approach was contrary to principle, and held that he must be regarded as having dissented from the approach of the majority in *McGhee*, which was to be preferred. The crucial question therefore is whether the defendant makes a substantial or material contribution to the causal process that results in the plaintiff's injury.

Secondly, there are cases involving 'pre-empted' or 'overtaken' causes. A famous textbook example of this type of case is where a woman, about to set out across the desert, has a lethal dose of poison put into her water keg by one enemy and the keg emptied by a second; ignorant of this, she sets out on her journey during the course of which she dies. The 'but for' test again threatens to mislead: if the keg had not been poisoned, the traveller would have died of thirst, while, alternatively, if the keg had not been emptied, she would have died from the poison. However, this is not a case like that of the converging fires where we can say that both factors were a cause, for the traveller in fact died of thirst and not of poison. In cases of this sort, we would say that the plan of the first enemy was 'pre-empted', 'overtaken' or 'neutralised' by that of the second. The secret here, as Wright (1985) points out, is to ask what actually happened, not what might have done.

Cases in which the plaintiff suffers successive injuries, the effects of which overlap, cause significant difficulties of analysis in this context. In fact, the question that arises is not generally one of causation, namely whether the defendant caused actionable injury to the plaintiff; there is no doubt but that *some* actionable injury has occurred. Rather, the question is what value to attach to that injury; this is the question of the assessment or quantification of damages. Where the action is brought in respect of the second of the two injuries, the rule is that one must take one's victim as one finds her. In *Performance Cars* v. *Abraham* [1962] 1 QB 33, the plaintiff's Rolls-Royce was involved, in the space of two weeks, in two collisions each of which was caused by the fault of another. Either collision on its own would have necessitated a respray of the car. In an action against the second tortfeasor, the Court of Appeal rejected the owner's claim for the cost of the respray on the grounds that the loss did not flow from the defendant's wrongdoing: at the time of the second collision, the vehicle was already in need of a respray.

Where the action is brought in respect of the first of two successive injuries, the courts have adopted a pragmatic distinction between cases in which the second injury is tortious and those in which it is innocent. In *Baker* v. *Willoughby* [1970] AC 467, the plaintiff was first run down by the defendant's negligent driving, suffering a stiff leg, and then shot in the same leg in a hold-up, after which the leg had to be amputated. With his stiff leg, the plaintiff had suffered a loss of mobility and a consequent reduction in his earning capacity; the loss of the leg, on its own, would have been sufficient to produce that same (and greater) loss of mobility and reduced earning capacity. The House of Lords rejected the argument that the defendant's negligence could only be regarded as the cause of that loss up to the time of the second incident, the second injury 'obliterating' the effect of the first. Lord Reid, speaking for the majority of the court, held that both injuries were concurrent causes of the disability from the time of the shooting onwards and that the defendant therefore remained liable in respect of the period after the shooting. He thus treated the issue purely as one of causation and ignored the principle that, in assessing damages, the aim is to put the plaintiff into the position she would have been in had the tort not happened. This aspect of his speech attracted much criticism in the subsequent decision of the House of Lords in *Jobling* v. *Associated Dairies* [1982] AC 794. This case differed from *Baker* in that the second injury was the onset of a natural disease and not the tortious conduct of a third party. The defendant employers had been responsible for injuring the plaintiff's back and thereby reducing his earning capacity. Subsequently, the disease rendered the plaintiff totally unfit for work. Again the House of Lords had to consider whether the defendants continued to be liable for that reduced earning capacity in respect of the period after the second event, the onset of the disease. This time their Lordships took account of the aim of an award of damages and held that the plaintiff would be over-compensated if able to recover for the continuing loss. Accordingly, the defendants' liability ceased at the time of the onset of the disease. Yet, although the members of the House of Lords criticised the reasoning of Lord Reid in *Baker*, they accepted that that case might be correctly decided on its facts and were not prepared to rule out the possibility that the result reached in *Baker* might be appropriate in cases involving successive tortious injuries. This seems fair: as Lord Keith pointed out in *Jobling*, where two successive tortfeasors are liable to the plaintiff, 'it would be highly unreasonable if the aggregate of both awards were less than the total loss suffered' (p. 815).

9.3 **Proof of Causation in Fact**

In typical cases of negligence, e.g. where the plaintiff is injured in a car accident, proof of factual causation is a simple matter; witness accounts and physical examination of the accident scene will make it tolerably clear what happened. However, as we move away from paradigmatic instances of negligence liability, we come across cases in which no number of witnesses could produce evidence enabling us to determine unequivocally how the plaintiff was injured. In such cases, all we can do is talk in terms of probabilities. Typical of cases of this sort are those that involve disabilities that arise after medical treatment or exposure to some toxic substance. An example that provoked tremendous political controversy in the USA arose out of the use in the Vietnam war of the chemical Agent Orange, a defoliant employed as part of a modern-day 'scorched earth' policy by the US Army (see *Agent Orange Litigation* 597 F. Supp 740 (1984)). After the war, veterans claimed that exposure to the chemical as it was sprayed over the forests of Vietnam had caused them serious health problems and had produced congenital disabilities in their offspring. They sought to pin responsibility on the various manufacturers of Agent Orange whom they alleged had improperly failed to warn of the risks inherent in the use of the chemical. However, the veterans faced an uphill battle in making out a case for compensation for, although there was evidence that the incidence of health problems of those exposed to Agent Orange was abnormally high, there was no evidence that any individual had suffered those problems as a consequence of that exposure rather than through natural causes. Nor was there evidence as to which company had manufactured the particular quantities of Agent Orange with which each individual came into contact. These difficulties of establishing causation in individual cases forced the veterans to settle out of court for a level of compensation that fell far short of their original expectations.

The Agent Orange case neatly illustrates two different problems that plaintiffs might face in seeking to establish causation. First, there is the problem of the 'indeterminate plaintiff'. This arises in cases where, in a group of people suffering similar injuries, it is not clear whose injury resulted from the defendant's negligence as opposed to some other, non-tortious factor. This difficulty faced many of those involved in the Agent Orange litigation, as there was a pre-existing 'background risk' of contracting, without any contact with the chemical at all, many of the conditions from which the plaintiffs suffered. Secondly, there are cases in which each of a number of defendants is known to have injured a proportion of the class of victims but there is no way of identifying the individuals for whose injury each is responsible; such cases present the problem of the 'indeterminate defendant'. Again, the Agent Orange litigation provides an illustration: there was no evidence available with which to prove that it was one manufacturer rather than another that had produced the particular quantities of Agent Orange to which individual veterans had been exposed.

The normal rules of proof in civil litigation require the plaintiff to prove on the balance of probabilities that she has a good cause of action against the defendant. In cases that raise the problem of the indeterminate plaintiff or defendant, these rules may be thought to deprive those within the group affected of reasonable compensation and to weaken the incentive on the defendant to take due care. Accordingly, efforts have been made in many jurisdictions to get around the normal rules, e.g. by awarding damages to represent the chance that the defendant caused the plaintiff's injury. In England, however, the courts have for the most part been hostile to such innovations (see also *Wilsher* v. *Essex Area Health Authority* [1988] AC 1074, above (9.2)).

The issue of damages for 'loss of a chance', designed to reflect the degree of probability of the defendant's fault being the cause of the plaintiff's injury, was raised before the House of Lords in *Hotson* v. *East Berkshire Area Health Authority* [1989] AC 750. The case concerned a teenage boy who had fallen from a tree in his school playground. He was subsequently taken to hospital where staff negligently failed to appreciate the extent of his injuries, with the result that treatment was delayed for several days. After the incidents, the boy was found to be suffering from a permanent disability (avascular necrosis) in his hip joint. Medical evidence suggested that it was likely that this disability would have resulted from the fall anyway, but that there was a 25 per cent chance that the boy would have recovered had he been treated promptly. On this evidence, it was clear that the boy would fail to satisfy the burden of proving on the balance of probabilities that his disability was caused by medical negligence; consequently, the claim was presented as one for the loss of the chance that the boy might have recovered and the damages sought were limited to 25 per cent of the amount to which the boy would have been entitled had full liability been accepted. This argument succeeded at trial and before the Court of Appeal, but was robustly rejected by the House of Lords: it was necessary to prove, on the balance of probabilities, that the injury itself resulted from the negligence.

It is necessary to take care to distinguish the all-or-nothing question of causation, in relation to which the plaintiff must prove on the balance of probabilities that the defendant's negligence caused actionable damage, from the question of quantum (i.e. the assessment of damages); in assessing the value to place on the plaintiff's injury, the courts do indeed make adjustments in respect of the probability of various contingencies that might aggravate or alleviate the effect of the injury (see generally Ch. 22). The question of causation is logically prior to that of quantum, for it makes no sense to value the plaintiff's claim until it is clear that the plaintiff in fact has an action; as Lord Bridge explained in *Hotson*, 'Unless the plaintiff proved on a balance of probabilities that the delayed treatment was at least a material contributory cause of the avascular necrosis he failed on the issue of causation and no question of quantification could arise' (p. 782).

The distinction between issues of causation and quantification calls for particular care in cases of pure economic loss, for the actionable damage is not so readily identifiable here as in cases of physical harm. If solicitors should negligently fail to commence an action on behalf of their client within the limitation period, the solicitors may be liable for the amount of the client's claim, discounted by the probability of its success (cf. *Kitchen* v. *Royal Air Force Association* [1958] 1 WLR 563). It is implicit in this that the client's actionable injury is the loss of the claim, and that the cause of action accrues at the time of that loss; the probability of success is taken into account only in putting a value upon that injury, i.e. in relation to quantification, not causation. The same principle would apply when the solicitors' negligence causes their client to miss out on the opportunity of a favourable business deal *(Allied Maples Group Ltd* v. *Simmons & Simmons* [1995] 1 WLR 1002; *pace* Lunney, 1996–97): as the deal had been 'a substantial chance rather than a speculative one' (p. 915, per Stuart-Smith LJ), the client had therefore 'lost something of substance' (p. 925, per Hobhouse LJ) and it was necessary only to value that loss, taking account of the probability of the deal actually being concluded. The statutory claim for loss of dependency under the Fatal Accidents Act 1976 (see Ch. 22), which is in effect a claim for pure economic loss, raises equivalent issues: the dependant must establish a cause of action by proof, on the balance of probabilities, that the deceased was killed by the wrongful act of the defendant and that she stood in a relationship of dependancy with the deceased; in assessing the value of that dependency, however, a discount should be made to reflect the probability of its continuing (as in *Davis* v. *Taylor* [1974] AC 207, where the deceased had been separated from his dependant spouse at the time of his death, but there was a realistic chance of a reconciliation.

The cases cited so far deal with the problem of the indeterminate plaintiff in which the evidential difficulty is in differentiating the effects of the defendant's negligence from that of innocent background factors. The problem of the indeterminate defendant, by contrast, has been curiously neglected by English lawyers. Where a plaintiff has undoubtedly been injured by another's negligence and the question is simply how, if at all, to allocate responsibility for that loss among a number of people who have behaved carelessly, the policy considerations are rather different from those that govern the case where it is by no means clear that the plaintiff has been made worse off by negligence. This observation explains the House of Lords' pragmatic departure from ordinary principles in the case of *Baker* v. *Willoughby*, noted above (see 9.2); we should not rule out the possibility that English courts might be prepared to accept equivalent innovations in the law of evidence to deal with the problem of the indeterminate defendant, which is closely-related to that arising in *Baker*. Cases in the United States and Canada have resorted to a reversal in the burden of proof in order to deal with hunting accidents in which there was no evidence as to which of two hunters fired the shot that injured the plaintiff, with the result that the loss was apportioned equally between them both (*Summers* v. *Tice* 199 P 2d 1 (1948); *Cook* v. *Lewis* [1952] 1 DLR 1). More radically, the Californian Supreme Court was prepared to hold pharmaceutical concerns liable in proportion to their market share when it was not clear which of them was the source of a generic drug that had injured the plaintiff (*Sindell* v. *Abbott Laboratories* 607 P 2d 924 (1980)). It will be interesting to see the reaction of English courts to such innovations if suggested to them in appropriate cases.

9.4 Legal Causation

When we seek to identify the cause of a particular event, we do not ordinarily try to compile a list of all the factual causes of that event. What we do is pick out one or other of them as particularly significant. Thus, in the example of the car accident given above, we might say that the cause of the accident was the icy road surface or drunken driving, but it would not be particularly illuminating to isolate the fact that all cars involved had petrol in their tanks, even though, indisputably, this was a necessary condition for the accident. Not everyone will pick out the same factors: our choice is determined by who we are and what we are trying to prove. This is shown by the following example (see Honoré, 1983): a man lives with his wife in an unhappy marriage, comes home drunk, quarrels with her, takes out a revolver which he possesses without a licence, and shoots her, whereupon she consults a quack who treats her unsuitably and she dies. To a marriage reformer, the cause of her death is the state of divorce law; to a teetotaller, it is drink; to a pacifist, possession of the weapon; to an upholder of medical interests, the activity of the quack. Ordinary people, however, have no time for this dry intellectualism: their response is more instinctive. Headlines in the tabloid press would declare 'Wicked husband in brutal wife murder', and this would no doubt be the common response. By and large, the law takes the tabloid line.

The 'tabloid line' reflects a highly individualistic political theory which demands that people take full responsibility for their deliberate actions and trusts in their ability to control the physical world around them. Accordingly, in selecting the legal cause from a number of factual causes, the law grants special status to deliberate human acts. Furthermore, it homes in on the deliberate human act that most closely precedes the outcome in question and will generally look no further for its cause. In doing so, the law assumes that the choice whether or not to bring about the outcome lay entirely in the hands of the last actor: it refuses to let her 'pass the buck' and will not hold anyone else responsible for her actions. One product of this approach is that the pre-existing susceptibility of the plaintiff to injury of the type suffered is considered immaterial (see the 'thin skull' rule, 10.4). Another is the tendency to treat deliberate interventions by third parties, and deliberate risk-taking by the plaintiff, as intervening acts negativing causal connection between the defendant's wrongdoing and the plaintiff's injury. The Latin phrase *novus actus interveniens* is often used to denote an intervening act which negatives causal connection.

According to Hart and Honoré (1985), 'the free, deliberate and informed act or omission of a human being, intended to exploit the situation created by defendant, negatives causal connection' (p. 136). Hence, where the defendant local authority flooded the plaintiff's home, which had to be vacated during repairs, and squatters entered the vacant property and caused damage, the local authority could not be said to have caused the plaintiff's loss (*Lamb* v. *Camden London Borough Council* [1981] QB 625). Although there is a tendency in such cases to view the reasonable foreseeability or likelihood of the intervention as the test of *novus actus interveniens* (see, in particular, *Home Office* v. *Dorset Yacht Co* [1970] AC 1004, 1030 per Lord Reid), the stronger modern view is that the voluntary character of the intervention suffices to negative causal connection irrespective of how foreseeable it was. Exceptionally, however, the courts may recognise a special duty to prevent a third party causing harm; in such cases, the defendant is not strictly speaking the *cause* of the harm, but the law accepts as sufficient a weaker causal relationship, namely that in which the defendant is said by Hart & Honoré to *occasion* the harm (as in the *Home Office* case: see further 6.4).

Of course, not all deliberate acts intervening between a defendant's wrongdoing and the plaintiff's injury will negative causal connection. Acts of irresponsible agents such as infants and those with mental disabilities will rarely do so (see *Kirkham* v. *Chief Constable of Greater Manchester* [1990] 2 QB 282). Even the deliberate acts of a responsible agent will not do so if those acts cannot be regarded as 'voluntary'. Where a pedestrian is knocked down by a car, taken to hospital and given emergency treatment which is known to be highly dangerous, her death in the course of this treatment will still be regarded as a consequence of the accident. The reason for this is that the doctors' actions in administering the emergency treatment cannot truly be said to be voluntary: their choice to pursue that course of action was not free but was forced on them by the circumstances. This will be true in all situations where the intervening act was done either out of self-preservation or out of a praiseworthy desire to save the lives of others (see 7.1: 'Rescuers').

A case that illustrates this, as well as demonstrating the tendency of the courts to obscure the issue by recourse to bewildering metaphors, is *The Oropesa* [1943] P 32. Two ships, the *Oropesa* and the *Manchester Regiment*, had been involved in a collision at sea for which they were both partly to blame. The weather was rough and, in view of the damage his ship had sustained, the master of the *Manchester Regiment* feared she might not stay afloat. He began to ferry his crew across to the *Oropesa* by boat; on its second trip, with the master and the deceased crew member whose family brought the action on board, the boat overturned and the deceased was drowned. The Court of Appeal had to consider whether the act of setting off in the boat negatived the causal connection between the negligence of the *Oropesa* and the death of the deceased. In reaching the conclusion that it did not, Lord Wright, who delivered the leading judgment, explained his approach in the following cryptic, but oft-cited, passage (p. 39): 'To break the chain of causation it must be shown that there is something which I will call ultroneous, something unwarrantable, a new cause which disturbs the sequence of events, something which can be described as either unreasonable or extraneous or extrinsic.' As Hart and Honoré remark, 'It would have been simpler to say that the acts were done partly for self-preservation and partly in pursuance of what was at least a moral duty to save the lives of those on board' (p. 148).

It is not only deliberate acts intended to exploit the situation created by the defendant that may negative causal connection; it appears that reckless or grossly negligent interventions may do so as well, although mere negligence does not have this effect. Let us return to our example of a pedestrian knocked down by a car. Suppose now that she died in hospital only because the hospital staff, mistaking her for another patient, gave her the wrong operation. The staff cannot be said to have exposed her to risk any more voluntarily than before: they were still acting under the pressure of the circumstances. Yet the treatment was so wholly wrong that it would be unjust to hold the negligent driver responsible for her death. In *Rouse* v. *Squires* [1973] QB 889, a lorry jack-knifed as a result of its driver's negligence and caused an obstruction of the road; shortly afterwards, a second lorry, driven at excessive speed, was unable to brake in time to avoid the obstruction and skidded into the deceased, who had stopped to offer assistance. The Court of Appeal held that the second driver's negligence did not relieve the first driver of all responsibility for the death, of which he remained a joint cause. Cairns LJ, however, distinguished those (like the second driver) whose negligence consisted in driving too fast or not keeping a proper lookout from 'those who deliberately or recklessly drive into the obstruction' (p. 898).

Knightly v. *Johns* [1982] 1 WLR 349) may be regarded as falling within Cairns LJ's exception. The plaintiff police motorcyclist was injured in the aftermath of an accident caused when the first defendant negligently overturned his motor-vehicle at the exit from an underground carriage-way. The defendant police inspector, arriving to take charge at the scene, forgot to close off the tunnel at its entrance and ordered the plaintiff to ride back down it, against the flow of traffic (the other carriageway being closed for maintenance), in order to do so; the plaintiff was struck by an oncoming motorist who was driving without negligence. The Court of Appeal held that the defendant driver could not be regarded as responsible for the plaintiff's injury. Stephenson LJ accepted that not every intervening error or act of folly would negative causal connection, but ruled that the folly here was so out of the ordinary as to have that effect: 'too much happened here, too much went wrong, the chapter of accidents was too long and varied to impose on the first defendant liability for what happened to the plaintiff. . .' (p. 367).

The same principles apply where the intervening act is not that of a third party but that of the plaintiff. In *McKew* v. *Holland & Hannan & Cubitts (Scotland) Ltd* [1969] 3 All ER 1621, as a result of the defendant's admitted fault, the plaintiff suffered an injury which caused his left leg to give way suddenly and without warning. Shortly afterwards, the plaintiff lost control of the leg while descending a steep flight of stairs that did not have a handrail; to avoid falling headfirst, he threw himself from the stairs but broke his right ankle on landing. The House of Lords accepted that his decision to jump, while perhaps an error of judgement, was not such as to break the chain of causation given the need for a split-second reaction to the danger; only an action that was 'so utterly unreasonable that even on the spur of the moment no ordinary man would have been so foolish as to do what he did' would have such an effect (p. 1624, per Lord Reid). Nevertheless, their Lordships ruled that the causal connection was negatived by the plaintiff's prior conduct in unreasonably placing himself in a position where he might be confronted with an emergency. Lord Reid stated: 'if the injured man acts unreasonably he cannot hold the defender liable for injury caused by his own unreasonable conduct. His unreasonable conduct is novus actus interveniens' (p. 1623). This dictum should not be thought to entail that any intervening fault whatsoever on the part of the plaintiff will negative causal connection, for that would undesirably trespass upon the defence of contributory negligence. It is submitted that only conduct amounting to a reckless disregard for the plaintiff's personal safety should have this effect.

In exceptional circumstances, causal connection may be negatived by a natural events rather than an intervening human action. If the ambulance taking the accident victim to hospital is hit by a falling tree, causing her additional harm, there is no prospect of attributing this further injury to the person who was responsible for the initial accident; it was a mere coincidence, simply her bad luck. The test here is whether the conjunction of the two accidents was reasonably foreseeable. An example is provided by *Carslogie Steamship Co.* v. *Royal Norwegian Government* [1952] AC 292): the plaintiff's ship, the *Heimgar*, was damaged in a collision caused by negligence attributable to the defendant government; temporary repairs rendered her seaworthy but, while steaming to the USA for permanent repairs, she suffered further damage in a heavy winter storm. It was held that the storm damage was a 'supervening event' and not in any sense a consequence of the collision; therefore the defendant could not be held responsible for the loss of chartered hire for the period in which the heavy-weather damage was being repaired. As Hart & Honoré point out, regardless of whether the storm could be regarded as unforeseeable in itself, it was mere coincidence that it happened to damage the vessel while *en route* for repairs (pp. 164–8).

In summary, causal connection between the defendant's negligence and the plaintiff's injury is negatived if the injury results from (a) a voluntary intervening act by the plaintiff or a third party; (b) a grossly negligent or reckless intervening act by the plaintiff or a third party; or (c) an abnormal natural occurrence. This, essentially, is the thesis advanced by Hart & Honoré. The most common attack on this thesis is that it introduces policy considerations into what should be a purely factual concept (see, for instance, Wright, 1985). However, Hart & Honoré are surely right in maintaining that the process of selection from among causally relevant factors is appropriately termed 'causal' because it merely reflects the distinction we make in ordinary speech between 'mere conditions' and 'the cause' of an event. This, of course, is not to insist that the causal enquiry is value-free. Indeed, as our values change, it may be possible to discern some difference in our, and the law's, use of causal language. Thus it may be that the advance of collective values at the expense of the individualistic values of pre-welfare state Britain may prompt the law to relax its insistence that deliberate acts negative causal connection and to hold responsible those who provide the opportunity for others deliberately to cause harm. To some extent, this has already happened with regard to landowners and public authorities (see 6.4 and 6.7).

Summary

9.1 The defendant's negligence will be treated as a 'cause in fact' of the plaintiff's injury if it was a necessary element of a set of conditions together sufficient to produce that injury. The 'but for' test is often employed as a simple guide as to whether the requirement of causation in fact is satisfied.

9.2 The 'but for' test is not able to deal with cases of multiple causation and in such cases we have to employ the underlying notion of causation in fact. However, even if the defendant's action is treated as causally relevant, it may be that the policy of the law relating to the assessment of damages requires the court to take account of the fact that the plaintiff's loss would have occurred in any event because of some other (non-tortious) factor.

9.3 The plaintiff must prove, on the balance of probabilities, that her loss was caused by negligence rather than by natural causes. It is not possible to evade this requirement by framing the claim as one for the 'loss of a chance'.

9.4 Not all causes in fact are treated as the cause of the plaintiff's loss in law. An intervening act or event may negative causal connection between the defendant's negligence and the plaintiff's injury.

Exercises

9.1 What is the "but for" test? Does it always identify all the factors that may be treated as the cause of the plaintiff's loss? Does it identify them specifically enough or do we need to supplement it with different principles of causation?

9.2 How, if at all, can *Baker* v. *Willoughby* be reconciled with *Jobling* v. *Associated Dairies*?

9.3 Your employer is required to issue you with a safety harness when you work above ground level but has never done so. You are pig-headed and there is a chance that you would have refused to use one even if it was provided. If you were injured in a fall that would have been avoided had you been wearing a harness, how would a court decide if your injury was caused by your employer's neglect?

9.4 Explain the difference between the problem of the indeterminate plaintiff and the problem of the indeterminate defendant. Should the same considerations govern both?

9.5 How do the courts decide if the causal connection between the defendant's negligence and the plaintiff's loss is negatived by an intervening act or event?

9.6 Is there sufficient causal connection in the following situations:

(a) A hits B and leaves her on the beach where she is drowned by the incoming tide.

(b) C hits D and leaves her on the beach where she is murdered by a robber.

(c) E crashes her car into a lamp post. A police officer negligently directs traffic around the obstruction and a collision ensues in which F is killed.

(d) G carelessly leaves the door of her house unlocked. Thieves walk in, break down a thin partition wall and steal property from H's house next door.

9.7 To what extent do the law's principles of causation reflect matters of policy?

10 Remoteness of Damage

10.1 The *Wagon Mound* Test of Remoteness

In order to recover damages in respect of injury caused by another's negligence, you must establish that injury of that type was a foreseeable consequence of the negligence. This rule was laid down by the Privy Council in the case *Overseas Tankship (UK) Ltd* v. *Morts Dock & Engineering Co Ltd, The Wagon Mound* [1961] AC 388; although the English courts were not in strict law bound by the decision, it was nevertheless reasonably foreseeable that they would accept the principle, as one contemporary commentator wryly predicted (Goodhart, 1966). The rule is one of a number of mechanisms by which the law limits liability for the consequences of one's negligence; most notable among the others are the principles concerning selection from among causally relevant factors and those concerning the existence and scope of the duty of care.

In *The Wagon Mound*, a fire started in Sydney Harbour had damaged a wharf belonging to the plaintiffs. The fire had begun when oil, which had carelessly been allowed to overflow from the defendant's ship, the *Wagon Mound*, was accidentally set alight. The Privy Council held that, while it was foreseeable that the oil spillage might foul the plaintiff's wharf, it was not foreseeable that the oil would be set alight and cause fire damage to the wharf. The claim in respect of fire damage was disallowed. It was not enough that some damage to the plaintiff's wharf was foreseeable; the plaintiff had to establish that damage of the type that actually occurred was foreseeable.

The justification for the rule is that it ensures that the defendant is not penalised excessively for her default. Under the law as it stood before the *Wagon Mound* decision, it appeared that a defendant would held liable for all the consequences of her negligence so long as they were 'direct'. This requirement, which was attributed to the decision of the Court of Appeal in *Re Polemis* [1921] 3 KB 560, strikes many as obscure and seems to do no more than reiterate the fact that an intervening act or event may negate the causal connection between the defendant's wrongdoing and the plaintiff's loss (for an alternative analysis of *Re Polemis*, see Clerk and Lindsell, 1995, para. 7–187). In *The Wagon Mound*, Viscount Simonds suggested that the rule in *Re Polemis* might give rise to 'palpable injustice':

> '[I]t does not seem consonant with current ideas of justice or morality that, for an act of negligence, however slight or venial, which results in some trivial foreseeable damage, the actor should be liable for all consequences, however unforeseeable and however grave, so long as they can be said to be "direct".'

The *Wagon Mound* rule of remoteness applies elsewhere in the law of tort, for instance in the law of nuisance and under the rule in *Rylands* v. *Fletcher* (1868) LR 3 HL 330 (see *Cambridge Water Co* v. *Eastern Counties Leather Co* [1994] 2 AC 264). However, it does not apply where the defendant intends to inflict injury on the plaintiff: in torts such as deceit and the economic torts, in which intentional injury is the gist of the tort, the plaintiff can recover in respect of all the direct consequences of the defendant's wrong under the rule in *Re Polemis* (see *Smith New Court Securities Ltd* v. *Scrimgeour Vickers (Asset Management) Ltd* [1996] 4 All ER 796).

10.2 The Concept of Foreseeability Examined

Foreseeability in the context of the *Wagon Mound* rule of remoteness plays a rather different role from when it is employed in order to determine whether a defendant was negligent (in breach of duty). Its place in the latter enquiry is as one of a number of factors – others being the gravity of the possible injury and the burden of guarding against it – which must be considered before we can say whether certain behaviour was reasonable or not. The degree of foreseeability required before the defendant is branded negligent varies in relation to those other factors: running a risk of a certain probability will be reasonable in some circumstances but not in others. In contrast, the stipulation that the harm the plaintiff has suffered must be of a type that was foreseeable requires a court to look at the issue of foreseeability in isolation and to demand the same degree of foreseeability whatever the circumstances of the case.

That foreseeability is used in different senses in these two contexts is established by the case of *Overseas Tankship (UK) Ltd* v. *The Miller Steamship Co, The Wagon Mound (No. 2)* [1967] 1 AC 617. This arose out of the same set of circumstances as the first *Wagon Mound* decision, but dealt with a claim by a different plaintiff. The fire in Sydney Harbour damaged not only the wharf belonging to Morts Dock, the plaintiffs in the first action, but also ships belonging to The Miller Steamship Co, the plaintiffs in the second. As we have seen, the Privy Council held in the first case that it was not foreseeable that the oil would be set alight and cause fire damage to the wharf. In the second case, different evidence was led, causing the trial judge to take a different view of the facts of the case. He held that it was in fact foreseeable that the oil might catch fire and the Privy Council held that he was perfectly entitled so to do. The trial judge went wrong, however, in going on to hold that this risk was too small to attract liability. This was an error because, once it had been decided that fire damage was a foreseeable possibility, the question was whether a reasonable person would have run that risk. In determining this, the degree of risk could not be looked at in isolation but had to be considered in the light of other factors such as the cost of averting the danger. The trial judge had not appreciated this and, while he had correctly analysed foreseeability in the remoteness context, he had fallen into error when it came to looking at it from the point of view of breach of duty. On the facts of the case, as the risk was not far-fetched, and as it could have been eliminated without expense simply by stopping the discharge, the Privy Council held the defendant shipowners liable (see Dias, 1967).

10.3 The 'Type of Loss' Requirement

As we have seen, the plaintiff must show that the type of loss she suffered was foreseeable. It was for this reason that the plaintiffs in the first *Wagon Mound* case failed: their actual loss (the fire damage to the wharf) was of a different type from that which was foreseeable (damage by oil fouling). However, while the plaintiff must prove that loss of the type she suffered was foreseeable, she need not prove that loss of the same extent was foreseeable. Neither need she prove that the exact chain of events leading to her loss was foreseeable. The leading case is *Hughes* v. *Lord Advocate* [1963] AC 837. Road works being carried out by the Post Office were left unattended during a teabreak. There were paraffin lights around the site. Two boys sneaked onto the site to play. One of them knocked over a lamp which fell into a manhole and caused a violent explosion; the boy was badly burnt. The House of Lords accepted that the explosion had been unforeseeable but held that the boy's injury was not too remote as it was foreseeable that he might have been burnt by contact with the oil in the lamp. The foreseeable risk that did not eventuate and the unforeseeable risk that did were both of the same type. As Lord Guest remarked, 'I cannot see that these are two different types of accident. They are both burning accidents and in both cases the injuries would be burning injuries' (p. 356).

It will be readily apparent that the crucial question is how widely defined is the relevant 'type of harm'. The lack of clear guidance on this question of definition has caused the courts to adopt a variety of different approaches, from the narrow and restrictive to the generous and expansive. The case of *Tremain* v. *Pike* [1969] 1 WLR 1556 provides an example of the narrow definition of the relevant type of harm. The plaintiff, a herdsman at the defendants' rat-infested farm, came into contact with rats' urine in the course of his employment and contracted Weil's disease. His claim for damages was rejected by the High Court: Payne J held that the defendants ought to have foreseen the possibility of some illness or infection arising from the infestation but decided that the contraction of Weil's disease itself was unforeseeable and therefore too remote to be actionable. Such an approach will strike many as inequitably restrictive, given the defendant's undoubted negligence and the plaintiff's lack of alternative recourse in respect of his injury.

Recently, however, the House of Lords has signalled a much more expansive approach, at least in cases involving personal injury rather than property damage. In *Page* v. *Smith* [1996] AC 155 (see further 4.3), the House of Lords had to determine precisely what harm had to be foreseeable in a case involving 'nervous shock'. By a majority, their

Lordships denied that *The Wagon Mound* entailed that the risk of nervous shock should be specifically foreseeable (albeit that the desirability of limiting the number of claims by 'secondary victims' necessitated, as a matter of policy, a more restrictive approach at the duty stage in such cases) and effectively treated personal injury as a single, indivisible type of harm. Lord Lloyd (with whom Lord Ackner and Lord Browne-Wilkinson agreed) stated that it was necessary to satisfy only the following test of foreseeability, namely 'whether the defendant can reasonably foresee that his conduct will expose the plaintiff to the risk of personal injury, whether physical or psychiatric' (p. 197). He added: 'There is no justification for regarding physical and psychiatric injury as different "kinds of damage".'

His Lordship did not specifically advert to *Tremain* v. *Pike* or any other case taking a narrow approach to the 'type of harm' criterion in relation to personal injury, but such cases may now be regarded as impliedly overruled. The same seems also to apply to cases in which the unforeseeable *manner of causation* of the plaintiff's personal injury has been held to preclude liability on grounds of remoteness. In *Doughty* v. *Turner Manufacturing Co Ltd* [1964] 1 QB 518, the plaintiff suffered burns in an accident at work when the cover of a cauldron of molten liquid was inadvertently knocked into the cauldron. The cover reacted with the molten liquid and caused an explosion in which the plaintiff was injured by liquid dispelled from the cauldron. The Court of Appeal held that, even accepting that injury might foreseeably have resulted from splashing caused by the cover's falling into the cauldron, the actual events that occurred were wholly unforeseeable and hence too remote from the original inadvertence (see also *Crossley* v. *Rawlinson* [1982] 1 WLR 369). This reasoning is clearly inconsistent with the decision of the House of Lords in *Page* v. *Smith*, for the distinguishing feature of nervous shock cases is not so much the nature of the injury but the manner of its causation (see 4.1), and the House of Lords specifically denied that the fact that the plaintiff's injury was caused by psychiatric rather than physical means could warrant a finding that it was too remote. This, of course, is not to deny that liability might be denied without reference to the foreseeability of the injury's causation, e.g. on the grounds that no injury at all was foreseeable or that the plaintiff was not a foreseeable *victim* of the defendant's negligence (cf. Clerk and Lindsell, 1995, para. 7–190).

In contrast with cases of personal injury, cases of property damage must, it seems, be subdivided into a set of different types. The *Wagon Mound* decision provided that damage by fire is a different type of harm from damage by fouling, while the Privy Council's criticism in that case of *Re Polemis* (in which a plank's falling into a ship's hold unexpectedly caused a fire) suggests that fire damage is a different type of harm from impact damage. The more expansive approach adopted in cases of personal injury, relative to that applied where the loss is property damage, may be justified on the basis of the comparative value of the interest to be protected. The law rightly values personal integrity above the interest in property.

10.4 The 'Thin Skull' Rule

The 'thin skull' rule is a potentially significant exception to the requirement that the type of harm suffered by the plaintiff must have been foreseeable. Where the plaintiff suffers foreseeable injury as the result of the defendant's negligence and this triggers off an unforeseeable reaction which is attributable to the plaintiff's pre-existing susceptibility, there is authority to suggest that the plaintiff can recover in respect of both foreseeable and unforeseeable consequences of the negligence. In such cases, the principle enunciated by Lord Parker CJ in the leading case of *Smith* v. *Leech Brain & Co Ltd* [1962] 2 QB 405 is that 'a tortfeasor takes his victim as he finds him'. The case concerned an accident at the defendant's iron works in which Mr Smith was hit on the lip and burnt by a piece of molten metal. As he had a premalignant condition, he was abnormally susceptible to cancer; shortly afterwards a cancerous growth, which proved to be fatal, formed at the site of the burn. The court allowed Mr Smith's wife to recover damages in respect of his death regardless of the unforeseeable nature of his fatal cancer; it was sufficient that the burn he had suffered was foreseeable. In the view of the court, the Privy Council in *The Wagon Mound* did not have any intention of making inroads into the 'thin skull' doctrine.

Two interpretations of this decision are possible. The narrow view is that it is wholly entailed by the *Wagon Mound* approach, which provides that if damage of a particular type is foreseeable it is immaterial that the extent of the damage sustained is not. Given that personal injury must now be treated as a single, indivisible type of harm (see *Page* v. *Smith*), it appears that the deceased in *Smith* v. *Leech Brain* did indeed suffer a foreseeable type of harm, for the court accepted that personal injury *of some type* was foreseeable; the unforeseeable cancer was a matter affecting only the *extent* or gravity of that injury. The alternative and more expansive view is that the decision in *Smith* v. *Leech Brain* represents an exception from the *Wagon Mound* doctrine, applicable where a foreseeable loss triggers another loss, of a different and unforeseeable type, as a result of the pre-existing susceptibility of the plaintiff or the plaintiff's property. Suppose the defendant were negligently to drop a plank into the hold of the plaintiff's ship. It is foreseeable that the plank might fall upon the plaintiff's goods in the hold, causing them damage. But if the bottom of the hold were unsound and should spring a leak, causing water damage to the goods, this would seem to be damage of a different sort. Should the plaintiff be able to recover in respect of the unforeseeable water damage on the basis that it was triggered by the conjunction of the foreseeable impact and the pre-existing unsoundness of the hold? It is submitted that the plaintiff should not recover in such a case for, on such facts (as in many cases of property damage), the damage is best regarded as a commercial risk against which the plaintiff might be expected to take out insurance; accordingly, the first interpretation of *Smith* v. *Leech Brain* is to be preferred.

11.5 **Impecuniosity**

Where the plaintiff incurs expenses in seeking to mitigate a loss sustained as a result of the defendant's negligence, those expenses that are attributable exclusively to the plaintiff's impecuniosity are deemed too remote. In *Liesbosch Dredger (Owners)* v. *Edison (Owners)* [1933] AC 449, a vessel called the *Edison* negligently caused the loss of a dredger known as the *Liesbosch*. The *Liesbosch* was under contract to carry out certain work and, in order to complete these contracts, the owners of the *Liesbosch* were obliged to secure the use of a substitute dredger. In the long run, it would have been cheaper to buy the substitute rather than hire it, but the financial position in which the owners found themselves initially precluded this. The House of Lords declined to allow the owners to recover the hire charges, limiting their damages to the cost of acquiring a replacement dredger; the hire charges were incurred as a result of their want of means and as such were too remote or, alternatively, they resulted from an independent cause. The decision apparently contradicts the principle of *The Wagon Mound* that, if the type of harm suffered is foreseeable, its precise extent is immaterial, and it is perhaps best considered as a somewhat anomalous exception to that principle.

The impecuniosity rule is limited to cases in which extra expense incurred by the plaintiff was attributable solely to her want of means, and does not apply where it might be ascribed to 'commercial good sense'. In *Dodd Properties (Kent) Ltd* v. *Canterbury City Council* [1980] 1 WLR 433, the plaintiffs sought compensation in respect of damage caused to their garage by the defendants' building operations nearby. The damage was suffered in 1970 but the plaintiffs postponed carrying out repairs until after judgment had been given against the defendants in 1978, by which time the cost had soared. One of the reasons for this delay was the fact that the plaintiffs were very short of cash. The trial judge followed *Edison* in holding that the delay was due to the plaintiffs' impecuniosity, and therefore they could only recover the cost of repairs as they would have been in 1970. The Court of Appeal reversed this ruling, Megaw LJ distinguishing *Edison* on the grounds that '[t]he "financial stringency" which would have been created by carrying out the repairs was merely one factor among a number of factors which together produced the result that commercial good sense pointed towards deferment of the repairs' (p. 453). Among the other factors was the concern that, if the defendants were not found liable, the plaintiffs' limited resources might be better spent on another project.

Summary

10.1 The plaintiff must establish that her loss was of a type that was the foreseeable consequence of the defendant's negligence. This is known as the *Wagon Mound* rule of remoteness.

10.2 The use of the concept of foreseeability in this context is rather different from its use as one of the factors determining whether the defendant was in breach of duty.

10.3 It is not enough that some loss to the plaintiff was the foreseeable consequence of the defendant's negligence: the same type of loss as that suffered by the plaintiff must have been foreseeable. The categorisation of different 'types' of loss has proved problematic.

10.4. The 'thin skull' rule, by which the plaintiff is allowed to recover in respect of the unforeseeable consequences of the defendant's negligence when those consequences were attributable to the plaintiff's pre-existing susceptibility, is of uncertain status in the modern law and arguably adds nothing to what is entailed by the *Wagon Mound* rule of remoteness.

10.5 Where the plaintiff incurs expenses in seeking to mitigate a loss sustained as a result of the defendant's negligence, those expenses that are attributable exclusively to the plaintiff's impecuniosity are deemed too remote.

Exercises

10.1 What is the difference between the *Wagon Mound* and *Polemis* test of remoteness? Which torts take which test?

10.2 How does the role of the concept of foreseeability in the context of remoteness of damage differ from its role in the context of breach of duty?

10.3 According to what criteria do the courts decide if the harm that eventuates is of the same type as that which was foreseeable?

10.4 What is the 'thin skill' rule? Does it apply to 'thin wallet' cases (i.e. those in which the plaintiff's loss is aggravated by her own impecuniosity)?

11 Defences

The defences we consider below are in fact of general application in the law of tort, but we deal with them here partly for convenience and partly because they are most frequently encountered in practice in the context of negligence litigation.

11.1 Voluntary Assumption of Risk: Introduction

We begin by looking at what is popularly known as the 'free will' defence, which arises where the plaintiff is found to have voluntarily assumed the risk of injury. In fact, this label indicates a group of related defences rather than any single principle. The defence of consent, which arises most frequently in relation to the intentional interference with the person, is considered elsewhere (see 16.7); here we shall consider waivers of liability (exclusions and disclaimers) and the defence expressed by the Latin maxim *volenti non fit iniuria* (see 11.2 and 11.3). The former deals with actual agreements to assume the risk of negligent injury, the latter with conduct from which it may be inferred that the plaintiff willingly took that risk upon herself. Unlike contributory negligence, which functions only as a partial defence, both doctrines act as a total defence to tortious liability.

The free will defences have played a significant role in the history of tort law though that role has decreased in recent times (see Cornish and Clark, 1989, pp. 499–500, 509–10). The product of an earlier and more individualistic age, the defences were used to shield entrepreneurs in post-Industrial Revolution Britain from claims by the victims of increasing industrialisation. Employees injured as a result of dangerous conditions at work were held to have voluntarily assumed the risk of that injury on the grounds that they were aware of the dangers; no heed was paid to the economic pressures that forced them to endure those conditions. Equally, the railway companies protected themselves against claims from passengers hurt in train crashes by issuing tickets only on terms that the companies were not to be liable for such injury. Gradually, however, the tide turned. The courts realised the harsh social consequences of regarding employees as having 'volunteered' to work in dangerous conditions: this could only be true if the employees had accepted additional wages as 'danger money' (see *Bowater* v. *Rowley Regis BC* [1944] KB 476). And reform of the defence of contributory negligence, making it a partial defence by providing for apportionment of responsibility between the parties, further reduced the role of the free will defences which were seen as harsh and inflexible on account of their 'all-or-nothing' basis.

Recent years have also seen the introduction of various statutory limitations upon the operation of the common laws free will defences. The most important of these, the Unfair Contract Terms Act 1977, is considered below (see 11.4); a couple of other notable examples are noted here. By the Road Traffic Act 1988, s. 149, the defences of exclusion of liability, disclaimer of responsibility and *volenti non fit iniuria* are declared to be unavailable in actions for negligence brought by any passenger in a compulsorily insured vehicle against the driver of that vehicle. This rule seems to rest on the underlying sentiment that, as any damages award would be met.out of the considerable resources of an insurance company, it would be unduly harsh to prevent even an extremely foolhardy passenger from recovering anything at all. It remains possible, however, to raise contributory negligence, e.g. against a passenger who accepts a lift from a driver who is clearly drunk (cf. *Owens* v. *Brimmell* [1971] QB 859). Another statutory restriction on the free will defences is to be found in the Consumer Protection Act 1987, s. 7, which prohibits reliance upon any provision which purports to exclude or limit the liability imposed by the Act in respect of damage caused by defective products; the statute does not expressly advert to the defence of *volenti* and the predominant view is that this defence may be raised in an action under the Act (see 15.7).

Before going on to consider the elements of the defences of waiver of liability and *volenti non fit iniuria*, it must be stressed that the question whether the defendant has been careless at all must be considered prior to the question whether the plaintiff, by reason of her agreement or conduct, should be precluded from recovering compensation for the consequences of any carelessness. This has not always been appreciated by the courts, who on occasion have made erroneous and unnecessary use of the principles of voluntary assumption of risk. This fault is particularly evident in cases which deal with injuries suffered by participants in, or spectators at, sporting events. The issue was fully discussed in *Wooldridge* v. *Sumner* [1963] 2 QB 43 in which a professional photographer covering the National Horse Show sought to recover damages after being knocked down by the defendant's horse; the horse had been taken too fast into a corner by its rider and had careered into a seating area. The Court of Appeal denied that principles of voluntary assumption of risk had any application in the case: the only question was whether the rider had taken reasonable care in the circumstances. Because the circumstances were those of a fast-moving competition, not every error of judgement or lapse of skill would amount to a departure from the standard of the reasonable participant. Something akin to a reckless disregard of the spectator's safety was required and the rider's conduct fell far short of this. The courts preference for analysing these cases in terms of breach of duty rather than voluntary assumption of risk has the important practical consequence of preventing the result of the case from depending on the identity of the plaintiff: as the free will defences can only be employed against responsible agents who have the capacity to assume the risk in question, where does this leave the infant spectator struck in the face by the football or the passer-by outside the ground hit when the ball is kicked over the fence? If liability to such plaintiffs is to be denied, it can only be on the basis that the defendant did nothing wrong rather than that the plaintiff voluntarily assumed the risk.

11.2 Voluntary Assumption of Risk: Waivers of Liability

A person may voluntarily assume the risk of harm by agreeing in advance not to sue the person by whose negligence the harm is caused. Often this agreement will be contained in a contract as an exclusion clause: one only has to think of the small print on airline tickets or car-hire forms for examples of this. However, there need not be any contract and it will be sufficient that the plaintiff freely exposes herself to the risk after being informed that the defendant takes no responsibility for any harm that occurs; this is known as a disclaimer of reponsibility. Thus, if the plaintiff enters premises after seeing a notice stating that entry is at her own risk, or relies upon financial information or advice after being told that this was given without responsibility, then she will be denied compensation if she is injured on those premises or loses money as a result of relying upon the information or advice (subject to the operation of the Unfair Contract Terms Act – see 11.4). The reason for giving effect to these non-contractual disclaimers is that the defendant might have relied on the plaintiff's agreement to those terms in placing herself in a position of potential liability (see Jaffey, 1985). As in the law of contract, the existence of the requisite agreement is tested objectively. It is not necessary that the plaintiff *in fact* consented to – or even took notice of – the provision in question; the question is only whether the defendant took reasonable steps to communicate the disclaimer to her (*Ashdown* v. *Samuel Williams & Sons Ltd* [1957] 1 QB 509).

Strictly speaking, exclusions and disclaimers are dependent upon the existence of an agreement to waive one's legal rights, not merely to run the risk of injury. Indeed (in contrast with the defence of *volenti*) the plaintiff need not have any knowledge of the precise risk that may eventuate provided that there is a clear intention to absolve the defendant from liability for harm howsoever it is caused. The waiver may be express or implied; in the latter case, a number of surrounding circumstances may be relevant in deciding whether the plaintiff has truly agreed to give up the right to sue. In *Nettleship* v. *Weston* [1971] 2 QB 691, the plaintiff agreed to give informal driving instruction to the defendant in a car owned by the defendant's husband. He had previously enquired whether he was insured against injury in the event of an accident, and had been told (correctly) that he was. He suffered injury when the defendant, owing to her inexperience, crashed the car. The court declined to accept the defence that the plaintiff had voluntarily assumed the risk of injury. Far from being a case in which the plaintiff had expressly waived his rights to sue, his request for information about the insurance position showed that he had expressly contemplated exercising those rights.

Where parties are linked together by a chain of contracts and subcontracts, the effectiveness of exclusions of liability contained in those contracts is prima facie restricted by the doctrine of privity of contract. But strict adherence to the doctrine has caused commercial inconvenience and has given rise to attempts to circumvent the privity requirement (for a discussion of the resultant problems in the law of contract, see McKendrick, 1994, ch. 7.6). In the law of tort, two issues arise. First, when, if ever, may the plaintiff in a tort action be bound by an exclusion clause in the defendant's contract with a third party? In principle, it should be possible for the contractual exclusion to the third party to act concurrently as a non-contractual disclaimer of responsibility to the plaintiff, at least where the plaintiff has reasonable notice of it (see, e.g., *Smith* v. *Eric S Bush* [1990] AC 831; in the exceptional cases in which the duty to the plaintiff is derived by extension from a voluntary assumption of responsibility by the defendant to a third party, it seems that it may not even be necessary for the plaintiff to have notice of the relevant exclusion or disclaimer: see *White* v. *Jones* [1995] 2 AC 145, 268 per Lord Goff, considered above at 5.6). Secondly, can the defendant seek to evade the doctrine of privity of contract by taking advantage of an exclusion clause in the plaintiff's contract with a third party? This is a more difficult question. English law knows no doctrine of vicarious immunity (*Scruttons Ltd* v. *Midland Silicones Ltd* [1962] AC 446), but the courts have shown a great deal of ingenuity in discovering collateral contractual relationships between plaintiff and defendant in order to give effect to the exclusion (see especially *The Eurymedon* [1975] AC 154). A simpler solution, however, is to treat the exclusion accepted by the plaintiff as relevant to the question whether it is fair, just and reasonable to recognise a duty of care; although this approach is most evident in the cases dealing with pure economic loss, there is no reason why it should not be applied to cases of physical damage as well (see *Norwich City Council* v. *Harvey* [1989] 1 All ER 1180; cf. the approach of the Supreme Court of Canada in *London Drugs Ltd* v. *Kuenhe & Nagel International Ltd* (1992) 97 DLR (4th) 261).

11.3 *Volenti non fit iniuria*

The Latin maxim *volenti non fit iniuria* states that those who voluntarily accept the risk of injury through another's negligence have no legal claim if that risk eventuates. The scope of this defence is not clearly defined and has generated much debate. Although it has sometimes been doubted whether the defence may be raised in an action for negligence (see, e.g., *Wooldridge* v. *Sumner* [1963] 2 QB 43, 70 per Diplock LJ), the predominant modern view is that it can (see, e.g., *Morris* v. *Murray* [1991] 2 QB 6). There is also controversy as to whether the conceptual basis of the defence is the plaintiff's implied consent to run the risk of injury, or simply the unreasonableness of her conduct; it is submitted here that there is ample authority for bringing both types of case within the scope of the *volenti* doctrine.

The defence may be analysed as having three elements: knowledge of the risk in question (in Latin, the *sciens* element); a voluntary exposure to the risk (the *volens* element); and – most elusively – an *assumption* of the risk. Let us take the knowledge requirement first. This serves to distinguish the defence from that of exclusion or other waiver of liability (see *White* v. *Blackmore* [1972] 2 QB 651). A notice at the entrance to farmland stating 'The owner disclaims all liability for injury howsoever caused' would be effective as a waiver of liability (subject to the Unfair Contract Terms Act), but in order to trigger the defence of *volenti* it would have to specify the type of risk that would be encountered by the entrant (e.g. 'Danger! There is a big and bad-tempered bull in this field. Enter at your peril.'). The plaintiff must have actual knowledge of the risk: it is not enough that such knowledge may be imputed to the plaintiff on the basis that a reasonable person in her position would have known of the risk; nor is it enough, in a case when the plaintiff is intoxicated at the relevant time, that the plaintiff would have known of the risk if sober, for she must be 'capable of appreciating the risks' (*Morris* v. *Murray* [1991] 2 QB 6, 16 per Fox LJ, see below).

Secondly, the plaintiff must *voluntarily* expose herself to the risk. The concept of voluntariness here is given a narrower definition than it has in the criminal law where it refers to the conscious control of a person's bodily movements. In tort, the term refers to the absence of constraints upon the person's freedom of action. For instance, an act will be non-voluntary if it is done in order to avert danger to life or limb (see especially the so-called 'rescuer' cases: 7.1). In *Haynes* v. *Harwood* [1935] 1 KB 146, horses left unattended in a public place by the defendant's servant were startled and ran off down a crowded street. The plaintiff police constable saw that people in the street were in considerable danger and averted that danger by grabbing hold of the horses and bringing them to a stop. As a result of this act of bravery he suffered injury. The court ordered the defendant to pay him compensation, declining to find that the police constable had voluntarily exposed himself to the risk of harm. In such cases, the defendant's conduct, although deliberate, is not 'voluntary'.

Finally, we turn our attention to the meaning of the key phrase 'assumption of liability'. This entails something more than that the plaintiff freely exposed herself to the risk of injury. The plaintiff must do something that warrants the conclusion that the loss should be left to fall on her if the risk eventuates. Precisely what this might be is not entirely clear from the authorities. The narrowest view is that there must be an express or implied waiver of liability by the plaintiff. But a contrary and, it is submitted, better view, suggests that the risk may be assumed even in the absence of a waiver in two types of case: first, when the plaintiff either agrees that the defendant should do the very conduct which was alleged to constitute the negligence; secondly, when the plaintiff exhibits a reckless disregard for her personal safety going beyond mere contributory negligence.

Must There Be a Waiver of Liability?

In *Nettleship* v. *Weston* [1971] 2 QB 691, 701 Lord Denning MR stated: 'Nothing will suffice short of an agreement to waive any claim for negligence'. However, this view must be treated with some caution. In the first place, it gives rise to certain doctrinal difficulties. If, which seems to be asserted, the defence of *volenti* is no more than a subcategory of the defence of waiver, it is hard to see the justification for the other requirements of the defence. One can effectively waive liability for negligently inflicted injury 'howsoever caused', so why should the defence of *volenti* require knowledge on the part of the plaintiff of the type of risk to be encountered? Additionally, the fact that the defence of *volenti* may be negated by constraints on the plaintiff's action which render her conduct non-voluntary seems to contradict the rule, applicable to contractual waivers and probably to notices, etc., as well, that only a very limited range of factors (e.g. incapacity) will negate agreement to an exclusion or disclaimer. Even putting these doctrinal difficulties aside, it is submitted that Lord Dennings approach does not satisfactorily account for the actual application of the doctrine in many of the decided cases (see especially *Morris* v. *Murray* [1991] 2 QB 6, below) and that the search for even an implied waiver of liability often leads to artificiality. The following analysis proceeds therefore on the basis that other factors more satisfactorily account for the application of the defence than a simple waiver of liability.

Agreement to the Conduct Constituting the Negligence

It appears that the defence of *volenti* is triggered where the plaintiff consents to the defendant's performance of the very act or acts alleged to constitute negligence (and not merely to the careless performance of the agreed acts). In *Imperial Chemicals Industries Ltd* v. *Shatwell* [1965] AC 656, two brothers, George and James Shatwell, were employed by ICI as shotfirers, whose job it was to detonate explosives at a quarry belonging to the company. One day, when testing a series of some fifty explosives wired together, they found that one of the detonators in the circuit must have been a dud. They decided to test the detonators by passing an electrical current through each of them in turn. The law's mythical 'reasonable man' might have thought it safer to retreat some distance before doing this, but the Shatwell brothers, acting contrary to company regulations, carried out the testing from close at hand. The predictable result was an explosion in which both men were injured. George commenced legal proceedings against ICI, alleging the company was vicariously liable for James's negligence. The House of Lords ruled that George had voluntarily assumed the risk of injury and hence could recover nothing, emphasising the brothers' deliberate disobedience of the company rules and their knowledge of the risk involved. We might go further and suggest that this was a particularly strong case of *volenti* because George had in fact agreed to every aspect of the conduct that he subsequently alleged to amount to negligence.

Reckless Exposure of Oneself to the Risk of Injury

Although cases like *ICI* v. *Shatwell* may legitimately be seen as based upon consent, not specifically to relieve the defendant of liability but to the defendant's performance of the relevant acts, others are not amenable to this analysis; at most, the plaintiff can be said to have consciously and voluntarily encountered the risk that the defendant might act negligently, but this does not address the question of whether the plaintiff has forfeited the right to sue for that negligence. It is submitted that the answer to this question, in the residual category of cases with which we are now concerned, turns simply upon the reasonableness of the plaintiff's conduct. The defence can have no application where the plaintiff acts reasonably, even if aware of the risk that the defendant might act without due care and skill (see *Nettleship* v. *Weston*). Nor ought it to intrude on that sphere in which it is enough to reduce the level of damages payable to reflect the plaintiff's contributory negligence. There are, however, some cases in which the plaintiff's lack of care for her own safety goes beyond mere negligence and amounts to recklessness. Because apportionment of liability under the Law Reform (Contributory Negligence) Act 1945 must reflect the plaintiff's 'share' in responsibility for the damage, courts are not able to rule that even an extremely foolhardy plaintiff has been 100 per cent contributorily negligent (for then responsibility for the accident would rest entirely with the plaintiff and not be shared at all); nevertheless, the same result may be achieved through the defence of *volenti*.

A clear example of this type of case is provided by *Morris* v. *Murray* [1991] 2 QB 6. The plaintiff and defendant, after drinking all afternoon at public houses, agreed to go flying in the defendant's light aircraft, which was kept at a local flying club. It seems that shortly after take-off the defendant lost control of the aircraft, which stalled and then dived to the ground. The defendant was killed and the plaintiff severely injured. At the autopsy, the defendant was found to have drunk the equivalent of 17 whiskies prior to the flight (more than three times the limit permitted for a car driver). In the plaintiff's action for damages, the defendant's estate raised the plea of *volenti*, and this was held to be good by the Court of Appeal. The plaintiff had embarked upon the flight without compulsion and, despite his intoxication, with adequate knowledge of the risks involved: he was 'merry' rather than 'blind drunk'. This amounted to 'great folly' and was distinguishable from cases in which the plaintiff accepted a lift in a motor vehicle from a person who was clearly drunk (cf. *Dann* v. *Hamilton* [1939] 1 KB 509, which held that *volenti* did not apply in such circumstances; motoring cases are now governed by the Road Traffic Act 1988, s. 145: see 11.2), as Fox LJ explained (p. 17):

> 'It seems to me . . . that the wild irresponsibility of the venture is such that the law should not intervene to award damages and should leave the loss where it falls. Flying is intrinsically dangerous and flying with a drunken pilot is great folly. The situation is very different from what has arisen in the motoring cases.'

The emphasis here in determining whether the plaintiff has assumed the risk of injury is not so much the plaintiff's agreement to absolve the defendant from liability but his recklessness (or 'wild irresponsibility') in exposing himself to risk (cf. the approach of Stocker LJ, who emphasised the requirement of consent). It is submitted that this is the better approach, and that in such cases the *volenti* defence is the legal equivalent of the 'playing with fire' doctrine in popular morality: if you play with fire, you cannot complain if you get your fingers burnt.

11.4 Unfair Contract Terms Act 1977

The scope of the various defences involving a voluntary assumption of responsibility is significantly restricted by the Unfair Contract Terms Act 1977. Although its name may suggest otherwise, the Act in fact applies to liabilities in tort as well as in contract, and casts its net over non-contractual provisions such as notices that attempt to limit liability, as well as over contract terms. Put briefly, the Act operates against all attempts to exclude or limit business liability for negligence. This short definition has three elements which we consider in turn – 'exclusions and limitations', 'business liability', and 'negligence' – before turning to the question of the effect the Act has when it does in fact apply.

Exclusions and Limitations

A defendant might attempt to exclude or limit her liability in various ways. In many cases, the most prudent course would be to make it an express term of a contract with the plaintiff that she should agree to waive any rights against the defendant in the event that she is injured by the defendant's fault. If contracting with the plaintiff is not practicable, then the defendant might put up a notice to the same effect where it will be seen by the plaintiff. For instance, a landowner might put a sign at the entrance to her grounds making it clear that those coming on to her land do so at their own risk. These are obvious attempts to exclude liability; less obvious are ingenious efforts to avoid the operation of the Act by trying to prevent any duty of care coming into existence at all, rather than by seeking to exclude liability in respect of an admitted breach of duty. You will recall that liability under the rule in *Hedley Byrne* v. *Heller* is often said to depend on an 'assumption of responsibility' by the defendant towards a plaintiff. Could all those facing possible *Hedley Byrne*-type liabilities escape the operation of the Act by the simple expedient of telling those who might rely on their advice 'I assume no responsibility towards you'? The answer – it is now clear – is 'No'. In *Smith* v. *Eric S Bush* [1990] AC 831; see also 5.4), the surveyor who prepared the valuation report that Mrs Smith relied on in purchasing her house put words to that very effect on the front of his report; the House of Lords declined to accept the argument that the Unfair Contract Terms Act could not bite on such a provision. Their Lordships took the view that, if the effect of a provision was to exclude or limit liability, it did not matter one jot how that provision was phrased.

Business Liability

The scope of the Act, in so far as it applies to liabilities in negligence, is restricted to cases of 'business liability'. This phrase is given a technical definition in s. 1(3) of the Act. Originally, the Act applied to all liabilities arising out of business activities or from the occupation of premises used for business purposes of the occupier, with 'business' referring not only to commercial ventures but also to the activities of public bodies. In 1984, the reference to liabilities arising out of the occupation of 'business premises' was amended to take account of the objections of farmers who thought it unfair that they should not be entitled to exclude their liabilities towards members of the public strolling across their fields and who threatened to restrict access to their land in response. Section 1(3) was accordingly amended, by the Occupiers' Liability Act 1984, so as to ensure that those injured on account of the dangerous state of land they had entered for recreational or educational purposes might be prevented from suing the landowner by an appropriate notice: liability in such circumstances would no longer be regarded as a 'business liability'. However, the amendment makes it clear that, where granting access to land for recreational or educational use falls within the business purposes of the occupier, the Act still applies. Hence, while Farmer Giles is free to exclude his liability towards those who wander through his fields without worrying about the provisions of the Act, Lord Fauntleroy cannot do the same to those who pay an entrance fee to stroll through his ornamental gardens.

Negligence

A brief glance at the Act gives the impression that it only prevents the exclusion or limitation of liabilities in the tort of negligence. This is somewhat misleading, because s. 1(1) of the Act gives an extended definition of the word 'negligence'. As well as covering liabilities in the tort of negligence, the word also refers to breach of all other common law duties to take reasonable care as well as to breach of the common duty of care imposed by the Occupiers' Liability Act 1957. Curiously, 'negligence' is not said to cover breach of the duty owed to trespassers imposed by the Occupiers' Liability Act 1984. Perhaps this is because this duty is a legal minimum that cannot ever be restricted at all (see 14.8).

Effect of the Act

Having considered the circumstances in which the Act will apply, let us turn now to look at what effect the Act has in such circumstances. This can be dealt with briefly. Everything depends on the type of loss of which the plaintiff complains. Where that loss is death or personal injury, the Act prevents any exclusion or limitation of liability at all (s. 2(1)). Where the plaintiff merely suffers property damage or pure economic loss, then s. 2(2) allows the defendant to exclude or restrict her liability, but only in so far as the contractual term or notice in question satisfies the requirement of reasonableness (i.e. that it was fair and reasonable that the term should be included in the contract or, in the case of a notice, that it was fair and reasonable to allow reliance upon it: s. 11). It is not possible exhaustively to catalogue all the factors that may be taken into account in assessing the reasonableness of an exclusion or restriction of liability: different factors will be relevant depending on the circumstances. An example of how this enquiry is carried out can be found in *Smith* v. *Eric S Bush*, in which the House of Lords considered the reasonableness of the surveyors' attempted exclusion of liability. In deciding that the notice was not reasonable, their Lordships took account of the inequality of bargaining power favouring the surveyors, the 'low-risk' nature of the task they were performing and the ease with which they could obtain liability insurance. Had the property been destined for commercial use, however, their Lordships felt that the result might have been different.

11.5 Contributory Negligence

Until 1945, contributory negligence operated like voluntary assumption of risk to bar a plaintiff's claim completely. This rule, which operated no matter how trivial the plaintiff's fault, came to be regarded as unduly harsh and the courts devoted considerable ingenuity to defeating its effect. Pressure for reform was met with the introduction – in the Law Reform (Contributory Negligence) Act 1945 – of a new regime that gave a court freedom to reduce an award of damages 'to such an extent as the court thinks just and equitable having regard to the claimant's share in the responsibility for the damage' (s. 1(1)). As we have seen (11.3), the word 'share' prevents the plaintiff being found 100 per cent contributorily negligent.

The defence does not depend on the plaintiff owing the defendant a duty of care: the only question is whether the plaintiff had taken due care in ensuring her own safety. This is assessed according to an objective standard, attaching weight to much the same factors as determine whether a defendant was in breach of duty. Hence, the degree of care demanded of someone placed in an emergency situation by the defendant's negligence is lower than that demanded of one who can respond in a considered fashion (see *Jones* v. *Boyce* (1816) 1 Stark 493). The words of the statute make it clear that the rules of contributory negligence only operate where there is some causal link between the plaintiff's conduct and the harm she suffers: if she is injured in a head-on car crash, it would be no defence for the negligent driver of the other vehicle to point to the fact that she had been driving without brake lights.

The defence of contributory negligence represents a powerful weapon in the hands of defence lawyers during the out-of-court settlement process (see 22.5). As judges are left with a great deal of discretion as to the

appropriate level of deduction to make in individual cases, raising the
defence may contribute to the uncertainty playing on the plaintiff's mind
and induce her to accept an early, and hence low, offer of settlement.
Plaintiffs are fearful of the risks inherent in personal injury litigation.
Their concern is not only that they might lose their case, but also that they
might not win it handsomely enough. If the defendant has made a
payment of an offer of settlement into court, and if the damages eventually
awarded to the plaintiff are lower than that payment, then the court will
penalise the plaintiff for continuing with her case by declining to make the
usual order for costs against the losing defendant in respect of the period
after the payment into court. In such circumstances, the more uncertainty
surrounding the plaintiff's prospects of success, the greater the 'downside
risk' will weigh in her mind. Things are improved somewhat by the courts'
willingness to lay down fixed percentage reductions in certain frequently
occurring types of case, a practice first approved by the Court of Appeal in
Froom v. *Butcher* [1976] QB 286. For instance, the standard deduction
where a car driver injured in a crash would have escaped injury had she
been wearing a seat-belt is 25 per cent. Use of these fixed percentage
reductions makes it more difficult for defence lawyers to 'bully' injured
plaintiffs into accepting a low offer of settlement.

11.6 Illegality

The English law of tort recognises a defence of illegality. It would
undermine the authority of law if unlawful activity were condoned by the
award of damages to those who break the law. Furthermore, depriving
law-breakers of a remedy in damages might serve to make them think
twice about pursuing their wrongful conduct. Yet the law does not go so
far as to brand all those who have in the past engaged in unlawful
conduct, or even those engaging in unlawful conduct at the time of their
loss, as 'outlaws' for the purposes of tortious compensation. It would be
draconian, for instance, to disallow wholly a claim for damages following
a traffic accident just because the plaintiff was breaking the speed limit at
the time the defendant negligently veered into her path. Sometimes
illegality will defeat a claim and sometimes it will not, and the question of
when precisely it will do so has provoked much controversy.

The English courts have varied between two approaches: some have
applied a 'public conscience' test, asking whether allowing recovery would
be an affront to the public conscience; others have declared it impossible
to determine an appropriate standard of care where two parties to a joint
illegal enterprise have absolved each other from acting according to
normal standards (the 'no standard of care' approach). The latter
approach can be illustrated by reference to a popular hypothetical
example in which two safeblowers set out to burgle a house, only for one
of them to detonate the explosives too soon, injuring the other. In such a
case, it is alleged, it would be impossible for a court to prescribe what
precautions the burglars should have taken for they have no way of

knowing how burglars might respond to the exigencies of the situation (footsteps upstairs, police sirens wailing in the distance, etc.). In *Pitts* v. *Hunt* [1991] 1 QB 24, the majority of the Court of Appeal expressed a preference for the 'no standard' approach, at least in the case of a joint criminal enterprise. The plaintiff, Pitts, and his friend, Hunt, had spent the night drinking at a disco before setting off home on a motorcycle, driven by Hunt with Pitts riding pillion. Encouraged by Pitts, Hunt drove in a dangerous manner designed to frighten other road users. The motorcycle crashed: Hunt was killed and Pitts was injured. The Court of Appeal held that Pitts's claim for damages against Hunt's estate was barred by the defence of illegality; in the view of the majority of the court, it was impossible to set a standard of care for a course of criminal conduct. Dillon LJ expressly rejected the public conscience test as unsatisfactory: first, the reaction of the public to the compensation of wrongdoing plaintiffs might be affected by irrational considerations (such as factors of an emotional nature); secondly, it was impossible to draw a graph of moral turpitude that would separate those plaintiffs who should succeed from those who should not. It may be objected, however, that, whatever the defects of the public conscience test, the 'no standard' approach of the majority is also flawed (see the powerful arguments of Brennan J in *Gala* v. *Preston* (1991) 172 CLR 243). It is a fiction to say that it is impossible to determine a standard of care for those involved in unlawful ventures: even if we take the case of the safeblowing burglars, it is not hard to see that, by any standard, it is careless for the burglar with the plunger to detonate the charge while the other is attaching gelignite to the safe. Furthermore, the courts are well used to altering their view of the conduct required of the defendant in the light of the exigencies of her situation: a police officer engaged in a high-speed car chase need not obey the same rules of the road as ordinary drivers. In any case, this approach can have no application where only the plaintiff, and not the defendant, was involved in a criminal venture (e.g. the cat-burglar who plunges to the ground when the tiles of the defendant's roof give way; cf. *Revill* v. *Newbery* [1996] 1 All ER 291, below).

In truth, the courts have responded to the problem of the wrongdoing plaintiff in a way that is more intuitive than reasoned and, to this extent, their approach may be thought to approximate to the 'public conscience' test. A number of factors seem to be of particular importance. First, the court may take account of the interest which the law broken is designed to protect. Where the plaintiff's wrongdoing consists in a breach of a law passed for her own benefit, the court is unlikely to deprive her totally of her remedy. This argument is most likely to succeed in the context of workplace accidents arising out of an agreement between employer and employee to 'cut corners' in breach of the law relating to health and safety at work (see *Progress and Properties* v. *Craft* (1976) 135 CLR 651).

Secondly, the relative fault of the parties seems to be a material consideration: the defence is more likely to arise where the plaintiff's conduct involves real moral turpitude rather than, say, the breach of a merely administrative regulation; conversely, where the defendant's wrongdoing goes beyond mere negligence and amounts to recklessness or gross negligence, this may preclude the operation of the defence. This seems to be the best explanation of the striking decision of the Court of Appeal in *Revill* v. *Newbery* [1996] 1 All ER 291 in which the septuagenarian defendant was held liable in damages to the plaintiff burglar whom he unintentionally shot while trying to deter the latter from breaking into his allotment shed (see also 13.8). The Court of Appeal, in a decision that attracted much adverse press comment, declined to apply the defence of illegality but upheld the trial judge's decision to reduce the level of damages by two-thirds on account of the plaintiff's contributory negligence. Although the court made allowance for the fact that the defendant's judgement was clouded by fear, it held that his actions went so far beyond what was reasonable force in the circumstances as to be clearly dangerous and bordering on the reckless (p. 302, per Millet LJ), given especially that the defendant had fired from inside the shed through a hole in the door and was effectively blindfolded in that he had no means of knowing for sure whether the gun was pointing at anyone. It should not be concluded, however, despite some rather ambiguous remarks in the decision, that the use of excessive force in self-defence or the prevention of crime will always amount to an actionable civil wrong: such conduct may well result in a criminal liability for the defendant (although it did not here: Mr Newbery was acquitted) but it is a different matter to allow the plaintiff to recover damages for injuries sustained in the course of the criminal enterprise.

Lastly, the closeness of the link between the plaintiff's injury and her unlawful conduct is a matter to be taken into account. In the example of the safeblowing burglars (above), the injured party would be unable to recover if she was blown up by her colleague: her injury would have been sustained in the course of criminal conduct. Neither would she get compensation if she sustained her injury in a crash which brought to an end their high-speed getaway: this was a risk that she brought upon herself (see *Ashton* v. *Turner* [1981] QB 137). However, she would probably succeed in a suit against her accomplice if the latter crashed the getaway car well away from the scene of the crime when there was no longer any immediate pressure to avoid detection: in this case, her injury would be merely coincidental to her wrongdoing.

So far we have looked at cases in which illegality bars the plaintiff's claim in its entirety. In other cases, the courts have ruled out only part of the plaintiff's claim on the grounds that it would offend public policy to allow recovery of particular heads of damage (e.g. where the plaintiff requests damages for loss of earnings derived from her career as a burglar: see *Burns* v. *Edman* [1970] 2 QB 541). The courts would describe their approach to this sort of case as pragmatic, though others would regard it as merely arbitrary. A striking example is *Meah* v. *McCreamer* [1985] 1 All ER 367, [1986] 1 All ER 943. The litigation arose out of a car crash caused by McCreamer's negligence, in which Meah suffered brain damage which brought on a change in personality. Some years later, Meah perpetrated a number of violent sexual attacks, for which he was convicted and imprisoned; he was also successfully sued by two of the victims of the assaults. In two successive cases against McCreamer, he sought damages first in respect of the time he spent in prison and then in respect of the compensation he was required to pay his victims. Although both claims were founded on the same criminal conduct, Woolf J allowed only the first, arbitrarily disqualifying the second as offensive to public policy.

Summary

11.1 The defence of voluntary assumption of responsibility operates as a total bar to the recovery of damages. It only comes into play if the defendant was in fact careless and care should be taken not to invoke the defence unnecessarily in cases where the defendant has done nothing wrong. The role of the defence has diminished as a result of legislative changes.

11.2 A person may voluntarily assume the risk of harm by agreeing in advance not to sue the person by whose negligence the harm is caused (e.g. by accepting a contractual exclusion clause or a non-contractual disclaimer of liability).

11.3 The Latin maxim *volenti non fit iniuria* expresses a related principle by which a person may be held to have voluntarily accepted the risk of injury through another's negligence. It requires proof of knowledge of the risk in question, a voluntary exposure to the risk, and (most elusively) an 'assumption' of the risk.

11.4 The ability of the defendant to make out a defence of voluntary assumption of risk has been restricted by the Unfair Contract Terms Act 1977. The Act, which applied to cases of business liability, prevents exclusion or limitation of liability for negligently causing death or personal injury, and subjects exclusions or limitations of liability in respect of other losses to a test of reasonableness.

11.5 Since 1945, the defence of contributory negligence has operated to reduce, by an amount considered just by the court, the damages recovered by a plaintiff who shared responsibility for her injury.

11.6 Where the plaintiff was engaged in unlawful activity at the time of her injury, she may be barred from recovering damages by the defence of illegality (e.g. in the case of a joint unlawful venture).

Exercises

11.1 In what circumstances will the defence of voluntary assumption of risk arise? Is the defence based exclusively on agreement?

11.2 Do you agree with Lord Reid (in *ICI* v. *Shatwell*) that voluntary assumption of risk is 'a dead or dying defence'? If so, why is this the case?

11.3 Would the case of *Hedley Byrne* v. *Heller* (see 5.3) still be decided the same way now that the Unfair Contract Terms Act 1977 has come into force?

11.4 What advantages are there in developing a set of tariffs to deal with commonly recurring types of contributory negligence?

11.5 What significance, if any, is attached to the fact that the plaintiff in a tort action was engaged in illegal activities at the time when the injury was sustained?

11.6 Is the law justified in precluding entirely any claim by a young man injured in a tragic accident, albeit one which resulted from his fooling around on a motorcycle after an evening's drinking (*Pitts* v. *Hunt*), at the same time as recognising a liability in damages to the burglar shot by a terrified septuagenarian who was merely defending his property (*Revill* v. *Newbery*)?

11.7 F and G, both aged 14, decide to go cycling on their tandem one afternoon. After cycling for a while, they decide to stop for some liquid refreshment and go into an off-licence where they are served by H. F asks for a six-pack of Lodgers Extra Strength lager for each of them, adding jokingly that 'Cycling up the hills should be a good deal easier after drinking that lot.' H sells them the lager. F and G get back on their tandem and cycle several more miles, drinking as they go. Rather the worse for alcohol, they decide to start a 'Mexican wave', which involves each of them in turn standing up on the pedals and waving her hands in the air. As they are doing this, F, who is steering, loses control of the tandem and both are involved in a head-on collision with J. J's car is dented and one of the tyres is punctured. Nevertheless, J decides to drive F and G to the hospital. However, on the way, she loses control of the car because of the punctured tyre. The car crashes into a ditch, causing extensive damage to the bodywork but no further injury to those in the car. J asks her neighbour K, who is a keen DIY car-repairer, if she would fix the bodywork on his car. K replies that she 'will have a go.' K makes a mess of the job and J has to have the car repaired professionally at considerably greater cost than would have been necessary before K had done any work on it. Advise the parties as to their rights and liabilities in tort.

Part II

Interference with the Person and Personal Property

12 Interference with the Person and Personal Property

12.1 Overview

Having considered the tort of negligence, we begin now our discussion of the remaining torts that feature on the typical tort syllabus. As we stated above, these are to be grouped according to the interests they may be said primarily to protect (see 1.3). Here we deal with torts that protect against interference with the person and personal property. Subsequent parts of the book deal with interest in land (Part III) and interests in reputation and privacy (Part IV). In each of these areas, we consider the impact made by the tort of negligence and the distinctive contribution made by other tortious causes of action.

In the context of interference with the person and with personal property, the tort of negligence has had a significant impact. As a practical matter, it has tended to marginalise the older common law torts. As a matter of strict law, it has led the courts to regard the distinctive features of other torts as anomalous, and consequently to eliminate those features. However, a number of older common law torts continue to play a valuable role in the law today. The most important of these are listed below:

Trespass to the person is the label affixed to a group of torts, actionable without proof of damage, which deal with 'direct' violations of the person or of personal liberty. The group consists of *assault*, *battery* and *false imprisonment*. These are considered in Ch. 16.

Wrongful interference with goods (not considered elsewhere in this book) is also a name given to a group of torts, this time dealing with injury to personal property rather than to the person. Among them are *trespass to goods*, which consists in any unjustified 'direct' interference with goods (e.g. snatching your wallet, kicking your dog or ramming your car) and *conversion*, which consists in unjustified and wilful taking away, detention, disposal or destruction of goods in a manner inconsistent with the rights of another. If nothing done to the goods is inconsistent with another's rights, the only action is in trespass. Thus my stealing your ball is both a trespass and conversion, but my grabbing your ball to throw it at someone else is only a trespass, for I am not questioning your rights over it.

Liability for animals, an example of strict liability (i.e. liability without fault), developed in the early days of the common law. It was expressed in two common law rules, the first concerning *cattle trespass*, the second dealing with the infliction of harm by dangerous animals whose vicious propensity was known – actually or imputedly – by their keeper (the *scienter* action). The old common law actions have been abolished, and the principles of strict liability in relation to the keeping of animals codified, by the Animals Act 1971.

The emergence of the tort of negligence, and of the ideology that underpins it, has influenced the legal development of the other torts and led to their marginalisation in practice. These processes are evident when we consider the relationship between negligence and trespass to the person. The influx of notions of negligence into the legal definition of trespass is traced below (see 16.1). As trespass became increasingly assimilated to negligence, it was tempting to regard as anomalous those exceptional cases in which liability might arise in the former but not in the latter (e.g. where the plaintiff suffers no damage). The result has been an attempt to eradicate those anomalies by treating unintentional interference with the person as giving rise to liability in negligence alone (*Letang* v. *Cooper* [1965] 1 QB 232; see 16.2) As a matter of practice, however, negligence had long since supplanted trespass as the principal action for personal injuries. Although negligence could not be regarded as a comprehensive and self-contained tort until *Donoghue* v. *Stevenson*, liability for negligence in various contexts was established centuries before. In such contexts (e.g. running-down cases on the highway), it was preferable for plaintiffs to frame their actions in negligence, as the scope of the action of trespass was limited and uncertain. Crucially, there were doubts as to whether the requirement of trespass that the interference be caused by 'direct' means was satisfied where a collision on the highway was caused by negligence rather than by wilful conduct (see Baker, 1990, pp. 466–7). By way of contrast, actions for negligence came to be allowed in respect of both 'direct' and 'indirect' damage (see *Williams* v. *Holland* (1833) 10 Bing 112) and so the risk of losing one's case on the pleadings was reduced.

Weir (1992) has noted wryly that 'Negligence is always trying to edge out the other torts . . . [but] . . . a few torts have managed to survive the competition' (p. 313). The torts considered in the subsequent chapters of this part of the book may be numbered among them. They are not mere historical relics. The various forms of trespass to the person (see Ch. 16) retain a practical importance in the protection of civil liberties and the vindication of individual rights. Furthermore, various statutory torts provide a more satisfactory remedy than the tort of negligence. One reason for this is that the availability of an action in negligence may be limited by restrictions on the scope of the duty of care (as was the case in relation to occupiers' liability: see Ch. 13). Another reason is that a number of statutes impose liability that is 'strict', in the sense that negligence on the part of the defendant need not be established (see Ch. 14 and 15).

12.2 Fault-Based and Strict Liability

When considering the role of fault in tort liability throughout history, three phases can be distinguished.

1. Early tort actions seem little concerned with fault. This was probably because the age was unmechanical and it was difficult for people at the time to conceive of harm being caused other than intentionally. If the fact that the defendant took all reasonable care was recognised as an excuse, this does not appear in the law reports of the time (see Baker, 1990, pp. 456–9).

2. With increasing industrialisation all this changed. Accidents at the workplace and on the roads, railways and shipping routes became frighteningly common. Infant industry, its existence still precarious, feared being crippled by liabilities imposed by the law of tort. To limit these liabilities, it adopted the standard 'No liability without fault'. Where industry was not threatened, by contrast, liability might well be recognised as strict, as was the case with the *scienter* action.

3. The advent first of workers' compensation schemes (1897) and then of the social welfare state (1946) reflected a change in society's attitudes to its responsibilities for the unfortunate. Industry was now established and producing enough wealth to safeguard its future even if it were exposed to an increased level of tortious liabilities. Many people came to feel that industry had a responsibility towards those who were injured by its activities, irrespective of whether anyone was at fault. In a startling piece of judicial innovation, the courts in *Rylands* v. *Fletcher* recognised strict liability in respect of damage caused by the escape of water from a reservoir used to power the defendant's mill (see Ch. 19). The courts also began to recognise liability for the breach of strict statutory duties imposed upon employers and others, even when no statutory remedy was prescribed (see Ch. 15). The spirit of reform has enveloped the legislature as well, notably in the field of product liability (see Ch. 14).

The rationale of strict liability is that it is unfair for the community at large to benefit at the expense of the individual. The community benefits from risky activities carried out in industrial and other spheres, activities which have their inevitable cost in the injuries suffered by employees, consumers and others. The wealth generated by industry could well be employed to provide compensation for the victims of the machine age. The rationale of strict liability can be contrasted with that of negligence liability. Whereas the latter focuses upon the defendant's wrong and treats that as the reason for requiring him to compensate the victim, strict liability accepts that the defendant's conduct might be blameless – even for the public benefit – but nevertheless requires him to compensate the victim as the price of pursuing his activities. The compensation paid may be viewed as a tax on, or licence fee for, those activities.

12.3 Compensation for Personal Injuries

As we have just seen, a more general response to increasing welfarism than the recognition of strict liability in certain areas was the introduction of workers' compensation schemes and subsequently of social security benefits. Once the principle of compensation out of public funds and irrespective of fault became established, a collision of ideals between the social welfare state and the common law of tort was inevitable. The continuing relevance of the law of tort as a means of providing compensation for personal injuries was now open to doubt.

The centrepiece of any discussion of the role of tort law in compensation for personal injury is the report of a Royal Commission on Civil Liability and Compensation for Personal Injury, chaired by Lord Pearson, which was presented to Parliament in 1978. The Commission had been set up in 1972 amid public concern about the Thalidomide cases. These cases had fuelled debate about the place of tort law in modern society and had stimulated a number of calls for tort law's abolition. Providing ammunition for those making such calls were the reports of government-appointed teams of inquiry in New Zealand (1967) and Australia (1974), both chaired by Mr Justice Woodhouse. The reports concluded that tort claims in respect of personal injury should be abolished and replaced by comprehensive schemes providing compensation irrespective of whether anyone else could be proved to be responsible for the injury. These factors generated the expectation that the Pearson Commission would recommend the abolition of the tort system in respect of accidental injury. However, this was not to be.

The Pearson Commission took the view that its terms of reference precluded it from considering whether tort should be abolished. It had been directed to consider when and how compensation should be paid in respect of death or personal injury caused at work, on the roads, by defective products or services, on other people's premises or otherwise through the acts or omission of another. Because a large proportion of injuries, notably many of those suffered in the home, fell outside these terms, the Commission felt unable to recommend a comprehensive scheme dealing with all personal injury. Having reached this controversial conclusion, it was inevitable that the Commission would base its detailed recommendations on the assumption that tort should continue to have a major role in any accident compensation strategy. As the Commission pointed out, unless a comprehensive compensation scheme were in operation, 'the abolition of tort for personal injury would deprive many injured people of a potential source of compensation, without putting anything in its place'. Accordingly, the Pearson Commission recommended the retention of a 'mixed system' of accident compensation.

12.4 The Mixed System of Accident Compensation

The mixed system that the Pearson Commission wished to perpetuate was and is one in which social security is the primary method of providing compensation and the role of tort law is supplementary. As a system of compensation, tort law suffers from a number of limitations in comparison with social security, being of limited scope, costly and prone to delay. In terms of the scope of its coverage, it is social security which ensures that the needs of the vast majority of those who have been injured are met. The Pearson Commission found that, whereas over 1.5 million of those suffering personal injury receive social security payments, only 215 000 (6.5 per cent) of them obtain tort damages. Those whose condition stems from illness rather than accident are particularly unlikely to recover in tort. As Stapleton (1986a) points out, even those who suffer from 'man-made disease', and who are therefore potential tort claimants in that they at least have a defendant to pursue, may find their case runs up against insurmountable obstacles. In particular, it may prove impossible to establish more than the fact that exposure to a certain substance *may* cause injuries of the sort suffered by the claimant, which is not sufficient to satisfy the causal requirement that the plaintiff was *in fact* injured in a certain manner (see 9.3).

In terms of cost, tort again suffers in comparison: lawyers charge breathtaking fees, insurance companies devote considerable resources to handling claims and valuable court time is taken up with determining liability and assessing damages. Taking all such factors into account, the Pearson Commission estimated that the operating costs of the tort system amount to about 85 per cent of the value of tort compensation payments; the equivalent figure for social security was about 10 per cent. These costs suggest that tort law is an inefficient means of channelling compensation to accident victims. The same story emerges from a consideration of the length of time it takes for accident victims to receive compensation. Although, according to the Pearson Commission, almost half of all tort claims are settled within a year, those alleging substantial losses often take considerably longer (frequently more than five years). A long delay before receiving compensation may place considerable demands on the resources of the victim, especially as he may be in no condition to work, and may detrimentally affect his quality of life. This is exacerbated in the case of those whose condition may actually require them to spend money: someone who is crippled after an accident, for instance, may have to make alterations to his house in order to get about it freely. By way of contrast with the law of tort, victims of accidents or illness begin to receive social security benefits as soon as they need them.

Advocates of the tort system would argue, however, that the expense of running the system is justified. Adherents to notions of corrective justice, for example, maintain that those injured by another's fault have a claim to greater compensation than the bare minimum support provided by the social security system, even if their injuries are similar to those of people who have to make to without such support. (This view seems to underpin much of the Pearson Commission's thinking; contrast Cane, 1993, ch. 7.) A different school of thought holds that the expense of the tort system is warranted on the grounds that the threat of liability serves to deter wrongdoing and leads to the most efficient utilisation of society's resources. For a comprehensive analysis of the competing theories, see Cane, 1993, ch. 18.

12.5 **The Pearson Commission Proposals**

As the Pearson Commission thought that recommending a comprehensive compensation system was beyond its remit and was committed to the continuation of a mixed system, its proposals for reform were rather limited. They amount to an effort to tinker with the tort system rather than a major overhaul. The Commission's aims were fourfold: (a) to make sure that tort compensation did not overlap with social security payments; (b) to give priority within the tort system to the most seriously injured and ensure that their interests were adequately looked after; (c) to introduce pockets of strict liability; and (d) to consolidate or extend 'no-fault' schemes of limited scope in certain areas.

(a) The Prevention of 'Overlap'

In a mixed system of compensation, there is a danger that benefits from one source will simply duplicate those from another. The result is overcompensation. To guard against the possibility of overlap between the two partners in the mixed system of compensation approved by the Pearson Commission, the Commission made a number of recommendations: the value of social security payments should be deducted in full from damages awards (implemented in part by the Social Security Act 1989; see 22.10); private medical expenses should only be recoverable where the plaintiff could show that for medical reasons it was reasonable to incur them (not implemented); and the value of being maintained by the NHS (the 'hotel element') should be taken into account in the assessment of damages (implemented by Administration of Justice Act 1982, s. 5; see 22.8).

(b) Prioritising the Most Serious Cases

The Pearson Commission aimed to give priority within the tort system to those who would need it most by making radical changes to the law relating to the assessment of damages (see Ch. 22). First, many minor cases were to be removed from the system altogether by imposing a threshold in relation to non-financial loss. The Commission recommended that no damages should be recoverable for non-financial loss suffered during the first three months after the date of injury. Its rationale for this restriction was that it would leave the tort system free to concentrate on serious and continuing losses. Secondly, the Commission recommended that no damages for non-financial loss should be recoverable for permanent unconsciousness: the award of such damages could perform no useful purpose because the plaintiff would not be able to derive enjoyment from their use. Thirdly, the Commission proposed that, in cases of death or serious and lasting injury, compensation for post-trial financial losses should be paid on a periodic basis rather than in a single lump sum. The extra expense which would result from the operation of a system of periodic payments would be justified by the fact that the plaintiff would be more accurately compensated for what he had lost, namely his income, and better protected in the event of a change in his circumstances. None of these proposals has as yet been implemented.

(c) Strict Liability

The Pearson Commission considered that, in general, negligence should remain as the basis of liability in tort. However, the Commission recommended the introduction of strict liability regimes in respect of rail transport, defective products, vaccine damage, and things and activities involving exceptional risks (see Cane, 1993, pp. 88–93). The rationale behind this piecemeal approach is unclear; certainly, it was never fully explained by the Commission. Its reasons for emphasising the role of 'fault' as a precondition of tort liability seem largely sentimental and amount to little more than a repeated assertion that it would be unfair to hold those who cause accidents innocently liable to their victims. This ignores both the justifications for the imposition of strict liability (see 12.2) and the fact that much tort liability is already strict (e.g. breach of statutory duty: Ch. 15; vicarious liability: see Ch. 21). Even the tort of negligence manifests some characteristics of strict liability, for the standard of care it demands is that of the reasonable person and this may result in the imposition of liability even though there was nothing a particular defendant could have done to prevent the injury in question (see 8.2).

The only area in which the Pearson Commission's proposals on strict liability have properly been implemented is that of product liability, on which the UK was required to act as a matter of EC law (see Ch. 14). In relation to vaccine damage, the government, on which the strict liability was to fall, pre-empted the Commission's proposals by announcing that, subject to certain qualifications, severely vaccine-damaged children would be given lump sum payments of £10 000 (now increased to £30 000). Cane (1993) comments that the preferential treatment of vaccine-damaged children as compared with other disabled children seems to owe more to political action than any satisfactory moral distinction (p. 93):

> 'It appears that in this case, as in some others, preferential treatment for a small group was the result of a well conducted political campaign which played on public sympathy for particularly heart-rending cases.'

(d) 'No Fault' Compensation Schemes

The Pearson Commission advocated the consolidation or extension of 'no fault' compensation schemes in three areas. No fault schemes provide accident victims with compensation regardless of whether their injuries were the result of anyone else's fault. In this, it resembles strict liability. It differs from strict liability, however, in that the money paid as compensation comes from a central fund rather than directly from the person who caused the accident. The Pearson Commission approved the basic structure of the existing industrial injuries scheme, although it recommended some improvements (the benefits are now payable in the form of Statutory Sick Pay and other related benefits). It suggested that a new scheme be introduced for those injured on the roads. This has not been done, although the issue was raised again for consideration in the Lord Chancellor's Department following a recommendation in the *Civil Justice Review* (1987). Finally, the Pearson Commission submitted that a new social security benefit should be introduced for severely handicapped children (not implemented). In each of these areas, injured people were to retain their rights to tort compensation.

12.6 Comprehensive Compensation Schemes

The piecemeal approach of the Pearson Commission to the institution of no fault compensation schemes contrasts with efforts to implement comprehensive schemes elsewhere. As we have noted, the introduction of such schemes was first seriously considered in the common law world in New Zealand and Australia. The New Zealand accident compensation scheme was introduced in 1974 by legislation that at the same time abolished any claim to compensatory damages in tort for accidental personal injury; proposals to introduce a similar scheme in Australia were scuppered shortly afterwards as a result of a change in government.

The New Zealand scheme set out to achieve compensation and deterrence objectives (see 2.5) more effectively than under a mixed system. Its fundamental precept was that of comprehensive entitlement to compensation. Compensation was to be paid to all those suffering 'personal injury by accident'. This phrase included injuries suffered because of medical misadventure as well as occupational disease, though not ill health generally. The compensation provided by the scheme was to be paid on a periodic basis and was to be earnings-related. However, a limit was set to awards in respect of lost income at 80 per cent of pre-accident earnings subject to an overall maximum figure; the scheme's focus upon pre-accident earnings meant that no allowance could be made for prospects of promotion or other contingencies. Provision was made for the award of lump sums up to specified maximums in respect of non-financial losses. The scheme was to be paid for by levies on employers, the self-employed and vehicle licence holders, as well as out of general taxation. This allowed a deterrence element to be built into the scheme. Employers with good safety records could have a proportion of their contributions to the scheme refunded, while those with bad safety records might incur penalty rates (though some remain sceptical about the effectiveness of these mechanisms).

The scheme became the envy of many in other countries. Its combination of the principle of comprehensive entitlement with administrative costs that proved to be very low (around 6 per cent of the sums paid out) led to it being treated as a model of enlightened reform. In so far as the scheme attracted criticism, it was for failing to go far enough, and many pressed for its extension to all cases of disease as well as accidental injury. Such calls ignored the financial strains that the burden of ensuring comprehensive compensation was already imposing on the scheme. These strains were such that major changes in the scheme became necessary. The Accident Rehabilitation and Compensation Insurance Act 1992, described in its preamble as '[a]n Act to establish an insurance-based scheme to rehabilitate and compensate in an equitable and financially affordable manner those persons who suffer personal injury', made several significant reforms in an effort to cut costs. First, it abolished the right to recover a lump sum in respect of non-pecuniary losses, replacing it with a weekly independence allowance for those left with significant disabilities. Secondly, it gave a restricted definition to the concept of compensatable personal injury in order to reduce uncertainty about the scope of entitlement to compensation and to reverse the effect of a number of judicial decisions which had had the effect of extending the right to compensation in various respects (e.g. in relation to medical misadventure, nervous shock and stress). Lastly, the new scheme will be financed by premiums levied upon the ordinary taxpayer as well as upon those who subsidised the original scheme, while provision has been made for the 'experience rating' of premiums, in an effort to promote the deterrence objectives of the scheme more effectively than under the old system of penalties and bonuses.

The reforms made to the New Zealand scheme should place it on a sounder financial footing and thereby enable it to demonstrate the economic feasibility of operating such a scheme. It may, however, be queried whether the reforms serve to exclude so many cases from the scope of the scheme that they promote a return (albeit limited) to the tort litigation that the scheme was designed to abolish. Only time will tell whether the New Zealand experience can provide a model for the introduction of a comprehensive compensation scheme in this country.

Summary

12.1 The emergence of the tort of negligence has put other torts concerned with interference with the person and personal property into the shade. Many of the latter have been assimilated to negligence in some measure. Nevertheless, they retain practical importance in some fields (e.g. the protection of civil liberties). Furthermore, tort liabilities imposed by statute may be more stringent than those in negligence.

12.2 Although the ideology expressed by the tort of negligence has dominated legal thinking since the time of the Industrial Revolution, the welfare values of the last hundred years or so have questioned whether fault should be a prerequisite of liability. The result has been the judicial recognition and legislative creation of pockets of strict liability.

12.3 Increasing welfarism has also focused attention on the way accident victims are dealt with by society. The role of tort law in providing compensation for personal injury, and its relationship with social security, was considered by the Pearson Commission.

12.4   The Pearson Commission recommended the retention of a mixed system of compensation for personal injuries in which social security would play the major role, but tort law would continue to provide − at a cost − higher levels of compensation for the privileged few.

12.5   The reforms proposed by the Pearson Commission were designed to ensure there was no overlap between tort damages and social security benefits, to prioritise the most serious cases in the tort system and to introduce areas of strict liability and no fault compensation. Many of these proposals have yet to be implemented.

12.6   A more radical solution to that found in the Pearson Report would be the institution of a comprehensive no fault compensation scheme. In such a scheme, an example of which exists in New Zealand, the entitlement to compensation would be available even to those whose injuries were not caused by fault and the awards would be paid from public funds.

Exercises

12.1   What is strict liability? Can its imposition ever be justified?

12.2   What was the Pearson Commission? What were the principal recommendations that it made? Did these recommendations go far enough?

12.3   What is meant by talk of the 'mixed system' for compensation for personal injuries? Does every part of that system perform the task of compensating the needy satisfactorily? Does any part of that system perform any other tasks (Please specify.)

12.4   What reforms would you advocate for the system of compensation for personal injuries?

---

13   Occupiers' Liability

13.1 Introduction

This chapter is concerned with the liability of an occupier of premises for injury caused or damage done to persons or their property while on the premises. The law in this area is now statutory and is governed by the 1957 and 1984 Occupiers' Liability Acts. This chapter does not deal with the situation where things done an the occupiers' premises affect other premises; this is the province of the law of 'nuisance' and *Rylands* v. *Fletcher* (see Ch. 19 and 20). The 1957 and 1984 Acts replaced a somewhat complex regime of common law, distinct from that developed from *Donoghue* v. *Stevenson*, under which an occupier owed different standards of duty depending on the status of the person who came onto his land. Those entering under a contract were owed the highest duty, while progressively lower duties were owed to those entrants the law classified as invitees, licencees or trespassers. The position today is that the Occupiers' Liability Act 1957 governs liability to lawful visitors and the 1984 Act governs the duty owed to those entrants loosely referred to as 'trespassers'. In the first part of this chapter we will examine the Occupiers' Liability Act 1957.

13.2 Scope of the Occupiers' Liability Act 1957

The 1957 Act abolishes the common law categories and provides that all lawful entrants are owed the same 'common duty of care'. This duty is owed by the occupier to his visitors 'in respect of dangers due to the state of the premises or to things done or omitted to be done on them' (s. 1(1)(a)).

Before analysing the central concepts of occupier, visitor and 'common duty of care', a number of points should be made about the scope of the Act. First, the provisions enacted apply to regulate the obligations of a person occupying or having control over, 'any fixed or moveable structure, including any vessel, vehicle or aircraft' (s. 1(3)(a)). Thus, while immoveable, landed property is clearly within the Act, so too are moveables such as ships and aircraft. Other less permanent structures such as diving boards, scaffolding and ladders and (in Australia) even a car have also been held to be premises. Second, the obligations of an occupier extend beyond a duty not to cause personal injury to a visitor and cover damage to property suffered on the premises whether the property be that of the visitor or of a person who is not himself a visitor (s. 1(3)(b)). Third, liability under the Act may also arise in respect of omissions (s. 1(1)). Thus, in one case, owners of a public park, who knew that golf balls were regularly hit there but did nothing to stop it, were held liable to a visitor to the park injured by a golf ball struck by a third party.

Finally, there is a division of opinion on the question whether the Act covers so-called 'activity' duties as well as 'occupancy' duties. The difficulty arises from the wording of section 1(1)(a), which provides that the Act regulates the duty of an occupier to his visitor in respect of 'anything done or omitted to be done [on the premises].' In addition to injury caused by the defective state of the premises, the Act is clearly apt to cover *conduct* on the premises that causes a continuing source of danger thereby rendering it unsafe (occupancy duties). However, less clear is whether the Act applies to all claims for injuries suffered on the occupier's premises arising from every kind of activity or omission on them irrespective whether they are connected with the safety of the premises as such (activity duties). Notwithstanding support for the view that the Act does cover 'activity' duties (see, for example, Pearson LJ in *Videan* v. *British Transport Commission* [1963] 2 QB 650, 679) the majority view is that activities are excluded (Law Commission, *Report on Liability for Damage or Injury to Trespassers and Related Questions of Occupiers' Liability* (Law Com No 75, 1976), at para 23; *Revill* v. *Newbery* [1996] 1 All ER 291). The distinction between the two may, however, be both fine and somewhat artificial. Thus, if A hires out his land for a shooting party and a visitor is shot by one of the guns then A may be liable under the Act but A would not be liable under the Act for negligently shooting a visitor if at the time he was out shooting on his own land. Further, for most practical purposes, the distinction should not be of any importance because injuries caused negligently on the occupier's premises will in any event be governed by common law negligence under which the duty owed is the same.

13.3 Who is an Occupier?

The Act does not attempt a definition of 'occupier', but instead, in s. 1(2), provides that an occupier is a person who would have been treated as such at common law. The leading case on the definition of an occupier is *Wheat* v. *Lacon* [1966] AC 552. In that case the defendants were owners of a public house, the management of which they entrusted to a manager. By virtue of the service agreement, the manager was entitled to live in a flat above the public house and to take in paying guests. There was no direct access between the pub and the flat, both parts having separate entrances. W and his wife were paying guests of the manager. W was fatally injured when he fell down an unlit and defective staircase in the flat. W's wife sued the defendants and the main issue was who was in occupation of the flat. The House of Lords held that, in determining who the occupier was, the important question was who had sufficient degree of control over the premises such that he ought to be under a duty of care to those who come lawfully onto the premises. Applying this test the court said that the defendants were to be treated as occupiers for the purposes of the Act.

Although it is clear that the important question is one of control, it is more difficult to determine what is a sufficient degree of control for the purposes of the Act. While an owner in occupation would no doubt have sufficient control, *Wheat* v. *Lacon* makes clear that an absentee owner may also retain sufficient control to be an occupier. In Lord Denning's speech in *Wheat* v. *Lacon*, he said that the defendants, although not in actual occupation, retained sufficient control because they had only granted a contractual licence to the manager to occupy the flat and had retained a right to enter to do repairs. This right was enough to make them occupiers. If, however, the defendants had let the flat to the manager, granting him a right of exclusive occupation, they would not have been occupiers of the flat for the purposes of the Act. In such circumstances the defendants would be treated as having parted with all control over the premises.

Wheat v. *Lacon* makes clear a further point, namely that it is possible for two or more persons to be in occupation, for the purposes of the Act, at the same time. Thus, if the plaintiff had sued the manager it appears from the speeches of Lords Denning, Morris and Pearson that they would have held the manager also to be in occupation for the purposes of the Act.

To conclude, the question of occupation is to be decided in each case on the particular facts having regard specifically to the degree of control exercised by the defendant over the premises. As has been seen, particular legal relationships or the fact of absentee ownership cannot be conclusive one way or the other but are no doubt factors to be taken into account.

13.4 **Who is a Visitor?**

The occupiers' duty under the 1957 Act is owed to lawful visitors. The Act does not define visitors but provides in s. 1(2) that a visitor is a person who would at common law have been treated as an invitee or licensee. These two categories cover a wide range of entrants and essentially encompass all those who enter with the express or implied permission of the occupier.

While this group is very wide the Act also makes specific provision for other classes of entrant who were not invitees or licensees at common law and these deserve some mention. First, at common law, those entering under a contract (such as hotel guests or workmen carrying out building work), although not classified as invitees or licensees, were nevertheless afforded a high degree of protection. Section 5(1) of the 1957 Act now provides that in the absence of a specific term of the contract dealing with the duty owed to the contractual entrant there will be implied a term that he is owed the common duty of care. The parties are, however, free to negotiate different terms which may provide that a more or even less onerous duty is owed. Terms which seek to limit or exclude the duty may, of course, fall foul of the Unfair Contract Terms Act 1977.

Second, s. 2(6) provides that 'persons who enter premises for any purpose in the exercise of a right conferred by law are to be treated as permitted by the occupier to be there for that purpose, whether they in fact have his permission or not.' Thus, a policeman entering a house in the execution of a warrant to search or a fireman entering to fight a fire are within the Act. Section 2(6) was not, however, intended to expand the range of persons who are to be treated as visitors. Thus, those using a public (*McGeown* v. *Northern Ireland Housing Executive* [1995] 1 AC 233) or private (*Holden* v. *White* [1982] 2 WLR 1030) right of way, who were not treated as either licensees or invitees at common law, are not, because of s. 2(6), to be treated as visitors. That is not to say, however, that those using private or public rights of way are wholly without protection. A person using a *private* right of way may be owed a duty under the Occupiers' Liability Act 1984 and a person using a *public* right of way may have an action against the owner of the land over which the right of way exists for breach of the ordinary duty of care in negligence (*Thomas* v. *British Railways Board* [1976] QB 912). But, as the House of Lords made clear in *McGeown* v. *Northern Ireland Housing Executive* (see above), the owner's liability in respect of both public and private rights of way will only arise in respect of positive misfeasance; he is under no duty to maintain any right of way in a safe condition. Such a conclusion was justified by Lord Keith on the ground that,

> '[R]ights of way pass over many different types of terrain, and it would place an impossible burden upon landowners if they not only had to submit to the passage over them of anyone who might choose to exercise them but were also under a duty to maintain them in a safe condition.'

Whether the acquisition of a public right of way over a path always extinguishes the common duty of care that would otherwise be owed to the occupier's visitors is not clear. Owners of shopping malls, to which the public are obviously invited, often dedicate land as a public right of way. In the absence of the right of way visitors to the mall would obviously be 'visitors' for the purposes of the Act. It is surely absurd to suggest that merely by dedicating access to such shops as a public right of way the owners could evade liability for injury caused by the state of the premises.

As already mentioned, invitees and licensees were those people who entered with the express or implied permission of the occupier. Where the occupier *expressly* invites a person onto his premises, it is generally clear that that person is a lawful visitor for the purposes of the Act. Significant problems may, however, arise in determining whether a person has the *implied* permission of the occupier to be on the occupier's premises.

It is a question of fact whether or not a person's entry has been impliedly permitted and the onus of proving this rests on the person who asserts it (*Edwards* v. *Railway Executive* [1952] AC 737, 747 per Lord Goddard CJ). To take a simple example, a person who walks up an occupier's front path with the intention of paying a social visit, or of trying to sell something to the occupier, will be treated as having the occupier's implied permission to be there (*Robson* v. *Hallet* [1967] 2 QB 939). It may be that even where he enters for his own purposes, for example if his hat is blown off into the occupier's front garden and he enters to retrieve it, he will still be held to be a visitor. However, it is clear that a licence, whether express or implied, can be withdrawn provided this is done clearly and that the licensee is given a reasonable time to leave the premises.

When we move from the rather obvious examples mentioned above, it is somewhat more difficult to discern when the courts will hold that a person's entry has been impliedly permitted. The courts have on a number of occasions made it clear that such permission should not be implied lightly. Thus, mere knowledge that persons are entering the occupiers' premises will not generally be enough (*Edwards* v. *Railway Executive*). What must be shown is that in spite of this knowledge the occupier took no steps or took insufficient steps to keep the visitor out. This can be illustrated by the case of *Lowery* v. *Walker* [1911] AC 10. People were in the habit of using the defendant's field as a shortcut on their way to the railway station. Although the defendant gave them no express permission to do so, he knew they used it as a short cut and he took no steps to stop them. The defendant, without any warning, put a savage horse into the field which attacked and injured the plaintiff. On the facts, the House of Lords held that the plaintiff was a lawful visitor.

Where child entrants are concerned, the judicial warnings against being too ready to imply permission have largely been ignored. The courts have, particularly where the child was 'enticed' onto the land by some attractive object (for example, *Cooke* v. *Midland Great Western Railway* [1909] AC 229 (a railway turntable); *Glasgow Corporation* v. *Taylor* [1922] 1 AC 44 (poisonous berries)), been relatively quick to imply permission in cases where, had an adult been injured, no such permission would have been implied. This willingness to imply a licence is attributable to at least two factors: first, until relatively recently trespassers were treated very harshly by the law, and, second, children are often meritorious, or at least attractive, plaintiffs. Since the enactment of the Occupiers' Liability Act 1984 trespassers are treated far less harshly than they had been at common law and it is probable, therefore, that courts will feel under less pressure to imply the fictitious licences that were necessary to do 'justice' in the past.

Two further problems in relation to implied permission deserve mention. The first arises where, in contravention of an express prohibition by an employer in occupation of certain premises, an employee or independent contractor invites onto the premises a person who is then injured. This situation arose in *Ferguson* v. *Welsh* [1987] 1 WLR 1553 where the House of Lords held that in such circumstances the injured person would be a lawful visitor *vis-à-vis* the employer provided he honestly and reasonably believed that the employee or independent contractor was entitled to invite him onto the premises. In *Ferguson* v. *Welsh* a local council engaged S to do some demolition work. The contract between them expressly prohibited S from subcontracting the work. In breach of this, S arranged with W to do the work. The plaintiff, who was working for W, was injured as a result of unsafe working practices being adopted. One of the issues considered by their Lordships was whether, *vis-à-vis* the council, the plaintiff was a lawful visitor. The House of Lords held that he was. The plaintiff had no reason to know anything about the details of the contract between the council and S and thus it was reasonable for him to believe that both S and W were entitled to invite him onto the premises.

Second, even where a person has the permission of an occupier to enter premises such permission may be limited by time, space or circumstance. As Scrutton LJ said in *The Calgarth* [1927] P 93, 'when you invite a person into your house to use the stairs, you do not invite him to slide down the bannisters' (p. 110). However, the application of this limitation has been approached in a common-sense way. In one case, for example, a customer in a public house wandered into a private part of the building looking for a lavatory, and in so doing fell down some stairs and suffered injury. The court held he was not behaving unreasonably in looking where he was looking, even though he had no express permission to be there, and that, therefore, he remained a lawful visitor (*Gould* v. *McAuliffe* [1941] 2 All ER 527n).

13.5 The Common Duty of Care

Section 2(1) of the Occupiers' Liability Act 1957 provides that the duty which an occupier owes his visitor is the common duty of care. This is defined in s. 2(2) as 'a duty to take such care as in all the circumstances of the case is reasonable to see that the visitor will be reasonably safe in using the premises for the purposes for which he is invited or permitted by the occupier to be there'. This duty, as Lord Denning pointed out in *Roles* v. *Nathan* [1963] 1 WLR 1117, is really the same as the ordinary duty of care in negligence and thus the factors mentioned in the chapter on breach of duty, such as the nature of the danger, the length of time the danger was in existence, the steps necessary to remove the danger and the likelihood or otherwise of an injury being caused, are equally relevant here. However, the Act also draws attention to two specific matters that are to be taken into account when considering the degree of care required.

First, s. 2(3)(a) provides that 'an occupier must be prepared for children to be less careful than adults'. This gives statutory recognition to a fact of life that the courts have always taken into account, namely, that what may not be a danger to adults may nevertheless be a danger to a child. Thus the courts have held that it is careless for a local authority to plant a shrub with poisonous berries in a public park to which children have access, because it is known that children are attracted by bright berries and may try to eat them (*Glasgow Corporation* v. *Taylor*). Were an adult to eat one of the berries it is unlikely that the court would allow recovery because it is simply not foreseeable that an adult would be so foolhardy as to eat one. Whether or not something is likely to attract a child and therefore become a danger in circumstances where it would not be a danger to an adult is a question of fact to be decided in the light of all the circumstances. What needs to be emphasised is that where an occupier knows, or ought to know, that children are in the habit of frequenting a particular place he must take account of that fact, and may be required to take greater care than he would do if children did not have access. Having said that, the courts have made it clear that occupiers may in some circumstances be entitled to rely on children being supervised by their parents: an occupier should not have to be an insurer for irresponsible parents. Thus, while it may be expected that young children will be left unaccompanied in designated play areas, it is less foreseeable that they will be left to wander wasteland or building sites (*Phipps* v. *Rochester Corporation* [1955] 1 QB 450). As Devlin J said in that case:

> '[T]he responsibility for the safety of little children must rest primarily on the parents; it is their duty to see that such children are not allowed to wander about by themselves, or at least to satisfy themselves that the places to which they do allow their children to go unaccompanied are safe for them to go to. It would not be socially desirable if parents were, as a matter of course, able to shift the burden of looking after their children from their own shoulders to those of persons who happen to have accessible bits of land.'

The second specific matter highlighted in the Act is found in s. 2(3)(b), which provides that 'an occupier may expect that a person in the exercise of his calling will appreciate and guard against any special risks ordinarily incident to it, so far as the occupier leaves him free to do so'. This subsection was extensively considered by the Court of Appeal in *Roles* v. *Nathan*. A central heating boiler produced a great deal of smoke when lit. On the advice of a heating engineer, two chimney sweeps were engaged to clean the flues. The engineer warned the sweeps of the dangers presented by fumes when the boiler was lit and told them not to clean the flues at such a time. The sweeps however disregarded this warning and were subsequently killed by the fumes given off. The action brought by their widows failed because, as Lord Denning put it, 'the householder could reasonably expect the sweeps to take care of themselves so far as any dangers from the fumes are concerned'. This was a special risk ordinarily incident to the work of a sweep. If, however, the sweeps had been injured when a bench they were sitting on having a teabreak collapsed, the occupier may well have been liable. The risk of a bench breaking is not one ordinarily incident to a sweep's work and, thus, there is no reason why the sweeps should not in such a case be treated as any other visitor.

Section 2(3)(b) will not automatically absolve the occupier from liability when a person 'exercising his calling' is injured. This is illustrated by its application to cases where firemen have suffered injury while fighting a fire on the defendant's premises. In *Salmon* v. *Seafarer Restaurants* [1983] 1 WLR 1264 firemen were injured at a fire negligently started by the occupier in his fish and chip shop. The defendants sought to argue that there is always some risk involved in fire-fighting and that they should only be liable where they failed to warn the firemen of some exceptional risk not ordinarily incident to the job. Woolf J, however, rejected this argument and stated that an occupier would be liable where

> 'it can be foreseen that the fire which is negligently started is of a type which could first require firemen to extinguish the fire and where because of the nature of the fire they will be at risk even though they exercise all the skill of their calling'.

The majority of states in the United States have adopted a different approach. Relying on concepts such as assumption of risk by the fire-fighter, a desire to avoid imposing overburdensome liability on the occupier, and the danger of discouraging property owners from seeking assistance from emergency services, courts have generally held that firemen (extended to police officers and other professional 'risk-takers'; *Berko* v. *Freda* (1983) 459 A 2d 663 (police officers) *Anicet* v. *Gant* (1991) 580 So 2d 273 (public employee caring for the violent insane persons)) cannot recover unless the defendant's negligence creates undue risks of injury beyond those inevitably involved in fire-fighting (*Krauth* v. *Geller* (1960) 157 A 2d 129).

In considering whether the occupier has discharged the common duty of care, s. 2(4) of the Act lists two further matters to be taken into account. First, s. 2(4)(a) provides that 'where damage is caused to a visitor by a danger of which he had been warned by the occupier, the warning is not to be treated without more as absolving the occupier from liability, unless in all the circumstances it was enough to enable the visitor to be reasonably safe'. Clearly if a notice is illegible or unintelligible it will not be enough and, in considering this, account must be taken of the capabilities of those who the occupier knows or ought to know are likely to see or hear the warning. Even if the warning is clear, this may not be enough to comply with the occupier's duty which is to make the premises reasonably safe. If, for example, to reach the occupier's front door his visitors have to cross a bridge over a river on his land and the bridge is rotten, the occupier is unlikely to be absolved from liability by putting up a notice warning that the bridge is rotten. This does not enable his visitors to be reasonably safe if it is the only way to get to the front door. Conversely, if there are two bridges, only one of which is safe, and a notice which says, 'this bridge is dangerous, use the other one', the occupier may not be in breach of his duty towards his visitors because the warning enables them to be reasonably safe (*Roles* v. *Nathan*, *per* Lord Denning).

Second, s. 2(4)(b) provides:

> 'where damage is caused to a visitor by a danger due to the faulty execution of any work of construction, maintenance or repair by an independent contractor employed by the occupier, the occupier is not to be treated without more as answerable for the danger if in all the circumstances he had acted reasonably in entrusting the work to an independent contractor and had taken such steps (if any) as he reasonably ought in order to satisfy himself that the contractor was competent and that the work had been properly done.'

This section was considered by the House of Lords in *Ferguson* v. *Welsh* where their Lordships rejected the plaintiff's argument that, having regard to s. 2(4)(b), the council had failed to discharge the common duty of care which they owed to him. In so doing, their Lordships considered a number of problems concerning the interpretation of that section. First, the plaintiff had argued that the council should not be able to rely on the section because the work it had engaged S to do was 'demolition' and this was not within the ambit of the section which refers to 'any work of construction, maintenance or repair'. In rejecting this argument the House of Lords held that 'a broad and purposive' approach should be taken to the meaning of these words and that 'demolition' was embraced by the word 'construction'. Second, it was argued that an occupier did not discharge the common duty of care where he employed someone he knew or ought to have known was incompetent. While this argument was accepted as correct in principle, it was rejected on the facts of the case. There was not enough evidence to suggest that the council ought reasonably to have doubted the honesty or competence of S. Had the council known that S was in the habit of adopting dangerous working practices, it is unlikely that it would have been held to have discharged the common duty of care. Finally, it was argued that the council ought to have supervised the conduct of the work. Again, this was rejected on the facts. The council did not have any reasonable grounds to suspect S was anything other than competent and this was not the type of work where supervision would ordinarily be required. However, there may be cases where work is of such technical difficulty that the occupier's common duty of care will not be discharged unless a specialist is employed to supervise the work and to make sure that it is completed properly.

13.6 Defences

The area of defences generally is dealt with in Chapter 11 and as a result only matters specifically relevant to the liability of occupiers are mentioned here.

First, by s. 2(5), the Act expressly preserves the general defence of *volenti non fit iniuria*. Second, the Act does not specifically mention whether a visitor's own lack of care can be taken into account in reducing damages. However, the courts have in a number of cases applied the Law Reform (Contributory Negligence) Act 1945 to reduce damages. Thus, it seems clear the defence of contributory negligence is available to an occupier. Finally, s. 2(1) of the Act specifically allows an occupier the freedom 'to extend, restrict, modify or exclude his duty to any visitor or visitors by agreement or otherwise'. However, such freedom is limited in three important ways. The first, and most important limitation is by the Unfair Contract Terms Act (see 11.4). The second limitation is found in s. 3(1) of the Occupiers' Liability Act 1957, which provides that, where an occupier is bound by contract to permit persons who are strangers to the contract to enter or use the premises, he owes them the common duty of care and the occupier cannot by that contract restrict or exclude this duty. Thus, if A puts K up as a lodger in his flat, he cannot stipulate that he will not be liable for any injury suffered by any person visiting K as a consequence of a defect in the premises. Finally, where a visitor is a 'contractual entrant' the occupier's ability to limit his liability to his visitor may be restricted by the Unfair Terms in Consumer Contracts Regulations 1994 (see McKendrick, 1994, pp. 280f).

13.7 Liability to Trespassers

The law governing the duty of care owed by an occupier to a trespasser was left unaltered by the 1957 Act and, until the House of Lord's decision in *BRB* v. *Herrington* [1972] AC 877, the law was as laid down in *Robert Addie & Sons (Collieries)* v. *Dumbreck* [1929] AC 358. In *Addie*, it was held that the occupier had to do some act either deliberately intending to harm the trespasser or at least with reckless disregard for his safety, before a trespasser could succeed in an action against him. The harshness of this principle was to a large extent alleviated by the House of Lords in *BRB* v. *Herrington*, where it was held that trespassers were owed the 'common duty of humanity'. Their Lordships did not, however, make clear precisely what they meant by this and in particular how it differed from the ordinary duty of care in negligence or that arising under the 1957 Act. Subsequent cases indicated that the duty was somewhat higher than the old common law duty owed to trespassers but lower than the ordinary duty of care in negligence. Dissatisfaction with the uncertainty of the principle lead the, then, Lord Chancellor, Lord Hailsham, to ask the Law Commission to consider, 'in the light of the decision of the House of Lords in *BRB* v. *Herrington*, the law relating to liability for damage or injury suffered by trespassers'. The Law Commission recommended that legislation was needed to clear up the uncertainty (Law Commission, 1976) and the Occupiers' Liability Act 1984 was the result.

13.8 The Occupiers' Liability Act 1984

The Occupiers' Liability Act 1984 replaces the common law as laid down in *Herrington*. It places occupiers ('occupier' having the same meaning under the 1984 Act as it does under the 1957 Act) under a duty to 'persons other than his visitors' to take such care as is reasonable in all the circumstances to see that they do not suffer injury on the premises provided certain conditions are satisfied. In this section we use the term 'trespasser' as shorthand for 'persons other than [the occupier's] visitors'. However, note that the Act does in fact apply to more than just 'trespassers': the duty is owed to 'persons other than his visitors'. Thus, in addition to those who enter an occupier's premises without that person's express or implied permission (trespassers properly so called), the Act also applies to those using private rights of way (*Holden* v. *White* (*supra*)) and those exercising rights under National Parks legislation (National Parks and Access to the Countryside Act 1949, s. 1(4)), but not to those using the highway (Occupiers' Liability Act 1984, s. 1(7)).

As is the case under the 1957 Act, the duty owed under the 1984 Act is owed in respect of any risk of their suffering injury by reason of 'any danger due to the state of the premises or *to things done or omitted to be done on them*' (s. 1(1)(a); (emphasis added). In *Revill* v. *Newbery* [1996] 1 All ER 291, the Court of Appeal held that the Act did not apply where the defendant carelessly shot the plaintiff burglar who was trying to get into his shed. Although the Act could apply to both dangers arising from the state of the premises and from activities conducted on the land, s. 1(1)(a) was only intended to impose liability on an occupier *qua* occupier. Here the fact that he was an occupier was irrelevant to his liability.

The duty owed under the 1984 Act does not, unlike under the 1957 Act, extend to damage done to the entrant's property (s. 1(8)). Thus, if A entered B's land as a trespasser riding his scrambling bike, and due to a danger on B's land A fell off, he may be able to recover for any personal injury suffered in the accident but cannot recover for any damage done to the bike. Presumably in such a case the common law position accepted in *Herrington* would apply to the property damage though it is somewhat unsatisfactory to talk in terms of a breach of the duty of common *humanity* where only property damage is suffered (Winfield and Jolowicz, 1994, p. 245).

The Act provides in s. 1(3) that a duty is owed by an occupier to a trespasser provided:

'(a) he is aware of the danger or has reasonable grounds to believe that it exists;

(b) he knows or has reasonable grounds to believe that the other is in the vicinity of the danger concerned or that he may come into the vicinity of the danger . . .; and

(c) the risk is one which in all the circumstances of the case, he may reasonably be expected to offer the other some protection.'

The phrasing of ss. 1(3)(a) and 1(3)(b) creates some difficulty. Does a duty only arise if the occupier had *actual* knowledge of the existence of the danger and a similar knowledge of the presence or likely presence of the trespasser? Or, is it enough that a reasonable man would have, or ought to have, such knowledge? The language used is unclear, providing as it does that the occupier must know or be aware or 'have reasonable grounds to believe' that the danger exists and that the trespasser is in the vicinity or is likely to come into the vicinity. The better view is that the occupier must either have *actual* knowledge of the danger or actual knowledge of facts from which a reasonable man would draw the inference that the danger existed and that the person was in the vicinity or was likely to come into it. This is not the same as saying that it is enough that a reasonable man ought to know of the danger and likely presence of the trespasser.

This view is supported by the decision of the Court of Appeal in *White* v. *St Alban's City Council* (1990) *The Times*, 12 March. The plaintiff was injured while taking a short cut to get to his car, which was parked in the defendants' car park. Although the defendants were aware of the danger and had taken steps to prevent any injury arising from it by blocking off access to the short cut, they had no evidence that the short cut was ever used to get to the car park. The court held that s. 1(3)(b) was as a result not satisfied. Further, the court acknowledged that this would have been the case even if a reasonable man in the position of the occupier would have been aware that the short cut was in fact used.

The content of the duty owed under the 1984 Act is governed by s. 1(4). This provides that the occupier owes a duty to 'take such care as is reasonable in all the circumstances of the case to see that [the trespasser] does not suffer injury on the premises by reason of the danger concerned'. The duty owed is akin to the ordinary duty of care in negligence and, as a result, unlike under *BRB* v. *Herrington*, questions of the resources of the individual defendant will be irrelevant. However, in considering whether the duty has been breached, it is to be remembered that what constitutes reasonable care will vary according to the circumstances. Thus, for example, the duty will be less easily breached with respect to a burglar than with respect to a child who wanders into an occupier's garden to have a look at the fish in a pond.

By virtue of s. 1(5), the duty owed may be discharged when warning of a danger is given. As is the case under the 1957 Act, a warning will not in every case be sufficient to discharge the duty owed by an occupier. However, it is more likely to be effective to discharge the duty owed to a trespasser than to a lawful visitor. The reason for this is that whereas a lawful visitor may have no choice but to run the risk of being injured on the premises, the trespasser will usually have that choice.

In principle, the general defences available to an action in negligence should also be applicable to an action under the 1984 Act. However, some doubt was cast on this by the unsatisfactory decision of the Court of Appeal in *Revill* v. *Newbery* (Weir, 1996). While the court accepted that an occupier sued by a trespasser could plead contributory negligence, it refused to allow the defendant to plead *ex turpi causa non oritur actio* (see 11.6). By enacting s. 1, Parliament made clear that an occupier cannot treat a burglar as an outlaw. Indeed, it set out the scope of the duty that an occupier owes a trespasser. Yet, the court held, to allow the defendant to rely on the defence would have the effect of turning burglars into outlaws.

It is true that Parliament did decide that trespassers should not, as a class, be treated as outlaws. But it is does not follow from the fact that Parliament recognised a duty to trespassers generally, that the behaviour of some trespassers can never be so bad that their claims ought not to be totally barred. The existence of a duty of care and any defence barring a claim based on that breach of duty are logically distinct. Thus, it is submitted that there should have been no reason why the defendant should not have been entitled to rely on the defence. This point becomes stronger when account is taken of the fact that the 1984 Act was enacted to protect 'innocent trespassers', such as those who accidentally blunder onto another's property, and children. It hardly seems likely that Parliament would have bothered to enact a statute mitigating the 'harshness' of the common law just to protect someone like the plaintiff in *Revill*.

Finally, it should be noticed that the Act makes no provision as to whether the duty owed to trespassers can be excluded. As a matter of policy it could be argued that the duty imposed by the Occupiers' Liability Act 1984 should be seen as an irreducible minimum imposed by the law which cannot be excluded. The problem with such an argument is that in certain circumstances, it would leave a lawful visitor, to whom the duty has been properly excluded in a worse position than a trespasser. This may lead lawful visitors, where there is an exclusion clause, to seek to argue that they are trespassers. The courts could deal with this problem either by holding that the duty under the 1984 Act can be excluded, or, and this, it is argued, is the better solution, by holding that the 1984 Act provides an irreducible minimum duty which cannot be excluded as against either visitors or trespassers.

Summary

13.1 The law relating to the liability of an occupier of premises for injury caused or damage done to persons or their property while on the occupier's premises is governed by the Occupiers' Liability Acts 1957 and 1984. These Acts replace a complex regime of common law rules distinct from that developed from *Donoghue* v *Stevenson*.

13.2 The Occupiers' Liability Act 1957 governs the liability of occupiers to their lawful visitors and certain other entrants in respect of dangers due to the state of the premises and to things done or omitted to be done on them.

13.3 An occupier is a person who has sufficient degree of control over the premises such that he ought to be under a duty of care to those who come onto the premises. It is possible for more than one person to be an occupier. An occupier need not live in the premises of which, for the purposes of the Act, he is an occupier.

13.4 A 'lawful visitor' is a person who enters with the express or implied permission of the occupier. The Act also expressly provides that persons entering premises under a contract and those entering as of right are afforded the same protection as lawful visitors. An occupier may limit permission to enter.

13.5 The duty owed by an occupier to his lawful visitors is the common duty of care. This is very similar to the ordinary duty of care in negligence. The Act requires two specific matters to be taken into account when considering the standard of care required. These are, first, that children may be less careful than adults and, second, that a person should guard against risks ordinarily incident to his calling. In considering whether the duty has been discharged, regard is to be had to any warning given. Furthermore, in considering whether an occupier is to be held liable for acts of an independent contractor, regard must be had to his selection and supervision of the independent contractor.

13.6 The same general defences available in an action under the ordinary law of negligence apply with regard to the Occupiers' Liability Act 1957. An occupier may extend, restrict, exclude or modify his liability to a lawful visitor, to the extent that the law leaves him free to do so. The Unfair Contract Terms Act, s. 3 (1) of the Occupiers' Liability Act 1957 and the Unfair Terms in Consumer Contracts Regulations 1994 substantially curtail this freedom.

13.7 The law relating to the liability owed to trespassers is now governed by the Occupiers' Liability Act 1984. The Act replaces the common law test as laid down by the House of Lords in *BRB* v *Herrington*.

13.8 Occupiers owe a duty of care to trespassers and certain other entrants in respect of dangers due to the state of the premises and to things done or omitted to be done on them. The duty is only owed to a trespasser if the criteria set out in s. 1(3) are satisfied. The standard of care imposed is to take reasonable care to see that the trespasser does not suffer injury while on the premises.

Exercises

13.1 How is 'occupier' defined for the purposes of the Occupiers' Liability Acts 1957 and 1984?

13.2 Would an action against the manager have succeeded in *Wheat* v. *Lacon*?

13.3 Are all their Lordships in *Wheat* v. *Lacon* agreed on the basis on which the defendants were occupiers *vis-à-vis* the plaintiff's husband?

13.4 How is 'lawful visitor' defined for the purposes of the 1957 Act? Why are those persons exercising a public or private right of way not lawful visitors?

13.5 In what circumstances will the courts hold that an entrant has the implied permission of the occupier to be there? Why are the courts more ready to find such permission exists in the case of children than in the case of adults?

13.6 What factors, along with those specifically mentioned in the Act, will the courts take into account when considering whether or not the common duty of care has been broken?

13.7 Was it fair in *Phipps* v. *Rochester Corporation* to refuse to allow the child to recover anything? Would a different approach have been fairer?

13.8 A fireman is injured at a fire negligently started by the occupier. What factors will be relevant in deciding whether or not the occupier is liable?

13.9 In what circumstances would it be unreasonable, (a) for an occupier to entrust work to an independent contractor? (b) for an occupier not to supervise an independent contractor?

13.10 Is property damage recoverable under the 1984 Act? If it is not recoverable under the Act, would an action succeed at common law?

13.11 What degree of 'knowledge' must be possessed by the occupier before a duty will be owed to a trespasser?

13.12 Is it possible to exclude the duty imposed upon an occupier by the 1984 Act?

14 Product Liability

14.1 Product Liability at Common Law

The most famous product liability case of all is perhaps the most famous in all of the law of tort: no defective product has ever since achieved the notoriety of Mrs Donoghue's bottle of ginger beer and its alleged contents, the decaying remnants of a snail. In deciding that case, Lord Atkin laid down the following test of liability for products in the common law of negligence:

> '[A] manufacturer of products which he sells in such a form as to show he intends them to reach the ultimate consumer in the form in which they left him, with no reasonable possibility of intermediate examination, and with the knowledge that absence of reasonable care in the preparation or putting up of the products will result in injury to the consumer's life or property, owes a duty to that consumer to take that reasonable care.' (*Donoghue* v. *Stevenson* [1932] AC 562, 599)

The case allowed consumers rights against manufacturers of defective products that they lacked under the law of contract. Contract law provided consumer plaintiffs with very powerful remedies against those defendants with whom they could establish privity of contract. Most significantly, contractual remedies were available even where the defendant was in no way at fault as liability for breach of contract is, in general, strict. The common law of contract was buttressed by the Sale of Goods Act (now of 1979, as amended) which implied terms into contracts of sale that the goods sold were of 'satisfactory quality' and reasonably fit for any purposes made known by the buyer to the seller (ss. 14–15). However, the doctrine of privity of contract limited the value of contractual remedies in two respects. In the first place, liability could only arise in favour of someone who had 'bargained for' the goods. That is why Mrs Donoghue was unable to sue in contract: her bottle of ginger beer had been bought for her by a friend. Secondly, it is the seller of the good, not the manufacturer, who is held liable to the consumer in the law of contract. Had Mrs Donoghue bought the bottle of ginger beer herself, it would have been Minchella, the cafe-owner, and not the manufacturer, who would have had to compensate her. The cafe-owner would then have had to sue his supplier, initiating a series of actions for breach of contract which would continue until the 'contractual chain' led to the manufacturer. This is at best a clumsy way of fixing liability on the manufacturer and is unfair to any seller who cannot identify his supplier or whose supplier has gone out of business. The tort of negligence avoids both these problems.

The development of the tort of negligence served the interests of consumers well. Although in theory the burden of establishing fault lay on the consumer, in practice the presence of a defect in a product gave rise to an inference of negligence. Furthermore, it was no excuse for a manufacturer to say that his quality control system was as good as could be and the defect could only be the result of human error: through the doctrine of vicarious liability, the manufacturer would be liable for the errors of his employees. These principles were relied upon in the Australian case of *Grant* v. *Australian Knitting Mills* [1936] AC 85, which went on appeal to the Privy Council. Mr Grant had suffered a severe skin complaint after wearing a new pair of woollen underpants and he sued the manufacturer, alleging that traces of chemicals used in the manufacturing process had been left in the wool. The Privy Council found that Mr Grant was entitled to damages and Lord Wright, who delivered the advice of the Privy Council, described how the case was approached (p. 101):

'If excess sulphites were left in the garment, that could only be because someone was at fault. The appellant is not required to lay his finger on the exact person in all the chain who was responsible, or to specify what he did wrong. Negligence is found as a matter of inference from the existence of the defects taken in connection with all the known circumstances.'

The 50 or so years since that decision have shown that the courts have preferred to uphold the spirit of Lord Atkin's 'neighbour principle' rather than seek a literal application of his words quoted above. Failure to fit in with Lord Atkin's precise words has not resulted in a total denial of liability: courts have assured themselves of a degree of flexibility to meet the circumstances of each case. Hence the possibility of intermediate inspection, for example, will not prevent a duty of care from arising, although it may cause the harm caused by a product to be regarded as too remote (see *Aswan Engineering Establishment Co* v. *Lupdine Ltd* [1987] 1 WLR 1).

14.2 Reform: The Consumer Protection Act 1987

Despite these developments, well-publicised tragedies arising from the use of defective products stimulated pressure for legislative reform. In particular, the Thalidomide tragedy of the late 1960s and early 1970s, in which hundreds of babies were born without limbs as the result of an unforeseen side-effect of a drug their mothers had taken during pregnancy, gave rise to public concern and prompted consideration of the issue by law-review bodies. Ultimately, reform was accomplished as part of EC law. A 'Products Liability' Directive (85/374/EEC) was adopted in 1985, obliging member states to implement its provisions in their domestic legislation. This was done in the UK by Part I of the Consumer Protection Act 1987. The goals of the new statutory products liability regime were spelled out in the recital to the European Directive: '[l]iability without fault on the part of the producer is the only way of solving the problem, peculiar to our age of increasing technicality, of a fair apportionment of the risks inherent in modern technological production'. However, sceptics predict that, in terms of consumer protection, the new scheme is flawed because it will be no easier to prove that a product is defective than that it was negligently manufactured (especially when the effect of the development risks defence is considered as well; see 15.7 and Stapleton, 1986b). On the other hand, proponents of the reform claim that the new scheme provides a speedier and therefore cheaper remedy for consumers (see Jolowicz, 1987). In any case, the consumer will be left no worse off than before: the statutory remedy exists alongside the existing remedies in contract and tort. Thus, those injured by a product they themselves have bought, for example, will still be able to sue for breach of the implied warranty of quality in the contract of sale.

One final introductory point to note about the Consumer Protection Act is that, under EC law, it must fully implement all the provisions of the Directive. Should it not do so, the European Court of Justice might call upon the UK to amend its legislation. The UK has sought to avoid this by inserting an 'interpretation clause' in the Act: s. 1(1) states that Part I of the Act shall be construed 'as is necessary in order to comply with the product liability Directive'. This clause was intended to allow courts to comply with EC law by adopting a generous interpretation of any provision in the statute that appears, on its face, to be too narrow. It might also have an unintended effect: a court may well decide that the Act shall not be construed as providing any remedy that is not necessary in order to comply with the Directive, thus precluding it from interpreting the statute as being more radical in effect than the Directive (cf. Stapleton, 1994, pp. 60–5).

14.3 Meaning of 'Product'

The basic definition of a product is found in section 1(2) of the Act: ' "product" means any goods or electricity and . . . includes a product which is comprised in another product'. This last limb of the definition encompasses the component parts of larger products as well as the raw materials of which products are made: if you were to buy a car, the engine and tyres would be regarded as products no less than the car as a whole, and you would be able to sue the manufacturers of these component parts if the parts were defective and caused you injury. The same would be true with regard to the manufacturers of the metal and tyre rubber used as raw materials if the defect were traced to them.

'Goods', in turn, is defined in the Act: s. 45(1) says the term is to include 'substances, growing crops and things comprised in land by virtue of being attached to it and any ship aircraft or vehicle'. The precise limits of the definition of 'goods', and therefore of the definition of 'products', will be hard to determine. Take, first of all, the case of buildings and building materials. On its face, the definition of 'goods' seems to encompass these things on the basis that a building is a thing attached to land. However, it is arguable that a building is better regarded as 'land' itself, rather than a thing 'attached to land'. This interpretation is supported by the Directive, Art. 2 of which defines 'products' as meaning all moveables, which it contrasts with immoveables, although it allows that moveables remain products even if incorporated into an immoveable. From this, it appears that the building materials (the bricks, beams, tiles, etc.) that are used in constructing a building were, being moveables, meant to be covered by the Directive, even where incorporated into a building. Conversely, the building itself, being an immoveable, falls outside the scope of the Directive, and therefore of the Consumer Protection Act.

A second hard case concerns the information contained in goods like books and computer software (see Whittaker, 1989). Suppose you buy a chemistry text book which contains details of a particular experiment. You are directed to mix two chemicals together in a certain proportion. You follow the instructions to the letter but, because of a misprint, you mix the wrong chemicals and cause an explosion. Can you claim that the textbook was a defective product because of the misprinted information it contained and therefore sue for any injuries you suffered? It seems widely accepted that the answer to this question is 'Yes'. Any doubts about this must surely be laid to rest by consideration of the following example: a traffic light is wired up incorrectly so that it shows red when vehicles should go and green when they should stop; an accident is the result. No one would deny that the traffic light was a defective product. Far removed as this example may seem from the case of a chemistry experiment detailed in a textbook, it is in fact indistinguishable in principle: in both cases, the product is the source of information (how to conduct an experiment, when to cross an intersection) upon which people place reliance.

14.4 Meaning of 'Defect'

The Consumer Protection Act does not hold a producer liable for all the harm caused by his products: he may only be liable if his product is defective. It is more accurate to speak of liability under the Act as 'defect liability' rather than 'strict liability'. The test of defectiveness is found in s. 3(1): 'there is a defect in a product . . . if the safety of the product is not such as persons generally are entitled to expect'. Three preliminary points should be noted. In the first place, the test refers to the safety of a product, not to its usefulness. The Consumer Protection Act gives no remedy in respect of products that simply do not work: for this, the consumer must look to the law of contract. Secondly, the test is framed in terms of consumer expectations rather than in terms of whether the producer exercised reasonable care and skill (the test in negligence). It is perfectly possible for a product to be regarded as defective even though the producer took all reasonable steps to ensure its safety. Finally, the court must consider what consumers are entitled to expect: the test is one of legitimate expectations, which are not necessarily the same as actual expectations.

In determining what consumers are entitled to expect about the safety of a product, 'all the circumstances shall be taken into account'. This is the phrase used in s. 3(2), which goes on to list certain of those circumstances. In paragraph (a), there is a list of a number of factors which relate to the way the product is marketed or presented (see Schlechtriem, 1989). It seems that the way a product is advertised may be held to affect the legitimate expectations of consumers. If, for example, a car of a particular model is marketed as having advanced anti-locking brakes, it might be regarded as defective if its brakes were in fact no better than those in the standard model. This paragraph also requires regard to be had to any instructions or warnings accompanying the product: a product that is potentially dangerous may be perfectly safe if used correctly. For instance, many drugs are lethal if taken in large quantities: these would not be regarded as defective if the correct dose were clearly stated and a warning against exceeding that dose prominently displayed. Paragraph (b) refers to the use one might reasonably expect the product to be put to. The wording of this paragraph makes it clear that a product may be regarded as defective because its misuse was predictable. Hence, bottles of drugs might be declared defective if not fitted with child-proof tops. Finally, paragraph (c) requires the court to look at the time the product was supplied by the producer: the fact that products supplied more recently have additional safety features built in as standard does not require the court to hold an old product to be defective simply because it lacks those features. If a car were marketed today with no safety belts, it would undoubtedly be regarded as defective; however, a vintage car would not be so regarded as the importance of safety belts was not recognised at the time the car was supplied by its manufacturer.

The new statutory scheme has been criticised by some as being little more effective as a consumer remedy than the law of negligence. These critics draw particular attention to the deficiencies of the consumer expectations test when it comes to dealing with design defects as opposed to production errors. In the case of a production error (where something goes wrong during the manufacturing process so that the product does not end up as intended), the law of negligence afforded consumers adequate protection since the mere presence of such an error suggested an inadequate sysytem of quality control or human error (see 14.1). However, the law of negligence was not an effective weapon against products that were dangerous because, although they ended up as intended, the original design was unsafe; in other words, they suffered from a design defect. Such cases present courts with very difficult choices. Suppose a drug company discovers a cure for cancer. This new wonder drug is effective in many cases, but a small proportion of those who use the drug suffer severe side-effects. What right has the judge to say that the harm to the few outweighs the benefit to the many? By and large, courts have viewed the imposition of liability in cases like this as the task of Parliament; they do not have the time and money to look at all the possible ramifications of such a decision, while the adversarial system prevents them from listening to all interested parties. This problem will surface under the new statutory scheme as well because, in determining the safety consumers are entitled to expect from a product, courts will have to consider whether the benefits of that product outweigh its costs. Critics of the new scheme believe, probably correctly, that judges will be no more willing to hold producers liable for deliberate design decisions than they were under the common law, and that consumers will suffer as a result. In truth, really effective consumer protection requires strict liability, not merely defect liability, for the manufacturers of products (see Stapleton, 1986b).

14.5 Who Can be Liable Under the Act?

The primary liability under the Act is upon the producer of a product. 'Producer' is defined in s. 1(2) as one who manufactures a product, or wins or abstracts it, or carries out any process upon it to which essential characteristics of the product are attributable. This definition gives rise to a number of complexities which centre around the crucial distinction drawn in s. 1(2) between products which have been 'manufactured, won or abstracted' and those which have not. In the case of products not 'manufactured, won or abstracted', liability under the Act will only arise if 'essential characteristics' of that product are attributable to any process which has been carried out on it. This leaves us with a three-stage inquiry. First, we have to ask whether the product we are concerned with has been manufactured, won or abstracted. Secondly, if the answer to that question is 'No', we have to determine whether any 'process' has been carried out upon the product. Lastly, in such cases we have to decide whether that process has given the product certain 'essential characteristics'.

To conduct the first part of our enquiry, we have to know what the words 'manufactured, won or abstracted' mean. Clearly anything that is man-made comes within the meaning of 'manufactured': the word itself means, literally, 'made by hand' but clearly extends to things made by machine. It seems equally clear that substances like coal that are mined come within the definition of those that are 'won or abstracted'. On the other side of the line come agricultural products, which appear in s. 1(2) as an example of products that are not 'manufactured, won or abstracted'. Beyond these paradigm cases, there is considerable doubt as to where to draw the line between those products which are, and those which are not, 'manufactured, won or abstracted'. In order to ensure effective consumer protection, courts should be encouraged to take a broad view of this phrase so that, for example, blood taken for transfusion should be treated as 'abstracted' from the blood donor.

Passing over these difficulties, we discover more obscurity when we come to the second stage of our enquiry. At this stage we have to ask whether a product which has not been 'manufactured, won or abstracted' has had any process carried out on it. Shells washed up on the seashore are certainly not 'manufactured, won or abstracted': if they are polished, can they be said to have undergone a process? Again, courts should be encouraged to adopt a generous interpretation: anything that is done deliberately to a product, in an attempt to adapt it for some use, should count as a process.

A further complexity is added by s. 2(4) of the Act (cf. Stapleton, 1994, pp. 303–5). Where the product in question is game or agricultural produce, the process must be one that can be described as an industrial process if liability is to arise. The word 'industrial' suggests that the process must be on a large and continuous scale and involve the use of machinery. It would, for instance, exclude the making of a few pots of home-made jam in a domestic kitchen. However, in requiring that the process be industrial, the Act might be narrower than the Directive, which speaks only of an 'initial process'. This seems to refer to whatever process is first carried out on a product, be it industrial or not. An English court might feel entitled to give a broad interpretation to the word 'industrial' in order to give effect to the Directive.

The third issue is whether the process carried out on the product has given it 'essential characteristics'. This phrase gives rise to enormous problems of definition. Take the simple example of a carrot. Is it an essential characteristic of a carrot bought from the supermarket that it has had its leaves removed and all the dirt shaken off it? What if it has been sorted into a selection of carrots of the same size and put in a plastic bag? Or if it has been peeled and washed? Or grated? Our intuition tells us that the fact that carrots have been grated is an essential characteristic of those carrots. Equally, we are inclined to view a carrot bought from the supermarket as just a carrot unless we have paid more for it because it has, for instance, been peeled and washed. However, when it comes to formulating a rule to distinguish these cases, and to apply to borderline cases, we come unstuck. It seems likely the courts will address this issue in a very impressionistic way, relying on the notorious 'elephant test': 'Don't ask me to describe it, but I know one when I see one.'

The justification for 'channelling' liability to the producer of the products is that he is best placed both to absorb the loss (typically by taking out insurance) and to do something about the defect by making his product safer. However, a number of other people may, depending on the circumstances, be treated as equivalent to the actual producer of a product and be held liable under the Act. These are anyone who 'has held himself out to be the producer of the product' (e.g. supermarkets who sell 'own-brand' goods), anyone who imported the product in question into the EC ('the importer'), and anyone who has at any time supplied the defective product to another. In the case of suppliers, liability will arise only if they are unable to identify their supplier or, alternatively, the importer or actual producer of the product. These provisions are found in s. 2(2),(3) of the Act.

14.6 Who Can Recover Under the Act?

As a general rule, anyone who suffers personal injury or property damage that is caused by a defective product may recover to the full extent of his loss. The Act makes no distinction between those who are injured while using the product and those who are mere bystanders injured by someone else's use of the product. The main restrictions on the right to recover relate to property damage. No compensation may be awarded in respect of property damage in three cases. The first case is given in s. 5(2): where the damage is to the product itself or to any product supplied with the product in question comprised in it, no liability arises under the Act. This provision means that, if you buy a car which is fitted with a faulty engine that blows up, you cannot claim under the Act for the cost of a replacement engine: the engine is 'the product itself'. Neither can you recover for the cost of repairing the bodywork should that be damaged by the explosion: this is damage to a product (the car) which was supplied with the defective product (the engine) 'comprised in it'. This corresponds to the rule in the common law of negligence that damage to the product itself is pure economic loss and not recoverable (though note the possibility that at common law certain things might be regarded as 'complex structures' so that damage to one part of the structure, even though caused by another part of the same structure, would still be regarded as damage to 'other property': see 5.2). The second case in which property damage gives rise to no liability is where the damaged item is not both of a type that is ordinarily intended for private use and intended by the plaintiff mainly for his own private use (s. 5(3)). Hence, a barrister has no claim under the Act if a leaky pen damages his courtroom attire, but he would have if the pen were to damage the clothes he uses for lazing about the house. The final case is where the total property damage complained of is valued at no more than £275. This case is dealt with by s. 5(4) of the Act, the purpose being to cut out trivial claims for property damage.

The simple word 'cause', of course, obscures a great many complicated issues (see Ch. 9). Of particular note in the present context is its use in Civil Law countries, in which it encompasses rules of remoteness or 'legal cause'. It would seem to be possible for an English court to justify applying the *Wagon Mound* foreseeability rule in cases under the Act, and perhaps the principle of *volenti non fit iniuria* too, on the grounds that these rules are entailed by the word 'cause' (see Chs. 10–11).

14.7 Defences

The Act lists a number of specific defences in s. 4(1)(a) to (f):

(a) '[T]he defect is attributable to compliance with any requirement imposed by or under any enactment or with any Community obligation. . .'

Suppose statute requires children's toys to be coated with a certain flame-resistant substance. Many children prove allergic to the substance and suffer severe rashes. The manufacturer would have a defence under this paragraph. However, if the statute did not require, but merely permitted, him to use that substance, the defence would not avail him. The statutory permission would, however, almost certainly be conclusive proof that the product was not defective.

(b) '[T]he person proceeded against did not at any time supply the product to another. . .'

This paragraph effectively excludes waste products from the operation of the Act. A manufacturer cannot be liable under the Act for harm resulting from his discharge of waste into a river. However, should a manufacturer sell his waste products, or even give them away, then he will fall within the definition of supply in s. 46(1) and may be liable for any harm that they cause.

(c) The supply was not with any business motive falling within s. 4(1)(c).

Liability only attaches to those who produce products with what might loosely be called a business motive. This result is ensured by s. 4(1)(c) which allows a defendant a defence that he at no time supplied the product in the course of business or with a view to profit. Thus, if you give your home-made jam to be sold off for charity in the local church fête, you will not be liable under the Act if it makes those who eat it sick, though you may still be liable in the common law of negligence. Equally, if you bring back souvenirs from your holiday in Australia which you give to your relatives, you will face no liability under the Act if they prove to be dangerous even though you have imported and supplied the goods.

(d) The defect did not exist in the product at the time it was supplied by the defendant.

This defence protects a manufacturer whose product has become dangerous because it has been interfered with after it has left his control. However, certain products should be designed so they cannot be interfered with (e.g. containers for prescription drugs should have child-proof tops) and a product might be regarded as defective because it lacks this design feature.

(e) '[T]he state of scientific and technical knowledge at the [time the product was supplied by the producer] was not such that a producer of products of the same description as the product in question might be expected to have discovered the defect if it had existed in his products while they were under his control. . .'

Suppose a pharmaceutical firm admits that one of its drugs it has now taken off the market has been discovered to have serious side-effects, but claims that no one could have predicted those side-effects at the time the drug was put on the market. Even if the drug could be regarded as defective because the risk of the side-effects outweighed the benefits of the drug, the manufacturer might still escape liability by arguing that the state of scientific knowledge at the time the drug was marketed did not allow that risk to be detected. This defence, contained in s. 4(1)(e) of the Act, is often known as the 'development risks' or 'state of the art' defence (see Newdick, 1988; Stapleton, 1994, pp. 236–42)).

The defence was included in the Directive after enormous pressure from manufacturers, particularly in the pharmaceutical industry. They alleged it would be unfair to hold them liable for risks they could not be expected to detect, and that to do so would impede technological innovation. Member states were left to choose whether or not they would include this defence in their domestic legislation; the UK was among those countries that did. However, the form in which the defence appears in the Consumer Protection Act seems more generous to producers than the Directive would allow. Whereas the Directive stipulates that the defence will only avail a producer where 'the state of scientific and technical knowledge at the time when he put the product into circulation was not such as to enable the existence of the defect of the defect to be discovered' (art. 7), the defence in s. 4(1)(e) of the Act requires only that the state of knowledge was such that 'a producer of products of the same description as the product in question might be expected to have discovered the defect'. This is more generous than the Directive in that it asks what might reasonably be expected of producers of a particular product rather than what was possible given the state of scientific knowledge. This difference between Act and Directive leaves the UK at risk of prosecution in the European Court for failing properly to implement the Directive.

(f) The defect in the product is wholly attributable to the design of another product in which it was comprised or to compliance with instructions given by the producer of that other product.

Note that, even though a manufacturer who supplies component parts or raw materials to another to be incorporated into a more complex product may escape liability under the Act by virtue of this defence, he may yet be liable under the common law. This may be so if he should have known better than the subsequent producer and pointed out the errors of his ways.

Outside the s. 4 defences, the defendant may rely on the defence of contributory negligence. Express reference is made to this defence in s. 6(4). Yet the defence of *volenti non fit iniuria*, which often arises on the same facts, is not mentioned at all in the Act: it may be that it is encompassed by the concept of 'legal cause'. One defence is expressly ruled out by the Act: by virtue of s. 7, the defendant cannot rely on any provision that purports to exclude or limit liability under the Act.

Summary

14.1 At common law, consumers have remedies in respect of harm caused by defective products under the law of contract (within the constraints imposed by the doctrine of privity) and the tort of negligence.

14.2 The Consumer Protection Act 1987 was enacted in order to comply with the European 'Products Liability' Directive, which was a response to public concern after disasters such as the Thalidomide tragedy. Its most notable feature is that it removes the need for those injured by a product to establish fault on the part of the producer. The extent to which the Act will in practice improve on the common law of negligence is, however, disputed.

14.3 Under the Act, 'product' means any goods or electricity, including component parts and raw materials. The term 'goods' probably includes building materials (but not the buildings into which they are incorporated) and sources of information such as books and computer software.

14.4 The test of defectiveness under the Act is whether the product is as safe as persons generally are entitled to expect (the 'consumer expectations' test). This test is the source of many criticisms of the Act which allege it is insufficiently radical. Such criticisms have most force in the context of design defects.

14.5 The primary liability under the Act is upon the producer of a product, though 'own-branders', importers and suppliers (in some circumstances) may be held liable.

14.6 Anyone who suffers injury or property damage caused by a defective product can recover under the Act, though there are some limitations on the recovery of property damage.

14.7 The Act lists a number of specific defences, of which the most important and controversial is the 'development risks' defence. The exclusion of liability under the act is prohibited.

Exercises

14.1 What are the comparative advantages and disadvantages of the law of contract and the tort of negligence as remedies in respect of defective products?

14.2 Does the Consumer Protection Act 1987 actually advance the interests of consumers?

14.3 What problems does the definition of 'product' under the Act give rise to?

14.4 Explain how design defects differ from production errors. Do the courts approach them in the same way? If not, why not?

14.5 What goals were the framers of the legislation trying to achieve in selecting those who could be liable under the new products liability regime?

14.6 What do the limitations imposed on the recovery of property damage under the Act tell us about the interests that the law is trying to protect?

14.7 What is the 'development risks' defence? Should it be allowed?

14.8 What improvements, if any, could still be made to the law of product liability?

15   Breach of Statutory Duty

15.1 Introduction

Each year Parliament enacts a substantial number of statutes that impose duties on public bodies, private individuals and others. Some of these statutes specifically create a detailed scheme of civil liability of a tortious nature. The Occupiers' Liability Acts 1957 and 1984, the Animals Act 1971 and the Consumer Protection Act 1987 are all examples. Claims brought under these statutes are often described as actions for breach of statutory duty. While there is nothing inherently wrong with this description, claims under these statutes do not create any of the problems normally associated with the tort of breach of statutory duty. The creation of an express tortious action in these cases is clear and the person who has suffered loss has his remedy in the statute.

Our concern in this chapter is with those statutes that impose duties but that are either silent on the question whether Parliament intended a civil action to lie for breach of that duty, or provide some other sanction for such a breach. If the breach of the statute is determined to give rise to an action then the common law treats this as a nominate tort (*Thornton* v. *Kirklees Metropolitan BC* [1979] QB 626, 642). The difficulty faced by the courts is to determine which statutes do, and which do not, give rise to such liability. A tortious remedy is obviously available where Parliament has made express provision for it, but it does not follow from the fact that Parliament has included no provision for such a remedy that none exists.

It might be thought that, given the enormous volume and disparate coverage of modern legislation, Parliament would articulate clearly whether or not it intends there to be a civil remedy. Unfortunately, it does not always do so. It is true that Parliament does sometimes make clear that no civil remedy lies for breach of statute (for examples, see: Health and Safety at Work Act 1974, s. 47(1); Safety of Sports Grounds Act 1975, s. 13; Guard Dogs Act 1975, s. 5(2)(a)). There are also examples where a statute states expressly that breach of duty constitutes a tort (Building Act 1984, s. 38; Resale Prices Act 1976, s. 25(2), (3); Race Relations Act 1976, s. 57; Sex Discrimination Act 1975, s. 66). Too often, however, legislation is enacted that makes no express provision either in favour or against the provision of a civil remedy. The difficulty which this failure to provide for the consequences of a statutory breach presents the courts prompted Lord Du Parcq to say in *Cutler* v. *Wandsworth Stadium Ltd* [1949] AC 398:

> 'To a person unversed in the science or art of legislation it may well seem strange that Parliament has not by now made it a rule to state explicitly what its intention is in a matter which is often of no little

importance, instead of leaving it to the courts to discover by a careful examination and analysis of what is expressly said, what that intention may be supposed probably to be . . . I trust, however, that it will not be thought impertinent . . . to suggest respectfully that those responsible for framing legislation might consider whether the traditional practice, which obscures, if it does not conceal, the intention which Parliament has, or must be presumed to have, might not be safely abandoned.' (p. 410)

Lord Du Parcq's suggestion has not, unfortunately, been taken up. It may be that this is for political reasons: Staughton LJ suggested in the Court of Appeal in *M* v. *Newham BC* [1994] 4 All ER 602, 627 that it might be politically embarassing to make clear in a statute that there should be no common law remedy where a public authority fails to perform its statutory duty. Whatever the reason, the difficulty of ascertaining Parliament's intention remains and it is with that issue that this chapter is concerned.

15.2. Inferring the Existence of the Tort

The problem that the courts face in any case where the statute is silent on whether or not there should be a civil remedy is to discern the intention of Parliament on a matter that has not been expressly resolved by the language of the statute. The courts must determine whether Parliament did or did not *intend* to confer an action on this particular plaintiff. Although the factors to be considered by the court in answering this question are relatively well settled, their application in any particular case is unlikely to be straightforward. Indeed Lord Denning protested in one case that, '[t]he dividing line between the pro-cases and the contra-cases is so blurred and so ill-defined that you may as well toss a coin to decide it.' (*Ex Parte Island Records Ltd* [1978] Ch. 122, 135) A number of attempts have been made to bring some order and consistency to the problem of whether or not a civil remedy was intended.

In some early cases on breach of statutory duty, courts went so far as to hold that where Parliament has created a duty by statute the common law should provide a remedy to a person injured by breach of it (*Couch* v. *Steel* (1854) 3 El & Bl 402). Thus Coke said, 'whensover an act of Parliament doth generally prohibit any thing the party grieved shall have his action for his private reliefe' (2 Inst 163). A relatively modern expression of this approach can be found in the judgment of Greer LJ in *Monk* v. *Warbey* [1935] 1 KB 75. His Lordship said (p. 81), ' prima facie a person who has been injured by the breach of a statute has a right to recover damages from the person committing it unless it can be established by considering the whole of the Act that no such right was intended to be given.' However, to the extent that *Monk* v. *Warbey* ever represented the law it can no longer be supported.

Until very recently the approach most favoured by the courts was based on the application of two presumptions which were first stated by Lord Tenterden CJ in *Doe dem. Murray, Lord Bishop of Rochester* v. *Bridges* (1854) 1 B & AD 847. There he said:

> '[A]nd where an Act creates an obligation, and enforces the performance in a specified manner, we take it as a general rule that performance cannot be enforced in any other manner. If the obligation is created, but no mode of enforcing its performance is ordained, the common law may, in general, find a mode suited to the particular nature of the case.' (p. 859)

Modern support can be found for this approach in *Lonrho Ltd* v. *Shell Petroleum Co Ltd* [1982] AC 173. However, in *Lonrho* Lord Diplock, with whom the other Lords agreed, articulated two exceptions to the presumption against actionability where the statute provides a specific mode of enforcement, e.g. through a criminal penalty:

> 'One starts with the presumption . . . that 'where an Act creates an obligation, and enforces the performance in a specified manner . . . that performance cannot be enforced in any other manner' . . . there are two exceptions to this general rule. The first is where . . . it is apparent that the obligation or prohibition was passed for the benefit or protection of a particular class of individuals . . . The second exception is where the statute creates a public right (i.e., a right to be enjoyed by all those of Her Majesty's subjects who wish to avail themselves of it) and a particular member of the public suffers . . . 'particular, direct and substantial' damage 'other and different from that which was common to all the rest of the public'.' (p. 185)

The approach may be justified on the basis that the presumptions tell the legislature how a court will respond to the use of different legislative drafting techniques. The court assumes that the legislature knows what the presumptions are and, if it gives no express direction as to actionability, it is assumed that the legislature has done this with full knowledge of what the judicial response will be. As Stanton (p. 33) has put it, 'In effect, the judicial intent is attributed to the legislature.'

In several of the most recent cases, courts have emphasised that Lord Tenterdon's presumptions are merely 'indicators' of Parliament's intention and have adopted a much more fluid approach to the recognition of private rights of action, treating a number of factors or indicators as relevant to the discovery of the legislative intent (*X* v. *Bedfordshire County Council* [1995] 2 AC 633, p. 731; *Olotu* v. *Home Office* [1997] 1 All ER 385). No one indicator is conclusive in favour or against liability. As Lord Browne-Wilkinson made clear in *X* v. *Bedfordshire CC*, 'There is no general rule by reference to which it can be decided whether a statute does create such a right of action but there are a number of indicators.' (see also in *Olotu* v. *Home Office* [1997] 1 All

ER 385, p. 393 per Lord Bingham CJ). Thus, as is the case in the tort of negligence (when deciding whether a duty of care is owed), determining whether an action lies for breach of statutory duty is a complex question. The courts will have regard to several indicators that may be treated as more or less compelling according to the circumstances. In the next section we consider some of the factors that the courts are likely to consider in any particular case.

15.3 Ascertaining Parliament's Intention

Where the Statute Provides an Alternative Method of Enforcement

Where a statute provides for a penalty to be paid for a breach of the duty a presumption will arise that this was the only remedy intended. In *Atkinson* v. *The Newcastle and Gateshead Waterworks Co* (1877) LR 2 Ex.D 441 the defendants were, by s. 42 of the Waterworks Clauses Act 1847, under a duty to keep water in their pipes under a certain pressure. Failure to comply with this section subjected the defendants to a penalty of £10. In breach of the section the defendants failed to maintain this pressure; as a result of which firemen were unable to save the plaintiff's house from being gutted by fire. The plaintiff brought an action for damages for breach of the section. The Court of Appeal held that the plaintiff's action failed since the penalty was intended to be exclusive. It cannot have been the case, according to the court, that Parliament intended the defendants to become 'gratuitous insurers of the safety from fire . . . of all the houses within the district over which their powers were to extend'. Such a 'presumption' may also exist where the statute provides an administrative remedy by way of complaint to a minister or some administrative tribunal (*Scally* v. *Southern Health and Social Services Board* [1991] 4 All ER 563).

Where the Statute is Passed for the Benefit of a Particular Class of Persons

Where a provision is passed for the benefit of a particular class of persons the traditional approach is that a contrary presumption will arise and that an action for breach of statutory duty will lie. In *Groves* v. *Lord Wimborne* [1898] 2 QB 402, a workman was injured because of a failure to fence a dangerous piece of machinery. The Court of Appeal held an action would lie for damages despite the fact that the statute provided only for a penalty. Section 5(3) of the Factory and Workshop Act 1891 (now s. 14 of the Factories Act 1961) provided that, '[a]ll dangerous parts of the machinery . . . shall either be securely fenced, or be in such position or of such construction as to be equally safe to every person employed in the factory as it would be if it were securely fenced'. This section, the court said, was passed for the benefit and protection of a specified group, namely employees. In the words of Vaughan Williams LJ, 'where a statute provides for the performance by certain persons of a particular duty, and someone belonging to a class of persons for whose benefit and protection the statute imposes the duty is injured by failure to perform it, prima facie, and, if there be nothing to the contrary, an action by the person so injured will lie against the person who has failed to perform the duty'. So also in *Ex Parte Island Records Ltd*, a majority of the Court of Appeal held that musicians had a right of action for breach of section 1 of the Dramatic and Musical Performers' Protection Act 1958. Section 1 provides that 'if a person knowingly – (a) makes a record, directly or indirectly from or by means of the performance of a dramatic or musical work without the consent in writing of the performers . . . he shall be guilty of an offence under this Act. . .'. Although the only 'remedy' provided by the Act was a criminal penalty, the Court held that the Act was passed for the protection of a particular class of individuals, namely, musical performers and, therefore an action would lie for breach of statutory duty.

Where, however, the duty is imposed for purposes of a general or social nature and not for the benefit of a particular class an action will not generally lie. So in *Atkinson* v. *The Newcastle and Gateshead Waterworks Co*, the obligation to maintain the water in the pipes at a certain pressure was held to be owed to the public in general and not to any member of the public whose property was damaged as a result of the breach. One of the leading cases on this point is *Cutler* v. *Wandsworth Stadium Ltd* [1949] AC 398, which raised the question whether an action for breach of statutory duty lay in respect of breach of s. 11(2)(b) of the Betting and Lotteries Act 1934. This section provided that, '[T]he occupier of a licensed track . . . (b) shall take such steps as are necessary to secure that . . . there is available for bookmakers space on the track where they can conveniently carry on bookmaking in connection with dog races run on the track. . .'. The appellant, a bookmaker, claimed injunctions prohibiting the respondents from excluding him from the track and also requiring them to secure a space for him where he could conveniently carry on bookmaking. The House of Lords refused to grant the injunctions sought. The purpose of the Act was to protect the public interest by regulating the operation of betting at dog tracks. Any benefit which accrued to bookmakers was wholly incidental to this purpose. The Act was not intended to confer a right upon an individual bookmaker who presented himself at the stadium to demand a place on the track.

While the question whether a statute was passed for the benefit of a particular class of persons is undoubtedly treated by the courts as a relevant factor in deciding whether a civil action for breach of statutory duty was intended, it is important for two reasons not to give too much emphasis to this question. First, as was made clear by the House of Lords in *X* v. *Bedforshire CC*, the mere fact that legislation is introduced primarily for the protection of a limited class of persons does not mean that a cause of action will always exist. Such a 'purpose' is only a 'pointer in favour of imputing to Parliament an intention to create a private law cause of action' (p. 378 per Browne-Wilkinson). Other factors may dictate against the existence of a cause of action (cf. *R* v. *Deputy Governor of*

Parkhurst Prison, ex parte Hague [1992] 1 AC 58). Second, whether or not
a statute is held to have been passed for the benefit of a particular class of
persons or the public at large is inevitably a question of impression. In
Cutler, for example, was it not strongly arguable that the Act had been
passed for the benefit of bookmakers, among others? It could legitimately
be said that bookmakers constituted a sufficiently identifiable group and
possessed sufficiently common interests to constitute a defined group. As
we have already mentioned, the real issue in all these cases is whether
Parliament intended not merely to benefit a class of the public but to
create a cause of action for breach of statutory duty.

The Availability of Alternative Remedies

Where the statute creates a duty but makes no provision as to the method
of enforcement, the traditional approach was to presume that a tortious
remedy for breach of statutory duty was intended: *ubi jus ibi remedium*
(where there is a right there is a remedy). An example of this can be seen in
the case of *Dawson* v. *Bingley UDC* [1911] 2 KB 438. By s. 66 of the Public
Health Act 1875, every urban authority was required to provide fire-plugs
and to identify clearly their position in some way (see now s. 13 Fire
Services Act 1947 which imposes a duty on fire authorities to ensure
supply of water for firefighting). No penalty or other remedy was provided
for breach of this section. The defendants put up a notice which failed to
indicate the true position of the fire-plug. A fire broke out at the plaintiff's
premises to which the fire brigade were called. They spent some
considerable time trying to locate the fire-plug and as a result the
plaintiff's property suffered greater damage than it would otherwise have
done. The Court of Appeal held that the plaintiff's action for damages for
breach of statutory duty should succeed. Where, as here, the statute was
silent as to the mode of enforcement 'the legislature is to be taken as
intending the ordinary result; and the proper remedy for breach of a
statute is an action for damages. . .'.

Although the Court of Appeal in the *Dawson* case had little difficulty in
deciding that on the facts Parliament had intended there to be an action
for breach of statutory duty, difficulties may arise where although the
statute provides no method of enforcement there is already an existing
legal remedy, either of a private or public law nature. In such cases is there
still a presumption of actionability?

Where there is an existing private law remedy, the prevailing view seems
to be that Parliament cannot have intended to provide an action for
breach of statutory duty. So, for example, in *Scally* v. *Southern Health and
Social Services Board* [1991] 4 All ER 563 the House of Lords (adopting
the reasoning of Kelly LJ in the Court of Appeal; [1991] 4 All ER 573n)
held that no remedy in damages for breach of statutory duty lay for
breach of an employer's statutory duty to give his employee information
about pensions and pension schemes (Contracts of Employment and
Redundancy Payments Act (Northern Ireland) 1965, s. 4(1)). A full and
effective remedy already existed in the form of recourse to a tribunal which

was empowered to order that the information be given. So too in *Phillips* v. *Britannia Hygenic Laundry Co* [1923] 2 KB 832, the Court of Appeal decided that breach of the Motor Car (Use and Construction) Order 1904, which governed the conditions to be met by motor cars on the highway, did not give rise to an action for breach of statutory duty. One of the reasons given by the court for refusing to impose such liability was that rights of road users 'have always been sufficiently protected by the common law' (per Bankes LJ).

It is suggested that this reluctance to recognise a claim for breach of statutory duty where an alternative remedy already exists is sensible. Where there is already a remedy in damages it is unlikely that Parliament intended to duplicate that remedy. However, it should be noted that the availablity of an alternative private law remedy has never been treated as decisive. As Ormrod LJ made clear in *McCall* v. *Abelesz* [1976] QB 585, such a 'formula, though useful, must be cautiously applied for it purports to do just what Lord Simonds declined to do in *Cutler's Case*, namely to formulate a set of rules' (p. 595). So, for example, an action was held to lie in *Groves* v. *Lord Wimborne* [1898] 2 QB 402 notwithstanding that an action would have existed in negligence for breach of the employer's non-delegable duty and in *Monk* v. *Warbey* [1935] 1 KB 75, where the defendant allowed an uninsured driver to drive a vehicle without insurance contrary to Road Traffic Act 1930, s. 35, this was held to give rise to an action for breach of statutory duty notwithstanding the fact that the plaintiff had a private law remedy in negligence against the (uninsured) driver. It may be, as Weir has pointed out (Weir, 1996, p. 207), that the decision is justifiable because it fits well into the policy of the law that 'victims of *negligence* on the highway should not only be entitled to compensation, but should actually receive it.' However, the case was distinguished in *Richardson* v. *Pitt Stanley* [1995] 1 All ER 460 (criticised by O'Sullivan, [1995] CLJ 241) where the Court of Appeal held that the Employers' Liability (Compulsory Insurance) Act 1969, which made it an offence for an employer to fail to insure against liability for injury sustained by its employees in the course of their employment, did not give rise to an action for breach of statutory duty. One of the reasons given was that the employer's liability for the injury was already well provided for under the common law, whereas in *Monk* v. *Warbey* the owner of the motor vehicle would, absent the statute, have had no direct liability to the injured party.

Where the only remedy is a 'public law' remedy via an application for judicial review the cases are less consistent. In *R* v. *Deputy Governor of Parkhurst Prison, ex parte Hague* [1992] 1 AC 58 Lord Jauncey considered the existence of a public law remedy was relevant to the question whether an action for breach of statutory duty was intended and refused to find that breach of the Prison Rules was actionable at the instance of the plaintiff. A similar conclusion was reached by the Court of Appeal in *Olotu* v. *Home Office*, where the plaintiff had, in breach of the Prosecution of Offences Act 1985 and reg. 5(3)(a) of the Prosecution of Offences Act (Custody Time Limits) Regulations 1987, been detained for 81 days after the expiry of her custody time limit. The court, in that case, treated the availability of public law proceedings for habeas corpus and mandamus as a 'strong indicator' that no action for breach of statutory duty was intended. However, in other cases the existence of the general remedy of judicial review has not deterred the courts from finding that a statute was intended to give rise to an action for damages. There is much to be said for the approach taken in *Hague*. Parliament must surely be presumed to know of *all* existing remedies, whether of a private or a public law nature. It seems unsatisfactory to ignore the existence of such rights in considering whether or not Parliament intended there to be an action for breach of statutory duty. Yet against that it might be argued that the public law remedy is of little use to the plaintiff who wants damages rather than, say, mandamus.

The Ambit of Discretion

In considering whether an action should lie, the courts have in a number of cases given considerable weight to the nature of the duty imposed on the defendant. Where the duty imposed is of a very broad nature giving a large measure of discretion to the person on whom the duty is imposed it is unlikely to give rise to an action for breach of statutory duty. Thus, in *X* v. *Bedfordshire CC* one of the reasons for refusing to allow an action for failure to bring care proceedings (Children and Young Persons Act 1969, s. 2) or failing to take a child into care (Child Care Act 1980, s. 2) was that the duties imposed were made conditional upon the exercise by the local authorities of subjective judgement that they had good grounds for doing so. Lord Browne Wilkinson found it

'impossible to construe such a statutory provision as demonstrating an intention that even where there is no carelessness by the authority it should be liable in damages if a court subsequently decided with hindsight that the removal, or failure to remove, the child from the family either was or was not 'consistent with the duty to safeguard the child'' (p. 379).

It will be recalled that in the tort of negligence, when considering the liability of public authorities, courts have drawn a distinction between policy and operational decisions (see 7.2). Broadly speaking it is only in respect of the latter that a duty of care can arise. Similarly, where a statute entrusts policy matters to a particular person or body, it is unlikely that a court will find that any duty thereby imposed gives rise to an action for breach of statutory duty. As Lord Browne-Wilkinson said in *X* v. *Bedforshire CC*:

'Where Parliament has conferred a statutory discretion on a public authority, it is for that authority, not for the courts, to exercise the discretion; nothing which the authority does within the exercise of the discretion can be actionable at common law. If the decision complained of falls outside the statutory discretion, it *can* (but not necessarily will) give rise to a common law liability. However, if the factors relevant to the exercise of the discretion include matters of policy, the court cannot adjudicate on such policy matters and therefore cannot reach the conclusion that the decision was outside the ambit of the statutory discretion. Therefore a common law duty of care in relation to the taking of decisions involving policy matters cannot exist' (p. 371).

By way of contrast to cases where the statute grants a wide discretion, the courts have shown themselves willing to infer the existence of the tort where a penal statute enacts a safety standard to protect against personal injury (an area of considerable practical importance, see, for example, *Groves* v. *Lord Wimborne* [1898] 2 QB 402). The willingness of the courts to allow an action in the case of industrial safety legislation probably stems, at least in part, from a desire to give monetary compensation to an injured workman and to ensure that employers do not evade safety standards imposed by statute (see also *Monk* v. *Warbey* [1935] 1 KB 75 in the context of road traffic cases). Whatever the reason, most industrial safety legislation has been interpreted to give rise to an action for the tort of breach of statutory duty. Where, on the other hand, the effect of allowing an action for breach of statutory duty would be to protect the plaintiff against an economic loss the courts have been markedly less willing to find that a civil action was intended. In *Cutler*, for example, to have given bookmakers a right of action would have protected the bookmaker against an economic loss, i.e. the loss of business as a result of being excluded from the track (see also *Richardson* v. *Pitt-Stanley*).

Where the Enactment is Purely Regulatory

Where an enactment is purely regulatory, contravention of a duty laid down by the statute is unlikely to give rise to an action for breach of statutory duty. As Lord Browne-Wilkinson said in *X* v. *Bedfordshire CC*;

> 'Although the question is one of statutory construction and therefore each case turns on on the provisions of the relevant statute, it is significant that your Lordships were not referred to any case where it has been held that statutory provisions establishing a regulatory system or a scheme of social welfare for the benefit of the public at large had been held to give rise to a private right of action for damages for breach of statutory duty' (p. 364).

Thus, in *Hague*, for example, Lord Goff, in deciding that breach of the Prison Rules was not actionable, gave as a reason that the Prison Rules are 'regulatory in character and were never intended to confer private rights on prisoners in the event of breach'. So too in *Olotu* the Court of Appeal, in holding that there could be no action for breach of the custody time limit prescribed under s. 22 of the Prosecution of Offences Act and regulation 5(3)(a) of the Prosecution of Offences Act (Custody Time

Limits) Regulations 1987, laid considerable stress on the regulatory function of the provisions. The object of the Act and regulations made thereunder was to expedite the prosecution of criminal offences and, if such expedition was lacking, to ensure that defendants did not languish in prison for excessive periods. The elaborate scheme of duties backed up by administrative procedures made it impossible to infer that Parliament intended there also to be a cause of action for breach of statutory duty.

The Insurance Position

A factor which may on occasion be mentioned by a court is that of the insurance position. In *Atkinson*, for example, the Court of Appeal were clearly influenced by the burden that would be imposed on the defendant if they were to allow an action for breach of statutory duty. The effect of allowing such an action would be to make the defendants gratuitous insurers against fire of all the houses in their area. In this situation it was thought that the householder was a better loss bearer than the defendants because he was more likely to have insurance and to be able to obtain it more cheaply to cover such an eventuality. Similarly, the courts have generally been unwilling to allow a civil action for breach of any road traffic legislation. This unwillingness reflects the view that to allow an action in such cases may be too harsh on the defendant. For example, having a defective rear light is an offence under road traffic legislation. This is the case even where the light has gone out while the defendant is driving the motor vehicle and had no way of knowing that the light was no longer functioning. The refusal to allow an action in such cases may also reflect the view that the plaintiff can easily acquire insurance to protect himself against non-negligent accidents and the loss should, therefore, fall on him. Against this, it might be argued that the defendant will be, or should be, insured and, as he is also the cause of the loss, that he is the more suitable loss-bearer. This view can be seen reflected in *Monk* v. *Warbey* [1935] 1 KB 75. The Court of Appeal held in that case that the failure to insure was actionable and its decision is surely justifiable on the basis that the very purpose of the section was to ensure that third-party insurance was available to protect accident victims. Where, as here, that insurance had not been taken out the court were justified in giving the victim the additional protection of an action against the owner of the vehicle. *Monk* v. *Warbey* is, however, almost the only case where a breach of road traffic legislation has been held to give rise to a tortious action and it seems unlikely that such actions will be extended any further.

Where the Statute Creates a Public Right and the Plaintiff Suffers Special Damage

In *Lonrho* Lord Diplock mentioned a second exception to the 'presumption' of non-actionability where the statute provides a penalty. This arose according to his Lordship where the statute creates a public right and a particular member of the public suffers 'special' damage. It is not, however, altogether clear in what circumstances this 'exception' is to apply. The widest view would treat all criminal and administrative law duties as creating public rights, any violation of which causing special damage would be actionable by the individual affected. The actual decision in *Lonrho* shows that this is too broad an interpretation of Lord Diplock's words. An Order in Council had been made making it a criminal offence to supply oil to what was then Southern Rhodesia. It was alleged by the plaintiffs that, in breach of this Order, the defendants had supplied oil to Southern Rhodesia. The plaintiffs argued that as a result of this they had suffered loss and claimed damages in respect of the breach. The House of Lords held that the plaintiffs had no civil action for breach of this Order. Lord Diplock, delivering a speech with which the other Lords agreed, held that no public right was created. The whole purpose of the Order was to withdraw a pre-existing right, i.e. to trade with Southern Rhodesia, and not to create a right to be enjoyed by the general public. While it is the case that not every breach of a 'public' right causing special damage gives rise to liability, the exact circumstances in which such a breach does give rise to liability is far from clear. More detailed discussion of this point should be sought in specialist texts: see Stanton (1986).

15.4 Elements of the Tort

Persons Protected and Risk Covered

Once it has been determined that an action for breach of statutory duty lies the court must decide whether the damage suffered is recognised by the statute in question. This is a question of judicial interpretation. The leading case is *Gorris* v. *Scott* (1874) 9 Exch 125. An Order was made in pursuance of the Contagious Diseases (Animals) Act 1869 requiring sheep or cattle being transported by ship from any foreign ports to ports in Great Britain to be put in pens of certain dimensions. The defendant did not have any such pens on board his ship and the plaintiff's sheep were washed overboard in a storm and drowned. The plaintiff brought an action for damages for breach of the Order. The court held that the plaintiff's action should fail. The statute had been passed, according to the judges, merely for 'sanitary purposes, in order to prevent animals in a state of infectious disease from communicating it to other animals with which they might come into contact'. The purpose of the statute was not to prevent them being drowned.

The Duty Imposed

Second, it must be considered what the content of the duty imposed is. The answer to this question depends upon the interpretation of the statutory language used. The wide variety of language used in different statutes has meant that a variety of different standards have been imposed.

Some statutes impose strict or even absolute duties; others, however, impose more qualified, 'negligence' duties. There is no rule of thumb used to determine which duty has been imposed. Each statute must be construed carefully to determine what the standard imposed is. The following cases are illustrative.

Statutes imposing absolute standards are rare. However, an example of an absolute duty can be seen in the case of *Galashiels Gas Co Ltd* v. *Millar* [1949] AC 275 (HL, Sc). By s. 22(1) of the Factories Act 1937 it was provided that, 'every hoist or lift shall be properly maintained'. The House of Lords held that the section imposed an absolute duty to maintain a lift in an efficient state. Proof of any failure in a lift mechanism, therefore, established a breach of duty, even if it was impossible to foresee the failure before the event or explain it afterwards. Here liability is truly independent of fault.

More often a statute will impose a qualified duty. For example, s. 29(1) of the Factories Act 1961 provides, '[T]here shall, so far as is reasonably practicable, be provided and maintained safe means of access to every place at which any person has at any time to work. . .'. There are many reported cases which interpret qualified standards of this type. Space considerations, however, preclude full consideration being given to these. The point that must be recognised is that it is always necessary to turn to the statute to discover what the content of the duty imposed on the defendant is. One case may be cited by way of illustration. In *McCarthy* v. *Coldair Ltd* [1951] 2 TLR 1226 an employee fell when a short ladder he was ascending slipped. He claimed that his employer was in breach of what is now s. 29(1) of the Factories Act 1961. The employer was held to be in breach of his duty. It was accepted by the court that it would not ordinarily be reasonably practicable to station a man at the foot of a short ladder, because this would be a disproportionately expensive way of avoiding a small risk. However, in light of the fact that the ladder was being used on a semi-glazed floor which had been splashed by paint, the court felt that the risk was greatly increased such that it would be reasonably practicable to take the steps suggested by the worker.

15.5 **Reform**

The approach taken by English courts to the question whether an action for breach of statutory duty lies has been the subject of criticism. First, it is argued that adoption of a presumption or 'indicator' approach to determine Parliament's intention is misguided because in most cases the silence of the statute on the question of civil liability points to the conclusion that Parliament either did not have the problem in mind or that it deliberately omitted to provide for it. Second, the matters considered by the courts are unhelpful in that they serve to produce no clear result. The courts are thus left with considerable discretion as to whether liability should be imposed. Third, it is hard to explain why it is that the so-called indicators are relevant in assessing Parliament's intention. For example, why should it be the case that an action should be presumed where a duty is owed to a particular class but not where it is owed to the general public. It is surely strange that a duty which Parliament considers to be so important that it provides that it should be owed to the public at large will generally not give rise to an action whereas a less important duty owed to a particular class will, prima facie at least, be presumed to give rise to an action.

As a result of this dissatisfaction various alternatives have been suggested. The Law Commission has argued for a statutory presumption that an action will lie unless express provision to the contrary is made in the statute (Law Commission, 1969). This suggestion attracted severe criticism when placed before Parliament and seems unlikely to be adopted. It does at least have the merit of introducing clarity into a notoriously unclear area but it does so, according to its critics, by imposing unacceptably wide liability. The main criticism was that the suggested presumption of actionability pays no attention to the areas in which it would operate. Rights and duties should be imposed only where they are shown to be required. This Law Commission proposal ignores this. It might be argued, however, that it would have the merit of focusing Parliament's attention on the question of actionability and would at least answer the criticism that Parliament's intention was being frustrated.

An alternative approach is to regard breach of statutory duty as a particular species of negligence. Any breach of such a duty should be treated either as negligence *per se* or as evidence of negligence. Under this approach breach of statutory duty is no longer considered a nominate tort but is instead subsumed under the tort of negligence. This is the approach favoured in most American jurisdictions (where the view adopted by the majority of States is that breach of a statutory duty is *per se* negligence) and in Canada (where breach of statute is evidence of negligence only). Perhaps the strongest argument in favour of the 'statutory negligence' approach, in either of its forms, is that it gets rid of the necessity for the courts to ascertain what was Parliament's intention. English courts would no longer be able, were such an approach to be adopted, to shield their decisions from public scrutiny behind the presumptions. At present, however, it seems unlikely that this approach will be adopted.

Summary

15.1   In this chapter we have sought to answer the question when statutes that impose duties but are either silent as to whether a civil action should lie for breach or impose some other form of liability for breach give rise to a civil action for breach of statutory duty.

15.2   In determining whether a statute gives rise to a civil action for breach of statutory duty, the courts seek to determine whether Parliament intended there to be an action.

15.3   In ascertaining the intention of Parliament the courts consider a number of indicators. These include, but may not be limited to: (a) provision of an alternative method of enforcement; (b) a legislative intention to benefit a particular class of persons; (c) the availability of alternative remedies independent of the statute; (d) the ambit of discretion; (e) the regulatory character of the enactment; (f) the insurance position, and; (g) the creation by the statute of a public right, interference with which carries special damage to the plaintiff.

15.4 Once it has been determined that an action for breach of statutory duty lies, the court must decide whether the damage suffered is recognised by the statute in question. The court must also determine what the content of the duty imposed is.

15.5 A number of proposals have been made to reform the law relating to breach of statutory duty. They have involved either the replacement of the existing presumptions with a new one (Law Commisssion) or treating breach of statutory duty as a particular species of negligence.

Exercises

15.1 I'm the Parliamentary Draftsman,
I compose the country's laws,
And of half the litigation
I'm undoubtedly the cause. (J.P.C., *Poetic Justice*, 1947)

Is this true? (see Williams, 1960, from where this 'poem' is taken)

15.2 What factors do the courts take into account in determining whether a statute gives rise to an action for breach of statutory duty?

15.3 What effect does the existence of a private or public law remedy have on the question whether Parliament intended there to be a civil action?

15.4 What policy considerations, if any, do the courts take into account in considering whether a statute was passed for the benefit of a particular class of persons? Does the fact that a statute was passed to benefit a particular class of persons mean that an action will always lie?

15.5 Why have the courts not imposed civil liability for breach of statutory duty in the area of motor vehicles?

15.6 What proposals for reform have been suggested? Which do you prefer?

16   Trespass to the Person

16.1 Introduction

In most societies, protection of an individual's bodily integrity is likely to rank high on the agenda of interests considered worth protecting. It is perhaps understandable, therefore, that one of the earliest remedies provided by English law was for forcible wrongs against the person. Such wrongs were remediable by commencing an action using a writ of trespass. The writ of trespass emerged in the thirteenth century. It originally existed in a semi-criminal form and if the defendant did not appear to answer the writ he would be outlawed while, if convicted, he was liable to a fine or imprisonment in addition to being liable to the plaintiff in damages. However, by the end of the medieval period the tort action had shed its criminal characteristics. In the civil law the writ of trespass dealt with direct interference with the person in three types of case which correspond to the modern torts of assault, battery and false imprisonment.

By the eighteenth century trespass was differentiated from the other main writ providing a remedy for tortious misconduct, namely the action of trespass on the case (later simply called case), by its requirement that the interference be direct. Case provided a remedy where the harm was indirectly caused. The tendency in later years, however, has been to associate case with negligently caused harm and trespass with intentional wrongs. The main cause of this belief is the fact that the modern law of negligence is derived from the action on the case. As case was associated with negligence, so trespass came to be seen as a tort of intention. However, unlike negligence, which provides a remedy for both indirectly and directly caused harm, trespass has still retained the requirement that the harm must be directly caused.

16.2 Trespass and Negligence

The essence of trespass to the person is that it affords a plaintiff protection against direct invasions of his bodily integrity. In this regard the early common law imposed a very strict responsibility on the defendant. Although it is doubtful that a person would ever have been liable in trespass where he was totally without fault, it was certainly once true that where the plaintiff had established a direct interference the defendant would be liable unless he could establish some justification or excuse. However, in 1959 it was clearly established that in order to succeed in trespass it was not enough for the plaintiff simply to prove a direct invasion of his bodily integrity. In *Fowler* v. *Lanning* [1959] 1 QB 426 the plaintiff's statement of claim alleged that on a certain date and at a certain place 'the defendant shot the plaintiff' and that by reason thereof the plaintiff suffered injury. The defendant objected that this statement of claim disclosed no cause of action in that it did not allege that the shooting was intentional or negligent. Diplock J held that to succeed in trespass it was not enough to prove a direct act (the defendant shot me); the plaintiff had in addition to prove that the direct act was done intentionally or negligently.

The result of *Fowler* v. *Lanning* is that where the injury is unintended, whether it is a direct or indirect consequence of the defendant's act, the plaintiff will only succeed where he can show that the defendant's conduct was unreasonable (i.e. negligent). Thus, in most cases of unintentional injury the plaintiff will bring his action in negligence rather than trespass because there is no need in negligence, unlike trespass, to prove that the injury was a direct consequence of the act. To a large extent, therefore, the rules of negligence have overtaken those of trespass where the defendant's act is unintentional.

Difficulties, however, remain in determining the true relationship between trespass and negligence. In particular, can an action for trespass still be brought where the defendant's act was unintentional? This question is important in cases where the plaintiff suffers no damage because, unlike negligence where *damage* is the gist of the action, the tort of trespass is actionable *per se* (i.e. without proof of damage). The point was considered by the Court of Appeal in *Letang* v. *Cooper* [1965] 1 QB 232. The defendant negligently drove his Jaguar car over the legs of the plaintiff, who was sunbathing in a car park. More than three years after the accident the plaintiff sued the defendant in negligence and trespass. The plaintiff admitted that her action in negligence was time barred by the Limitation Act 1939 but argued that her alternative claim in trespass was not. Her argument succeeded at first instance but was rejected by the Court of Appeal. One reason given for the decision was that the three-year limitation period applicable to actions for personal injury in negligence also applied to *any* cause of action, including trespass to the person, whereby damages for personal injuries were claimed. This part of the decision must now be seen as wrong in light of the decision of the House of Lords in *Stubbings* v. *Webb* [1993] AC 498. Lord Griffiths, who delivered the leading judgment, held that an action for trespass did not fall within s. 11 of the Limitation Act 1980 but within s. 2. Section 11, which provides for a basic period of limitation of three years (which can be extended: sections 14 and 33), applies to 'any action for damages for negligence, nuisance or breach of duty . . . where the damages claimed by the plaintiff . . . include damages in respect of personal injuries to the plaintiff or other person'. Section 11 was intended to be limited to causes of action for personal injury caused by *accidents*; personal injury caused by a trespass to the person was not accidental and therefore did not come within the section (for a criticism of *Stubbings* v. *Webb*, see Mullis (1997). An alternative ground for the decision in *Letang* does, however, remain of continuing importance. Lord Denning MR, with whom Danckwerts LJ agreed, held that where the defendant inflicts the injury unintentionally no action would lie for trespass. He agreed with the judgment of Diplock J in *Fowler* v. *Lanning*, but said (at p. 240):

> 'I would go this one step further: when the injury is not inflicted intentionally, but negligently, I would say that the only cause of action is negligence and not trespass. If it were trespass, it would be actionable without proof of damage; and that is not the law today.'

In Lord Denning's opinion, therefore, trespass is truly an intentional tort in that only the intentional application of force can give rise to an action in trespass. Where the act is unintentional the correct and only cause of action is negligence.

Lord Denning's opinion that a cause of action will only lie in trespass where a person intentionally applies force directly to another has not found universal support. For example, Diplock LJ in *Letang* v. *Cooper* itself accepted that trespass could be committed negligently but thought that there were no significant differences between an action for unintentional (but negligent) trespass and an action in negligence. Also, in Canada and Australia support still exists for the view that there may be a negligent trespass. While the point still remains open, the better view is that expressed by Lord Denning. In the first place little is lost to the plaintiff by depriving him of a right to sue in trespass where the application of force is unintentional. If damage is suffered he has an action in negligence. Where no damage is suffered it is almost inconceivable that the plaintiff would want to bring an action. In the second place, Lord Denning's view achieves a welcome clarification of the law classifying liability according to the mental state of the defendant.

16.3 Assault and Battery

Where a person intentionally and without the other's consent applies force directly to another, this constitutes a battery. Where a person intentionally makes a threat that causes another reasonably to apprehend the immediate infliction of a battery on him, that is an assault. It should be noted that in some of the cases courts use the word *assault* to describe what is in essence a *battery*. The reason for this is because most assaults end in a battery and the result is often described as an assault and battery or just an assault. Despite this terminological confusion, the distinction between the two torts is fairly clear. Thus, it is an assault for A to point a loaded gun at B who fears being shot but if A fires the gun and the bullet hits B that is a battery. It is an assault for A to drive a car at B such that B fears being hit but it is a battery to hit him. Often battery and assault go together, but they need not. For example, if A sneaks up behind B without B hearing him and hits him over the head there is a battery but no assault. Similarly if A shakes his fist at B that is an assault but not a battery.

Although extensively analysed in the context of criminal law, the meaning of 'intention' has not been much discussed in tort cases. If it can be shown that it was the defendant's *purpose* to apply force directly to the plaintiff then liability would be established. Proof that he knew with substantial certainty that the above consequences would occur would also be sufficient to ground liability. However, an intention to *injure* is probably not necessary. Provided it can be established that the defendant intentionally applied force directly to another, then liability is established even if the consequences were not intended (*Wilson* v. *Pringle* [1986] 2 All ER 440). More difficult is the question whether recklessness will suffice. There is little or no authority on this question but such as there is (*Ball* v. *Axten* (1866) 4 F & F 1019) is not inconsistent with the view that recklessness may be sufficient. There is also no English authority on the question whether the transferred intent doctrine, recognised in the criminal law context, applies in trespass actions. American cases have recognised the existence of such a doctrine (*White* v. *Davis* (1982) 18 BR 246 (Bkrtcy, Va)) and some courts have even been prepared to allow the transfer of intention from one intentional tort to another. Thus, in one case (*Altieri* v. *Colasso* (1975) 362 A 2d 798), where the defendant threw a stone in the direction of A intending to frighten (*assault*) him (A) but hit B the court held the defendant liable to B for battery.

Battery

As we have seen, there is no requirement in establishing a battery that the defendant intended to cause *harm*. All that the plaintiff need show is that the defendant intended to touch the body of the plaintiff. This might be thought to give rise to intolerable difficulties. Is it, for example, a battery if I shake your hand in greeting, or if I slap you on the back in congratulations when you tell me your examination results? An early attempt to distinguish acceptable from unacceptable touchings was made by Holt CJ in *Cole* v. *Turner* (1704) 6 Mod 149 where he said, 'the least touching of another in anger is a battery.' While there is nothing inherently wrong with this statement in that if A touches B in anger his act will generally amount to a battery, some behaviour not committed in anger will still be a battery. Examples of such behaviour might include an unwanted kiss or restraining someone to question them, but not retraining them merely to attract their attention (*Collins* v. *Wilcock* [1984] 1 WLR 1172). Despite the fact that the test is plainly inadequate to explain all the cases, Holt CJ's words were held by the Court of Appeal in *Wilson* v. *Pringle* [1987] QB 237 to lay down the appropriate test. Croom Johnson LJ held that for there to be a battery there must be 'something in the nature of overt hostility'. Hostility, he said should not be equated with ill-will or malevolence: an act can be 'hostile' even if not committed in anger. Instead he appears to suggest that it means little more than an objectionable touching. This, it is suggested, is not very helpful; all it does is restate the very question that needs to be answered.

A better approach is that suggested by Robert Goff LJ in *Collins* v. *Wilcock*. There he said that a touching will only amount to a battery where it does not fall within the category of physical contacts 'generally acceptable in the ordinary conduct of general life.' Thus being jostled in the underground during the rush-hour would not be a battery, whereas an unwanted kiss or perhaps an over-exuberant shove in the back may be. Although this approach was thought impracticable by Croom Johnson LJ in *Wilson* v. *Pringle* Lord Goff (as he has become) restated his views in the House of Lords in *F* v. *West Berkshire Health Authority* [1990] 2 AC 1, 73 where he explicitly rejected any requirement of 'hostility' as unnecessary. It is likely, therefore, that this will be the approach adopted in future cases.

Historically, a cause of action in trespass only lay where the the touching was the direct or immediate result of the plaintiff's act. This requirement was well stated by Blackstone J. in *Scott* v. *Shepherd* (1773) 2 Black W 892 where he said, 'where the injury is immediate, an action in trespass will lie; where it is only consequential, it must be an action on the case.' Thus it has been said that, where a person throws a log of timber onto the highway and another person falls over it and is injured, this injury is only consequential and an action for trespass will not lie. By way of contrast, if the log were to hit someone that would give rise to an action in trespass because the contact would be direct and immediate. In the modern law the plaintiff is still required to show that the touching was the direct result of the defendant's act, but the courts have stretched the concept of directness so far that it is doubtful whether today this requirement provides a substantial hurdle for many plaintiffs. The facts of *Scott* v. *Shepherd* itself illustrate the broad nature of the concept. The defendant threw a lighted squib made of gunpowder into a covered market where a large number of people were collected. The squib fell onto B's stall and he picked it up and threw it onto C's stall; C likewise threw it away and in doing so hit the plaintiff. The court, by a majority, held that an action for trespass would lie. The intermediate acts of B and C were, somewhat surprisingly, found not to have broken the chain of directness between the defendant and the plaintiff.

In the more recent case of *DPP* v. *K* [1990] 1 WLR 1067, K, a 15-year-old schoolboy, took some concentrated sulphuric acid out of a chemistry lesson and took it to the lavatory. On hearing footsteps outside the lavatory door he poured the acid into a hand and face drier. Another pupil turned the drier on and was badly burnt when acid spurted out. K was convicted of assault occasioning actual bodily harm. Although the case has subsequently been held to be wrongly decided on another ground, it is no less interesting from our point of view because it appears to have been assumed that the contact was the direct, as opposed to consequential, result of the defendant's act. Surely, this is a case where the touching was consequential on the act of the plaintiff in putting the acid into the drier. If the case is correctly decided on this point then leaving a log on the highway over which someone falls should also be seen as the direct cause of the plaintiff's harm, as should the setting of a trap for the plaintiff. While other, generally older cases, have taken a narrower view as to the meaning to be ascribed to the word 'direct', the requirement no longer appears to be a serious bar to recovery and could be abandoned (as it has been in the United States).

Assault

The essence of an assault is the making of a threat that places the plaintiff in reasonable apprehension of an immediate battery to himself. It is not every threat, however, that will suffice to give rise to liability. Clearly, if A points a loaded gun at B, the pointing of the gun will suffice. In such a case by virtue of the pointing of the gun the plaintiff reasonably apprehends the infliction of an immediate battery. Would the position be any different if A, without a gun, had said 'I am going to shoot you dead'? In other words can the speaking of words amount to an assault? Though such authority as there is is inconclusive, the view most often cited is that of Holroyd J in *Mead's and Belt's Case* (1823) 1 Lewin 184. He said there that, 'no words or singing are equivalent to an assault. . .' This view reflects the fact that in many cases the uttering of mere words will not give rise to fear of an *immediate* battery. In our example, the speaking of the words 'I am going to shoot you dead' by a person without a gun would probably lack immediacy. The speaker would have to go away, find a gun and then return before he could put the threat into effect.

The fact that mere words are used should not, however, mean that in every situation there will be no assault. For example, if a mugger were to say to his victim, 'your money or I will beat you up' this could amount to an assault even in the absence of any threatening gestures by the mugger. Similarly, if the defendant, who was engaged in beating up A, were to say to the plaintiff, 'you are next' this too could amount to an assault. What is important, therefore, is not how the threat is conveyed but whether what is conveyed is enough to place the plaintiff in reasonable apprehension of an immediate battery.

Although older English decisions emphasised the immediacy requirement, more recent (criminal) cases suggest that the mood of the courts towards verbal (and non-verbal) threats may be changing. In the recent case of *R* v. *Ireland* [1997] 1 All ER 112 (which involved an appeal against a successful criminal prosecution on three counts of assault occasioning actual bodily harm contrary to s. 47 of the Offences Against the Person Act 1861), the Court of Appeal held that the making of a large number of telephone calls to three women and remaining silent when they answered was capable of amounting to an assault. The exact basis of the decision is not entirely clear but it appears that the court thought that it was sufficient that the telephone calls instilled fear into the women of suffering 'psychological' damage (see also *Smith* v. *Chief Superintendent, Woking Police Station* (1983) 76 Cr App Rep 234). Such a decision, if applied by a civil court, would effectively make the immediacy requirement redundant. Whether in the light of the enactment of the Protection From Harassment Act 1997 (which would provide protection against such behaviour; ss. 1

and 4)) it was wise for the court to 'stretch the ambit' of the crime of assault to punish this defendant must be open to doubt.

Words may not only amount to an assault: they may also have the effect of neutralizing a threat made by a gesture. In *Tuberville* v. *Savage* (1669) 1 Mod 3, T put his hand on his sword and said to S, 'if it were not assize-time I would not take such language from you.' These words were held to prevent the gesture from amounting to an assault. Their effect was to show that there was no intent. By way of contrast, a phrase such as, 'your money or your life' might (if the threat is sufficiently immediate) be actionable. While the words still negative intent, they do so only by demanding fulfilment of a condition by the plaintiff. The defendant should not be forced to 'buy' his safety by compliance with a condition and therefore such conditional threats ought to be actionable.

For there to be an assault the plaintiff must reasonably *anticipate* the infliction of a battery. Thus, where the plaintiff has no knowledge of the threat there can be no assault. This point is well illustrated by the American case of *McCraney* v. *Flanagan* (1980) 267 SE 2d 404. The plaintiff brought an action against the defendant for *assault* alleging that he had had intercourse with her without her consent. However, the plaintiff could remember nothing about the alleged assault though it was clear from the physical evidence that intercourse had taken place. The North Carolina Court of Appeals upheld the grant of summary judgment to the defendant. While a *battery* may well have have occured, an *assault* had not. As the court said:

> 'The tort of assault occurs when a person is put in apprehension of a [battery] and there is no evidence here that the plaintiff feared, or even knew, that such a contact might occur. She has no recollection at all of the events. Since the interest involved is a mental one of apprehension of contact, it should follow that the plaintiff must be aware of the defendant's act at the time . . .' (at 408–9)

However, there will be an assault if the plaintiff reasonably anticipates the infliction of a battery even if he is not *in fact* put in a state of fear or terror. It is the plaintiff's knowledge that is important and not the effect that this knowledge has on his mind.

A related, though distinct, question is whether there is an assault where, although the plaintiff thinks that the defendant is about to inflict a battery on him, the defendant does not in fact have the necessary means to do so. For example, if a person points an unloaded gun at another does this amount to an assault? In *Stephens* v. *Myers* (1830) 4 Car & P 350 Tindal CJ said, 'it is not every threat, when there is no actual personal violence that constitutes an assault, there must be, in all cases the means of carrying the threat into effect.' This approach finds support in *Blake* v. *Burnard* (1840) 9 Car & P 626 where Lord Abinger CB held that it was not an assault to point an unloaded pistol at another. However, while these cases have not been overruled, other cases (for example, *R* v. *St George* (1840) 9 Car & P 483) have held that such an act can amount to an assault. In principle, the better view is that expressed in *R* v. *St George*. Where a battery is, in all the circumstances, *reasonably* apprehended this should be enough to constitute an assault.

16.4 False Imprisonment

The tort of false imprisonment is committed when the defendant intentionally and without lawful justification restrains a person's liberty within an area delimited by the defendant. It is not necessary in order to establish the tort that a person be locked up in a prison or restrained within four walls. As was said in the *Termes de la Ley*:

> 'imprisonment is no other thing but the restraint of a man's liberty whether it bee in the openfield, or in the stocks or in the cage in the street or in a man's own house, as well as in the common gaole; and in all the places the party so restrained is said to be a prisoner so long as he hath not his liberty freely to goe at all times to all places wither he will without baile or mainprise or otherwise.'

Thus, preventing a person from leaving his own house, casting him adrift in a boat or taking hold of him in the street can all amount to false imprisonment.

In order for there to be a false imprisonment the restraint must be total. In *Bird* v. *Jones* (1845) 7 QB 742 the defendants enclosed part of Hammersmith Bridge and put seats in the enclosure for the use of paying spectators of a regatta. The plaintiff insisted on passing along the bridge through the enclosure and climbed over the fence of the enclosure without paying the charge. The defendants then refused to let the plaintiff go forward in the direction he wished to go but told him that he could go back and cross the bridge though not through the enclosure. The court held that this was no false imprisonment. In reaching this conclusion, Patteson J said (at 751–2) that there was no imprisonment where 'one man merely obstructs the passage of another in a particular direction, whether by threat of personal violence or otherwise, leaving him at liberty to stay where he is or to go in any other direction if he pleases. . .'

A difficult decision which at first sight appears to conflict with the decision in *Bird* v. *Jones* is that of *Robinson* v. *Balmain New Ferry Co Ltd* [1910] AC 295. The respondents operated a ferry service between Sydney and Balmain. On the Sydney side a turnstile with an exit and entrance was set up and a notice displayed stating that a penny had to be paid on entering and leaving the wharf. The appellant paid his penny to enter and then changed his mind and sought to leave without paying a further penny. The respondents prevented him from doing so. The Privy Council held that this was not a false imprisonment. How can this be so? Surely it was the case that the plaintiff was wholly restrained within the wharf? If so it would seem to be the case that an action for false imprisonment should have succeeded. One explanation of the case is that the appellant was never completely restrained; he could still have used the ferry, as he had originally intended to do, and gained his freedom unconditionally on the other side. Thus, his contractual path was never closed to him and he was not, therefore, falsely imprisoned.

While this may be a convincing explanation of the case, it is not clear that this was the reason given by the Privy Council for their decision. An alternative view of the reasoning of the court was that there was no false imprisonment because an occupier of premises is entitled to impose reasonable conditions on the manner in which an entrant leaves his premises. On the facts, the Privy Council held that it was reasonable for the ferry company to insist that all persons leaving the wharf paid one penny. The plaintiff had contracted to leave the wharf via the ferry and the payment of one penny was not an unreasonable condition to impose for his leaving by a different route.

A similar case was that of *Herd* v. *Weardale Steel Coal and Coke Co Ltd* [1915] AC 67. A miner employed by the defendants refused, in breach of his contract, to do certain work in his pit. His employers refused to take him to the surface for some time after a cage was available to do so. He sued for false imprisonment. The House of Lords held that his action failed. Clearly, the restraint here was total, the only way out was via the cage to the surface. The court, relying on the decision in *Robinson* v. *Balmain New Ferry Co*, held that the miner had gone down the mine on certain terms and it was not false imprisonment to hold him to the conditions he accepted when he went down. Both cases may, therefore, be authority for the proposition that a landowner's imposition of a reasonable condition on exit may negate false imprisonment.

Such a conclusion is, however, not without difficulty because if correct it seems tantamount to recognising an extra-judicial right to imprison for breach of contract. Yet *Sunbolf* v. *Alford* (1838) 3 M & W 247 establishes that English law does not allow a man to be imprisoned for debt. It has been argued, therefore, that these cases are not authority for the proposition that enforcement of a contractual condition may negate false imprisonment but are instead about consent. (Tan, (1981). While a person can consent to a deprivation of his liberty (as happened in *Herd* and *Robinson*) he can always, subject to considerations of reasonableness, revoke that consent. A person does not, by consenting to a deprivation of his liberty, tie his hands forever. Thus the issue in *Herd* and *Robinson* was whether the plaintiffs had effectively revoked their consent. It is established law that a revocation of consent need not in every case take immediate effect. The owner of premises who would be unreasonably inconvenienced if required to allow a visitor to leave at once can lawfully restrain him until such time as it is convenient to let him go. It is for this reason that the passenger on a bus has no right to insist on being allowed to alight between stops. This consideration may underlie the decisions in *Herd* and *Robinson* although, as Tan admits, the extent of the delay in these cases must have been close to the limit of what was permissible.

There may be a false imprisonment even in the absence of actual force or direct physical contact. Thus if a police officer informs a person that he is under arrest this, in the absence of lawful justification, will amount to a false imprisonment. It has even been held that requiring a person to come along to the police station and answer some questions may be sufficient. All that is required, therefore, is that there must be such constraint on the person's will that he believes that he is under restraint. The emphasis, is on the impression created in the victim's mind. Given this emphasis it is perhaps not surprising that differing views have been expressed on the question whether a person can be falsely imprisoned where he does not know that he is under constraint. Despite a old decision (*Meering* v. *Graham-White Aviation Co* (1919) 122 LT 44) suggesting that there cannot be liability in such circumstances, the more modern view is that there can be. In *Murray* v. *Ministry of Defence* [1988] 1 WLR 692 Lord Griffiths, with whom the other members of the House of Lords agreed, said that knowledge of the restraint was not an essential element of the tort. While in the absence of such knowledge the damages likely to be awarded will be nominal, 'the law attaches supreme importance to the liberty of the individual and if he suffers a wrongful interference with that liberty it should remain actionable even without proof of special damage.' The position adopted by English law should be contrasted with that taken by the American Restatement Second of Torts, s. 42 (1965). The rule expressed there is that there can be no imprisonment unless the plaintiff is aware of it at the time. Yet, as Prosser (1955) pointed out, such a position is rather harsh particularly where, as is certainly possible, substantial damage results to the plaintiff from the imprisonment. Is it really the case that a one-month-old baby locked in a bank vault for three days should have no action if it suffered illness as a result?

The essence of false imprisonment is, as we have seen, the restraint of a person without lawful justification. In most cases this restraint will be of a person who is lawfully at large. A difficult problem is posed by the question whether a person who is lawfully imprisoned can ever complain of false imprisonment in relation to acts subsequent to his lawful imprisonment. This matter was considered by the House of Lords in *R* v. *Deputy Governor of Parkhurst Prison, ex parte Hague* [1992] 1 AC 58 (see Mullis, (1991) pp. 396–8). Allegations were made against the prison authorities by two prisoners. H alleged that in breach of the Prison Rules he had been transferred to another prison and there segregated from other inmates for 28 days. W alleged that he had been falsely imprisoned by being placed in a strip cell overnight. The House of Lords held that no action for false imprisonment could lie in these circumstances. The prison authorities had a complete defence by virtue of s. 12(1) of the Prison Act 1952 which provides that, 'a prisoner . . . may be lawfully confined in any prison.' This section, their Lordships said, provided a complete defence for the restraint of a prisoner within the bounds of a prison by the governor or someone acting with the governor's authority. Thus where the prisoner was locked up in a part of the prison with the governor's authority there was no room for an argument that the prison authorities were liable for false imprisonment based on any 'residual liberty' of the prisoner's. They further held that holding a prisoner in intolerable conditions could not give rise to liability for false imprisonment because this was to confuse the *fact* of confinement with the *conditions* of confinement. The tort of false imprisonment was confined to remedying the former. They did accept, however, that an action for negligence might lie if a prisoner suffered injury as a result of such confinement. While no action lay on the facts of this case, the House of Lords did not wholly reject the possibility of an action being brought by a person who is lawfully imprisoned. The court said that if another prisoner, or a prison officer who acted in bad faith, locked up within the confines of a prison a person who was lawfully imprisoned, this could amount to false imprisonment.

Can a person (A) be liable for false imprisonment where it is not he but another (B) who imprisons the plaintiff? Where B is A's employee or agent and is acting under his instructions there is little doubt that A, as principal or employer, would be liable for the imprisonment. More difficult, however, are cases where B is neither A's agent or employee, but, acting on information given by A, B detains the plaintiff. The paradigm example of this is the case where a police officer arrests a person on the basis of information given to him by a member of the public. In such a case, could either the person who gave the information or the arresting officer be liable for false imprisonment? This was considered by the Court of Appeal in *Davidson* v. *Chief Constable of North Wales* [1994] 2 All ER 597, which held that it would only be in very rare circumstances that a person who gave information to the police would be liable for any subsequent imprisonment. This is surely correct. A decision by a police officer to arrest involves the exercise, on the part of the officer, of an independent discretion. The police officer does not in any real sense act as the informant's agent and the arrest decision is his. Sir Thomas Bingham MR made clear, however, that, if the informant went beyond the mere laying of information before the police for them to take such action as they thought fit and he took steps which, 'amounted to some direction, or procuring, or direct request or direct encouragement that they should act by way of arresting these defendants', then the informant may be liable.

16.5 Intentional Infliction of Physical Harm Other than Trespass to the Person: *Wilkinson* v. *Downton*

In *Wilkinson* v. *Downton* [1897] 2 QB 57 the defendant, by way of a practical joke, falsely represented to the plaintiff that her husband had met with a serious accident. The plaintiff, believing the story, suffered a violent shock to her system and subsequently became ill. She brought an action against the defendant claiming damages for her psychiatric injury. Wright J held that where a person wilfully does an act calculated to produce an effect on the plaintiff of the kind which was actually produced then a cause of action would arise in the absence of any legal justification. On the facts it was clear that the defendant must be treated as having intended to induce the psychiatric illness in the plaintiff and, therefore, the plaintiff's claim succeeded.

There have been few cases in English law in which the principle of *Wilkinson* v. *Downton* has been applied. In one (*Janvier* v. *Sweeney* [1919] 2 KB 316) the defendants, who were private detectives, told the plaintiff that unless she produced certain letters then in the possession of her employer they would disclose to the authorities that her fiancé was a traitor. She suffered a 'nervous illness' as a result of these statements. The Court of Appeal held, applying *Wilkinson* v. *Downton*, that her action for damages succeeded. In the more recent case of *Khorasandjian* v. *Bush* [1993] 3 WLR 669 the defendant subjected the plaintiff, an estranged former friend, to a campaign of harassment over a period of months. The plaintiff suffered considerable stress as a result of the defendant's behaviour and sought a *quia timet* injunction preventing him from, 'using violence to, harassing, pestering or communicating with' her. At first instance the judge granted the injunction and, by a majority, the Court of Appeal upheld the award. Such an injunction was justified according to the court on the basis, *inter alia*, of *Wilkinson* v. *Downton* which 'established that false words or *verbal threats* calculated to cause and uttered with the knowledge that they are likely to cause and actually causing physical injury to the person to whom they are uttered are actionable.' (per Dillon LJ, at 676; see also *Burris* v. *Azadani* [1995] 4 All ER 802)).

What then, in the light of these authorities, is the extent of the principle recognised in *Wilkinson* v. *Downton*? Clearly within the principle are those cases where the defendant makes a *false* statement intending to cause the plaintiff a psychiatric illness and where such an illness is in fact caused. It also applies to illness caused by verbal threats intended to frighten or terrify the plaintiff (*Khorasandjian* v. *Bush* and *Janvier* v. *Sweeney*). Although the injury in *Wilkinson* v. *Downton* resulted from a false *statement* there is no reason in principle why the principle should not extend to *acts* (*Khorasandjian* v. *Bush*).

Proof of intention to cause such harm does not appear to be indispensable. Such an intention may be inferred where the consequences which result are the natural and probable result of the defendant's conduct (*Wilkinson* v. *Downton*). There seems to be little reason to confine the principle to cases where a 'nervous' or psychiatric' illness is caused. Thus, if the defendant were to shout at a person riding a bicycle intending to cause him to fall off, any *physical* injury suffered in the subsequent fall would give rise to liability. Further, although some injury must be suffered (so mere distress would not be actionable) a court may issue a *quia timet* injunction in order to prevent the occurence of the tort in the future where there is 'an *obvious risk* that the cumulative effect of the continued and unrestrained further harassment . . .': would cause a recognisable psychiatric illness' (p. 677, per Dillon LJ).

The rule in *Wilkinson* v. *Downton* is descended from the action on the case and is not a form of trespass. It is for this reason that the plaintiff must prove actual loss. What then is the rule's relationship with the trespassory torts (assault, battery and false imprisonment)? At least three views appear tenable. First, liability under *Wilkinson* v. *Downton* should be confined to cases of intentionally but *indirectly* inflicted physical or emotional harm. Thus, it should be seen as a residuary form of liability for intentionally caused personal injury supplementing the trespass torts. Second, the tort recognised by *Wilkinson* v. *Downton* should be seen as a separate nominate tort broadly equivalent to the tort of intentional infliction of emotional distress recognised in Restatement Second of Torts, s. 46. Under that provision, which represents the law in the majority of states in America, liability is imposed where a person intentionally or recklessly inflicts emotional distress upon another and; (a) the actor's conduct is extreme and outrageous, and; (b) the harm intended is severe, and; (c) the actual resulting emotional harm is also severe. Although such a view has its attractions in that the well-developed American law on the subject could provide a basis for the development of English law (see Givelber, 1982), little in the existing case law suggests that such a development is likely. Finally, there is the possibility that *Wilkinson* v. *Downton* will be treated as giving rise to a general principle of liability for all intentionally inflicted harms (including economic losses) whether directly or indirectly caused. Such an approach would require a radical restructuring of the existing law and this appears unlikely. For the moment, therefore, it seems likely that the principle will continue to be treated as a separate complementary form of liability covering cases of intentionally but indirectly caused *physical* harm.

16.6 Damages

Unlike negligence, where proof of damage is an essential element in the cause of action, trespass to the person is actionable *per se* (without proof of any damage). Substantial damages may, therefore, be awarded even where there is no physical injury simply for invasion of the right itself. Thus, a person who is falsely imprisoned is entitled to damages for the loss of his liberty regardless of whether the imprisonment caused him any physical or economic harm and a person who is the victim of a battery is entitled to damages for the invasion of his bodily integrity even if he is not harmed but only affronted, upset or embarassed. Additionally, exemplary damages may be awarded where the trespass occurred either as a result of arbitrary conduct by a government official, or as a result of a deliberate or reckless breach of the law done with a view for gain (see 22.2). The fact that exemplary damages can be awarded in respect of arbitrary conduct by a government official gives trespass an important role in the protection of the liberties of the citizen against infringement by the state.

16.7 Defences to Trespass to the Person

Once the plaintiff has proved the direct interference that constitutes the trespass, it is for the defendant to justify his action by reference to one of the defences. There are a number of defences to trespass to the person of varying degrees of practical importance. Thus, the exercise of disciplinary powers by parents over children can be a defence provided the force used is reasonable. At common law, teachers and others *in loco parentis* had a similar defence. However, corporal punishment has now been rendered actionable in state schools by the Education (No 2) Act 1986, s. 47 and in other schools, if 'inhuman or degrading', by the Education Act 1993, s. 35. Statutory authority can also be a defence and so, in limited circumstances, can contributory negligence (see 11.5) and illegality (see 11.6). The fact that criminal proceedings have already been taken against the defendant may also, in certain circumstances, relieve him of civil liability (Offences Against the Person Act 1861, ss. 42–5). Probably the most important defences in practice are the powers of arrest conferred on police officers, and the more limited powers conferred on private citizens, by the Police and Criminal Evidence Act 1984. Where a police officer or a private citizen carries out a lawful arrest he will commit neither a false imprisonment nor a battery. Reference should be made to texts on constitutional law or civil liberties for details of the powers of arrest. Three defences – consent, self-defence and necessity – are considered in more detail below.

Consent

Where a person consents either expressly or impliedly to a trespass to his person no action will lie. There is some debate over the question whether consent is strictly speaking a defence at all because a defence is something that it is for the defendant to prove. In *Freeman* v. *Home Office (No 2)* [1984] QB 524 McCowan J held that the burden of proving absence of consent was on the plaintiff thereby implying that absence of consent is an essential element of trespass to the person. While this is probably the prevailing view in English law today (cf, the view in Australia, where McCowan's view has been rejected), it is suggested that Winfield and Jolowicz (1994) are correct when they say (at 724) that 'as a practical matter, however, the defendant may need to lead evidence to lay a foundation from which the court will infer consent as a specific issue in his statement of claim.' In this sense, therefore, consent may be treated as a 'defence'.

Consent can be given expressly, for example, where a patient signs a consent form to an operation. Alternatively, consent may be implied. An example of implied consent can be found in the old American case of *O'Brien* v. *Cunard* (1891) 28 NE 266 where the court held that by standing in line and holding out her arm the plaintiff impliedly consented to being vaccinated (but see Shalleck *et al* (1992)). Similarly, participants in 'violent sports' impliedly consent to the risks ordinarily incidental to such sports. They do not, however, consent to excessive violence or to deliberate unfair play. The line between the two is, however, by no means easy to draw.

The relevance of consent in a civil action may differ from that in criminal proceedings. While certain consensual activities may be considered so contrary to public policy that they are treated as criminal, it might nevertheless be wrong to allow one consenting participant to sue another. Thus, in the infamous case of *R* v. *Brown* [1992] 2 All ER 552 the Court of Appeal held that the participants in homosexual sado-masochistic 'games' could not rely on the defence of consent to negate their criminal liability. Much stress was laid by the court on the public interest that people should not injure each other for no good reason. While this is clearly a relevant matter when considering a criminal prosecution it is less clear that it is relevant in a civil action where the court is primarily concerned with the reciprocal rights and liabilities of the parties inter se (Skegg, 1988, pp. 38–40). Thus, had one of the participants in the activities brought an action for battery it is suggested that his consent should amount to a complete defence. A more difficult question is whether a 16 year old man successfully prosecuted for having 'unlawful sexual intercourse with a girl under the age of sixteen' (Sexual Offences Act 1956, s. 6), to which consent is not a defence, could rely on the defence if sued for battery. The purpose of making such an act criminal must, at least in part, be to protect the girl from her own consent. Should this, therefore, be a case where the defendant cannot rely on consent as a defence? (See Restatement Second of Torts, s. 892C.)

For consent to be valid it must be genuine. Thus, consent obtained by duress would be no defence. So, for example, consent to sexual intercourse obtained by threats of violence would not be valid. But the mere fact that the plaintiff may feel under 'pressure' to give consent does not necessarily mean that any consent given will not be valid. In *Freeman* v. *Home Office (No 2)* [1984] QB 524, for example, the Court of Appeal held that the consent given by a prisoner to medical treatment was genuine. The institutional pressures imposed in those circumstances were held not to negative the consent given.

Consent will not be valid unless the plaintiff understands the nature and purpose of the touching. In *Chatterton* v. *Gerson* [1981] QB 432 Bristow J said that 'once [a person] is informed in broad terms of the nature of the procedure which is intended and gives her consent, that consent is real . . .' The difficulty is to determine what information is relevant to the 'nature' and 'purpose' of the touching and what is merely collateral to it. In circumstances where the consent was induced by deceit or given under a misapprehension as to the nature and purpose of the touching the courts have held that the consent was vitiated. In *R* v. *Williams* [1923] 1 KB 340, for example, it was held that there was no valid consent by a woman to sexual intercourse where she was told that this was therapy for her voice. There the deceit was as to the nature and purpose of the touching.

More uncertainty surrounds the situation where the plaintiff is aware of the nature and purpose of the touching but unaware of its harmful consequences. This issue was considered in *R* v. *Clarence* (1888) 22 QB 23. The defendant had sexual intercourse with his wife with her consent. Unknown to the wife, the defendant had gonorrhoea and she became infected. The defendant was charged with 'assault occasioning actual bodily harm' and 'unlawfully and maliciously inflicting grievous bodily harm'. Thus, it was necessary to prove that the defendant's wife had not consented to the touching. The court held that the woman's consent was valid even though she had no knowledge of her husband's condition.

Despite, or perhaps because of, its antiquity this case has attracted much academic criticism. Grubb and Pearl (1990) have argued that the case should be narrowly confined. *Clarence* was a decision relating to a criminal prosecution for a serious offence and given the prevailing social and sexual mores of the time it was not surprising that the result was reached. It should not, however, be treated as authority for the proposition that in a civil action for trespass to the person consent to a touching will always be valid if the person touched knows the nature and purpose of the touching but does not know of its potentially harmful consequences. It is suggested that two situations need to be distinguished. Where, *unknown to the plaintiff*, the defendant intends to cause the harmful consequences, or where he is reckless or negligent as to those consequences, then consent should not be a defence. However, where the harmful consequences are not a reasonably foreseeable consequence of the consented-to touching then the defendant should be able to rely on the defence of consent. Thus, if A, knowing he has Aids, has intercourse with the plaintiff intending to infect him, consent to the sexual act should not bar recovery by the plaintiff. However, if when A and B are indulging in 'horseplay', something 'snaps' when A picks B up causing B to be paralysed, then consent should amount to a defence to any action brought by B against A. Unless it could be said that B was negligent as to the consequences caused, B's consent to indulge in the 'horseplay' should bar his recovery (see *Hellriegel* v. *Tholl* (1966) 417 P 2d 362).

Finally, something should be said about consent in medical cases as this is probably the most important area of the defence's operation. As a general rule, the principles explained above apply equally to medical cases. Indeed, many of the leading authorities involve medical treatment. Thus, provided the broad nature of the proposed operation is explained to a patient any consent given will excuse what would otherwise be a battery (see, for example, *Chatterton* v. *Gerson*). Particular difficulties arise, however, in medical cases in three types of case: the treatment of children, the treatment of the mentally handicapped or ill and the treatment of the unconscious. In the case of children, s. 8 of the Family Law Reform Act 1969 provides that a minor between the ages of 16 and 18 can give an effective consent to surgical, medical or dental treatment as if he were an adult. As regards a child who has not reached his sixteenth birthday, the House of Lords held in *Gillick* v. *DHSS* [1986] AC 112 that a child can give effective consent to medical treatment providing he has the ability to understand what is involved in the medical procedure proposed. In *Gillick* itself, Lord Scarman said that in relation to contraceptive advice and treatment this would involve not only understanding the reasons for the doctor touching the child and the purposes behind the touching but also an understanding of the wider social and moral implications. In the case of a very young child, consent must be sought from a proxy (usually a parent) in order for the touching to be lawful.

As far as mentally disordered or ill persons are concerned the position is more difficult. Clearly, such persons may be unable to give a real consent if they are not able to understand any explanation given to them as to the nature and purpose of the touching. This is obviously the case with regard to unconscious patients. Patients of both classes are, in law, incompetent to consent to medical treatment. In *F* v. *West Berkshire Health Authority* [1990] 2 AC 1 the House of Lords held that treatment of such patients could not be justified by any extension of the notion of implied consent; it would be a pure fiction to suggest that such patients impliedly agreed to medical treatment in their best interest. The English courts have also resisted adopting the American concept of 'substituted consent' whereby courts seek to ascertain from the evidence what the person himself would do if competent (see *per* Lord Mustill in *Airedale NHS Trust* v. *Bland* [1993] 1 All ER 821, where he described such consent as 'meaningless' and see Kennedy and Grubb, 1994, Chs. 4 and 16). However, medical treatment may be justified on the ground of necessity. This point is considered below.

Self-Defence

Where a person hits another in defending himself from an attack by that other person he may be able to plead self-defence as a justification. The defence may succeed even where no physical touching has actually been effected by the aggressor. So, for example, if a person threatens another with a gun the defence would succeed if the threatened person sought by force to disarm the aggressor. A reasonable apprehension of threatened aggression is all that is required to justify the use of reasonable force in self-defence. Provocation is not, however, a defence but may be relevant either to show the defendant believed he was being attacked or in mitigation of damages (but see Lord Denning MR in *Murphy* v. *Culhane* [1977] QB 94).

In addition to proving that he was justified in using force to defend himself, the defendant must also prove that the force used was reasonable. This is in essence a question of fact and the answer given will depend on such factors as the degree of violence offered, its immediacy and whether any weapons were used. It was held not to be self-defence in *Cook* v. *Beal* (1697) 1 Lord Raym 177, for example, for the defendant to draw his sword and cut off the hand of a person who had merely struck the defendant. Having said that, the use of even lethal force may be justified if the initial attack is sufficiently violent. Although in many situations the best form of defence is retreat, there is no *duty* on the defendant to retreat in the face of an assault. The fact that the person attacked did not retreat is however a factor to be taken into account in determining whether the action he took was reasonable.

In addition to the right to defend oneself if attacked, a trespass to the person may be justified if the defendant acts in defence of other persons or even to protect his property. It is clear that a person may defend any member of his family. As with self-defence the force used must be reasonable. It is suggested that it is also legitimate to use force in protection of persons other than one's own family. Nobody should have to stand idly by and watch a person seriously assault another because he is afraid of a civil action being brought against him for trespass.

A similar principle applies in relation to protection of property. A person is entitled to use reasonable force to defend land or chattels in his possession. So, for example, an occupier of land may use reasonable force in ejecting a trespasser. As with the defence of another person the force used must be reasonable. In *Collins* v. *Renison* (1754) Say. 138 Ryder CJ held that overturning a ladder on which the plaintiff was standing in order to eject him from the defendant's property was not justifiable. As the judge put it: 'the overturning of the ladder could not answer the purpose of removing the plaintiff out of the garden; since it only left him upon the ground at the bottom of the ladder, instead of being upon it.' It may be that these cases should now be considered as a special application of the principle of necessity (see below).

Necessity

In *F* v. *West Berkshire Health Authority* [1990] 2 AC 1 Lord Goff acknowledged that English law recognises a principle of necessity that 'may justify action which would otherwise be unlawful. . .' The cases on necessity, he said, could be conveniently divided into three different categories. First, there are cases of public necessity. A typical example of this category would be where a person pulls down another man's house in order to prevent the spread of a catastrophic fire. Second, there are cases of private necessity. Typically these occur where a person damages another's property or inflicts injury to another in order to save his own person or property. Finally, there is a series of cases concerned with action taken as a matter of necessity in order to assist another person without his consent. As an example of this category Lord Goff suggested the case of a man who forcibly seizes another to drag him from the path of an oncoming vehicle. As Fleming (1992) has pointed out, the defence of necessity involves 'more obviously than any [other] a hard choice between competing values and a sacrifice of one to the other' (p. 94). Its basis lies in a mixture of altruism, public protection and the maintenance of 'solid' social values. As a result, determining when it applies will be no easy task.

Most of the cases on public necessity are cases that justify trespass to land or to chattels and are, therefore, not compelling authority on the question whether public necessity justifies the infliction of a trespass to the person. In principle, however, there seems to be no reason why, given an appropriately strong case, it should not. For example, consider the case of a fire chief who, in attempting to prevent the spread of a fire to a hospital, orders that a burning house causing most danger to the hospital be pulled down. He knows that there are three people trapped in the house and that if he pulls down the house they will almost inevitably be killed. Would the inevitable killing of the three occupants in the house be justified by the saving of the patients? Can the taking of one or more lives ever be justified on the ground that it is neccesary to save others? It is suggested that, provided the fire chief's action was reasonable in all the circumstances, he should be able to rely on the defence of public necessity.

Yet, even if it is accepted that the fire chief's decision can be justified by necessity, it might be asked whether, in such a case, the 'community' should not have to make good the plaintiff's loss. It is surely wrong in principle to force one individual to suffer for public purposes without just compensation. Such a conclusion has been reached in a number of states in the USA. Thus, in *Wegner* v. *Milwaukee Mutual Insurance Co* (1991) 479 NW 2d 38 the Supreme Court of Minnesota held that damage done to the plaintiff's house by the police when attempting to arrest a suspect who had fled there was compensable. The court commented that, 'in situations where an innocent party's property is taken, damaged or destroyed by the police in the course of apprehending a suspect, [it] is for the *municipality* to compensate the innocent party for the resulting damages. The policy considerations in this case center around the most basic notions of fairness and justice . . . We do not believe that the imposition of [the whole] burden of the loss on the innocent citizens of this state would square with the underlying principles of justice.' (p. 48, *per* Tomljanovich J). While, an obligation to pay compensation binds the Crown when acting under its prerogative powers (see *Burmah Oil Co Ltd* v. *Lord Advocate* [1965] AC 75, it is doubtful whether in England the obligation to compensate extends any further.

As with public necessity, cases of private necessity justifying the infliction of harm are very rare. Most of the cases on private necessity concern trespass to land or chattels carried out to protect the defendant's own land or chattels. In principle, however, private necessity may justify a trespass to the person except that the circumstances in which the defence will succeed are likely to be more limited than for public necessity. The courts are less likely to be sympathetic to one who acts for wholly selfish reasons rather than for the benefit of the general public. For example, a person who pulls an innocent third party in front of him as a shield against an attack by another is extremely unlikely to be able to rely on necessity.

Finally, there are the cases where the defendant acts for the purpose of protecting the plaintiff's own health or property. As we have seen, any unconsented-to touching is prima facie, actionable. Yet in some cases respecting a patient's wishes may mean having to stand by and watch that person die. Does the principle of sanctity of life allow the patient's wishes to be overruled? It is beyond the scope of this book to consider this very difficult issue in any detail, but two situations are illustrative. First, if a prisoner determines to go on hunger strike and, in order to prevent his death, the prison authorities force-feed him, should they be able to rely on the defence of necessity if sued for battery? In *Leigh* v. *Gladstone* (1909) 26 TLR 139 Lord Alverstone CJ had directed a jury that prison officials had a duty to preserve the life and health of those in their custody, if necessary by force-feeding them. However, this view was rejected by Lord Keith in *Airedale NHS Trust* v. *Bland* (*supra*). His Lordship commented that, 'the principle of sanctity of life . . . is not an absolute one. It does not authorise force feeding of prisoners on hunger strike' (at 861; see also *Secretary of State for the Home Department* v. *Robb* [1995] 1 All ER 677, discussed by Kennedy, 1995. A second, more difficult case, involves the situation where a pregnant woman refuses a Caeserian operation for religious or other reasons (or even for no good reason). Without such an operation both she and the unborn child will undoubtedly die. Though this issue could arise in an action for battery brought after a 'forced' operation, the more usual way such a question would be considered would be by way of an application to the court for a declaration that such an operation was lawful. If such an application was made should a court grant the declaration? In a number of cases such a declaration has been granted though the exact basis on which intervention is justified has not been made clear (see, for example, *Re: S* [1992] 4 All ER 671). The different result reached in the two above-mentioned situations is by no means without difficulty. However, though there are formidable arguments against forcing treatment on a competent adult, it is submitted that intervention is justified in the type of case under discussion in order to save the life of the unborn child.

The defence of necessity may also have an important role to play in the case of treatment of incompetent (including unconscious) patients. In *F* v. *West Berkshire Health Authority* the House of Lords upheld a declaration made by a judge allowing the sterilisation of a mentally incompetent woman. Such treatment, although not consented to, could be justified on the principle of necessity. Lord Goff said that for the defence to succeed there must have been (a) a necessity to act in circumstances where it was not practicable to communicate with the assisted person and (b) the action taken must have been such as a reasonable person would in all the circumstances take, acting in the best interests of the assisted person. In determining what is in the best interests of the assisted person, Lord Goff said that in non-medical cases the test was that of the reasonable man. In medical cases, however, the principles set out in *Bolam* v. *Friern Hospital Management Committee* [1957] 2 All ER 118 should be applied. Provided a doctor acts in accordance with a responsible and competent body of medical opinion, he will not be liable.

Summary

16.1 The modern trepass to the person torts – assault, battery and false imprisonment – are derived from the ancient writ of trespass which provided a remedy for directly inflicted intentional interference with the person.

16.2 A cause of action will only lie in trespass where a person *intentionally* applies force directly to another. Where force is applied negligently the action is in negligence (cf. Diplock LJ in *Letang* v. *Cooper*).

16.3 Where a person intentionally and without the other's consent applies force directly to another, that is a battery. Where a person intentionally makes a threat that causes another reasonably to apprehend the immediate infliction of a battery on him, that is an assault. Directness is a requirement in both assault and battery. A touching will only amount to a battery where it falls outside the category of generally acceptable physical contacts. For there to be an assault some conduct is usually required to cause the plaintiff to apprehend the infliction of a battery.

16.4   The tort of false imprisonment is committed when the defendant intentionally and without lawful justification restrains a person's liberty within an area delimited by the defendant. The restraint must be total, though it is not necessary for a person to be locked up in a prison. A person may impose reasonable conditions on the manner in which an entrant leaves his premises. It is not necessary that the imprisoned person knows that he is imprisoned. A change in the conditions of a lawful imprisonment cannot render the imprisonment unlawful.

16.5   Where a person intentionally, but indirectly, inflicts physical harm on another, that person may be liable on the basis of the principle in *Wilkinson* v. *Downton*.

16.6   The trespass torts are actionable without proof of damage.

16.7   A number of defences that apply generally in the law of tort apply equally to trespass to the person. Thus, illegality and statutory authority are both defences to trespass to the person. The use of reasonable force in defending oneself, one's property or another person may also justify a trespass. Probably the most important defences in practice are the arrest powers contained in the Police and Criminal Evidence Act 1984, consent, self-defence and necessity.

Exercises

16.1   If A negligently touches B's breasts, does this give rise to an action in trespass? If A touched B's breast deliberately but honestly thought that all women liked being touched in that way, would he be liable to B?

16.2   Is Lord Denning MR's judgment in *Letang* v. *Cooper* preferable to that of Diplock LJ in the same case?

16.3   A persuades B, who is 16 years old, to pose naked for him. A tells B that he intends to use the photographs to try to win a prestigious art prize. In taking the photographs A touches B's leg to show him how to pose. A subsequently publishes the photographs in a pornographic magazine. Would B have any action against A? (cf. *Kaye* v. *Robertson* [1990] FSR 62.)

16.4   Was the infliction of harm in *DPP* v. *K* direct? Could the directness requirement safely be abandoned?

16.5   A took his gun to a field where his family grew hay. A large amount of hay was piled up and A fixed a target to it and began firing. A had no way of knowing that B was asleep in the haystack. B was seriously injured. Is A liable?

16.6   A was sitting up a tree taunting B. B shook the tree causing A to fall. A was seriously injured. Is B liable?

16.7   A points a purple water pistol at B, and B, wholly unreasonably, is terrified. Is this an assault?

16.8   A's house has been burgled several times. He hears noises in his garden and goes outside with his gun to investigate. In the darkness he sees two boys in the south side of his garden. Intending to frighten them he points the gun in a northerly direction and fires. Unfortunately, A hits B, one of the boy's friends, of whom A was wholly unaware. Is A liable to B?

16.9   In *Robinson* v. *Balmain New Ferry Co Ltd* would the result reached by the court have been different if instead of the vessel going on a short journey, it had been bound for America? What would the result have been if the defendant had demanded £5 from the plaintiff before he could exit? How long could the defendants in *Herd* v. *Weardale Coal and Coke Co Ltd* have left the plaintiff down the mine? Are these two cases reconcilable with *Sunbolf* v. *Alford* (1838) 3 M & W 247?

16.10 A is walking down a road when he hears a cry from a house. 'Let me out', the voice says. A does nothing. B, the person who had cried out, sued A as well as the person who originally imprisoned him. Is A liable to B?

16.11 A goes to his doctor for a blood test for glandular fever. Without A's consent the doctor tests the blood for the HIV virus. Would the doctor be able to rely on the defence of consent?

16.12 Are there any circumstances in which a doctor should be able to treat a competent person against their express wishes?

Interference with Land

17 Interference with Land: Introduction

17.1 **Property, Tort and Crime**

A number of torts can be seen as an adjunct to the law of real property. Speaking in broad terms, we can say that legal rules relating to interests in land may be grouped under three headings. First, there are rules that determine who has precisely what interest in land. Secondly, there are rules that serve to protect those various interests in land against interference. Thirdly, there are rules that govern the passing on of those interests to others, for instance by sale or by inheritance. Rules under the first and third headings are primarily the concern of books on land law; those under the second, however, are the preserve of the law of tort. The torts of trespass and nuisance, in particular, are the means by which those with interests in land prevent their enjoyment of those interests being eroded unlawfully. In performing this function, the torts of trespass and nuisance also add flesh to the skeleton furnished by land law's list of interests in land: where land law specifies who has what interest in land, tort law specifies what in practice those interests entitle one to do.

Trespass is concerned with 'direct' encroachments on land; nuisance with interference that is 'indirect'. If I step on your land without your permission or deliberately place something on it (e.g. my rubbish) that is a trespass, whereas if I pollute your land with noise, smells and fumes, or let things inadvertently escape from my land onto yours (as where my wall falls down through disrepair), that is a nuisance. 'Nuisance' is used here in a technical sense to denote the unreasonable interference with the use and enjoyment of another's land.

Sometimes this tort is called 'private nuisance' in order to distinguish it from 'public nuisance' which is a crime of ill-defined scope: the courts have the power to label any conduct that causes annoyance to a substantial portion of the community a 'public nuisance' (see Spencer, 1989). Public nuisances need not have any impact on the use and enjoyment of land. Examples have included making a telephone bomb hoax, selling food that was unfit for human consumption and holding an ill-organised pop festival. A public nuisance, though primarily a criminal offence, will give rise to a concurrent tortious liability where an individual suffers 'special damage' as a result of the conduct in question. In view of the nebulous nature of public nuisance, our discussion of it is confined to its most common manifestation: obstruction of the highway (see 18.6).

A third type of nuisance is 'statutory nuisance'. Statutory nuisances, like public nuisances, are criminal offences. Under the Environmental

Protection Act 1990, Part III, a number of activities that are harmful to the environment are listed as statutory nuisances, and the courts are empowered to order the cessation of those activities. The creation of these offences is a crucial prong of environmental policy. Unlike public nuisance, there is no rule that a person who suffers special damage as the result of a statutory nuisance may bring an action for damages in tort. The facts that give rise to a criminal liability for statutory nuisance may, however, give rise to an independent tortious liability for public or private nuisance if they satisfy the requirements of those causes of action.

17.2 Trespass, Nuisance and Negligence

As elsewhere in the law, the expansion of the tort of negligence has had an impact on the more established torts, particularly the tort of nuisance. Many claims which involve the competing rights and duties of neighbouring landowners, and which historically would therefore have been viewed as the concern of the law of nuisance, are today brought under negligence. This tendency was most noticeable in relation to liability for the acts of third parties and natural hazards on one's land (see 18.5). In both these areas, liability in nuisance was slow to develop and negligence, which was thought for a time to treat the foreseeability of harm to the plaintiff as the sole criterion of liability (see 3.2), seemed to offer plaintiffs better prospects of success. It is now clear that foreseeability is not enough to establish liability in negligence in such cases. There is no advantage to be gained from framing one's action in negligence rather than nuisance (see *Goldman* v. *Hargrave* [1967]) 1 AC 645). Nevertheless, the liability of landowners for the acts of third parties and natural hazards on their land is now an established part of the tort of negligence (see 6.4) and has substantiated what Markesinis (1989) views as negligence's 'unstoppable tendency to subsume under its heading the role of older nominate torts'.

The effect of the rise of negligence is not only that negligence is in practice tending to take over the role of nuisance: it is also the case that doctrines of nuisance law have been infused with the 'fault principle' which negligence embodies. Areas of nuisance law in which liabilities had been imposed irrespective of fault (e.g. under the rule in *Rylands* v. *Fletcher*; see Ch. 19) – or, conversely, in which liability did not arise however reprehensible the conduct in question – came to be regarded as anomalous. Consequently, the courts took every opportunity to enlarge the category of cases in which liability turned upon the reasonableness of what was done and to stress that liability should not be imposed without proof of fault (see 18.3). Some commentators have responded to these developments by arguing that, in reality, 'nuisance is a branch of the law of negligence' (Williams and Hepple, 1984, p. 124; see 18.8). Nevertheless, the primary remedy for a nuisance is an injunction and the tort may therefore be regarded as more forward-looking, and more concerned with regulating a continuing relationship, than can negligence whose concern is only to compensate a loss that has already occurred.

The tort of trespass to land also pursues a range of objectives quite distinct from the goal of compensation for losses incurred (indeed, it shares with other types of action in trespass the characteristic that it is actionable without proof of loss). Today, its chief practical significance is as a means of maintaining the privacy of one's home against unwanted intrusion and of settling boundary disputes with one's neighbours, purposes for which the tort of negligence is not suitable.

Summary

17.1 The torts of trespass to land and private nuisance provide protection against interference with the use and enjoyment of land. Trespass deals with 'direct' interferences, private nuisance with interferences that are indirect. Private nuisance should not be confused with public nuisance, a crime that may incidentally give rise to tortious liability if 'special damage' is suffered as a result. Public nuisances need not be connected with the use of land.

17.2 Notwithstanding the tendency of the tort of negligence to subsume the role of the older nominate torts, it appears that trespass and nuisance perform independent roles as means to vindicate interests in land against interference and to regulate the continuing relationship of neighbouring landowners.

---

18 Private Nuisance

18.1 The Nature of Private Nuisance

The tort of private nuisance is 'primarily concerned with conflict over competing uses of land' (Fleming, 1992, p. 409). It is remedied by the award of damages, or by the granting of an injunction, or both (see Ch. 23). That much is clear. The task of mapping out the precise contours of the tort, however, has frustrated the legal mind from the early days of the common law. Confusion has undoubtedly been caused by a failure clearly to distinguish private nuisance, with which we are concerned here, from public nuisance, the crime of ill-defined scope which may exceptionally give rise to liability in tort (see Ch. 17.1). But even considered on its own, in isolation from public nuisance, private nuisance suffers from a lack of doctrinal clarity. One of the most ancient actions in the law of tort, it retains hints of its history in the days of the forms of action and many pockets of caselaw falling under the general rubric 'nuisance' strike us today as anomalous; the tort has yet to be united under a coherent thread of general principle, albeit that steps have been taken towards this goal.

The classic definition of private nuisance is given in Winfield and Jolowicz, 1994, p. 404: 'Private nuisance may be described as unlawful interference with a person's use or enjoyment of land, or some right over, or in connection with it'.

This formulation gives rise to a number of questions:

(a) What rights and interests associated with the use and enjoyment of land are protected by the tort of nuisance?
(b) When will interference with those rights and interests be treated as unlawful?
(c) Whose rights and interests are protected (i.e. who can sue for a private nuisance)?
(d) Who can be held liable for the unlawful interference?
(e) What defences might be raised to an action in private nuisance?

We now consider these questions in turn.

18.2 Protected Rights and Interests

The tort of nuisance protects a variety of aspects of the use and enjoyment of land. As such, it may be regarded as a necessary complement to the law of real property. Whereas the law of real property deals with the creation and transfer of interests in land, the tort of nuisance provides a mechanism by which those interests may be protected. It performs this function in tandem with the tort of trespass to land. While trespass to land only protects against the direct invasion of the plaintiff's property, nuisance deals with indirect interference.

As a rough generalisation, we may say that the tort of nuisance protects three aspects of the use and enjoyment of land. First, it guards against indirect physical invasions of the plaintiff's land. (Remember that direct invasions are dealt with as trespasses.) A simple example would be where branches from the defendant's tree overhang the plaintiff's land (see *Smith* v. *Giddy* [1904] 2 KB 448). Secondly, it provides a remedy in cases of physical damage on the plaintiff's land (even in the absence of physical intrusion), e.g. where a cistern is dislodged by vibrations from the defendant's electricity generator next door (see *Malone* v. *Laskey* [1907] 2 KB 141, considered below at 18.4). Lastly, it safeguards the plaintiff's so-called 'amenity interests'. The nature of such interests calls for further elaboration.

Interference with the use and enjoyment of land can take many forms and need not involve any physical invasion or physical damage. Owners and occupiers of land may suffer personal discomfort and inconvenience in various other ways in respect of which the tort of nuisance offers a remedy. The law thereby enables landowners to enjoy the amenities associated with their ownership of land. It has long recognised liability for interference with the enjoyment of land by smell (see *Wheeler* v. *JJ Saunders Ltd*, below at 18.3) and by noise (see *Kennaway* v. *Thompson* [1981] QB 88). But it cannot be assumed that all aspects of the use or enjoyment of land are capable of protection in the tort of private nuisance.

According to a celebrated dictum of Wray CJ, no action lies for blocking a pleasant view or prospect because 'the law does not give an action for such things of delight' (*Bland* v. *Moseley*, 1587, unreported). Although it has been suggested that this justification is 'more quaint than satisfactory' (*Dalton* v. *Angus* (1881) 6 App Cas 740, 824, per Lord Blackburn), the rule remains in the modern law. Its more convincing rationale is that to treat loss of prospect as a nuisance would unduly inhibit the construction of new buildings; indeed, as '[a] right of prospect . . . would impose a burthen on a very large and indefinite area' (ibid.), it could be used to frustrate all large-scale property development. As Lord Hardwicke LC famously remarked in response to a submission that English law recognised a right of prospect, 'Was that the case, there could be no great towns' (*AG* v. *Doughty* (1752) 2 Ves Sen 454).

Wray CJ's dictum that the law recognises no action in respect of 'things of delight' may be thought, despite the doubts expressed above, accurately to express the law's unwillingness to protect the merely recreational aspects of the use or enjoyment of land (at least in cases where there is no damage or physical intrusion). In *Bridlington Relay* v. *Yorkshire Electricity Board* [1965] Ch. 436, Buckley J noted that he had been referred to no case in which interference with a purely recreational facility had been treated as a nuisance. In his view, '[c]onsiderations of health and physical comfort and well being appear to me to be on a somewhat different level from recreational considerations' (p. 447). Nevertheless, he declined to hold that interference with purely recreational facilities and activities could never amount to a nuisance.

The law's reluctance to protect purely recreational interests is evident in the cases which consider whether interference with a television signal can constitute an actionable nuisance. In the *Bridlington Relay* case, Buckley J treated domestic television viewing as an almost entirely recreational matter, notwithstanding the educational or political content of some programmes, and held that it could not be regarded as so important a part of an ordinary householder's enjoyment of property that its disruption would amount to a nuisance (nor a fortiori would the commercial relaying of television signals). But this decision was given only qualified support by the House of Lords in *Hunter* v. *Canary Wharf Ltd* [1997] 1 All ER 426. Their Lordships were required to rule whether damages could be obtained in nuisance for interference with domestic television viewing caused by the construction of the tower at Canary Wharf (currently the UK's tallest building). They held that where, as here, the interference resulted from the presence of a 'tall and bulky' building or other physical obstruction there could be no private nuisance. The court was impressed by an analogy with the cases on 'loss of prospect': the same concern lest construction work be unduly inhibited arose where it was alleged that television interference was caused by the erection of a building in the line of sight between a television transmitter and the land affected. The court, however, reserved its opinion on the question whether interference caused *mechanically* or *electrically*, as in the *Bridlington Relay* case, could ever amount to a nuisance. (It should be noted that a Canadian court has declined to accept the *Bridlington Relay* principle: *Nor-Video Services Ltd* v. *Ontario Hydro* (1978) 84 DLR 3d 221).

Does the tort of private nuisance protect interests in privacy by recognising a right to be let alone within the boundaries of one's own property? Although *entry* into property is actionable as trespass, violation of the right to seclusion can take other forms, e.g. the surveillance of property with electronic devices or the publication of photographs taken with the aid of powerful zoom lenses. An official report by Sir David Calcutt QC (1993) has recently recommended the creation of a statutory liability for harm caused by such means, but the government has at present no plans to implement the proposal (see further 20.1). It may be, however, that the tort of nuisance can be developed to provide some protection. Admittedly, it is well established that it is not a nuisance to erect a building that gives a view of the hitherto unobservable activities of a neighbour (see *Browne* v. *Flower* [1911] 1 Ch. 219). But more recently Griffiths J has suggested that the harassment of constant surveillance of the plaintiff's house from the air, accompanied by the photographing of his every activity, might well constitute a nuisance (see *Lord Bernstein of Leigh* v. *Skyviews and General Ltd* [1978] QB 479; as this case involved a single incident, it could not give rise to liability). Furthermore, the Court of Appeal has recently held that the disturbance caused by a telephone pest is actionable in nuisance (see *Khorasandjian* v. *Bush* [1993] QB 727). However, the effectiveness of the remedy in nuisance as a means of protecting the interest in privacy is limited by the requirement that the person bringing the action must have an interest in the land affected (see 18.4).

Finally, it appears that the law of nuisance recognises a right to be free from distress or alarm caused by activities on neighbouring land. Liability may arise not only where distress or alarm arises from actual physical interference with the ordinary amenities of land ownership, e.g. where distress is caused by the impingement upon the senses of unpleasant smells or loud noises (see above), but also where the physical harm is only prospective, e.g. where alarm is generated by the reasonable fear of contagion (see *Metropolitan Asylum District* v. *Hill* (1881) 6 App Cas 193). Additionally, it seems that the law also provides protection against activities that cause purely mental distress or alarm. In *Thompson-Schwab* v. *Costaki* [1956] 1 WLR 335, the plaintiffs complained of the defendants' use of a neighbouring townhouse as a brothel. They alleged that the defendants, both prostitutes, used the house as a so-called 'resort' to which they would return with customers whom they had attracted from nearby streets. The house, although not far distant from streets with an unsavoury reputation, was in a good-class residential street. The Court of Appeal upheld the award of an interlocutory injunction pending full trial of the matter. It provisionally rejected the submission that a nuisance must affect the reasonable enjoyment of premises in a physical way and held that the perambulations of the prostitutes, and their use of the building as a brothel, constituted a prima facie private nuisance even if it could not be shown to be criminal. One could well imagine, declared Romer LJ, the effect of that activity on the minds of young people in the plaintiff households, to say nothing of the feelings of visitors. It is submitted that, while mere upset should not give rise to liability in nuisance, a response of righteous outrage might well indicate an interference with the reasonable enjoyment of premises.

18.3 Unlawful Interference

The rights and interests recognised by the tort of private nuisance are only protected against *unlawful* interference. The question of when interference with the use and enjoyment of land becomes unlawful is much disputed. Confusion has arisen from a tension between the apparent tendency of early common lawyers to lay down rights and duties in black-and-white terms and the modern urge to infuse all areas of the law of tort with the concept of reasonableness.

The early common lawyers seemed little concerned with notions of reasonableness and fault. Their maxim was 'sic utere tuo ut alienum non laedas' (use your property in such a way that you do not injure anybody else's). The rule was expressed in absolute terms, apparently leaving no room for a defence that the defendant had acted reasonably. Since at least the nineteenth century, however, there has been an increasing tendency to employ a reasonableness formula to balance the competing rights and interests of plaintiff and defendant. The picture today is something of a mess. Pockets of strict liability remain (see, e.g., *Wringe* v. *Cohen* [1940] 1 KB 229; see 18.6), as do instances of cases in which a person has an absolute and unqualified right to interfere with a neighbour's use and enjoyment of land and in which, therefore, there can be no liability in any circumstances (see, e.g., *Mayor of Bradford* v. *Pickles* [1895] AC 587). Many of these pockets concern what land lawyers know as 'natural rights' and easements; so-called 'water rights' and 'rights of support' are among the most important in practice (for more detailed discussion, see the first edition of this work at pp. 178–81). Such anomalies have, however, been greatly reduced in number over the course of time and the concept of reasonableness has emerged as the central pillar of the modern law of nuisance; in the modern law of nuisance, unlawfulness tends to be equated with unreasonableness.

A notable example of this trend relates to interference with the use or enjoyment of land caused by the forces of nature. For centuries, the courts denied that liability could arise where a landowner failed to prevent land in its natural condition, or wild animals on it, causing damage to neighbouring property. Thus in *Giles* v. *Walker* (1890) 24 QBD 656 it was held that it was no nuisance if thistle seeds were blown from A's land to B's, where they took root and did damage. Lord Coleridge brusquely dismissed the claim with the words: 'I have never heard of such an action as this' (p. 657). Times, however, have changed and the rise of the concept of reasonableness has made the courts more willing to impose liability for 'natural nuisances' that landowners might reasonably be expected to prevent. In *Leakey* v. *National Trust* [1980] QB 485, the Court of Appeal accepted this principle for the first time and held the owner of hill-top land liable when rocks and other debris fell naturally onto property below (see 18.5). It is disputed whether the earlier caselaw justified the court in *Leakey* in adopting a general rule of liability for natural nuisances (see Wedderburn, 1978); nevertheless it is undeniable that the tendency of the law – exemplified by *Leakey* – has been to discard the old classifications of specific rights and duties relating to the use of land, expressed in absolute terms, and to increase the role played by the standard of reasonableness.

Whereas in the tort of negligence the question of reasonableness surfaces in enquiring whether the defendant exercised reasonable care, in nuisance we ask whether there was *unreasonable interference* with the *plaintiff's* use and enjoyment of land, or alternatively whether the *defendant* was engaged in an *unreasonable use or uses* of land. However the issue is stated, the matters for consideration are essentially the same. The tort of nuisance applies 'a rule of give and take, live and let live' (*Bamford* v. *Turnley* [1860] 3 B&S 62, 84 per Bramwell B) and seeks 'the balance of convenience and inconvenience' as between the competing rights and interests of the two parties to the action (*Dalton* v. *Henry Angus & Co* [1881] 6 App Cas 740, 824 per Lord Blackburn). Although there is no limit to the circumstances which may be taken into account in determining whether there has been an unreasonable interference or user, the following factors have attracted particular attention and warrant separate treatment.

The Extent of the Interference

The more intrusive and longlasting the interference, the more likely it is to be considered a nuisance. Physical damage is a graver form of injury than mere personal discomfort, and some commentators go so far as to deny that the reasonableness of the defendant's user of land can never excuse physical damage of the plaintiff (see, e.g., Spencer, 1987). But private nuisance ought not to be treated as if it were divided into two torts, one dealing with physical damage and the other with personal discomfort (see *Hunter* v. *Canary Wharf Ltd* [1997] 2 All ER 426, 451 per Lord Hoffman), and the distinction between physical damage (and physical invasion), on the one hand, and personal discomfort, on the other, is best seen as one only of degree. Interference which results in physical damage is more likely to be regarded as unreasonable than that which causes mere discomfort, but ultimately everything should turn on a flexible application of the reasonableness test (see Salmond & Heuston, 1996, p. 57; cf. 'locality', below).

Nuisance's rule of give and take, live and let live assumes particular importance where the complaint is of personal discomfort or inconvenience. As a certain amount of noise and smell, for instance, must be tolerated as part of everyday life, the discomfort which the plaintiff alleges must be substantial. The question to ask – according to the much-quoted formula of Knight Bruce VC in *Walter* v. *Selfe* (1851) 4 De G & Sm 315, 322 – is:

'Ought this inconvenience to be considered in fact as more than fanciful, more than one of delicacy or fastidiousness, as an inconvenience materially interfering with the ordinary physical comfort of human existence, but according to plain and sober and simple notions among the English people?'

Often the duration of the interference will be a material factor. Many nuisances involve intrusions that continue for a significant period of time, but this is not to say that an isolated incident cannot give rise to a cause of action. Nevertheless, where the plaintiff complains of a single occurrence, it is necessary to demonstrate that the incident was attributable to a continuing state of affairs on the defendant's land (see *British Celanese Ltd* v. *AH Hunt Ltd* [1969] 1 WLR 959).

Locality

In *Sturges* v. *Bridgman* (1879) 11 Ch. D. 852, 856 Thesiger LJ famously remarked: 'What would be a nuisance in Belgrave Square would not necessarily be so in Bermondsey.' The point he was making is that the reasonableness of any use to which land is put will depend on, among other things, the character of the neighbourhood the land lies in ('the locality'): factories billowing out smoke might be all right in an industrial estate but not in an idyllic rural village.

This 'locality principle' applies only to cases of personal discomfort, not to cases of property damage. This was decided by the House of Lords in *St Helens Smelting Co* v. *Tipping* (1865) 11 HLC 642. In that case, noxious vapours from the defendant's smelting works damaged trees and shrubs on the plaintiff's land. The defendant alleged that, as almost the whole neighbourhood was devoted to copper smelting or similar manufacturing activities, those activities could be continued with impunity. Lord Westbury LC dismissed this argument. In his view, it was necessary to distinguish two types of case, the first being where the nuisance produces what he refers to as 'material injury to property' or 'sensible injury to the value of the property', and the second being where it merely produces 'personal discomfort.' Locality was relevant only in relation to the latter: 'If a man lives in a street where there are numerous shops, and a shop is opened next door to him . . . he has no ground for complaint, because to him individually there might arise much discomfort from the trade carried on in that shop' (p. 650). In relation to the former, however, locality was of no significance. It followed that the injury to the plaintiff's trees and shrubs in the case before him gave rise to a cause of action in nuisance, irrespective of whether the pollution from the defendant's works was exceptional for the locality.

Lord Westbury's ruling has been criticised on a number of grounds. First of all, the precise meaning of what he says is obscure. He talks of 'sensible injury to the value of property' and distinguishes this from 'personal discomfort', yet if land becomes uncomfortable to live on then its value will surely be diminished. Perhaps it is best to assume that Lord Westbury merely intended to draw a line between cases of physical damage and those of intangible loss. A more substantial criticism is that the apparently rigid distinction between material damage to property and mere personal discomfort prevents a flexible application of the standard of reasonableness and might produce arbitrary or undesirable results; where, for example, the parties live on an isolated mountainside on which rock falls are regular, it might be appropriate to expect landowners to put up with a certain amount of damage caused by falls from land higher up the mountain (see Buckley, 1996, pp. 9–10).

The character of a locality may be changed very rapidly by large-scale property development; where this is carried out lawfully, with the relevant planning permission, the reasonableness of any interference with the use or enjoyment of land will be assessed in the light of the neighbourhood's new character. Planning permission does not, however, act as a defence analogous to that of statutory authority (see 18.6) In *Gillingham Borough Council* v. *Medway (Chatham) Dock Co Ltd* [1993] QB 343, local residents complained of disturbance arising from traffic passing to and from the defendants' dockyard. The local council sought an injunction under the Local Government Act 1972, s. 222, to stop what it alleged was a public nuisance arising out of the private nuisance suffered by the local residents. Ironically, the council had, some nine years previously, granted planning permission to the defendants to develop a port at the site of the dockyard, even though it was fully informed as to the likely disturbance to local residents. (It seems that the council's legal action was motivated by a desire to avoid the payment of compensation for revocation of the permission.) Buckley J denied that planning permission acted as a defence in the same way as statutory authorisation but held that 'where planning consent is given for a development or change of use, the question of nuisance will thereafter fall to be decided by reference to a neighbourhood with that development or use and not as it was previously' (p. 361).

It must be noted, however, that not every grant of planning permission will serve to alter the character of a neighbourhood. In *Wheeler* v. *JJ Saunders Ltd* [1996] Ch 19, the Court of Appeal upheld that decision of Buckley J in the *Gillingham* case but distinguished it from the case at hand. Granting permission for a project on the scale of a commercial dockyard, as in the *Gillingham* case, might indeed effect a change in the character of the neighbourhood, but this would not be the case where the development was small-scale and involved merely an increase in the levels of an existing activity rather than a wholly new use. Thus, where, as in *Wheeler*, the defendants had merely been given permission to erect additional buildings to continue their pig rearing business, this could not be said to have effected a change in the character of the locality. It did not allow the defendants to create a fouler stench than that permitted before the grant of the planning permission.

Hypersensitive Activities

In the words of Lord Robertson, 'A man cannot increase the liabilities of his neighbour by applying his own property to special uses, whether for business or pleasure' (*Eastern and South African Telegraph Co* v. *Cape Town Tramways* [1902] AC 381, 393). It follows that one cannot complain about interference with abnormally sensitive activities where ordinary activities would not be affected, albeit that, where there is unreasonable interference with the ordinary use of land, this will justify liability even to an abnormally sensitive user (see *McKinnon Industries Ltd* v. *Walker* [1951] 3 DLR 577). The rule was applied by Buckley J in *Bridlington Relay Ltd* v. *Yorkshire Electricity Board* [1965] Ch. 436 in deciding that interference with the signals received by a television broadcast relay station, caused by a nearby electricity power line, did not amount to a nuisance. The judge pointed to the abnormal nature of the plaintiff's business which, if it were to prosper, required an exceptional degree of immunity from interference. This was not a case of interference with ordinary domestic television reception. (As an alternative, he was prepared to rule that television reception was not so important a part of the ordinary enjoyment of land that it should be protected at all: see 18.2.)

An exception is made to this rule where the plaintiff complains of interference by something which is inherently noxious. In *Cooke* v. *Forbes* (1867) LR 5 Eq 166, the plaintiff was in the business of making coconut matting which was hung out to dry after it had been bleached. He alleged that emissions of hydrogen sulphide from the defendant's premises dulled the colours of the matting, requiring it to be dyed again at considerable expense. The court disregarded the fact that the matting required such unusually delicate handling that the fumes might impair its value and concluded that the defendant was liable in nuisance. The later case of *Robinson* v. *Kilvert* (1889) 41 Ch D 88, however, makes it clear that the crucial factor in that case was the noxious nature of the interference; in other cases, the hypersensitivity of the plaintiff's activities would be a good defence. The plaintiff kept stocks of brown paper which he sought to sell at a profit; the defendant occupied the premises below in which he made paper boxes, for which he required heat and dry air. The heat passed into the plaintiff's premises and dried out his paper, causing it to lose weight; as the paper was sold by weight, the plaintiff suffered a loss of profit. The Court of Appeal viewed the plaintiff's business as exceptionally sensitive, for ordinary paper would not have dried out in the same way. Accordingly his action failed. *Cooke* was distinguished on the grounds that the hydrogen sulphide emitted from the defendant's premises was 'inherently noxious': this made the hypersensitivity of the plaintiff's activity irrelevant. (Note also that interference with a hypersensitive use of land may also give rise to liability where the defendant acts with 'malice': see *Hollywood Silver Fox Farm* v. *Emmett* [1936] 2 KB 468, below.)

Fault

In the modern law of private nuisance, 'fault of some kind is almost always necessary' in order to establish liability (*The Wagon Mound (No. 2)* [1967] 1 AC 617, 639 per Lord Reid; it appears that his Lordship inserted the word 'almost' to take account of the exceptional instances of strict liability, e.g. in cases involving natural rights and dangers adjacent to the highway). For this reason, nuisance adopts the same rule of remoteness as applies in negligence and the defendant is only liable for the foreseeable consequences of her unreasonable use of land (ibid). In nuisance, 'fault' need not involve the element of carelessness alleged in most negligence actions; more often, the defendant's user of land is deliberately continued in full knowledge of the plaintiff's objections to it, and the question for the court is whether the 'balance of convenience and inconvenience' favours the former or the latter. Nevertheless it seems to be legitimate to ascribe fault to the deliberate continuation of an interference which the law regards as unreasonable.

'[I]f the user [sc. of land] is not reasonable, the defendant will be liable, even though he may have exercised reasonable care and skill to avoid it' (*Cambridge Water Co Ltd* v. *Eastern Counties Leather plc* [1994] 2 AC 264, 299 per Lord Goff). In such cases, the defendant's fault consists simply in pursuing a user of land that should not in the circumstances be pursued at all (or pursued at the same level of intensity). This is not to say that the exercise of reasonable care is irrelevant to an action in nuisance, for an activity carried out carelessly may give rise to liability when none would arise if due care had been employed. The principal was clearly stated by Vaughan Williams J in the context of disturbance caused by demolition work (*Harrison* v. *Southwark and Vauxhall Water Co* [1891] 2 Ch 409, 413–4):

'[A] man who pulls down his house for the purpose of building a new one no doubt causes considerable inconvenience to his next door neighbour during the process of demolition; but he is not responsible as for a nuisance if he uses all reasonable skill and care to avoid annoyance to his neighbour by the works of demolition. Nor is he liable to an action, even though the noise and dust and the consequent annoyance be such as would constitute a nuisance if the same had been created in sheer wantonnesss.'

If the defendant's wanton or thoughtlessly inconsiderate behaviour makes it hard to justify her disturbance of the plaintiff, her case is even weaker if she acts maliciously out of a desire to harm the plaintiff. This is made plain by *Christie* v. *Davey* [1893] 1 Ch. 316. The plaintiffs' was a musical family. Mrs Christie and her daughter were music teachers; her son was a cellist. Mr Christie seems not to have been a musician and, as the judge remarked dryly, 'perhaps fortunately for himself is very deaf'. The defendant, who occupied the adjoining house, was disturbed by the noise, particularly of singing which he claimed was hard to distinguish from the howling of a dog. He wrote to the Christies in protest (this entertaining correspondence is well worth reading in the law report), but his complaints were ignored. In retaliation, he decided to pursue his own brand of musical studies. Whenever he heard the sound of music coming from the Christies' house, he would begin to bang on the wall, beat on trays and blow a whistle. North J found that this behaviour constituted a nuisance on account of the fact that the defendant had acted maliciously, for the purpose of annoying the Christies. The judge contrasted the noise made by the latter: their music-making had been a legitimate use of their house.

Mayor of Bradford v. *Pickles* [1895] AC 587 is a case that has given rise to controversy in this area. The source of the problem is a dictum of Lord Halsbury LC that 'Motives and intentions . . . seem to me to be absolutely irrelevant' (p. 594). This should not be taken as laying down a rule for the law of nuisance as a whole; indeed, Lord Halsbury expressly limited it to cases of the same type as that before him. The case arose out of the defendant's action in draining his land. This threatened to diminish the supply of water available for the domestic use of the inhabitants of Bradford, for a proportion of this supply was drawn from water that percolated under the defendant's land. The plaintiffs alleged that the defendant had acted maliciously, as his intention was to get the city to pay for the water. This motive was rightly held to be irrelevant, for this was a case involving 'natural rights', more specifically 'water rights', and it was well established that a landowner has an absolute natural right to abstract water percolating under his land no matter how unreasonable his behaviour appears to others. The decision dealt with one of the anomalous pockets of nuisance law in which the test of reasonable user or interference has no application (see above). This was acknowledged in *Hollywood Silver Fox Farm* v. *Emmett* [1936] 2 KB 468. In that case, the defendant threatened to fire his gun during the fox breeding season – saying

'I guarantee you will not raise a single cub' – if the farm continued to advertise its breeding activities which the defendant feared would put off potential purchasers of his land. When the farm refused to comply, the defendant carried out his threat with the result that some vixens ate their cubs and others did not mate at all. McNaughten J held that the defendant's malice made the disturbance actionable as a nuisance, rejecting the contention that *Mayor of Bradford* v. *Pickles* had any bearing on cases such as that before him; it was not applicable to cases in which unreasonable user or interference was the test of unlawfulness.

18.4 Who Can Sue?

In order to complain of a private nuisance, it is necessary to show an interest in the land affected by the defendant's unreasonable user. This rule, propounded in the leading case of *Malone* v. *Laskey* [1907] 2 KB 141, was recently put in question by the Court of Appeal but has been affirmed by the decision of the House of Lords in *Hunter* v. *Canary Wharf Ltd* [1997] 2 All ER 426. In *Malone* v. *Laskey*, the plaintiff lived in a house belonging to her husband's employer; she herself had no interest in the property. While she was making use of the lavatory, the cistern was dislodged by vibrations from the defendant's electricity generator next door and fell on top of her. The Court of Appeal held she could not sue in nuisance in respect of her personal injuries as she lacked any interest in land (neither could her husband sue in lieu).

Two recent decisions of the Court of Appeal declined, however, to recognise the 'interest in land' requirement advanced in *Malone*. In *Khorasandjian* v. *Bush* [1993] QB 727, Dillon LJ (with whom Rose LJ agreed; Peter Gibson J dissented) stated:

'To my mind, it is ridiculous if in this present age the law is that the making of deliberately harassing and pestering telephone calls to a person is only actionable in the civil courts if the recipient of the calls happens to have the freehold or a leasehold propriety interest in the premises in which he or she has received the calls. . . The court has at times to reconsider earlier decisions in the light of changed social circumstances. . . If the wife of an owner is entitled to sue in respect of harassing telephone calls, then I do not see why that should not also apply to a child living at home with her parents.'

This bold decision was subsequently followed by a differently constituted Court of Appeal in *Hunter* v. *Canary Wharf Ltd* [1996] 1 All ER 482, where Pill LJ (who gave the principal judgment) submitted that it was enough that the plaintiff could demonstrate a 'substantial link' with the property in question; the occupation of property as a home was therefore sufficient to enable the occupier to sue in private nuisance.

This decision was reversed by the House of Lords. Their Lordships (Lord Cooke dissenting) insisted that nuisance was 'a tort against land'

(p. 452, per Lord Hoffman), i.e. 'a tort directed against the plaintiff's enjoyment of his rights over land' (p. 435, per Lord Goff); an action might therefore be brought by the owner or tenant of the land affected, or even by a person who enjoyed exclusive possession of the land (approving *Foster* v. *Warblington UDC* [1906] 1 KB 648), but not by a licensee without exclusive possession. To recognise the latter's right to sue would be to effect a fundamental change in the nature and scope of the tort of nuisance and would give rise to practical difficulties. In the first place, the category of those enjoying a substantial link with the land was 'not easily identifiable' (p. 439, per Lord Goff): would it extend to a lodger or an au pair, and would it apply to workplaces as well as residences? Secondly, the efficacy of voluntary arrangements by which potential conflicts between neighbouring landowners might be avoided would be threatened, because it might be impracticable to reach agreement with every person whose occupation of the property was substantial (ibid; it might be added that there would be a real danger of a conflict of interests as between the occupants of the same property). Lastly, the extension of nuisance that was countenanced would transform it into a tort to the person and render redundant the sensible restrictions on the right to sue for personal injury that were imposed in the tort of negligence, e.g. by allowing liability for mere discomfort without damage (ibid). Their Lordships therefore preferred to overrule *Khorasandjian* v. *Bush* in so far as it held that a mere licensee could sue in private nuisance (it retains authority as a case on intentional harassment under the principle in *Wilkinson* v. *Downton*: see 16.5).

18.5 Who Can Be Liable?

Those whose activities cause unlawful interference with another's use or enjoyment of land will be liable in nuisance. For these purposes, the activities of an occupier of land include not only those carried out personally or by employees, but also those carried out by independent contractors, at least where the activities involve 'a special danger of nuisance' (*Matania* v. *National Provincial Bank* [1936] 2 All ER 633). This represents an exception to the normal rule of vicarious liability, which requires proof of a contract of employment before responsibility will arise (see Ch. 21). In *Matania*, the defendants employed independent contractors to make extensive alterations to their flat. The plaintiff's flat underneath was affected by dust and noise which gave rise to an actionable nuisance. The defendants were held liable for the actions of the contractors, whose activities were found to involve a special danger of nuisance, it being inevitable that the noise and dust would interfere with the plaintiff unless precautions were taken.

The liability on those who 'create' a nuisance extends beyond those in occupation of land themselves, however, and covers those who create nuisances while on somebody else's land or even on the public highway. Although doubts have been expressed on the latter score (see *Esso*

Petroleum Ltd v. *Southport Corporation* [1954] 2 QB 182, 204 (Devlin J), [1956] AC 218, 242 (Lord Radcliffe)) most of the authorities assume that a nuisance need not emanate from private land. Thus it has been held that striking workers mounting a picket in the road outside a factory may be liable in private nuisance (*Thomas* v. *NUM (South Wales Area)* [1986] Ch 20), as may the owners of an oil refinery in relation to the noise of lorries approaching and leaving the refinery on a road running by the plaintiff's house (*Halsey* v. *Esso Petroleum* [1961] 1 WLR 683).

An occupier of land may be liable for interference caused by trespassers and natural hazards on her land as well as for interference caused by her own activities (or those of her employees and independent contractors). In the idiosyncratic language of the tort of nuisance, she may face liability not merely for a nuisance she 'creates', but also for one that she 'adopts' or 'continues'. She adopts a nuisance if she makes any use of the thing that constitutes the nuisance; she continues it if she allows it to remain after she knew, or ought to have known, of its existence and when she could easily have put an end to it.

The leading case on liability in nuisance for the acts of a third party is *Sedleigh-Denfield* v. *O'Callaghan* [1940] AC 880. The defendants owned property on which they located a religious commune. The plaintiff owned the adjoining property. At the boundary between the two properties, there was a ditch which belonged to the defendant. Local authority workers laid a drainage pipe in the ditch, in so doing trespassing on the defendants' land which they had no permission to enter. The workers neglected to place a grid at the mouth of the pipe to keep it clear of refuse. All these activities were observed by the defendants' representative at the commune, Brother Dekker. Some three years later, after a heavy rainstorm, the pipe had become so obstructed with refuse that rainwater overflowed from the ditch and flooded the plaintiff's land. The House of Lords held the defendants liable for they had both continued and adopted the nuisance, either of which alone would have been sufficient to make them liable. Viscount Maugham explained the application of the principles to the facts of the case (p. 895):

'After the lapse of nearly three years, they must be taken to have suffered the nuisance to continue, for they neglected to take the very simple step of placing a grid in the proper place, which would have removed the danger to their neighbour's land. They adopted the nuisance, for they continued during all that time to use the artificial contrivance of the conduit for the purpose of getting rid of water from their property without taking the proper means for rendering it safe.'

For some time after this case, it was questioned whether the same duty of positive action on the part of an occupier of land might arise in the context of natural hazards rather than the acts of trespassers. Such a duty was finally recognised to be part of English law in the case of *Leakey* v. *National Trust* [1980] QB 485. The natural hazard in that case was debris in the form of rocks, soil, tree roots and the like that fell from the steep banks of a hill owned by the National Trust, Burrow Mump in Somerset, onto the plaintiff's property below. The falls threatened to damage houses on that property. The Court of Appeal held that a nuisance had been established. Megaw LJ, who delivered the leading judgment, said that it would be a grievous blot on the law if such a duty were not recognised. He countered fears that this might result in injustice where those affected by the hazard were much wealthier than those on whose land it arose by saying that the scope of the duty imposed on the latter was limited. In contrast to the objective standard of care generally imposed in the tort of negligence (see 8.2), the standard proposed by Megaw LJ was that of what the particular occupier could be expected to do. Where physical effort was required to avert an immediate danger, the standard would reflect the occupier's age and physical condition; where the expenditure of money was required, it would reflect her means. Megaw LJ even went so far as to suggest that the duty on the defendant might depend upon what it was reasonable to expect the plaintiff to do to protect herself, for instance by erecting a barrier on her own land or by paying for repairs on the defendant's. It is possible that the same rule limiting the scope of an occupier's duty of positive action will apply whether cases like *Leakey* are argued in nuisance or, as they might very well be, in negligence. This at least was the view of Lord Goff who, in *Smith* v. *Littlewoods Organisation Ltd* [1987] AC 241 doubted whether there could be any material difference between what was required of the occupier in nuisance and what was required in negligence.

The position of landlords merits separate attention as they may be held liable for nuisances arising on premises they have let out even though they neither occupied those premises nor created the nuisance. Such liability will arise where they let out the premises (a) with the knowledge that the tenant will create a nuisance, as in *Tetley* v. *Chitty* [1986] 1 All ER 663 in which a local authority let land for the specific purpose of go-karting which was inevitably going to disturb local residents; or (b) with the knowledge that a nuisance already existed at the date of the lease; or (c) retaining the right to enter and repair the premises if a nuisance arises. With regard to the last category of case, an additional claim is now possible under s. 4 of the Defective Premises Act 1972, which requires landlords who have a right to repair to take reasonable care to ensure that those who might be affected by defects in the state of the premises, whether on or off the premises, are reasonably safe. This makes the liability at common law largely redundant except in so far as *Wringe* v. *Cohen* (see 18.7) imposes a stricter duty in respect of artificial structures on the highway.

18.6 Defences

Prescription

No liability arises if the defendant has acquired a prescriptive right to commit a nuisance after having done so without objection from the plaintiff for a period of 20 years. This only applies to interferences which can develop into easements. It is possible to acquire an easement to discharge rainwater from your eaves onto your neighbour's land, or to send smoke through flues in a party wall, but it is doubtful whether the right to disturb your neighbour by smell or noise can be acquired as an easement (see Clerk and Lindsell, 1995, para. 18–113).

Statutory Authority

No liability will arise if the defendant is empowered by statute to carry out a certain activity of which the unavoidable consequence is interference with the plaintiff's use and enjoyment of land. Such interference is regarded as impliedly authorised even if it is not expressly permitted. In *London, Brighton and South Coast Railway* v. *Truman* (1886) 11 AC 45, a railway company was empowered to purchase station yards to accommodate cattle that were to be carried by rail. When it did so, occupiers of nearby houses complained of the noise of the cattle and drovers. The House of Lords held that a yard such as the defendants' had inevitably and of necessity to be located close to stations which in turn had to be located close to centres of population; in consequence, the yard would have been a nuisance wherever located and Parliament must have been taken to authorise that nuisance. Planning permission does not act as statutory authority, although it may prevent liability in nuisance arising by changing the character of the locality in question (*Wheeler* v. *JJ Saunders Ltd* [1996] Ch 19; see 18.3).

The policy behind the defence was described by Lord Roskill in *Allen* v. *Gulf Oil Refining* [1981] AC 1001 in the following terms (p. 1023):

> 'The underlying philosophy plainly is that the greater public interest arising from the construction and use of undertakings such as railways must take precedence over the private rights of owners and occupiers of neighbouring lands not to have their common law rights infringed by what would otherwise be an actionable nuisance. In short, the lesser private rights must yield to the greater public interest.'

In that case, the plaintiffs urged that, although Gulf Oil had been authorised to build a refinery on land acquired by compulsory purchase, the relevant statute said nothing about putting the refinery to use and, if it could not be operated without unreasonable disturbance of neighbouring landowners, then it should not be operated at all. Lord Diplock responded wryly: 'Parliament can hardly be supposed to have intended the refinery to be nothing more than a visual adornment to the landscape in an area of natural beauty. Clearly the intention of Parliament was that the refinery was to be operated as such' (p. 1014). Nevertheless, the House of Lords agreed that it was still open to the plaintiff landowners to prove that the interference caused by Gulf Oil's refinery was in excess of that which was the inevitable consequence of the operation of any refinery whatsoever on the land.

Plaintiff's Act

The defendant may be able to defend an action for nuisance by pointing out that the plaintiff was responsible for all or some of the injury she suffered. If the plaintiff, by word or deed, has shown her willingness to accept the interference, then a defence of voluntary assumption of responsibility would bar her claim; if she carelessly contributed to her own loss, then a defence of contributory negligence might reduce any damages payable to her. These defences will only avail a plaintiff if the defendant has done something unreasonable and the courts have been adamant that those who move to a previously inhospitable environment have done nothing unreasonable: it is no defence that the plaintiff 'came to the nuisance' (*Bliss* v. *Hall* (1838) 4 Bing NC 183). Those who move to inhospitable areas must, however, put up with whatever degree of personal discomfort, though not physical damage, is appropriate in the locality (see 18.3).

18.7 Nuisances On or Adjacent to the Highway

The public interest in freedom of passage along the highway has resulted in the courts imposing liabilities of exceptional stringency on those who impede that passage. Obstruction of the highway amounts to the criminal offence of public nuisance, and it may give rise to tortious liability if an individual suffers 'special damage' as a result. This liability was first recognised, and the special damage requirement explained, by Fitzherbert J in *Sowthall* v. *Dagger* (1535) (see Baker, 1990, p. 493). The judge considered a case where the highway was obstructed by a ditch dug across it. In his view, no one could complain about mere delay caused by the obstruction but, if a man fell into the ditch, he should be allowed to sue the person who had dug it in respect of this special loss. This liability is anomalous because, in contrast with cases in which a moving vehicle causes a collision, where negligence must be proved, the defendant will be liable if she intentionally caused the obstruction whether or not she could reasonably have foreseen damage to the plaintiff (see Newark, 1949). It is also anomalous in that the plaintiff may be able to recover pure economic loss resulting from the obstruction, – e.g. where, as in *Rose* v. *Miles* (1815) 4 M&S 101, she has to pay for alternative transport – thus evading the limitations on such recovery in the tort of negligence.

Another area in which ordinary principles of liability have been cast aside relates to the collapse of artificial structures adjacent to the highway. In *Wringe* v. *Cohen* [1940] 1 KB 229, 233 Atkinson J laid down the following rule:

'if, owing to a want of repair, premises upon a highway become dangerous, and, therefore, a nuisance, and a passer-by or adjoining owner suffers damage by their collapse, the occupier . . . is answerable, whether or not he knew, or ought to have known of the danger'.

He went on to exclude liability in cases where the collapse was caused by the act of a trespasser or 'a secret and unobservable act of nature, such as a subsidence under or near the foundations of the premises.' The liability arises even where the plaintiff suffers injury not on the highway but on private property. This indeed was the case in *Wringe* in which the Court of Appeal found the defendant liable when his wall collapsed and fell on to the roof of the plaintiff's shop next door. Once again, it seems unreasonable to have one rule when the nuisance is a threat to users of the highway and another when it is not.

18.8 The Relationship Between Nuisance and Negligence

Much controversy attends the issue of whether nuisance is best regarded as a branch of the law of negligence or as a wholly separate tort. The former view finds particularly persuasive advocates in Williams and Hepple (1984), pp. 123–7. To see whether they are right, we now consider a number of claims made by those who insist that negligence and nuisance are very different entities. As will be seen, the differences between the two are in many respects more apparent than real.

Nuisance Protects a Wider Range of Interests than Negligence

Admittedly, there are many interests not protected by a duty of care in negligence that are recognised in nuisance. Whereas negligence generally limits liability to cases of physical damage, nuisance can be employed to prevent interference with personal comfort by ensuring, for example, freedom from unreasonable noise and smells. Williams and Hepple, however, argue that this is simply a matter of terminology: 'Why should we not say that people are under a duty of care not to be noisy and not to allow a noxious escape of such a nature that the plaintiff cannot reasonably be expected to tolerate it?' In other words, nuisance might be encompassed within negligence if we were just prepared to recognise that unusually extensive duties of care are owed to owners and occupiers of land.

Liability in Nuisance is Strict Whereas Liability in Negligence Depends on Proof of Fault

We should at the outset make it clear that there are indeed cases of strict liability (i.e. liability irrespective of fault) that fall under the general heading of the tort of nuisance. But they are anomalies in the modern law, arising only in a few, narrowly confined areas, e.g. in relation to 'natural rights' (see 18.3) or dangers on the highway (see 18.7). In the vast majority of cases, interference with the use and enjoyment of land will only be regarded as actionable if it is unreasonable, and we have taken the view that this requirement of unreasonable user entails fault on the part of the defendant (see 18.3: 'Fault'). This position is supported by some distinguished legal figures: in *Sedleigh-Denfield* v. *O'Callaghan* [1940]

AC 880, 904 Lord Wright insisted that the 'liability for a nuisance is not, at least in modern law, a strict or absolute liability' and, in *The Wagon Mound (No. 2)* [1967] 1 AC 617, Lord Reid argued that 'fault of some kind is almost always necessary' for liability to arise.

One persistent source of confusion in this regard is a remark made by Lindley LJ in *Rapier* v. *London Tramways* [1893] 2 Ch. 588. Delivering judgment for the plaintiff in an action for nuisance in respect of the smell coming from the defendant's excessively large and overcrowded stables, he commented (pp. 599–600): 'At common law, if I am sued for a nuisance, and the nuisance is proved, it is no defence on my part to say, and to prove, that I have taken all reasonable care to prevent it.' (In the *Cambridge Water* case, Lord Goff made the same point: see 18.3: 'Fault') As Williams and Hepple point out, however, this does not mean that liability was being imposed without fault, for, if all else failed, the only reasonable course left to the defendant would be to close his stables down. This was clearly in the mind of Lindley LJ, because he says, 'If the defendants are right in saying that they cannot concentrate their stables to such an extent as is desirable without committing a nuisance to the neighbourhood, then they cannot concentrate their operations to such an extent' (p. 602). Their failure to cease or cut back their operations itself amounted to fault.

In summary, then, we can say that an interference will be regarded as unreasonable only if the defendant was at fault either in the way an activity was carried out or in carrying on with the activity at all. For this reason, it is appropriate to rely upon the *Wagon Mound* test of remoteness of damage in nuisance as well as negligence (*The Wagon Mound (No. 2)*; see Ch. 11).

'[T]he distinguishing aspect of nuisance, as compared with other heads of liability like negligence, is that it looks to the harmful result rather than to the kind of conduct causing it.' (Fleming, 1992, p. 401)

In negligence actions, we put the question: 'Did the defendant take due care?'; in nuisance actions, we ask: 'Was there unreasonable interference with the plaintiff's use and enjoyment of her land?' Despite this difference in emphasis, it would be wrong to conclude that negligence looks only at the defendant's conduct, and nuisance only at the plaintiff's injury. In fact, both torts look both at the nature of the damage suffered by the plaintiff and at the nature of the defendant's conduct. In negligence, the court compares the extent of the risk faced by the plaintiff with the ease with which the defendant might have eliminated that risk before deciding whether the latter took reasonable care. If the foreseeable risk to the plaintiff is greater than that to ordinary people (as in *Paris* v. *Stepney Borough Council*: see 8.3) then the defendant will be expected to alter her behaviour accordingly. Similarly, in nuisance, the court enquires not only into the extent of the interference with the plaintiff, but also into the motive with which the defendant acted: what might be reasonable if done with care might be a nuisance if done wantonly (see 18.3).

The Function of Negligence is to Allocate Losses after One-off Accidents Whereas the Function of Nuisance is the Provision of Guidelines to Neighbours in a Continuing Relationship

Neighbouring owners and occupiers of land are in a continuing relationship that is very different from the relationship between those involved in the paradigmatic instances of negligence, accidents on the roads and the like. They need much clearer guidelines as to how they should conduct their affairs than the simple injunction to take reasonable care not to injure their neighbours. In response to this need, categories of the law of nuisance have grown up in which the limits of what one can do with one's land are spelt out in black-and-white terms; the vague but appealing standard of reasonableness is put on one side (see 18.3). Consider the question of 'water rights'. The law provides that you may stop up your neighbour's water supply by abstracting that water as it percolates under your land no matter how ill your motive (*Bradford* v. *Pickles*); on the other hand, you may not take water from a stream that passes through your land to supply your factory if the result is that your neighbour's supply is diminished, irrespective of the importance of your business and of the difficulty of obtaining another supply (*Chasemore* v. *Richards* (1859) 7 HLC 349). To this extent, the law of nuisance gives occupiers and owners of land very clear guidelines as to what they can and cannot do with their land.

Yet in the majority of cases neighbours can get no clear guidance as to how they may use their land, for all is left to the court's view of what is reasonable in the circumstances. Admittedly, once the court has given its view, then the parties are bound to continue their affairs in accordance with this view, at least until the character of the neighbourhood changes sufficiently to justify a reassessment. But this is no more than what happens in many cases in negligence, for the parties to a negligence action may well be in a continuing relationship, such as that between employer and employee: a decision that it was negligent not to provide safety goggles or the like to employees may serve to lay down a standard for the future for a whole industry. In this, as in the other respects already highlighted, nuisance and negligence perform a common function in setting down legally binding standards of reasonable conduct.

Summary

18.1 The tort of private nuisance is primarily concerned with conflict over competing uses of land; it is remedied by the award of damages in respect of losses already incurred and by the grant of an injunction to prevent interference in the future.

18.2 The tort of nuisance protects a variety of aspects of the use and enjoyment of land, including freedom from physical intrusion or harm; particular difficulty arises in respect of the protection of so-called 'amenity interests'.

18.3 Where the reasonableness of an interference is relevant, this is assessed after consideration of its extent, the locality in which it takes place, the sensitivity of the plaintiff to interference of that kind, and the fault (if any) exhibited by the defendant.

18.4   The traditional requirement that the plaintiff in a nuisance action must have an interest in the land affected has recently been reasserted, precluding nuisance actions by those who merely reside on the property in question.

18.5   Liability is imposed on those who create, adopt or continue a nuisance, whether by their own acts or the acts of their independent contractors. In certain circumstances, landlords may be liable in respect of nuisances created on land they have let out.

18.6   Various defences may be raised to an action in nuisance, notably prescription and statutory authority. Although the unreasonableness of the plaintiff's conduct may give rise to a defence of contributory negligence or *volenti*, it is no defence that the plaintiff 'came to the nuisance'.

18.7   The public interest in free passage along the highway has resulted in the imposition of liabilities of exceptional stringency on those who cause obstructions. Such liabilities arise in the tort of public nuisance rather than private nuisance, as there is no interference with the use or enjoyment of any private property. Liability in public nuisance depends on proof of special damage. A stringent liability is also imposed under the rule in *Wringe* v. *Cohen* in respect of the collapse of structures adjacent to the highway.

18.8   It is a disputed question whether nuisance is best regarded as a branch of the tort of negligence or as an entirely independent tort. Careful analysis of the alleged differences between the two suggest that these are often more apparent than real.

Exercises

18.1   To what extent is nuisance a tort of strict liability?

18.2   What is the test of 'reasonable user'? Is it relevant in all cases of nuisance? What factors determine whether a user of land is reasonable?

18.3   What is the significance of *St Helen's Smelting* v. *Tipping*? Do you agree with the views of Lord Westbury LC in that case?

18.4   Can *Mayor of Bradford* v. *Pickles* be reconciled with *Christie* v. *Davey*?

18.5   Who may sue in the tort of nuisance? Is the law satisfactory on this issue?

18.6   In what circumstances will liability in the tort of nuisance be imposed on one who has not personally created the nuisance?

18.7   Will the mere fact that a defendant has statutory authority to carry out a particular activity absolve her of any liability in nuisance?

18.8   Is it a defence that the plaintiff 'came to the nuisance'? Should it be?

18.9   Should obstruction of the highway be any of the following: (a) a crime; (b) a tort; (c) the tort of private nuisance?

18.10 Is nuisance in reality nothing more than a branch of the tort of negligence? (For a problem on nuisance and the rule in *Rylands* v. *Fletcher*, please see the end of Chapter 19)

19 The Rule in *Rylands* v. *Fletcher*

19.1 Introduction

Rylands v. *Fletcher* (1866) LR 1 Exch 265, (1868) LR 3 HL 330 lays down a rule of strict liability for harm caused by escapes from land applied to exceptionally hazardous purposes. Although historically it seems to have been an offshoot of the law of nuisance, it is sometimes said to differ from nuisance in that its concern is with *escapes from* land rather than *interference with* land. Accordingly, some authorities hold that there is no requirement – like that in the tort of nuisance – that the plaintiff be the owner or occupier of the land affected by the escape, though the point is far from uncontroversial (see 19.4). If this is so, the rule in *Rylands* v. *Fletcher* may be thought to have a role in protecting not just interests in real property but also interests in the person and in personal property. But its possible development into a general principle of strict liability for ultrahazardous activities has been obstructed by a number of limitations on its scope, notably the requirement of escape.

The case concerned the flooding of the plaintiff's mine with water from the defendants' recently constructed reservoir. A coal seam had previously been worked on the site of the reservoir and, although the mine shaft had been filled up, water from the reservoir was able to escape down the shaft and from there to the plaintiff's mine. The existence of the disused shaft had not been discovered before the reservoir was filled with water and thus no precautions had been taken to guard against the risk which eventuated. The fault for this lay with the independent contractors the defendants had engaged to construct the reservoir; the defendants were not personally to blame. Furthermore, the general rule is that, while one may be vicariously liable for the acts of an employee, one is not responsible for the acts of an independent contractor (see Ch. 21). This difficulty, though, was avoided in the case by treating the defendants as personally liable irrespective of fault.

In the Court of Exchequer Chamber, Blackburn J set out the rule to be applied in such cases, together with the defences to it (his formulation was subsequently approved by the House of Lords in the same case):

> '[T]he person who, for his own purposes, brings on his land, and collects and keeps there anything likely to do mischief if it escapes, must keep it in at his peril, and, if he does not do so, he is prima facie responsible for all the damage which is the natural consequence of its escape. He can excuse himself by showing that the escape was owing to the plaintiff's default, or, perhaps, that the escape was the consequence of vis major, or the act of God.'

This formulation makes it clear that there are two essential ingredients of *Rylands* v. *Fletcher* liability: first, the bringing of a dangerous thing onto one's land (so as to apply it to a 'non-natural use of land'); secondly, the escape of that thing.

19.2 Non-natural Use of Land

The requirement that the defendant must bring something onto his land was inadvertently transformed in the House of Lords by Lord Cairns. He paraphrased Blackburn J's words, saying that the rule applied only to a 'non-natural use' of land, not to a case in which a substance had accumulated naturally on the land. Yet there is an ambiguity in the word 'natural' and, although Lord Cairns meant to exclude from the scope of the rule only those things which were present on the land in its natural state, 'the law has long departed from any such simple idea, redolent of a different age; and . . . natural use has been extended to embrace the ordinary use of land' (*Cambridge Water Co Ltd* v. *Eastern Counties Leather plc* [1994] 2 AC 264, 308 per Lord Goff; see also Newark, 1961). Hence no liability will arise in respect of a man-made object or accumulation so long as they could be described as 'ordinary' ('ordinary' sometimes being a synonym for 'natural'). What will be regarded as ordinary and natural will depend on the exact circumstances of the case. Changes in perceptions brought about by the passage of time must be taken into account: keeping a motor-car in one's garage might be unremarkable in the late twentieth century, but at the beginning of the century it might have been thought unusually dangerous (see *Musgrove* v. *Pandelis* [1919] 2 KB 43). So too must more transient shifts in community standards: in *Read* v. *Lyons* [1947] AC 156 it was held that it was 'natural' to use land for the manufacture of explosives at time of war.

An influential examination of the non-natural use requirement is to be found in the speech of Lord Moulton in *Rickards* v. *Lothian* [1913] AC 263, 280. In his view, '[i]t must be some special use bringing with it increased danger to others and must not merely be the ordinary use of the land or such a use as is proper for the general benefit of the community.' This requirement effectively robbed the rule in *Rylands* v. *Fletcher* of its primary justification, for strict liability is premised upon the belief that the rights of individuals should not be sacrificed in the furtherance of the public interest (see 12.2). It is precisely where land is put to 'such a use as is proper for the general benefit of the community' that strict liability should be imposed, as a 'licence fee' to be paid by those who are permitted to pursue the activity in question. Furthermore, Lord Moulton's view that hazardous activities could give rise to liability under *Rylands* v. *Fletcher* if beneficial to the community left the (supposedly) strict liability derived from that case hard to distinguish from liability in negligence: exposing others to danger without generating a countervailing benefit should, as a matter of logic, amount to negligence.

Although Lord Moulton's words have been cited with approval on many occasions, the House of Lords has recently cast doubt upon his approach. In *Cambridge Water Co Ltd* v. *Eastern Counties Leather plc*

[1994] 2 AC 264, 308, Lord Goff (who delivered the only substantial speech) criticised his suggestion that no liability could arise in respect of uses of land that are 'proper for the general benefit of the community': this threatened unduly to restrict the scope of the liability. Accordingly, on the facts before them, their Lordships rejected the view that the benefit to the local community provided by the provision of employment opportunities at an industrial leather tanning works precluded the operation of the doctrine. The defendants' operations involved the storage of substantial quantities of chemicals on industrial premises, which was 'an almost classic case of non-natural use' (p. 309 per Lord Goff); his Lordship added: 'I find it difficult to think that there could be any objection to impose strict liability for damage caused in the event of their escape.' Although the claim failed on other grounds (see below), the approach taken by the House of Lords to the issue of non-natural use will please advocates of strict liability because it presages a greatly increased role for *Rylands* v. *Fletcher* than was envisaged by Lord Moulton.

19.3 Escape

The requirement that the thing brought onto the land must have escaped from the land was authoritatively laid down by the House of Lords in *Read* v. *Lyons*. The plaintiff was injured in her employment as an inspector of munitions in the defendant's arms factory when an artillery shell exploded on the production line. Their Lordships held that the rule in *Rylands* v. *Fletcher* had no application to her case as she had been injured on the defendant's land; the shell had not escaped and injured her on neighbouring land.

Fleming has commented that '[t]he most damaging effect of the decision in *Read* v. *Lyons* is that it prematurely stunted the development of a general theory of strict liability for ultra-hazardous activities' (1992, p. 341). Such a theory has been adopted in many US jurisdictions (see Restatement of the Law of Torts, 2nd, ss. 519–25), but the Law Commission (1970a) has recommended against its adoption here in the light of fears that key terms such as 'especially dangerous' or 'ultra-hazardous' might prove uncertain of definition and give rise to practical difficulties in their application. In the *Cambridge Water* case, Lord Goff noted these misgivings but indicated in any case his provisional view that the courts should not take it upon themselves to develop such a theory. The decision whether and how to introduce strict liability for high-risk activities was better left to Parliament, which could by statute define the activities to be affected with greater precision than was possible at common law.

19.4 Remoteness of Damage

The plaintiff must prove that damage resulted from the escape from the defendant's land. In the *Cambridge Water* case, the House of Lords decided that the damage resulting from the escape must be foreseeable, though the escape itself need not be foreseeable. Their Lordships applied the rule of remoteness recognised in *The Wagon Mound (No. 2)*, holding that it was necessary to ensure consistency with the tort of nuisance from which the rule in *Rylands* v. *Fletcher* was originally derived (see 18.3). The case concerned the spillage of a chemical solvent used by the defendants, a long-established leather manufacturer, in its tanning process. The solvent seeped through the soil and contaminated water percolating below, which was the source of the water extracted from the plaintiff's borehole some 1.3 miles away. The solvent took approximately 9 months to reach the borehole. On these facts, it was not foreseeable that the seepage of the solvent into the soil would cause harm to the plaintiffs; as foreseeability of harm was a prerequisite of liability under the rule in *Rylands* v. *Fletcher*, no liability could arise. Notwithstanding this decision, liability under the rule in *Rylands* v. *Fletcher* remains strict and may even arise even where the defendant is engaged in a reasonable use of land which cannot be restrained by way of injunction.

19.5 **Parties**

The primary liability under the rule in *Rylands* v. *Fletcher* is upon the owner or controller of the thing that escapes. The escape need not be from that person's own land but can be from land she is merely licensed to use or indeed from the highway: in *Rigby* v. *Chief Constable of Northamptonshire* [1985] 1 WLR 1242, Taylor J said that he could 'see no difference in principle between allowing a man-eating tiger to escape from your land on to that of another and allowing it to escape from the back of your wagon parked on the highway'. The owner or occupier of land on to which the thing is brought may also be held liable (*Rainham Chemical Works* v. *Belvedere Fish Guano Co* [1921] 2 AC 465), though she may have a defence where the actions are those of a stranger (see 20.5).

It is clear that the owner or occupier of the land affected can sue in relation to the damage to her property. Two significant areas of doubt arise, however, when we consider the question of to whom the liability is owed. First, it is not clear whether it is possible to claim in respect of personal injuries as opposed to property damage. In *Read* v. *Lyons*, Lord Macmillan said that 'an allegation of negligence is in general essential to the relevancy of an action of reparation for personal injuries' and would not countenance *Rylands* v. *Fletcher* as an exception to that general rule. Yet the point cannot be regarded as decided, for none of the other judges in Read was prepared to express a view on the issue and the Court of Appeal had previously awarded damages for personal injury under the rule, as in *Hale* v. *Jennings Bros* [1938] 1 All ER 579 where the plaintiff, the tenant of a shooting gallery at a fairground, was injured when a chair, with its occupant, became dislocated from the defendant's rotating 'chair-o-plane' ride. Secondly, different opinions have been expressed as to whether the plaintiff must have a proprietary interest in the land invaded.

Again, the courts have awarded damages to those who had no interest in the land on which they were injured; for example, the plaintiff in *Shiffman* v. *Order of St John* [1936] 1 All ER 557 who was injured in Hyde Park when the defendants' flag-pole fell on him. A more recent decision, however, may give some support to the opposing view that the plaintiff must have an interest in the land invaded: where the business of cattle auctioneers was disrupted after local livestock was infected by foot-and-mouth disease which had escaped from the defendant's laboratories, Widgery J resisted the auctioneers' claim for compensation under the rule in *Rylands* v. *Fletcher* (*Weller & Co* v. *Foot and Mouth Disease Research Institute* [1966] 1 QB 569). The true basis of the judge's decision on this point is not clear, however, because he dealt with the issue very briskly and his words are equally consistent with what is perhaps a better rationale for the decision, namely that plaintiffs should not be able to evade the limits of liability for pure economic loss in the tort of negligence by suing under the rule in *Rylands* v. *Fletcher* instead. In any case, the point remains controversial, though it has been said that it is not open to the Court of Appeal to limit the rule to cases of interference with a proprietary interest (*Perry* v. *Kendricks Transport Ltd* [1956] 1 WLR 85, 92 per Parker LJ).

19.6 Defences

Blackburn J indicated three defences to liability under *Rylands* v. *Fletcher* in the passage extracted above (19.1). First in his list was default of the plaintiff. In extreme cases, no liability at all will arise as where it was the plaintiff's mining operations beneath the defendant's canal, performed with full knowledge of the likely consequences, that caused water to escape and damage his mine (*Dunn* v. *Birmingham Canal Co* (1872) LR 7 QB 244). More mundane instances of fault can be dealt with through the apportionment provisions of the Law Reform (Contributory Negligence) Act 1945 (see 11.5). The second defence indicated by Blackburn J was *vis major*, which in this context refers to cases in which the escape was caused by the independent acts of a third party. The act of a third party will be considered 'independent' unless it would not have occurred without the negligence of the defendant. Hence, in *Perry* v. *Kendricks Transport Ltd*, the Court of Appeal declined to hold the defendants liable when a motor-coach in their car park was set on fire by young boys: the motor-coach was not left in such a condition that it was reasonable to expect that children might meddle with it and cause the fire. Lastly, the defence of Act of God will arise where the escape was caused by some wholly unforeseeable natural event (e.g. an earthquake or hurricane). The question of whether exceptionally heavy rains or violent winds give rise to this defence is a matter of degree (compare *Nichols* v. *Marsland* (1876) 2 Ex D 1 with *Greenock Corporation* v. *Caledonian Railway* [1917] AC 556).

In addition to the defences listed by Blackburn J, the defendant may be able to rely upon the defences of necessity (see 17.7), consent to the non-natural user of land and statutory authority (see 18.5).

19.7 **Fire**

Notwithstanding the narrow approach to *Rylands* v. *Fletcher* liability evident above, the courts have shown some flexibility when it comes to cases in which things brought onto land catch fire and the fire escapes to neighbouring land. Although Blackburn J's words, taken literally, would seem to require the thing that escapes to be the same as the thing brought on to the land, in *Mason* v. *Levy Auto Parts of England* [1967] 2 QB 530, McKenna J accepted that the same rule of strict liability applies where the non-natural thing catches fire and the fire escapes from the land.

Section 86 of the Fires Prevention (Metropolis) Act 1774 confers a tortious immunity in respect of fires beginning accidentally on the defendant's land. This does not apply, however, when liability can be established on *Rylands* v. *Fletcher* principles or indeed in negligence (*Musgrove* v. *Pandelis* [1919] 2 KB 43). Even where a fire begins without any negligence or non-natural user, the defendant may lose her immunity under the Act if she negligently allows the fire to spread. Thus, in *Musgrove*, the defendant was held liable after the engine of his motor car caught fire on being started up in his garage; the crucial factor in the case was that the spread of the fire to the plaintiff's premises above the garage would not have occurred without his servant's negligence (an alternative ground for the decision was that keeping the car was a non-natural user of land which itself deprived the owner of any immunity: see 19.2). The converse is true when a fire is lit intentionally but in a controlled environment and subsequently spreads from the defendant's land without any fault on her part. In such circumstances, the statutory immunity may be raised. Hence, in *Musgrove*, Warrington LJ considered that if a lump of coal should jump unexpectedly from a fire lit in a domestic hearth the resulting conflagration should be regarded as having begun accidentally and the statutory immunity would apply.

A similar rule to that under *Rylands* v. *Fletcher* governs the liability of those engaged in dangerous operations involving the creation of fire. The leading case is *Honeywell and Stein Ltd* v. *Larkin Bros (London's Commercial Photographers) Ltd* [1934] 1 KB 191, in which contractors engaged to work in a cinema themselves employed photographers to record their handiwork on film. The primitive flashlights used by the photographers set fire to the cinema. The contractors were held liable for the fire damage, even though they were not personally at fault, because they had instigated the dangerous operation. This liability differs from that under *Rylands* v. *Fletcher* in three main respects. First, it applies even in the absence of a non-natural user of land. Secondly, there is no requirement of any escape from the land on which the dangerous operations are carried out. Lastly, it seems that the liability is not properly regarded as strict but a hybrid form of liability for which negligence must be shown, even if it is the negligence of an independent contractor (see Ch. 21).

Summary

19.1   *Rylands* v. *Fletcher* lays down a rule, originally formulated by Blackburn J in the Court of Exchequer Chamber, of strict liability for harm caused by the escape of dangerous things accumulated on land.

19.2   The defendant must be engaged in a 'non-natural use of land'.

19.3   The plaintiff must be injured by an escape from the defendant's premises: no liability under the rule can arise when she is injured on those premises.

19.4   It must be reasonable foreseeable that the plaintiff will suffer damage as a result of the escape, though the escape itself need not be foreseeable.

19.5   Both the owner or controller of the dangerous thing and (if they are not one and the same) the owner or occupier of the land from which it escapes may be held liable under the rule.

19.6   Defences which may be raised against the imposition of liability under the rule include default of the plaintiff, the independent act of a third party and act of God.

19.6   The escape of fire may give rise to a liability analogous to that under *Rylands* v. *Fletcher*. The tortious immunity conferred by the Fires Prevention (Metropolis) Act 1774 does not apply to cases that fall within the rule, or indeed to cases where a fire was started negligently. Even when fire does not escape from premises, something approaching strict liability may be imposed under the rule in *Honeywell and Stein* v. *Larkin Bros*.

Exercises

19.1   What are the ingredients of liability under the rule in *Rylands* v. *Fletcher*?

19.2   Is the imposition of liability without fault justifiable? To what extent have the courts paid heed to the objectives of strict liability in developing the rule in *Rylands* v. *Fletcher*?

19.3   Can liability for fire damage ever arise in the absence of negligence? If so, when?

19.4   D and E are neighbours in Meadow Lane. Four weeks ago, F started to sell roasted chestnuts from a mobile stall in the lane outside D and E's houses. Many passers-by have been inconvenienced by the fact that F's stall gets in their way; D and E have more particular grievances. D alleges that she can no longer host her regular wine appreciation evenings as the smell from the stall overwhelms the bouquet of the wines. E, who is trying to sell her property, has been told that the fact that 'a dirty old tramp' has set up a stall in the vicinity, 'spoiling the view' and 'making a terrible smell', means that she will have to reduce the price considerably. When E asks F to move on, the latter replies: 'There've been stalls like mine in the area for hundreds of years. You should value your heritage. Besides, I'm only here a couple of hours a night.' Angered by E's attitude, F starts to burn an even more pungent fuel than before. Yesterday sparks from F's stall set fire to D's hedge. D's gardener, G, who comes to work for D one afternoon a week, tried to put out the fire with the garden hose. However, her efforts to direct the jet of water at the fire were ineffectual as she is elderly and suffers greatly from arthritis. As a result, a fire spread to D's rubbish tip and thence to E's property where it burnt down an outhouse. Despite this damage, F vows to continue selling chestnuts from the same place in the future. Advise the parties as to their rights and liabilities in tort.

Part IV

Interference with Reputation

20   Defamation

20.1 Interference with Personality Generally

How much protection should English law give to 'interests in personality'? Should one person, for example, have a remedy when another makes untrue, or even true, statements about him which affect his sense of dignity or honour? Should one person be able to bring an action where another appropriates his name or picture for commercial use without his permission? Should a person be able to prevent another planting listening devices in his house or taking photographs of him by surreptitious means? These are vexed questions that have troubled lawyers, both practising and academic, for at least a hundred years. In this chapter we look principally at the law of defamation and the way in which it protects a particular interest in personality, namely a person's reputation. As we shall see, the law of defamation is primarily concerned with providing a remedy to a person who has been the victim of an untrue statement that lowers his reputation in the estimation of others. The law of defamation, however, leaves other interests in personality unprotected. It provides no protection in respect of private information, for example, where true but unflattering or even extremely damaging statements are made by one person about another. Nor does it protect the so-called 'seclusion interest' against violation. It also provides no protection of the interest in commercial exploitation of one's personality (e.g. the use of another's name or image for financial gain).

Although the protection given to interests in personality by the law of defamation is limited, there are other legal principles which may be used in order to protect interests in personality. First, the *interest in reputation* is protected not only by the tort of defamation but also by the torts of negligence and malicious falsehood. In *Spring* v. *Guardian Assurance plc* [1995] 2 AC 296 it was held that, in writing a reference about an employee, an employer owed him a duty of care. As Lord Goff said,

> 'the employer is possessed of special knowledge, derived from his experience of the employer's character, skill and diligence in the performance of his duties while working for the employer . . . [F]urthermore, when such a reference is provided by an employer, it is plain that the employee relies upon him to exercise due care and skill in the preparation of the reference before making it available to the third party. In these circumstances, it seems to me that all the elements requisite for the application of the *Hedley Byrne* principle are present' (p. 146–7).

Recognition that an action lies in negligence in such a case is of considerable significance for those inaccurately characterised in a reference. Those who commence an action for negligence are, unlike those who sue in respect of a defamatory statement, entitled to legal aid. Further, the law of defamation recognises that statements made on certain occasions may be 'privileged' (see below, 20.10–11). Statements made in references have always been assumed to be protected by qualified privilege, If, therefore, the action was brought in defamation the plaintiff would not succeed unless he could establish that the defendant was actuated by malice. Privilege is not a defence to negligence.

Although the tort of malicious falsehood primarily protects a plaintiff's interest in his property or trade, it may in limited circumstances be utilised by a plaintiff to protect his reputation. In *Joyce* v. *Sengupta* [1993] 1 WLR 337, the defendant newspaper published an article alleging that the plaintiff lady's maid had stolen letters from her employer, the Princess Royal. Rather than commencing her action in defamation, which as the Court of Appeal accepted was the obvious action, the plaintiff sued for malicious falsehood (for which legal aid is available). Clearly, the plaintiff's reputation had been lowered but she had also been injured in her trade, that of lady's maid. Where the same facts constitute both torts there is no reason why the plaintiff cannot choose to sue for malicious falsehood.

Second, the *interest in informational privacy* is protected by the action for breach of confidence which, in addition to protecting trade secrets, can be used to prevent the disclosure of true but private facts about oneself. For example, in *Argyll* v. *Argyll* [1967] Ch 302 a man was prevented from disclosing information given to him by his ex-wife during their marriage which concerned her private affairs. However, the equitable remedies available in respect of an action for breach of confidence are available only where the information (a) has the necessary quality of confidence about it; (b) is conveyed in circumstances importing an obligation of confidence; and (c) is used in an unauthorised way to the disadvantage of the person who communicated it. In addition to the action for breach of confidence, certain statutes may also prevent the disclosure of true facts. For example, section 49 of the Children and Young Persons Act 1933 prohibits the revelation in any report of juvenile proceedings of the name, address, school or any other particulars identifying any juvenile involved unless the court grants leave.

Third some, though very limited, protection has been given to the *interest in commercial exploitation of personality* by the tort of defamation. In *Tolley* v. *Fry* [1931] AC 333 the court used the law of defamation to provide what looks, in essence, like a remedy for the unauthorised appropriation of another's personality. A caricature of a well-known amateur golfer with a bar of Fry's chocolate in his back pocket was held to be defamatory of the golfer. In reality, the plaintiff appears to have been given an action, under the guise of defamation, restraining the unauthorised use of his picture for commercial purposes. Apart from this case, the courts have not shown themselves willing to allow an action for the unauthorised use of another's picture or name though, as Fleming (1992, p. 605) points out, 'the decision has potentially far reaching implications and could be stretched to serve as a basis for restraining the unauthorised use of anyone's name or picture for commercial use under the guise of protecting reputation.'

Finally, some protection is given to one's *interest in seclusion* by, *inter alia*, the torts of trespass, nuisance and *Wilkinson* v. *Downton*. Thus, an owner of land may be able to sue in trespass a photographer who sneaks onto his land to take photographs and an injunction may be issued against a campaign of harassment that is likely to cause another psychiatric illness (*Khorasandjian* v. *Bush* (16.5)). Additionally, a number of statutes provide protection against interference with one's seclusion interest. For example, s. 14 of the Post Office Act 1969 makes it an offence to open the letters of another without authorisation and s. 43(1)(b) of the Telecommunications Act 1984 makes it a criminal offence to make persistent telephone calls to annoy or cause needless anxiety. Of considerable significance in this area is the recent enactment of the Protection from Harassment Act 1997. In addition to creating two criminal offences (one to catch the most serious cases (where the victim fears for his safety, s. 4): the other to deal with less serious cases, s. 1), the Act creates a statutory tort of harassment (s. 3). This provision is widely drafted and allows a victim to obtain an injunction not only to stop behaviour that is already causing distress but also behaviour that may cause distress in the future. Breach of any injunction made is made a criminal offence, carrying the power of arrest (s. 3(3)).

It can be seen, therefore, that English law does protect interests in personality other than the right not to have untruths uttered to another about oneself. However, the protection offered is at best haphazard and gaping holes still exist. Are there really free speech implications that prevent there being an action for appropriation of personality for commercial use? So far as the interest in seclusion is concerned, increasing intrusion by the press into the private lives of politicians, members of the royal family and members of the public generally lead to the appointment of a committee chaired by David Calcutt QC in 1990 (Calcutt, 1990). That committee concluded that the case for a statutory tort of invasion of privacy had not been made out, but made several recommendations to strengthen the existing self-regulatory system of the Press Council. However, a further review carried out in 1993 (Calcutt, 1993) concluded that the recommendations suggested had not worked. Subsequently (1993), the Lord Chancellor's Department has published a consultation paper on whether there should be a statutory tort of infringement or privacy. So far, there has been no legislation forthcoming. However, while the press continues to irritate politicians and members of the royal family by disclosing details of salacious gossip, the likelihood of such an Act increases. Politicians are notoriously cavalier about free speech where their personal interests are affected. Certainly, while the inconsistencies and inadequacies of the existing law remain it is unlikely that the issue will go away. How far the law should protect interests in personality is likely to remain an area of great controversy.

If privacy rights are the subject of few protections in English law, the same cannot be said of the USA where the law relating to the protection of privacy is relatively well developed if erratically effective. Interestingly, the impetus for this development came from an article written in 1890 by Warren and Brandeis (Warren and Brandeis, 1890), which reviewed a number of, predominantly English, cases and concluded that they were based upon a broader principle that was entitled to separate recognition. Today the law in the USA may be said to encompass four distinct kinds of invasions of what may compendiously be called a right to privacy. The first form of invasion of privacy relates to the appropriation of another's name or likeness. Where, without the consent of the plaintiff, the defendant appropriates the plaintiff's name, picture or other likeness for his own benefit or advantage then an action will lie. While the action may protect the plaintiff's feelings, the effect of the decisions has been to 'create an exclusive right in the individual plaintiff to a species of trade name, his own, and a kind of trade mark in his likeness.' (Prosser and Keaton, 1984, p. 854). In addition to those cases where the defendant has appropriated another's name or likeness for his own purposes, the action has been held to exist in relation to the appropriation of a catchphrase (*Carson* v. *Here's Johnny Portable Toilets Inc* 698 F 2d 831 (1983)) and, in some states, to continue to subsist (for the benefit of the estate) after the other's death (*Memphis Development Foundation* v. *Factors Etc. Ltd* 616 F 2d 956 (1980)).

Second, most states recognise a right to be free from 'unreasonable intrusions'. An action may lie where a person, whether by physical trespass or not, interferes with another's interest in solitude or seclusion, either as to his person or to his private affairs or concerns (Restatement Second of Torts, s.652B). The tort has been held to extend to such matters as eavesdropping on private conversations and bugging, as well as to persistent and unwanted telephone calls. Third, if a defendant makes public private facts that would be highly offensive and objectionable to a reasonable person and the public has no legitimate interest in having the information made available, then an action may lie. The concept of legitimate public interest is 'inspired by the first amendment and therefore is interpreted expansively' (Anderson, 1994, p. 634). Thus, the public is usually legitimately interested in the goings on of public figures and officials. Finally, an action may lie where the plaintiff is placed in 'a false light in the public eye'. Such an action most typically exists where some view or utterance is falsely attributed to the plaintiff. Closely related to the tort of defamation, the action is subject to constitutional limitations in the interests of preserving freedom of speech. While, it is suggested, wholesale adoption of the American approach would not be sensible, there is much to be said for introducing an action for appropriation of personality for commercial use. Whether such an action really protects privacy as such, however, must be doubtful.

The remainder of this chapter looks at the protection afforded to a person's reputation by the law of defamation.

20.2 **The Law of Defamation**

The law has from the earliest times recognised the making of false statements about another as a wrongful act. The high value accorded to a person's reputation has led to virtually every legal system in the world affording it protection. In English law, this function is performed by the law of defamation. While a reputation is deservedly afforded substantial protection by the law, the need to protect reputation must be balanced against the competing demands of free speech. No system of law does or should offer absolute protection for reputation. This is particularly the case where the maker of the statement is discussing a matter of public interest. One of the concerns, therefore, of the law of defamation is to achieve a satisfactory balance between these two interests. The difficulty of achieving this balance has led to the development of an area of law of considerable complexity.

In order for a statement to be actionable in the tort of defamation a defamatory statement must be published about the plaintiff to a third person. In the case of slander actual injury must also be proved. Each of these elements of the tort will now be considered in turn.

20.3 **The Statement Must Be Defamatory**

A defamatory statement is one which adversely affects a person's reputation. Vulgar abuse or insulting name-calling will not generally be defamatory because such behaviour is usually only insulting to a person's pride and does not affect his reputation. However, as the recent case of *Berkoff* v. *Burchill* [1996] 4 All ER 1008 illustrates, those who indulge in gratuitous insult must take care if their statements are not to be characterised as defamatory. In that case, the Court of Appeal, by a majority, held that the statement that Mr Berkoff, the well-known actor and playwright, was 'hideously ugly' was capable of being defamatory of him because it might make him an object of ridicule in the eyes of the public.

Traditionally the test as to whether or not a statement was defamatory was whether the words complained of brought the plaintiff into 'hatred, ridicule or contempt'. However, the difficulty of bringing some statements which appeared to adversely affect a person's reputation within the traditional definition led Lord Atkin in *Sim* v. *Stretch* [1936] 2 All ER 1237 to put forward a broader test. He said:

'[T]he conventional phrase exposing the plaintiff to 'hatred, ridicule or contempt' is probably too narrow . . . I do not intend to ask your Lordships to lay down a formal definition, but after collating the opinions of many authorities I propose in the present case the test: would the words tend to lower the plaintiff in the estimation of right thinking members of society generally?'

Although this test is in almost universal usage it remains the case that there is no wholly satisfactory test of what is defamatory (see per Neill LJ, *Berkoff* v. *Burchill*).

Whether or not a statement is capable of being defamatory is a question of law for the judge. Whether or not it is in fact defamatory is one of fact for the jury (Fox's Libel Act 1792). It is the tendency of the words themselves, however, that is important and not the intention of the maker of the statement. Thus, words may be held to be defamatory notwithstanding that no defamatory meaning was intended (*Hulton* v. *Jones* [1910] AC 20).

In considering the standard to be applied when determining whether or not the words used are defamatory the courts have not been wholly consistent. The formulation most used is that of the 'right thinking man' or 'the good and worthy subject of the [Queen]'. The question asked is, therefore, whether the 'right thinking man' would construe the words in a way defamatory of the plaintiff. It may, of course, be a controversial question what the 'right thinking man' would think. For example, would the 'right thinking man' consider that an allegation that a woman had been raped, or that she was not a virgin when she married, lowered her in the estimation of society? Similarly, would a 'right thinking man' consider that an allegation of insanity or alcoholism lowered a person's reputation? It may be that the courts in considering what the 'right thinking man' thinks are inclined to look to what he *should* think rather than what he does in fact think. A good illustration of this tendency is seen in the case of *Byrne* v. *Deane* [1937] 1 KB 818.

In that case automatic gambling machines, which were kept illegally on the premises of a golf club, were removed by the police after someone had informed them of the machines' presence. A verse appeared soon after this on the notice-board of the club. The last two lines of the verse read, '[B]ut he who gave the game away, may he byrnn in hell and rue the day'. The issue for the Court of Appeal was whether the trial judge had been correct to leave to the jury the question whether the words were defamatory of the plaintiff, Mr Byrne, in the sense that they meant he was guilty of underhand disloyalty to his fellow members. The court held that the words were not capable of a defamatory meaning as no 'good and worthy subject of the King' could consider such an allegation against a person to be defamatory. Thus the case should not have been left to the jury.

As Greene LJ admitted in his judgment, many people in the country would not consider any moral reprobation attached to the playing of gambling machines. Thus, for them at least, the allegation made against the plaintiff – whom they might regard as officious – could be defamatory. Why should not the question of whether the words are defamatory be judged according to what they think? The answer given by the court to this is that it is always possible to discover a small group in society who would not find the words complained of defamatory. For example, among certain groups to describe someone as a 'professional thief' would be a compliment. The ordinary meaning of words cannot be left to such anti-social groups but must instead be considered by a more respectable body of opinion. However, it must not be assumed that a body of opinion is anti-social merely because it is opposed by the majority.

In deciding whether or not the words used are in fact defamatory the jury is asked to consider the meaning of the words in their 'natural and ordinary' sense. In many cases of course the words used only have one meaning and that meaning is clearly defamatory. However, a word may be capable in its ordinary usage of having more than one meaning. For example, in one case a woman was described as an 'international boot'. Three 'dictionary' meanings were considered; first, that a boot was a type of footwear (unlikely to have been the apprehended meaning!); second, that boot meant a physically unattractive person; finally, the meaning that was accepted by the jury, that boot meant a promiscuous person. Where more than one natural and ordinary meaning is possible and pleaded it is left to the jury to decide which meaning the words have. Even though a publication may convey different meanings to different readers the jury is required to determine the *single* meaning that the publication conveyed to the notional reasonable reader (*Charleston* v. *News Group Newspapers Ltd* [1995] 2 All ER 313).

In determining whether a particular statement is defamatory it must be read in context. Thus, if one statement in a larger publication appears to be defamatory of the plaintiff when looked at in isolation but is evidently not defamatory when looked at in context then no action will lie; 'the bane and the antidote must be taken together.' (per Alderson B in *Chalmers* v. *Payne* (1835) 2 Cr M & R 156, at 159) But, it is of course the case that not every reader reads with the same care. Reading a Sunday newspaper, for example, one's eye is inevitably drawn to some things and not others. Such publications are simply too large, and uninteresting, to read in full. Could a plaintiff written about in such a publication argue that, if *some* reasonable readers would conclude on reading part (for example, a headline) in isolation that it appeared to lower the plaintiff's reputation, an action could lie? This question was considered but answered in the negative by the House of Lords in the recent case of *Charleston* v. *News Group Newspapers Ltd* [1995] 2 All ER 313. The court recognised that readers of newspapers read selectively but nevertheless held that it was a fundamental principle of the law of defamation that the publication must be read as a whole.

In some cases the plaintiff may wish to allege that the meaning that ought to be attributed to the words is not their ordinary and natural meaning but is instead a meaning that can only be drawn by inference or implication, or perhaps only from the use of evidence separate from the statement itself. In both cases words or statements apparently innocent may yet be found to be defamatory. Where the words do not speak for themselves, the plaintiff may, if he is to succeed, have to prove the necessary innuendo. Innuendos are either 'true' or 'false'. Some words may have popular or slang meanings different from their ordinary and natural meaning; meanings in other words that do not speak for themselves. Such a meaning is referred to as a false (or popular) innuendo. Unlike a true innuendo, it does not need to be separately pleaded, but in the light of the (feigned?) judicial ignorance of slang such a course may be wise. A true innuendo is an innuendo by which the plaintiff alleges that the words bear a defamatory meaning distinct from their natural and ordinary meaning (which may be wholly innocent), which can only be established by reference to extrinsic evidence. Thus, although a statement may appear innocent, knowledge of facts separate from the statement may make it defamatory. Because a true innuendo constitutes a cause of action separate from any arising in relation to the words in their ordinary and natural meaning it must be separately pleaded.

An example of a false (or popular) innuendo can be seen in *Lewis* v. *Daily Telegraph* [1963] 2 All ER 151. Two newspapers published a story in which it was reported that officers of the London Fraud Squad were 'inquiring into the affairs of the R Co and its subsidiary companies'. Three possible meanings were considered by the House of Lords. First, that there was an investigation in progress. Second, that the plaintiffs were suspected of fraud. Finally, that the plaintiffs were guilty of fraud. Lord Reid held that in determining the meaning to be given to the words the question to be asked was what meaning would be conveyed to the ordinary person. Such a person 'does not live in an ivory tower and he is not inhibited by a knowledge of the rules of construction. So he can and does read between the lines in the light of his general knowledge and experience of world affairs.' Their Lordships held that only the first two meanings were possible. It was impossible in this case, they said, for the statement that an inquiry was taking place to convey the impression that the subject of the inquiry was *guilty* of fraud. Acceptance of the second meaning, that the plaintiffs were suspected of fraud, involves a false innuendo. No extrinsic evidence is required for this meaning to be attributed; it is simply an implication that can be drawn or an impression that may be gained from a reading of the words themselves.

Where the meaning that the plaintiff is seeking to establish can only be ascertained by the use of extrinsic evidence this is known as a true innuendo. A true innuendo arises solely from facts or circumstances that are not apparent from the words themselves and that give the words a meaning they would not ordinarily have. A good illustration of a true innuendo can be seen in the case of *Cassidy* v. *Daily Mirror Newspapers Ltd* [1929] 2 KB 331. In that case the defendants published a photograph taken of Kettering Cassidy, also known as Michael Corrigan, and another woman. Below the photograph were the words: 'Mr M. Corrigan, the race horse owner, and Miss X, whose engagement has been announced.' Mr Cassidy had told the photographer of this announcement. The action was brought by Mrs Cassidy, who was in fact the lawful wife of Cassidy; although they lived apart, Cassidy occasionally visited her. She argued that the words and picture were capable of meaning that 'Corrigan' was a single man and that, therefore, she was living in immoral co-habitation with him. The Court of Appeal held that the publication was capable of bearing this defamatory meaning. On their own, the words and picture were not defamatory. However, in the light of the extrinsic evidence that Cassidy was in fact married, a defamatory meaning was possible. It did not matter that the defendant newspaper did not know of the extrinsic facts, provided that the paper had been read by those who did and who understood the statement to apply to the plaintiff.

20.4 The Statement Must Be Published to a Third Person

The law of defamation is concerned, as we have seen, with the protection of a person's reputation in the eyes of other people. As a person's reputation is, in simple terms, the opinion or view that others hold of him, it follows that unless the statement is published to a third person there can be no damage to the person's reputation. If nobody but the maker of the statement and the person about whom the statement was made know of the contents of that statement, how can the statement have affected the person's reputation in the eyes of his fellow man? In light of this concern, English law requires that the defamatory statement must be published to someone other than the person whose reputation is impugned.

Publication, then, is the communication of a defamatory statement to someone other than the plaintiff. An unexpressed defamatory thought or even the writing of such a thought on paper will not be actionable unless and until it is actually communicated to another. The publication must also be made to a person capable of understanding the defamatory meaning. Where, for example, the statement is not defamatory on its face but is only defamatory when considered in the light of extrinsic evidence (a case of true innuendo) the hearer must know of the extrinsic facts that make the statement defamatory. More obviously, if a defamatory statement contained in a letter is written in a foreign language the recipient must be able to understand that language.

It is not necessary for the plaintiff to prove that the publication was intentionally made. As long as he can show that the defendant ought reasonably to have foreseen that the statement would come to a third party's attention the requirement of publication will be satisfied. Thus in *Theaker* v. *Richardson* [1962] 1 WLR 151 the defendant wrote a defamatory letter to the plaintiff who was a married woman. The letter, which was addressed to the plaintiff, was contained in a manilla envelope similar to the kind used for distributing election addresses. The plaintiff's husband opened the envelope thinking it was an election address. At the trial the jury found there had been a publication of a defamatory statement and awarded damages to the plaintiff. On appeal to the Court of Appeal, Pearson LJ said that the question that should be asked was, '[Was] his [i.e., the recipient's] conduct so unusual, out of the ordinary and not reasonably to be anticipated, or was it something which could quite easily and naturally happen in the ordinary course of events?' This was pre-eminently a jury question and because the jury had decided that the opening of the letter by the husband was something that could quite easily happen in the ordinary course of events the Court of Appeal would not interfere with its decision. By way of contrast, the Court of Appeal held in

Huth v. *Huth* [1914–15] All ERep 242 that, where a husband sent a defamatory letter to his wife, the fact that it had been opened and read by the butler did not constitute publication. As Lord Reading CJ said, 'it is no part of a butler's duty to open letters that come to the house of his master or mistress addressed to the master or mistress.'

Every repetition of a defamatory statement is a new publication and creates a fresh cause of action in the person defamed. The person repeating the statement will be treated in the same way as if he had originated it. Further, a defendant cannot escape liability simply by putting a prefix such as, 'it has been rumoured that . . .' or, 'I have been told that . . .', before the allegation and then asserting that it was *true* that there was such a rumour or that he had in fact been told what he had then repeated. Such a 'hearsay' statement is treated as if it were a direct statement; thus, the person who repeats the rumour will have to prove the truth of the allegation to escape liability and not just that there was such a rumour in existence (see, for example, *Stern* v. *Piper* [1996] 3 All ER 385). This principle is sometimes known as the 'rumour' doctrine.

Although every repetition creates a new cause of action, common sense dictates that liability must cease somewhere. While there may be good arguments of policy for holding liable those primarily involved in the publishing process (such as author, publisher and editor), less reason exists for imposing liability on those more tangentially involved (such as libraries, printers and booksellers). Those only tangentially involved have little control, if any, over the content of any publication and often have no reason to suspect that any statement it may contain might be defamatory. To expect them to read for libel every line of all the material that they distribute is clearly ridiculous. At common law such 'mechanical' publishers could rely on the defence of innocent dissemination. In *Vizetelly* v. *Mudies' Select Library Ltd* [1900] 2 QB 170 the 'defence' (whether it is really a defence or a failure to make out the 'publication' element of the cause of action is not clear) was held to be available where the defendant could prove (a) that he was innocent of any knowledge of the libel; (b) that there was nothing in the work or in the circumstances in which it came to, or was disseminated by, him which ought to have led him to suppose it contained a libel; and (c) that when the work was disseminated by him it was not by any negligence on his part that he did not know it contained a libel.

The exact scope of the defence was, however, by no means clear and recent changes in technology have made it still less so. The new s. 1 of the Defamation Act 1996 was enacted with the intention of codifying the existing law while, at the same time, modernising it. The defence can now be relied upon, *inter alia*, by the broadcaster of a live programme that contains the statement in circumstances where the broadcaster has no effective control over the maker of the statement (e.g. talk radio: s1(3)(d)); the operator, or provider, of access to a communications system (such as an Internet site) by means of which a statement is transmitted; and persons responsible for processing, making copies of, distributing or selling any electronic medium (such as CD-ROMs and floppy disks) in or on which the statement is recorded (s. 1(3)(c)). The conditions for the existence of the defence are found in s. 1(1) of the Act. This provides that a person shall have a defence if he shows that – (a) he was not the author, editor or publisher (defined in s. 1(2)) of the statement; (b) he took reasonable care (defined in s. 1(5)) in relation to the publication; and, (c) he did not know, and had no reason to believe, that what he did caused or contributed to the publication of a defamatory statement. This amounts, in part, simply to a codification of the common law defence. However, as Patrick Milmo QC has pointed out (1996), the new provision, in one important respect, has restricted the scope of the defence. At common law, the defence had been available to a distributor who had no knowledge that the publication in question contained the *libel*. Under s. 1(1)(c) of the Act, however, the defence is available only if he did not know, and had no reason to believe, that what he did caused or contributed to the publication of a *defamatory statement*. The distinction is important because while those such as newsagents and booksellers may be aware that publications they sell contain *defamatory statements*, they are frequently assured by the publishers that such statements are true; in other words, that there is no *libel*. At common law only where the risk of *libel*, and not simply the risk that the publication contained *defamatory statements*, was ignored would the defence not exist.

A related question was considered by the Court of Appeal in *Slipper* v. *British Broadcasting Corporation* [1991] 1 QB 283: is the original maker of the statement liable for subsequent republications of his statement by others? The Court of Appeal held that the law relating to republication in defamation cases is simply an example of the rule of causation encapsulated in the Latin phrase '*novus actus interveniens*' familiar throughout the law of tort (see 9.4). Thus, in any case involving the repetition of a libel the following question should be asked: was it a foreseeable or natural and probable consequence of the libel that the third party to whom it was published would repeat it?

20.5 Reference to the Plaintiff

The third essential requirement to found an action for defamation is that the statement refer to the plaintiff. Where the plaintiff is expressly mentioned by name there will usually be no difficulty. However, it is not essential that the plaintiff be expressly referred to. In *Morgan* v. *Odhams Press Ltd* [1971] 2 All ER 1156 for example, the plaintiff's claim succeeded despite the fact he was not expressly referred to. The defendants published an article that stated that a girl had been kidnapped by a dog-doping gang. The girl had in fact been staying voluntarily with the plaintiff around this time. At the trial the plaintiff produced several witnesses who said that they thought that the article referred to him. The House of Lords held that in determining whether the article referred to the plaintiff, the test to be adopted was to ask whether a 'hypothetical sensible reader who knew of the special facts' could reasonably come to the conclusion that the article referred to the plaintiff. Such a reader is not expected to read a newspaper article with the care that a lawyer would read an important legal document. It is accepted that he may read it quickly in order to get a general impression. What is important is the inferences that such a reader would draw from the article. On the facts of the case, despite the fact that a close reading of the article would have made it clear that it could not have referred to the plaintiff, their Lordships upheld the jury's decision.

The fact that the defendant in making the statement did not intend to refer to the plaintiff has been held by the courts to be irrelevant. In *Hulton* v. *Jones* [1910] AC 20 Artemus Jones, a barrister, brought an action against the defendants in respect of a newspaper article that he claimed referred to him. The article referred to 'Artemus Jones' a church warden in Peckham and cast imputations on his moral behaviour at a motor festival in Dieppe. The defendants argued that they had never intended the article to refer to the 'real' Artemus Jones but instead had intended to create a fictitious character. The House of Lords held that the defendants' intentions were irrelevant. Lord Loreburn said '[A] person charged with libel cannot defend himself by shewing that he intended in his own breast not to defame, or that he intended not to defame the plaintiff, if in fact he did both.' The test to be applied was to ask whether a reasonable person would consider in all the circumstances that the article referred to the plaintiff.

In *Newstead* v. *London Express Newspaper Ltd* [1940] 1 KB 377 the Court of Appeal applied the principle of *Hulton* v. *Jones* to the situation where the defendant had intended to refer to a person about whom the statements were true but the plaintiff said that the statement also referred to him and was defamatory. Provided a reader of the article would reasonably think that the statement referred to the plaintiff it is no defence for the defendant to prove that the words were intended to refer to another person of whom they were true.

Where words are spoken of a group of people proof that the article refers to a particular member of the group is likely to be difficult. If a person was heard to say 'all lawyers are thieves', such a statement would be unlikely to give rise to a cause of action on the part of any individual lawyer. The fact that proof of reference in such a case is difficult does not mean that no 'group defamation' will be actionable at the suit of a member of that group. In *Knuppfer* v. *London Express Newspapers* [1944] AC 116 the House of Lords was asked to consider whether the trial judge had been correct to hold that an unflattering article concerning the activities of a pro-German group referred to the plaintiff. The membership of the British branch of the organisation, of which the plaintiff was head, numbered about 24. The House of Lords held that the article could not be understood as referring to him. As Lord Atkin pointed out, there was no special rule to be applied where group defamation was concerned: 'the only relevant rule is that in order to be actionable the defamatory words must be published of and concerning the plaintiff.' He accepted that this was likely to be difficult in most group defamations. However, in two situations apparent 'group defamations' may be capable of referring to individual members of that group: first, where the words are spoken of a group which is so small or so ascertainable that the words spoken of the group are necessarily said of each individual member; second, where although the words purport to refer to a group they can in fact be read as applying to a particular individual (for instance, where his photograph appears next to the defamatory words).

20.6 **Damage: The Distinction Between Libel and Slander**

English law draws a distinction between libel and slander. Libel is a defamatory communication conveyed in some permanent form, most often writing; slander is a defamatory communication conveyed in some non-permanent form, such as by the spoken word. In the case of libel, damage need not be proved as it is presumed. In cases of slander, by contrast, proof of injury will generally be required before such a defamatory communication can give rise to an action. Although the basis of this distinction is historical there have been a number of modern attempts to justify its continued existence. It has been argued that, as libels are in a permanent form, they are likely to remain in currency for longer, to be read by more people, and have more significance attached to them. It has also been suggested that a libel conveys the impression of a more deliberate and calculated attack on reputation than does slander. Slanderous remarks are often made in the context of heated conversations and once made may be immediately regretted. Libel, however, usually requires the defendant to have sat down and given some thought to what he is writing. While there is some truth in much of the above, it is suggested that a slander may have just as serious an effect on a person's reputation as a libel. For example, a well-placed remark at a board meeting of a large company concerning the personal proclivities of the company's chairman could be just as damaging as an article in a major newspaper. It is surely such factors as the status of the person making the statement, the statement's seriousness and the circumstances in which it was made that are important rather than the permanence of the statement or the means by which it was conveyed.

Originally, the distinction between libel and slander lay in the difference between oral and written statements. However, as methods of communication have developed and changed this distinction is no longer, to the extent that it ever was, wholly satisfactory. How, for example, should we classify radio defamation? Does it make any difference whether the programme is live or recorded? Are defamatory statements made on the Internet, CD-ROMs, videotapes and television libels or slanders? Parliament has legislated in respect of some of these question but where it has not, some 'test' must be sought to distinguish between the two.

Although there are statements to the effect that libels are conveyed to the sense of sight, whereas slanders are conveyed to the ear, it is suggested that the best view is that permanence is the gist of the distinction. As Lopes LJ said in *Monson* v. *Tussauds Ltd* [1894] 1 QB 671:

'[L]ibels are generally in writing or printing, but this is not necessary; the defamatory matter may be conveyed in some other permanent form. For instance, a statue, a caricature, an effigy, chalk-marks on a wall, signs or pictures may constitute a libel.'

Further, as that case makes clear, while libels are most often written they need not be. In *Monson* v. *Tussauds Ltd*, for example, a wax model of the plaintiff was placed in an exhibition entitled 'the chamber of horrors'. This was held to be a libel.

As has been mentioned, slander generally requires proof of actual damage for it to be actionable. By contrast libel is always actionable without proof of any special damage. Proof of actual or special damage requires proof of some 'material' or 'pecuniary' loss. Thus, while mere loss of reputation has been held to be insufficient, loss of a job or lost trade would amount to special damage.

While slander generally requires actual damage to be proved, there are four exceptional situations where slander is actionable *per se*. These are: imputations of criminal conduct punishable with imprisonment (*Gray* v. *Jones* [1939] 1 All ER 798); imputations that the plaintiff is suffering from a contagious or infectious disease (*Bloodworth* v. *Gray* (1844) 7 M & G 334); imputations of unchastity against a woman (Slander of Women Act 1891); and imputations calculated to disparage the plaintiff in any office, profession, calling, trade or business (*Dakhyl* v. *Labouchere* [1908] 2 KB 325n).

20.7 Defences

In addition to certain general defences dealt with elsewhere in the book, such as voluntary assumption of responsibility and consent, the law of defamation has its own special defences. These defences must now be considered.

Justification

Where a plaintiff succeeds in showing that the words complained of are defamatory of him and have been published to a third party, the law presumes in his favour that such words are untrue. However, to such a claim the defendant can plead justification. The essence of the defence of justification is that the words complained of are 'true in substance and in fact'. The policy behind allowing justification as a complete defence was well put by Littledale J in *M'Pherson* v. *Daniels* (1829) B & C 263, 272, '[T]he law will not permit a man to recover damages in respect of an injury to a character which he either does not or ought not to possess.' Unlike other defences, such as fair comment or qualified privilege, the motive of the defendant in making the original statement is irrelevant. Thus, even where the defendant makes the statement with the express intention of damaging the plaintiff's reputation, if the words are true the defendant will escape liability.

In order to establish the defence the defendant must prove that the defamatory matter complained of is true. However, it is not necessary that every 't' should be crossed and every 'i' dotted. As Lord Shaw said in *Sutherland* v. *Stopes* [1925] AC 47:

'[T]he plea [of justification] must not be considered in a meticulous sense. It is that the words employed were true in substance and in fact . . . all that was required to affirm the plea was that the jury should be satisfied that the sting of the libel or, if there were more than one, the stings of the libel should be made out.' (p. 79)

Thus, if I accuse A of having stolen my car on 20 March from outside my house, proof that A had stolen my car would justify the sting of the accusation. The fact that A stole the car on 21 March from outside my office would not prevent reliance on the defence. Such minor inaccuracies in no way add to the seriousness of the charge against A.

In order for the plea of justification to be successful it must cover the meaning attributed by the jury to the words complained of. You will recall that the plaintiff may, and must if he wishes to rely on them, give particulars of defamatory meanings that arise by way of innuendo. In a similar fashion, a defendant who pleads justification must state the meaning which he seeks to justify. If the defendant fails to justify the meaning which the jury finds the words to have then the defence will fail: the fact that the defendant can prove some other meaning is irrelevant. Thus, in *Lewis* v. *Daily Telegraph* the fact that the defendant could justify the literal meaning of the words – that the company was under investigation by the police – would not have justified the innuendo meanings, namely that the company was suspected or guilty of misconduct.

A defamatory statement may contain more than one charge. At common law where more than one charge was alleged a plea of justification would only have been successful where the defendant justified the sting of all the charges. If A says of some person that 'he has murdered his father, stolen from his mother and does not go to church on Sundays' and A can prove the first two allegations but not the last, A will remain liable in damages in respect of the last charge. The common law was altered by s. 5 of the Defamation Act 1952. This provides:

'In an action for libel or slander in respect of words containing two or more distinct charges against the plaintiff, a defence of justification shall not fail by reason only that the truth of every charge is not proved if the words not proved to be true do not materially injure the plaintiff's reputation having regard to the truth of the remaining charges.'

Under this rule, in the example given above, failure to prove that the plaintiff does not go to church on Sundays would not be fatal to a defence of justification if it was felt by the jury that an allegation of failure to go to church on Sundays did not add to the gravity of the other charges.

The provisions of s. 5 are, however, applicable only in an action where the plaintiff relies upon a defamatory statement that contains two or more distinct charges. It would appear to be open to a plaintiff to complain simply of one allegation out of several made against him. Hence, the defendant would not be allowed to justify other defamatory allegations contained in the publication in the hope of persuading the jury that the defamatory statement was substantially true or to influence the jury to award lower damages. However, although the plaintiff may isolate one particular allegation in the expectation of being able to prevent the defendant justifying other allegations, the defendant will only be prevented from justifying other allegations where they are 'separate and distinct'. Where the allegations have a common sting the defendant will be allowed to adduce evidence of the truth of the other allegations in order to justify the common sting. In *Polly Peck (Holdings) plc* v. *Trelford* [1986] 1 QB 1000, O'Connor LJ held that whether allegations are 'separate and distinct' or have a common sting is a question of fact and degree in each case. In *Khashoggi* v. *IPC Magazines Ltd* [1986] 1 WLR 1412 a magazine article contained what purported to be an account of the plaintiff's life with her husband, an international arms dealer, before and after the dissolution of their marriage. The article contained a series of allegations regarding the plaintiff's sexual behaviour. The plaintiff objected to one of the allegations in the article suggesting that she had committed adultery with a friend of her husband. The Court of Appeal held that, although the defendants could not prove the allegation of adultery with that particular person, the article was capable of meaning that the plaintiff was guilty of promiscuity generally. Evidence of other 'affairs', therefore, was relevant in considering whether the common sting of the article could be justified.

Fair Comment

The defence of fair comment on a matter of public interest is, like justification, a complete defence to an action for defamation. The defence is an essential aspect of the greater right of freedom of speech and a safeguard allowing protest at the undemocratic exercise of power. These considerations are of such social importance that in the area covered by the defence they are taken to outweigh the competing claim of protecting a person's reputation. In order for the defence to succeed it must be shown: (a) that the words used are comment and not fact; (b) that the comments are on a matter of public interest; (c) that the comment is based on true facts; and (d) that the comment is 'fair'. Once the defendant has proved these points he will be entitled to rely on the defence unless the plaintiff can show that the defendant was actuated by malice.

Comments or Statements of Fact

In order to be able to rely on the defence the defendant must indicate with reasonable clarity that the statement is one of opinion as opposed to one of fact. Where there is any doubt as to whether the words are fact or comment the trial judge is required to decide whether the words are capable of being comment, the question whether they are in fact comment being left to the jury. How then are statements of fact to be distinguished from comment? The distinction is often elusive, but an approach that has some merit is that suggested by Sutherland (1992). There he says:

'[G]enerally, the issue . . . can be determined by examining the statement in isolation. If the statement is at least theoretically susceptible of proof by objective criteria, then it a statement of fact. If, on the other hand, it represents the statement of a moral or aesthetic judgement, then it constitutes opinion or comment.'

Thus a statement that 'A is a convicted burglar and is, therefore, unfit for public office' is a statement of opinion that A is unfit for public office based on a statement of fact that A is a convicted burglar. More difficult is a statement that A has been guilty of 'disgraceful conduct'. This has been assumed by more than one judge to be a statement of fact. Yet it is difficult to see that such a statement is susceptible of proof by objective criteria. Is it not in reality a statement of moral judgment?

Matter of Public Interest

The comment must be on a matter of public interest. A matter is of public interest 'whenever . . . [it] is such as to affect people at large, so that they may be legitimately interested in, or concerned at, what is going on; or what may happen to them or others . . .' (per Lord Denning MR in *London Artists Ltd* v. *Littler* [1969] 2 QB 375, p. 391). Discussion of national or local politics or the administration of justice clearly falls within this definition, as does discussion of the performance of the national football team and its manager, or the management of a public company.

While comment on both the substance of public debate and the conduct and behaviour of those engaged in such debate is essential in any democracy, care must be taken not to stray from comment on a person's conduct in their public capacity to comment on their private life. The private character of a person is of interest only in so far as it affects their capabilities or qualifications for public office. The mere fact of being in the public eye does not legitimise comment on every aspect of a person's character.

Based upon True Facts

A defendant must prove that his comment was based upon true facts. At common law failure to prove the truth of any material basic facts, as distinct from the comments on, or inferences drawn from, those facts, prevented the defendant relying on the defence.

However, this strict position is mitigated by s. 6 of the Defamation Act 1952. This provides:

'[I]n an action for libel or slander in respect of words consisting partly of allegations of fact and partly of expression of opinion, a defence of fair comment shall not fail by reason only that the truth of every

268 Interference with Reputation

allegation of fact is not proved if the expression of the opinion is fair comment having regard to such of the facts alleged or referred to in the words complained of as are proved.'

Thus where it is said of A that he is unfit for public office because he is a 'liar, a cheat and he has never held office before', failure to prove that the plaintiff has never held office before would not prevent the defendant relying on the defence. The comment is still fair comment having regard to such of the facts as have been proved. However, if the defendant had failed instead to prove that the plaintiff was a cheat, s. 6 would probably not provide a defence.

The facts on which the comment is based need not be fully set out in the publication complained of. In *Kemsley* v. *Foot* [1952] AC 345 the defendant wrote an article accusing the Beaverbrook Press of the 'foulest piece of journalism perpetrated in this country for a long time'. The defendant's article was headed 'Lower than Kemsley'. The plaintiff, a rival newspaper proprietor, alleged that the statement implied that his companies knowingly published false statements and that 'his name was a byword in this respect.' The defendant pleaded fair comment. The House of Lords held that a plea of fair comment may succeed provided there is a 'sufficient substratum of fact stated or indicated in the words which are the subject matter of the action.' On the facts there was a sufficient substratum of fact – namely, that the plaintiff was in control of the newspapers and that his conduct in this regard was in question – to justify leaving the defence to a jury.

The Comment Must Be 'Fair'
The question of the appropriate test to be applied in determining whether a comment was 'fair' had, until the decision of the House of Lords in *Telnikoff* v. *Matusevitch* [1992] 2 AC 343, become so shrouded with confusion that the two leading practitioner works on defamation suggested different answers. In *Telnikoff* the House of Lords, held that the test is a purely objective one: 'could *any* fair-minded man honestly express that opinion on the proved facts?'. It was for the *defendant* to prove that any fair minded man could hold the view expressed but he did not need to go further and prove that he honestly held that view. However, proof by the *plaintiff* that the defendant did not honestly hold the view expressed is good evidence of malice and malice, as we shall see, defeats the defence. The objective test applied here does not require an investigation into whether a *reasonable* man could hold that opinion. The test instead appears to be whether any fair-minded (i.e. honest, even if prejudiced) man could hold the view expressed. Thus, the test protects the views of the honest 'crank' as well as those commenting intelligently on matters of public concern.

Once the defendant has established that the subject matter is a matter of public interest, that the facts on which the comment is based are true and the comment is one any fair-minded man could make, he is entitled to rely on the defence unless the *plaintiff* can establish that the defendant was actuated by malice. As the question of malice arises in almost identical terms in relation to the defence of qualified privilege, the issue of what amounts to malice is considered later.

Absolute Privilege

In certain situations deemed to be of sufficient social or political importance the law allows a person to speak or write about others without restraint. Where an occasion is deemed to be of sufficient importance, statements made on that occasion will be absolutely privileged. This is a complete bar to an action for defamation no matter how false the wording may be or how malicious the defendant is. Because the effect of the defence is so drastic, preventing as it does a person from vindicating his reputation, the number of absolutely privileged occasions is small. The defence is not, however, designed to protect abusers of such occasions. Instead the immunity is granted to protect the makers of statements on certain occasions from being forced to defend themselves against unjustified accusations that they were actuated by malice.

The following are occasions of absolute privilege:

Parliamentary Proceedings
Article 9 of the Bill of Rights 1688 provides that, 'the freedome of Speech and debates or proceedings in Parlyament ought not to be impeached or questioned in any court or place out of Parlyament.' This has been held to have the effect that any statement made by members of the Houses of Parliament in the course of debates or other parliamentary proceedings (including standing committees: *Rost* v. *Edwards* [1990] 2 All ER 654) is absolutely privileged. The privilege does not, however, attach to all statements made by MPs wherever made: it is only those made within the environs of the Houses of Parliament that are protected.

While the courts have always been sensitive to claims of parliamentary privilege, two recent cases have raised important questions concerning the exact scope of the privilege. In *Prebble* v. *Television New Zealand Ltd* [1994] 3 All ER 407, the plaintiff, then Minister for State-Owned Enterprises in New Zealand, sued the defendants for alleging that he was involved in a conspiracy with other businessmen to purchase state-owned enterprises on unduly favourable terms. In seeking to justify these allegations, the defendants sought to rely on statements made in the House and other parliamentary materials. The Privy Council upheld the claim to privilege. First, the Board held that the privilege applied even when the questioning of statements made would not lead to the assertion of any legal consequences *against* the maker of the statement. Article 9 was not just passed for the purpose of preventing the assertion by the courts of a right to hold an MP criminally or civilly liable for what he had said in Parliament (for a contrary view, see the decision of the New South Wales Supreme Court in *R* v. *Murphy* [1986] 5 NSWLR 18). The basic intention of art. 9 is to ensure that, as far as possible, members of the legislature can speak freely without fear that what they say will later be held against them.

Any exception permitting statements to be questioned subsequently would undermine that purpose because at the time he was speaking an MP would not know whether there was later likely to be a challenge.

Second, the Privy Council held that in principle parliamentary privilege could arise where it was claimed by an MP who *initiated* the claim and not just where an MP asserted it as a defence. The privilege protected was that of Parliament itself and not its individual members: the fact that the maker of the statement was the initiator of the proceedings rather than the defendant, therefore, made no difference to the question whether article 9 was infringed. However, the Board accepted that, where the *plaintiff's* claim to parliamentary privilege would effectively exclude all the evidence necessary to establish a defence, a stay of the action may be appropriate, albeit that in this case the New Zealand Court of Appeal had been wrong to order one. This 'exception' was later relied upon by Owen J in *Allason* v. *Haines* (1996) 145 NLJ 1576 to stay an action brought by Rupert Allason MP. Unlike in *Prebble*, where the matters protected by privilege were marginal to the defendants' ability to justify the allegations, the matters denied to the defendants by privilege in *Allason* were central to their ability to justify the allegations made. Where, therefore, a defendant can show that the assertion of privilege makes a fair resolution of the action impossible, a stay of the action may be appropriate.

It would appear, however, that the decision in *Allason* v. *Haines* may not survive the enactment of s. 14 of the Defamation Act 1996 which was passed as a result of the difficulty Neil Hamilton MP had in instituting libel proceedings against the *Guardian* newspaper. Section 14 allows an MP, where his conduct, 'in or in relation to proceedings in Parliament, is in issue in defamation proceedings', to waive parliamentary privilege for the purposes of those proceedings. Thus, had Mr Allason waived privilege, his action could have proceeded. While an MP can waive the protection of privilege to commence proceedings and, if he so chooses, if sued (s. 14(1)), it should be noted that, if sued, an MP does not have to waive the privilege. Section 14(4) preserves the rule that *protects* a person from legal liability for words 'spoken or things done in the course of, or for the purposes of or incidental to, any proceedings in Parliament'. This is the case even if the MP had waived privilege under s. 14(1).

In addition to the protection afforded to the maker of the statement, s. 1 of the Parliamentary Papers Act 1840 provides that the court is compelled to stay any action brought against the publisher of any reports or papers published by order of or under the authority of either House of Parliament. As yet there is no similar provision with respect to the televising of Parliament, although, the broadcasting authority would certainly be protected by qualified privilege.

Judicial Proceedings

An absolute privilege attaches to all statements, whether oral or written, made in the course of judicial proceedings. All concerned in judicial proceedings, whether as one of the parties to the action, counsel, judge, members of the jury or witness are immune from an action for defamation. The privilege is not confined to proceedings before a court properly so called. It extends to 'tribunals', which, although not courts of justice, nevertheless act in a manner similar to courts. Also covered by absolute privilege are communications between solicitors and their clients, at least where such communications are made in contemplation of litigation.

By s. 15 of the Defamation Act 1996, 'A fair and accurate report of proceedings before a court . . . if published contemporaneously with the proceedings, is absolutely privileged.' The section is applicable to any court (which includes any tribunal or body exercising the judicial power of the State) in the United Kingdom, the European Court of Justice, the European Court of Human Rights and any international criminal tribunal established by the Security Council of the United Nations or by international agreement to which the United Kingdom is a party (s. 15(3)(a)–(d)).

High Executive Communications

Where a statement is made by one high-ranking member of the executive to another it will be protected by absolute privilege. In *Chatterton* v. *Secretary of State for India in Council* [1895] 2 QB 189 the Court of Appeal held that a statement made by the Secretary of State for India to an Under-Secretary of State was protected by absolute privilege. The court attached great importance to the need for independence in such officers and the interest of the public in allowing them to get on with their work unhindered by libel actions.

The scope of this head of privilege remains uncertain. While communications between ministers of state or between ministers and high-ranking civil servants are clearly within the scope, doubt exists as to how high-ranking the official must be and what executive bodies might be covered. Should the privilege extend, for example, to high-ranking officers in the police force or army? The best approach to this problem is to reserve the privilege, 'for those cases alone in which complete freedom of communication is so important that it is right to deprive the citizen of his remedy for all defamatory statements made about him including even those made maliciously' (Winfield & Jolowicz, 1994, p. 356). Beyond that, the privilege should not be extended.

Statements of Public Officials Protected by Statute

A number of statutes expressly provide that publications made by certain officials, such as the Parliamentary Commissioner for Administration (the 'Ombudsman') and the Director General of Fair Trading, are absolutely privileged. The underlying rationale of these statutes appears to be that the nature of the work of these individuals makes it likely that they will be subject to actions for defamation. To allow a defamation action against them would make their work intolerable and leave them looking over their shoulder fearful of such an action. To avoid this, and to facilitate the proper working of these individuals, an absolute privilege is needed.

Qualified Privilege

In addition to those occasions that to justify the application of absolute privilege, there are others that, while not of sufficient importance to attract absolute privilege, are nevertheless of sufficient importance to attract qualified privilege. As with absolute privilege, the reason for allowing statements made on such occasions to be privileged is 'the common convenience and welfare of society'. However, unlike absolute privilege, the protection given is not absolute. Where the plaintiff can show that the maker of the statement was actuated by malice the defence will be defeated.

It is impossible fully to categorise all the occasions on which qualified privilege arises. As the legal concepts used to determine the existence of the defence of qualified privilege have regard to such matters as the 'interests' and 'duties' of society, the matters considered worthy of protection are likely to change over time. What was considered to be of public interest at the end of the last century may not be of public interest today. The following classifications of qualified privilege should not, therefore, be taken as exhaustive.

Statements Made in Performance of a Legal, Moral or Social Duty
Statements made in the discharge of a legal, moral or social duty to a person who has a reciprocal interest in receiving them are protected by qualified privilege. The determination of whether a duty to communicate exists is a question solely for the judge. The state of mind of the maker of the statement is not relevant to this question. Honest belief in the existence of a duty cannot create a duty to communicate. Whether a legal duty to communicate exists is not usually a difficult question. Certain contracts or statutes may, for example, impose an obligation to make a statement or disclosure (see, for example, Human Fertilisation and Embryology Act 1990, s. 35). Disclosures made in order to comply with such an obligation would in all likelihood be protected by qualified privilege.

Problems have arisen in determining whether a social or moral duty to communicate exists. In *Stuart* v. *Bell* [1891] 2 QB 341, Lindley LJ suggested the following test:

> '[T]he question of moral or social duty being for the judge, each judge must decide it as best he can for himself. I take moral or social duty to mean a duty recognized by English people of ordinary intelligence and moral principle, but at the same time not a duty enforceable by legal proceedings, whether civil or criminal.' (p. 350)

The circumstances in which courts have held a moral or social duty to exist are extremely diverse. Where the statement is made in answer to an inquiry, the courts appear to be more willing to hold a duty to communicate exists. However, it does not follow that where there is no request there is no duty. For example, unsolicited warnings by one member of a family to another regarding the 'moral dangers' of a suitor have been held to attract qualified privilege (*Todd* v. *Hawkins* (1837) 8 C & P 88). The case of *Watts* v. *Longsdon* [1930] 1 KB 130 illustrates, however, that not all 'well-intentioned' interventions will be protected. There, the unsolicited repetition by an acquaintance to the plaintiff's wife of unsubstantiated information concerning the plaintiff's sexual conduct was held not to be protected. Other common examples of circumstances attracting qualified privilege include the writing of a reference for an ex-employee at the request of someone proposing to employ him and a banker's reference on the credit standing of one of its customers (both situations may, however, attract liability in negligence where privilege is not a defence: *Spring* v. *Guardian Assurance plc* [1994] 3 All ER 129).

The existence of a duty to communicate is not enough of itself to attract the defence. In addition the statement must be made to a person who has a legitimate interest to receive it. Without this reciprocity there can be no privilege. A person may have a legitimate interest to receive the contents of a statement by virtue of some legal or social relationship. For example, an employer has an interest in receiving a complaint concerning the fitness of an employee to do his job and a solicitor has an interest in receiving his client's instructions. The interest may also arise by virtue of the public position of the receiver. A police officer has a legitimate interest to receive information regarding the alleged commission of an offence. Similarly, it has been held that an MP is legitimately interested in the way a constituent was treated by a local solicitor. Where, however, the statement is published in a newspaper or on television to the general public, the courts have been less willing to uphold the existence of the privilege. Something out of the ordinary will be required to satisfy the courts that the public at large, and not just a section of the public, has sufficient interest to receive the information. An example might be where the information relates to a public emergency such as a scare (later unsubstantiated) over the safety of a particular food product (see *Blackshaw* v. *Lord* [1984] QB 1, per Stephenson LJ)

Statements Made in Furtherance or Protection of an Interest
Private Interest   Where a person makes a statement in protection of his own personal interests to a person who has a reciprocal interest to receive it, the statement will attract the defence of qualified privilege. As Lord Oaksey said in *Turner* v. *Metro-Goldwyn-Mayer Pictures Ltd* [1950] 1 All ER 449:

'[T]here is . . . an analogy between the criminal law of self defence and a man's right to defend himself against written or verbal attacks. In both cases he is entitled . . . to defend himself effectively, and he only loses the protection of the law if he goes beyond defence and proceeds to offence.' (p. 470)

Therefore, statements are protected if made in reply to an attack on a person's reputation or proprietary interests, or in protection of one's employer's interests. For example, if A is accused of theft by a police officer, A's reply that B was the thief would attract qualified privilege. By accusing B, there is no evidence that A has gone beyond what is reasonably necessary to defend his reputation.

The recent case of *Watts* v. *Times Newspapers Ltd* [1996] 1 All ER 152 makes clear that the personal interest 'defended' will affect the latitude given to the speaker. In that case, the defendant newspaper published an article defamatory of the plaintiff. Unfortunately, they accompanied the defamatory article with a photograph of another person (A) who shared the plaintiff's name. The newspaper agreed to publish an apology to A and suggested a neutral form of words. A, however, insisted on a form of words which, while making clear that he was not the person referred to, repeated the allegation against the plaintiff. The plaintiff sued both the newspaper and A in respect of, *inter alia*, the defamatory apology. The court held that while A was protected by qualified privilege, the newspaper was not. A was entitled, as a person defamed, to defend himself. Provided he did not overstep the bounds of reasonableness and include wholly irrelevant and extraneous material any response he made would be protected even if it included material not objectively necessary. The newspaper was, however, in a different position. While it was under a duty to right the wrong it had done to A, it did not follow from that that it could publish matter defamatory of the plaintiff. To fulfil its duty it need have done no more than publish an apology in the neutral terms it had originally suggested. As it chose to go further, it was not protected.

In order to attract privilege, the communication must be made to a person with a corresponding interest or duty to receive it. This point has already been discussed with regard to statements made in performance of a duty.

Public Interest   A defamatory statement has no claim to privilege merely because it concerns a matter of public interest. As Stephenson LJ said in *Blackshaw* v. *Lord*, '[N]o privilege attaches yet to a statement on a matter of public interest believed by the publisher to be true in relation to which he has exercised reasonable care' (p. 26). In order to attract the privilege, the nature of the matter published, its source, the position or status of the publisher and the position or status of the recipient must be considered to determine whether the publisher has a duty or interest to publish the matter to the intended recipient. Publication to the general public will only rarely be protected. In *Blackshaw* v. *Lord*, the Court of Appeal held that the publication by a national newspaper of unsubstantiated allegations that the plaintiff was involved in the loss of several million pounds of public money was not protected by qualified privilege. While publication of details of wastage of taxpayers money may attract qualified privilege, the public had no interest in the half-baked rumours and guesses published by the defendant. The circumstances where the publication of such suspicions or speculations would be justified are very rare; Stephenson LJ gave as examples where 'there is danger to the public from a suspected terrorist or the distribution of contaminated food or drugs.'

Common Interest   A communication on a matter in which the defendant and the recipient share a common legitimate interest is privileged. For the privilege to exist, both parties must be interested in some matter that concerns them both. Where the recipient's interest is mere idle curiosity or meddling in the affairs of others the defence will not be established. The common interest may be financial. All employees were said in *Bryanston Finance Ltd* v. *De Vries* [1975] 1 QB 703 to have an interest in the survival and prosperity of the business in which they are employed. Therefore communications made to them for the purpose of informing them about the affairs of the business would be privileged. Other examples include: statements made to a trade or professional association by one member about another or by a member of the public about the conduct of a member of the association; and statements by an employer to his employees as to why he had dismissed one of their workmates.

Statements Made in Certain Classes of Report
Fair and Accurate Reports of Parliamentary Proceedings   Fair and accurate reports of parliamentary proceedings are protected by qualified privilege. Thus reports in newspapers, on the radio or on television are privileged whether the whole statement or merely extracts from such a statement are published. A report is fair and accurate where it gives a substantially fair account of what took place. The fact that the report is not verbatim will not preclude reliance on the defence (Parliamentary Papers Act 1840, s. 3 as amended).

Fair and Accurate Report of Judicial Proceedings   A fair and accurate report of judicial proceedings, whether or not published contemporaneously, is protected by qualified privilege.

Statements Privileged by Virtue of Section 16 and Schedule 1 of the Defamation Act 1996   Section 16 of the Defamation Act 1996 (which replaces s. 7 of the Defamation Act 1952 as amended) provides that, 'The publication of any report or other statement made in Schedule 1 of this Act is privileged unless the publication is shown to be made with malice.' (s. 16(1)) The privileged reports and statements are divided into two categories (s. 16(2)): first, those comprising reports and statements privileged without explanation or contradiction (schedule 1, part I); and, second, those statements privileged subject to the publication of a reasonable letter or statement by way of explanation or contradiction (schedule 1, part II). Where such a letter or statement of explanation or contradiction is requested but the request is not, or is inadequately, complied with, then there is no defence. Unlike the position under s. 7 of the 1952 Act, the publication does not have to be made in a newspaper to attract the privilege, but no privilege attaches where the matter published is not of public concern or for the public benefit (s. 16(3)). Reference should be made to schedule 1 for the full list of protected reports and statements.

Malice

Where a defendant is proved to have been actuated by 'malice' the defences of fair comment and qualified privilege will be defeated. In broad terms a defendant will be found to have been so actuated where he desires to injure the person defamed and this is the predominant motive for the defamatory publication. In other words, malice involves the making of a statement with an improper motive. The motive with which a person publishes defamatory material can, of course, only be inferred from what he did or said. Evidence of malice may be found in the words themselves or from extrinsic facts. For example, use of intemperate language in conveying information to a person who has an interest in hearing the information may be evidence of malice. Similarly, evidence that goes to show that the defendant knew the statement was untrue at the time he made it (*Horrocks* v. *Lowe* [1975] AC 135), or evidence of previous ill-will between the parties, is evidence of malice. The burden of proving that the defendant was actuated by malice is on the plaintiff. It is for the judge to determine whether there is enough evidence of malice to be left to the jury and for the jury to decide whether the defendant was in fact malicious.

Where more than one person has been involved in the publication of the defamatory material difficult questions have arisen in relation to malice. Does the proof of malice against one co-publisher prevent the others from relying on the defences of fair comment or qualified privilege? In *Egger* v. *Viscount Chelmsford* [1965] 1 QB 248 the plaintiff sued all eight members and the secretary of a committee of the Kennel Club in respect of a letter written by the secretary on the instructions of the committee. The trial judge held that the letter was written on an occasion of qualified privilege and the jury found that five of the members were actuated by malice but that the other three and the secretary were not. The Court of Appeal held that the non-malicious members were not tainted by the malice of the malicious members. As Lord Denning put it, 'each defendant is answerable severally, as well as jointly, for the joint publication, and each is entitled to his several defence whether he be sued jointly or separately from the others.' While *Egger* v. *Viscount Chelmsford* was concerned with the defence of qualified privilege there seems to be no reason why the principle in the case should not apply to the defence of fair comment as well (but cf. Davies LJ).

Unintentional Defamation

Liability for a defamatory statement, as we have seen, does not depend on the intention of the maker of the statement. The fact that the writer or publisher intended to refer to someone other than the plaintiff, did not intend to refer to a living person, or did not have any idea that what he said was defamatory is irrelevant at common law to their liability: liability for defamation is strict. This may cause hardship for writers, publishers and others and s. 4 of the Defamation Act 1952 was enacted with the intention of mitigating that hardship. Unfortunately, the offer of amends defence (provided for in s. 4 of the Act) proved unsuccessful. This was due, at least in part, to the twin requirements that the offer of amends had to be made as soon as practicable after the complaint was received (which effectively ruled out investigation) and that the defendant had to show the publication took place 'innocently'. Words were treated as published innocently only where the publisher took all reasonable care in relation to their publication and either (a) he did not intend to publish the words about the plaintiff and did not know of circumstances by which they might be understood to refer to him, or (b) the words were not defamatory on their face and the publisher did not know of circumstances by virtue of which they might be understood to be defamatory of the plaintiff. In practice proof of innocent publication proved virtually impossible (see Milmo, 1995) and the defence has remained virtually unused.

The rules regulating the defence have now been substantially changed by ss. 2–4 of the Defamation Act 1996. By s. 2 a person who has published a statement alleged to be defamatory of another may make an offer of amends. An offer to make amends under the section is an offer (a) to make a suitable correction and sufficient apology to the person defamed, (b) to publish the correction and apology in a manner that is reasonable and practicable in the circumstances, and (c) to pay the aggrieved person such compensation (and costs) as are agreed or determined (s. 2(4)). Such offer cannot be made after serving a defence in proceedings brought against him by the aggrieved person (s. 2(5)).

Where such an offer is made and *accepted* the party accepting the offer cannot bring or continue proceedings in respect of the publication concerned (s. 3(2)). Where the parties agree on the steps to be taken in fulfilment of the offer the aggrieved party may apply to the court for an order that the other party fulfil the offer (s. 3(3)). If the parties do not agree on steps to be taken by way of correction, apology or publication, the party making the offer may take such steps as he thinks appropriate and in particular he may make the correction and apology in open court with the approval of the court and give an undertaking to the court as to the manner of their publication (s. 3(4)). Where the parties do not agree as to the amount to be paid by way of compensation, it shall be determined by the court on the same principles as damages in defamation proceedings though the court shall take account of the terms of the offer and its suitability (s. 3(5)). Where an offer is made and *not accepted* then the fact that an offer was made is a defence (s. 4(2)) unless the party making the offer knew or had reason to believe that the statement complained of: (a) referred to the aggrieved person or was likely to be understood as referring to him, and; (b) was both false and defamatory of that party (s. 4(3)). The person who made the offer of amends need not rely on it as a defence but if he does he cannot rely on any other defence (s. 4(4)).

That the new provisions are an improvement on the old is not in doubt. The fact that the defence is available even where the defendant knew the statement was defamatory (but thought it was true) and that the burden – to defeat the defence – is on the *plaintiff* to show that the defendant had no reason to believe the statement referred to the plaintiff or was false and defamatory of him will undoubtedly make the defence more attractive than the old one to newspaper defendants. However, the defendant can only rely on the defence where he makes an apology and agrees to pay damages. Clearly, difficult decisions will arise as to whether to try to justify the story before a jury (and risk a finding of liability and *jury*-assessed damages) or whether to apologise and obtain a judge-assessed amount.

20.8 **Damages**

Defamation actions are usually still tried by a judge and jury. Where that is the case, the assessment of the amount of damages is a matter for the jury. The primacy of the jury in this matter is well established and the courts have until relatively recently shown themselves unwilling to interfere with jury awards. However, the amounts awarded by juries over the last decade have caused considerable and increasing concern. This concern has lead to changes in the advice given to juries in defamation actions, in an attempt to introduce some measure of reality into the amounts awarded, and to the granting to the Court of Appeal (by legislation) of a power to overturn jury awards of damages and substitute their own. Section 8(2) of the Courts and Legal Services Act 1990 and Rules of the Supreme Court, Or. 59, r. 11(4) empowers the Court of Appeal, on allowing an appeal against a jury award of damages, to substitute for the award of the jury such sum as might appear to the court to be proper. In *Rantzen* v. *Mirror Group Newspapers (1986) Ltd* [1993] 4 All ER 975 the Court of Appeal interpreted this provision as entitling it to substitute an award whenever the amount awarded by the jury was such that 'no reasonable jury could have thought that the award was necessary to compensate the plaintiff and re-establish his reputation'. There have now been some three or four cases in which the Court of Appeal has substituted a sum for a jury award and in all those cases the court has substituted a figure of £50 000 or less; (thus e.g. *Gorman* v. *Mudd* (1992) CA Transcript 1076 compensatory damages reduced from £150 000 to £50 000, *John* v. *MGN Ltd* [1996] 2 All ER 35, compensatory damages reduced from £75 000 to £25 000 and exemplary damages reduced from £275 000 to £50 000).

In addition to the power to substitute its own award for that of the jury, the Court of Appeal has recently decided that the jury should be given more guidance than had heretofore been the case. In *John* v. *MGN Ltd* Sir Thomas Bingham MR held that a jury should be referred to: (a) sums awarded by the Court of Appeal in the exercise of their jurisdiction under s. 8(2) of the Courts and Legal Services Act 1990; (b) awards for pain and suffering and loss of amenity in personal injury action. His Lordship also held that counsel and the judge should be allowed make suggestions as to the appropriate award. Mentioning figures, his Lordship thought, would induce a mood of realism: '[t]he plaintiff will not wish the jury to think that his main object is to make money rather than clear his name. The defendant will not wish to add to the insult by underrating the seriousness of the libel' (p. 55). Short of actually removing the function of assessing damages from the jury (which is not such a bad idea) there is probably little else that can be done. Whether juries will now get the hint remains to be seen (it should be noted that the Law Commission, (1995) provisionally concluded that juries should continue to decide quantum (4.100) but thought they ought to be provided with greater direction (4.103)).

Damages in a defamation action are primarily intended to be compensatory. The jury is required to assess the sum required to vindicate the plaintiff's reputation and to compensate him for the injury to his feelings. However, in addition to compensatory damages, aggravated and exemplary damages may be available. The circumstances in which, and basis upon which, such damages are awarded is considered in the chapter on damages (22.2).

Summary

20.1 'Interests in personality' are protected by a number of legal mechanisms in English law. The primary tort in this area is the tort of defamation, which protects a person's reputation. However, additional protection is provided by the principles of negligence, breach of confidence, malicious falsehood, trespass, nuisance and passing off. Additionally, a number of statutes protect interests in personality. English law, however, knows no tort of infringement of privacy.

20.2 The tort of defamation is committed whenever a person publishes defamatory material about another to a third person.

20.3 A defamatory statement is one that 'lowers the plaintiff in the estimation of right thinking members of society generally'. In applying this test the courts tend to look to what right thinking members of society *should* think, rather than what they actually think. Words are often capable of more than one meaning. The plaintiff can seek to show that the words convey an impression or mean something different from their ordinary meaning ('false' innuendo). Alternatively, the plaintiff can argue that the meaning of the words can only be understood by having regard to extrinsic evidence ('true' innuendo).

20.4 The statement must be published to a third person. However, the statement need not have been intentionally published. Provided the defendant ought reasonably to have foreseen that the statement would come to the attention of a third person that is sufficient. Every repetition of a defamatory statement gives rise to a fresh cause of action. However, the original maker of the statement only remains liable for the repetition where it was foreseeable.

20.5 The defamatory statement must refer to the plaintiff. There is no need for the plaintiff to be expressly referred to. Provided a 'hypothetical sensible reader with knowledge of the special facts' would have thought that the statement referred to the plaintiff that is sufficient. A defamatory statement made about a group is not actionable unless the group is so small that the words can be treated as referring to all the group or the words can be treated as having been intended to single out the plaintiff.

20.6 English law draws a distinction between libel and slander. Libel is actionable without proof of damage. Slander, unless falling within one of the exceptional categories, requires proof of damage. There is no single test for distinguishing between libel and slander. However, a statement made in a permanent form and conveyed to the sense of sight will be treated as a libel, while a statement made in transitory form and conveyed to the ear will be treated as a slander.

20.7 In addition to certain general defences such as voluntary assumption of risk and consent, the law of defamation has its own special defences.

20.8 Where a plaintiff succeeds in showing that the words complained of are defamatory, their falsehood is presumed. Justification or truth is, however, a defence. The essence of a plea of justification is that the 'words are true in substance and in fact'. Where there are two or more distinct charges against the plaintiff the defence will not fail merely because one or more cannot be proved, provided the untrue words do not materially injure the plaintiff's reputation.

20.9 The defence of fair comment is, like justification, a complete defence. In order for the defence to succeed it must be shown: (a) that the words used are comment and not fact; (b) that the comment is on a matter of public interest; (c) that the comment is based on true facts; and (d) that the comment is fair. The plaintiff can rebut the defence by showing that the defendant was actuated by malice.

20.10 Some situations are deemed to be of such social or political importance that the law allows a person to speak or write about another without restraint. These are situations of absolute privilege and they include statements made by MPs in Parliament, statements made in judicial proceedings, high executive communications and statements made by certain officials.

20.11 Some occasions, although not of sufficient importance to attract absolute privilege, are nevertheless considered to be of sufficient importance to attract qualified privilege. Statements covered by qualified privilege are protected unless the plaintiff can show that the maker of the statement was actuated by malice. In broad terms a defendant will be found to have been actuated by malice where his motive is to injure the person defamed or he does not believe in the truth of what he says. Statements attracting qualified privilege include: statements made in performance of a legal, moral or social duty; statements made in furtherance or protection of an interest (whether that interest is a private interest, public interest or a common interest); and statements made in certain classes of report.

20.12 A defendant may make an offer of amends (Defamation Act 1996, s. 2). Whether or not it amounts to a complete defence depends upon whether the conditions of ss. 2–4 of the Act are satisfied.

20.13 Generally defamation actions are tried by a judge and jury. Where they are, the assessment of damages is a matter for the jury. Damages in a defamation action are primarily intended to be compensatory. However, exemplary damages may be awarded.

Exercises

20.1 Was Calcutt (1989) right to oppose the introduction of a statutory tort of infringement of privacy? Who would benefit from the enactment of such a tort?

20.2 Is it defamatory to state of a person that he is HIV positive? (See *Bloodworth* v. *Gray* (1844) 7 Man & G 334.) Does the right-thinking person provide a satisfactory concept to determine what is defamatory?

20.3 Was the House of Lords correct in *Lewis* v. *Daily Telegraph* to say that the words complained of could not convey the impression that the plaintiff was guilty of the allegations?

20.4 What is the difference between a true and a false innuendo?

20.5 Would an action lie against the maker of a television programme in respect of remarks made in a review in a newspaper that repeated the defamatory allegations made in the programme?

20.6 Should *Hulton* v. *Jones* and *Newstead* v. *London Express Newspapers Ltd* be followed today?

20.7 How satisfactory is the test for distinguishing between libel and slander? Should the courts continue to draw this distinction? Do the existence of the 'exceptional' cases, where slander is made actionable *per se*, make it unnecessary to continue to draw the distinction?

20.8 A writes that B has a number of convictions for theft and robbery. Additionally, he accuses B of having been convicted of rape. B brings a libel action in respect of the allegation that he has been convicted of robbery. This is untrue, though the other allegations are true. Would A be able to rely on the defence of justification? Would your answer be different if B sued in respect of the rape allegation where this was untrue, though the other allegations were true?

20.9 A writes of B, an MP, that he is a drunkard who beats his dog and that he is, therefore, unfit to represent his constituents. A beats his dog but is not a drunkard. Does B have any remedy?

20.10 Members of Parliament are so irresponsible that their historical right to say what they like in Parliament should be abandoned. Do you agree?

20.11 Juries have shown themselves to be so irresponsible when it comes to the award of damages that they should no longer perform this task. Do you agree? Is s. 8(2) of the Courts and Legal Services Act 1990 and Rules of the Supreme Court, Order 59 sufficient protection for a defendant?

20.12 Anarchy plc is the owner of *Your Investments*, a weekly magazine devoted to stock market comment and City gossip. Brian, a journalist on the magazine, was preparing an article about the takeover of Holy Securities Ltd by Satanic Securities plc, a company in which the principal shareholder was Robert, a well-known entrepreneur. The article, transcribed onto Brian's word processor, alleged that Robert had obtained control of Holy for Satanic by 'strong-arm' tactics and by threatening to expose the extra-marital affair of Holy's principal shareholder, David, to David's wife, Edna. Felicity, an executive employed by Anarchy plc to manage the magazine's affairs, saw the final draft of the article on the word processor screen when she went into Brian's office while he was out to lunch. Felicity was about to resign her job because she was unhappy with the way the magazine was being run. She was also a friend of Edna and decided to disclose the contents of the story to her and also to David's fellow shareholder, Gaynor. On receiving the information from Felicity, Edna became irate and telephoned a gossip magazine called *City Slicker*, informing the editor, Ian, that one of David's affairs was with a well-known rock singer whose name was 'synonymous with Satan'. These word appeared in a report in last week's *City Slicker*. In using the words Edna had intended to refer to a rock singer named Cyn with whom she thought David was having an affair. In fact David was having an affair with a rock singer called Devilla.

The edition of *Your Investments* containing the article was published last week. The allegations contained about Robert are untrue.

Advise the parties as to their rights and liabilities in tort.

Part V

General Principles of Tortious Liability

21 Vicarious Liability and Joint Torts

21.1 **Introduction**

As we have seen, liability in the modern law of torts is generally still dependent on proof of some notion of fault or blameworthiness. Liability will not, subject to certain well-known exceptions, be imposed on a person unless he has intentionally or negligently caused some loss or damage to the plaintiff. Thus liability is usually based on personal fault. However, a person may incur liability as a result not only of his own acts but also as a result of the acts of another. Vicarious liability is an example of just such a situation. Where certain criteria are satisfied, the law holds the defendant vicariously liable for the misconduct of another. This is the case even though the defendant is not himself in any way at fault. In this chapter we examine the criteria required to establish a vicarious liability and look at the justifications for a rule of law that appears to run counter to two basic principles of English law, namely that a person should not be liable in the absence of fault and that a person should only be liable where his act or omission caused the injury.

Vicarious liability may be defined as the liability imposed on one person (D) for the tortious act or omission of another (X) which causes loss to a third person (P). For one person to be vicariously liable for another's tort, certain requirements must be met. First, P must be injured or suffer loss as a result of a tortious act committed by X. This was for some time a source of judicial and academic debate in that some had argued that unless D himself owed P a duty of care, D could not be liable. X's acts were to be attributed to D, but D was not liable for them unless *he* owed P a duty of care. This view was known as the master's tort theory. It is clear today that the view expressed in the master's tort theory is not correct. All that is required is that X commits a tortious act which injures P. Second, some relationship must exist between the tortfeasor X and the defendant D. The relationship that most characteristically satisfies this requirement is that of master and servant or, as it would be more commonly called today, that of employer and employee. Third, there must be some connection between the tortious act and the relationship. This requirement is satisfied where the employee acts in the 'course of his employment'.

Where the requirements of vicarious liability are met the employer will be liable for the acts of his employee regardless of his own culpability and regardless of whether he owes the injured person any duty recognised by law. The liability of the employee in such a case is not extinguished but, for reasons of policy, the courts have considered it desirable to give the injured person an action against the employer. The employer is still entitled to proceed against his employee to recover any damages he has to pay. However, because the employee is unlikely to be able to satisfy any substantial claim and because of the danger to good labour relations an employer is unlikely to bring such a claim.

21.2 Justifications for Vicarious Liability

Despite vicarious liability being one of the longer established principles in English law, its existence is still considered by English lawyers to be somewhat exceptional and to require some special justification. The reason for this is, as we have seen, that the doctrine seems to run counter to two well-established principles of the law of tort. Various arguments of policy have been put forward from time to time to justify the doctrine's existence. Today the most accepted justification is that, as the employer derives an economic benefit from his employee's work, so he ought to bear any losses or liability incurred in the course of the enterprise. It is felt to be justifiable to impose liability on the employer, who in most cases is likely to have substantially greater means than his employee, because these losses are a normal incident of his business and he should therefore bear responsibility for them. He is also better able to spread the cost of the accident. Because the employer knows that he has to bear the cost of any accidents he will usually take out insurance to cover such losses and increase the price of his products to take account of the cost of the insurance. By this mechanism, rather than one person having to bear the whole of the loss, the loss is distributed among those who derive a benefit from either the sale or use of the product.

21.3 Employer and Employee Relationship

In order for a person to be vicariously liable for the tort of another the relationship between them must be governed by a contract *of* service. Where the person is employed under a contract *for* services the employer will not generally be vicariously liable for his torts. In the latter case the 'employee' is more properly known as an independent contractor and, in the absence of a personal non-delegable duty on the employer, the latter will incur no liability in respect of the torts of the independent contractor.

The courts have not found it easy to articulate a single test to answer the question whether a person is an employee or – which amounts to the same thing – whether a person is employed under a contract of service. The changing nature of employment, the increasing technicality of many jobs and professions and the complexity of corporate structures makes it considerably more difficult today, compared with one hundred years ago, to say of a person that he is definitely employed by a particular employer. For example, if a lawyer is seconded from his law firm to a government department does he remain employed by his law firm? Similarly, is a consultant, who normally only does private work, a servant of the local health authority if he does an operation for the authority under the National Health Service? It might be thought that the answer to the question of whether a person is an employee or an independent contractor will depend upon how the parties themselves have classified the relationship. However, while any classification made by the parties will be taken into account by the courts, it can never be conclusive.

The conventional test used by the courts for distinguishing an employee from an independent contractor is the 'control' test. The test was well expressed by Bramwell B in *Yewens* v. *Noakes* (1880) 6 QBD 530, 532–3, where he said, '[a] servant is a person subject to the command of his master as to the manner in which he shall do his work.' An employee is, therefore, employed under a contract of service if his employer can tell him not only what to do but also how to do it. Such a test is, however, only satisfactory in an agricultural or primitive industrial society where the employer has at least as much technical knowledge as the employee and is able to instruct him in how to do the work. In a modern, complex industrial society it is doubtful whether the test is capable of any sensible meaning except in its application to the simplest of jobs. People are employed today in many cases precisely because they have the technical knowledge and skill that their employer does not have. If a hospital authority told a doctor how to resuscitate a patient or a warehouse owner told a fork-lift truck driver how to drive his truck they would probably be told, in no uncertain terms, to mind their own business.

While the courts continue to use the 'control' test in its traditional formulation where that is appropriate, they have not hesitated to hold an employer liable even where the work on which the employee is employed is highly technical and the method of its performance is something of which the employer is ignorant. In order to do so what they have done is to re-interpret the 'control' test so that what they now look for is 'not so much the power to direct *how* the work shall be done but instead the power to control the employee in relation to the incidental features of his employment -what has been termed the 'when' and the 'where' of the work' (Atiyah, 1967, p. 47). Thus the courts, in seeking to answer the question of who is in 'control', have taken into account a wide variety of factors, such as who has the power of appointment and dismissal, who pays the wages, where the 'employee' works, who provides the 'tools of the trade', who pays national insurance contributions or deducts tax and whether the contract itself makes any provision as to the parties' relationship.

The case of *Ready Mixed Concrete (South-East) Ltd* v. *Minister of Pensions and National Insurance* [1968] 1 All ER 433 illustrates some of the factors the courts are likely to take into account in considering whether a contract of service exists. The case raised the question whether an owner-driver was employed under a contract of service for the purposes of s. 1(2) of the National Insurance Act 1965. Although not concerned with the question of vicarious liability it highlights the problem of identifying a contract of service in a modern 'atypical' employment context. A company organised a scheme for the delivery of ready-mixed concrete to its customers through so-called 'owner-drivers'. The contract with each driver provided, *inter alia*, that each driver was to buy the vehicle on hire-purchase from a finance company owned by the company; the driver was not to use the vehicle for any haulage business other than that of the company; the driver was not to make any alterations, change or sell the vehicle without the consent of the company; the driver was to make the vehicle available to the company at all times of the day and night and was generally to comply with all rules, regulations and reasonable orders given by the company. Mackenna J held, despite these provisions which were suggestive of a high degree of control by the company, that this was not a contract of service. While there were a number of provisions suggestive of such a contract, the fact that the driver owned the vehicle, was free to maintain the vehicle as he chose, to hire another driver in the event of holiday or sickness and to buy fuel where he chose were more in line with this contract being a contract of carriage. As Mackenna J put it, 'the ownership of the assets, the chance of profit and the risk of loss in the business of carriage are [the driver's] and not the company's.'

21.4 The Course of Employment

The existence of the relationship of employer and employee is not, however, a sufficient basis for liability in itself. The tort committed by the employee may have absolutely no connection with his employment and in such a case the employer will not be vicariously liable for his employee. For example, if an employee of an accountancy firm assaulted another person in a night club, the mere fact that he happened to be an employee is manifestly no ground for imposing liability upon his employer. In addition, therefore, to the requirement of a contract of service the employee must commit the tort in the 'course of his employment'.

Clearly, if the tort committed by the employee has been expressly authorised or ratified by the employer, the employer will be liable for the tort (though this will not be on the basis of vicarious liability but instead a distinct principle of agency that applies even outside the employment relationship). Such cases are probably rare and it is clear that the course of employment is not limited to such circumstances. However, articulating a clear test to determine whether a tort was committed in the course of employment is not an easy task. As Fleming points out (1992, p. 377);

'[T]he course of employment is an expansive concept which provides ample scope for policy decisions and, despite the vast volume of case law, has failed to acquire a high degree of precision. No statistical measurement is possible, and precedents are helpful only when they present a suggestive uniformity on parallel facts.'

The standard starting point adopted by the courts is the test set out in Salmond and Heuston (1996, p. 443). The authors there state that, in addition to torts authorised or ratified by the master, torts committed by an employee are within the course of employment provided they are 'so connected with acts which [the employer] has authorised that they may rightly be regarded as modes -although improper modes- of doing them.' (p. 443) The test makes clear that the employer is liable not only for those acts he has authorised but also for those acts which, although he has not directly authorised them, are nevertheless to be treated as wrongful and unauthorised modes of performing an authorised task. Where the employee embarks on an unauthorised, independent jaunt of his own the limit is exceeded. Until that moment in time he acts in the course of his employment. It is all a question of degree. If, for example, a company employs a person as a bus conductor he may still be acting in the course of his employment if he merely drives the bus out of the way of another bus while in the bus terminal. However, he will almost certainly be acting outside the course of his employment if he takes the bus out onto the streets in order to engage in a race with another bus-driver. In order to consider the application of the test a number of problem areas are now considered.

Frolics, Detours and Incidental Duties

In *Joel* v. *Morison* (1834) 6 C & P 501, 503 Parke B stated that an employee acts outside the course of his employment 'when embarking on a frolic of his own'. This clearly encompasses egregious behaviour entirely for the employee's own benefit. For example, if an employer instructs his employee to drive from London to Glasgow to deliver a parcel and the employee deviates via Land's End to pick up a friend it can be said that he has deviated from his route so extensively that he has gone on an entirely new journey and is acting outside the course of his employment. On the other hand if he stops off between London and Glasgow in order to buy himself lunch and negligently runs someone over in the restaurant car park he is likely to be treated as acting in the course of his employment. In this case the diversion from the most direct route would be likely to be treated as incidental to his employment. In *Century Insurance Co Ltd* v. *Northern Ireland Road Transport Board* [1942] AC 509 a petrol tanker driver lighted a cigarette while delivering petrol and then threw away the match causing an explosion which damaged the plaintiff's property. The House of Lords held that he was still acting within the course of his employment. Even though the act of lighting the cigarette was done purely for his own benefit and convenience and not for his employer's benefit, the act could not be treated as a wholly independent act but was instead an improper mode of doing that which he was employed to do.

Some difficulty has been experienced by the courts in dealing with cases of negligence committed by employees while on their way to work or while travelling between different workplaces on the instructions of their employer. In *Smith* v. *Stages* [1989] AC 928 the House of Lords, while recognising that it was impossible to provide for every eventuality, set out a number of presumptions. First, an employee travelling to or from work is, in ordinary circumstances, not acting within the course of his employment. Of course it may be said that in order to carry out a day's work he must travel to and from work and thus the travel should be seen as an incidental part of his work. The House of Lords was, however, of the view that, while a person was employed to work at his place of work, he was not in ordinary circumstances employed to travel from his home to his workplace. However, their Lordships recognised that, where a person is obliged to travel to work by means provided by his employer, he may be held to be acting within the course of his employment. Second, where an employee is instructed or required by his job (for example, if he is a travelling salesman) to travel from one workplace to another or from his home to a succession of workplaces and he is paid for this travelling he will usually be acting within the course of his employment. Finally, payment of wages while travelling or allowing the employee a discretion as to the mode and time of travel are factors to be taken into account but are not conclusive of the question whether a person is acting within the course of his employment.

Prohibited Conduct

If an employer expressly prohibits his employee from doing a particular act and the employee in breach of that instruction does that very act and injures another it might be thought that he would be acting outside the course of his employment. This is, however, not necessarily the case. Some prohibitions do, and some do not, take the employee outside the course of his employment. Whether or not a prohibition takes the employee outside the course of his employment depends on whether it limits the sphere of his employment or seeks only to deal with conduct within the sphere of employment. It is often a very difficult question which side of the line a prohibition falls, and fine judgements may be called for. In some cases the breach of a prohibition makes the employee's conduct so unconnected with his employment that he will be treated as acting outside the course of his employment. For example, if a company expressly forbade the drivers of its buses from racing other buses, an employee who caused an accident while racing a rival firm's bus would in all likelihood be treated as acting outside the course of his employment. On the other hand, if a company prohibits its employees from using their own cars for work unless they are properly insured, an employee driving his own, uninsured, car who causes an accident will not be acting outside the course of his employment as the prohibition merely affects the way in which he is to do his job. It does not restrict him in what he is employed to do.

As a general rule prohibitions which affect the manner, time or place of performance are not held to affect the sphere of performance and, therefore, breach of the prohibition will not take the employee outside the course of his employment. In *Rose* v. *Plenty* [1976] 1 All ER 97 Mr Plenty was a milk roundsman employed by the defendants. His duties included driving a float on his round and collecting money. He was expressly prohibited by the terms of his employment from employing children in the performance of those duties. In breach of this prohibition, he invited the infant plaintiff to help him and the plaintiff was injured when Plenty drove the float negligently. The Court of Appeal, by a majority, held that Plenty was acting within the course of his employment. The judges held that the prohibition affected only the sphere of employment in that it went only to the manner in which the work was to be performed.

Intentional Misconduct

As with express prohibition, it might be thought that if by intentional misconduct an employee injures another person that would take him outside the course of his employment. If a university lecturer was to strike and injure a student who was annoying him, in all likelihood the university would not be vicariously liable for the lecturer's tort. Striking a student can only with great difficulty be viewed as an improper mode of performing an authorised duty. Having said that, there are cases where even intentional misconduct by the employee may be within the course of his employment. Such cases are usually situations where the employee was prompted by a desire to further the interests of his employers and was acting with, what turned out to be unfortunate enthusiasm. In *Poland* v. *John Parr & Sons* [1927] 1 KB 236 Mr Hall, an employee of the defendants, honestly believed that the 12-year-old plaintiff was stealing sugar from his employer's wagon. Hall struck the child causing him to fall under one of the wheels of the wagon and the child was seriously injured. The Court of Appeal held that Hall was acting in the course of his employment. He had behaved reasonably in defence of his employer's interests and such defence was reasonably incidental to the duties he was employed to perform.

Where, however, the act of the servant goes beyond unfortunate enthusiasm or an error of judgment the courts have generally been careful to avoid imposing too heavy a burden on the employer. In *Poland* v. *John Parr & Sons*, for example, Atkin LJ said that the answer given by the court may well have been different had Hall shot the plaintiff. Similarly, in another case a dance hall 'bouncer' having lawfully ejected a customer from the hall, later wholly gratuitously struck him and injured him. The court held he was acting outside the course of his employment.

21.5 Liability for Independent Contractors

As a general rule employers are not liable for the acts of independent contractors whom they employ to do a particular task or series of tasks. The reason given for this qualification of vicarious liability is that the employer lacks detailed control over the independent contractor who is, in any event, better able to distribute the losses caused by his work than his employer. In many cases this is of course true. If a person hires a taxi to drive him from London to Heathrow he has little control over the way in which the driver drives and it is surely more appropriate to expect the taxi driver to insure against any losses caused by his negligence rather than the passenger. However, as McKendrick points out (1990) it may no longer be realistic to treat all 'independent contractors' in the same way. Some are without doubt large, well-organised organisations who are capable of including provision for insurance within their pricing policy. However, over the last few years there has been a vast increase in the number of home-workers and the 'self-employed'. Neither category may be 'employees' as that word has been defined by the courts and yet, unlike their employers, they may be unable to bear or shift any loss that may be caused by their negligence. This change in work patterns may suggest a need to re-evaluate the courts' traditional opposition to liability for independent contractors and indicate a need either for a wider view of who is an 'employee' or for a relaxation of the rules against recovery against an employer of an independent contractor.

Although the courts have traditionally refused to allow a plaintiff to recover damages against the employer of an independent contractor there are a number of exceptional categories where recovery has been allowed. In recent years the courts have shown themselves willing to expand upon these exceptions, though unfortunately they have not articulated the basis on which they have done so. The mechanism by which liability is imposed on an employer is that of the non-delegable duty. By saying that an employer owes such a duty, the courts mean that he cannot acquit himself of liability by exercising reasonable care in choosing an independent contractor to do the work. As Glanville Williams has pointed out (1956), there is unfortunately no coherent theory that explains when a duty will be classified as non-delegable. Nevertheless, there are now a substantial number of duties that are classified as non-delegable and in the remaining part of this chapter we will seek to identify some of these.

Unsurprisingly, many of the duties that have been classified as non-delegable are strict duties. For example, there are a number of strict *statutory* duties that cannot be discharged by the employment of an independent contractor (see, for example, many of the provisions of the Factories Act 1961). So also the duty imposed upon neighbouring landowners to prevent the escape of dangerous things imposed by *Rylands* v. *Fletcher* is a non-delegable duty, as are the strict duties to maintain premises abutting a highway and to provide lateral support for adjacent land (*Tarry* v. *Ashton* (1876) 1 QBD 314). An analogous case to *Rylands* v. *Fletcher* is the non-delegable duty owed by all those who engage independent contractors to do 'extra-hazardous' acts. In the leading case of *Honeywill and Stein Ltd* v. *Larkin Bros (London Commercial Photographers) Ltd* [1934] 1 KB 191 a cinema company engaged the plaintiffs to do some acoustic work in their theatre. The contractors employed photographers to take photographs of their work inside the theatre. At the time, the taking of flashlight photographs involved the ignition in a metal tray of magnesium powder which, on being ignited, flared up and caused intense heat. As a result of the negligence of the camera operator the magnesium ignited too close to the curtains and they caught fire causing damage. The Court of Appeal held that the contractors were liable for the harm done. Where, as here, an act 'in its very nature involved a special danger to others' the contractors could not discharge their liability simply by proving that they had hired a competent independent contractor.

In addition to the strict duties which the courts have classified as non-delegable, they have identified a number of situations in which breach of the non-delegable duty is dependent upon fault, albeit that of an independent contractor rather than an employee. In such cases, the duty is not merely to take reasonable care but to ensure that reasonable care is taken. Thus, proof by the employer that he took all reasonable care in selecting a competent independent contractor will not excuse him from liability if the independent contractor is careless. Examples of such duties include the obligation of employers to provide a safe system of work (*Wilson and Clyde Coal Co* v. *English* [1938] AC 57); of hospitals to care for their patients (*Cassidy* v. *Ministry of Health* [1951] 2 KB 343, per Denning LJ); and of school authorities to care for their pupils (*Carmarthenshire County Council* v. *Lewis* [1955] AC 549).

Finally, it must be pointed out that an employer is not liable for any 'casual' or 'collateral' acts of negligence of the independent contractor. The distinction between 'collateral' acts of negligence and those for which the employer is responsible is by no means clear. What appears to be meant is that the employer is liable only when the independent contractor commits the tort while engaged in doing that which he was actually employed to do. Thus, in *Honeywill & Stein Ltd* v. *Larkin Bros* the employer would probably not have been liable for the independent contractor had he managed to set fire to the curtains while throwing firecrackers.

21.6 Joint and Several Liability: The Distinction Between Joint, Several Concurrent and Separate Tortfeasors

Where damage is caused to the plaintiff by two or more tortfeasors he may be uncertain as to whom to sue. Must he sue all of them or can he sue one only? Can he recover the full amount of his loss from one of the tortfeasors or must he bring separate actions against each tortfeasor to recover from each their proportionate share of his loss? If the plaintiff is required to sue all those involved in causing him damage he may be faced with problems if, for example, one of the tortfeasors cannot be found or is uninsured or insolvent. On the other hand, if a plaintiff is allowed to recover all his loss from one tortfeasor, fairness would seem to dictate that that tortfeasor should have some right to contribution from the other tortfeasors. In the remainder of this chapter we examine some of the problems that arise where more than one tortfeasor causes damage to the plaintiff and also consider the rights of tortfeasors to claim contribution from each other.

There are three possible types of case where a person may suffer damage as the result of a tortious act committed by two or more tortfeasors. First, the same damage may be caused to the plaintiff by two or more tortfeasors acting in pursuance of a common design. This may happen in at least three classes of case; namely agency, vicarious liability and joint enterprise. Thus, for example, where two people were looking for an escape of gas and one lighted a match thereby causing an explosion, it was held that they were engaged on a joint enterprise and were jointly liable for the damage caused (*Brooke* v. *Bool* [1928] 2 KB 578). Similarly, where a master is vicariously liable for the tort of his servant, both are jointly liable for the damage caused by the servant's tort. Where two or more people *jointly* participate in causing the same damage the plaintiff may sue any of them separately for the full amount of the loss. Alternatively, he may sue all of them jointly in the same action. The liability of *joint* tortfeasors is, therefore, joint and several.

Second, two or more tortfeasors may cause the same damage to the plaintiff in circumstances where they are acting independently and, therefore, do not fall within the first category. In such a case the tortfeasors are known as several concurrent tortfeasors. Where, for example, two cars driven by A and B respectively crash into the plaintiff's car causing him 'whiplash' injuries, A and B are several concurrent tortfeasors. As with joint tortfeasors, each several concurrent tortfeasor is answerable in full for the whole damage caused to the plaintiff.

At common law there were two principal distinctions between joint tortfeasors and several concurrent tortfeasor. First, judgment against one joint tortfeasor, even if it remained unsatisfied, barred any subsequent action. Second, the release of one joint tortfeasor operated as a release of all. Neither of these rules applied to several concurrent tortfeasors. The first rule has now been abolished and the second much diminished in importance such that there is now little substantive distinction between joint and several concurrent tortfeasors.

Finally, where two or more persons not acting in pursuance of a common design cause different damage to the same plaintiff, they are treated as separate and independent tortfeasors. For example, as a result of A's negligent driving the plaintiff's wrist is broken and requires hospital treatment. At the hospital Dr B, who had been drinking heavily, bandages the plaintiff's wrist but does it so negligently that the plaintiff permanently loses all feeling in his arm. A may not be responsible for Dr B's negligence. A and Dr B are separate and independent tortfeasors who have caused different damage to the same plaintiff. The cases of *Performance Cars* v. *Abraham* [1962] 1 QB 33 and *Baker* v. *Willoughby* [1970] AC 467 (see 9.2) are also good examples of separate and independent tortfeasors. No special rules are required where two or more tortfeasors cause different damage to the plaintiff.

21.7 Contribution Between Tortfeasors

General Right to Claim Contribution

As a general rule the common law allowed no contribution to be claimed between joint or several concurrent tortfeasors even where one tortfeasor had satisfied the plaintiff's claim in full. This rule has, however, largely been reversed by statute. The rules relating to contribution are now found in the Civil Liability (Contribution) Act 1978. Section 1(1) of the Act provides that:

> 'Subject to the following provisions of this section, any person liable in respect of any damage suffered by another person may recover contribution from any other person liable in respect of the same damage (whether jointly with him or otherwise).'

The Act is not limited in its application to tort. It also applies where the legal basis of liability is 'breach of contract, breach of trust or otherwise'.

Who May Claim Contribution?

In order to be able to claim contribution, the person seeking contribution must either have been found by a court to have been liable or be able to show that liability could be established against him at trial (s. 1(6)). Where, therefore, no action could be brought against him because, for example, a limitation period has expired his claim for contribution will fail. However, if one of the tortfeasors has paid the plaintiff, he is still entitled to contribution even if he has ceased to be liable to the original plaintiff provided 'he was liable immediately before he made or was ordered or agreed to make the payment in respect of which contribution is sought' (s. 1(2)). If one of the tortfeasors settles his claim with the plaintiff, without admitting liability, he will only be able to claim contribution if he could prove that he was legally answerable (s. 1(4)).

From Whom May Contribution Be Claimed?

Section 1(1) provides that contribution is recoverable from anyone who is liable for the same damage. A person may still be liable to make contribution even where he has ceased to be liable to the plaintiff (s. 1(3)). For example, a person may have ceased to be liable to the plaintiff because the plaintiff waived his claim against that person or because the claim was settled. More commonly, the period of limitation within which the plaintiff must sue the defendant may have expired. Provided, however, the person seeking contribution brings the action against his co-defendant within two years from the date of judgment or settlement an action for contribution may still lie.

Assessment of Contribution

Section 2(1) of the Act provides that 'in any proceedings for contribution under s. 1 above the amount of contribution recoverable from any person shall be such as may be found by the court to be just and equitable having regard to the extent of that person's responsibility for the damage in question.' The assessment of the amount of contribution payable is made by having regard only to the parties before the court: the negligence or contributory negligence of a party not before the court cannot be taken into account. In determining the 'responsibility for the damage' the courts have looked at both the blameworthiness of the tortfeasor and the extent to which that person's act directly caused the loss. Thus, the question of responsibility is assessed on the basis of fault plus causation and not simply moral blameworthiness.

Where the amount of damages payable by one of the tortfeasors to the plaintiff has been limited by agreement or by virtue of the operation of the Law Reform (Contributory Negligence) Act 1945 then the maximum amount recoverable in contribution is that limited or reduced amount (s. 2(3)).

Summary

21.1 Vicarious liability may be defined as the liability imposed on an employer (D) for the tortious act of his employee (X) that causes loss to a third party (P). For one person to be vicariously liable for the tort of another three conditions must be satisfied. First, the relationship of employer and employee must exist. Second, the employee must commit a tort. Third, the tort must be committed within the course of the employees employment.

21.2 The most commonly accepted justification for the principle of vicarious liability is that as the employer derives a benefit from his employees' work so he ought to bear any losses or liability incurred in the course of the employment. Other justifications have, however, been put forward.

21.3 In order for the employer to be liable for the torts of his employee a contract *of* service, as opposed to a contract *for* services, must exist. Traditionally, the 'control' test was used to establish this relationship. However, the more modern approach is to look at all the terms of the contract and the surrounding circumstances in order to see whether a contracts *of* service exists.

21.4 The tort must be committed by the employee *in the course of his employment*. Torts are committed by the employee within the course of his employment where they are so connected with acts which the employer has authorised that they may be rightly regarded as modes, albeit improper modes, of doing that which the employee was employed to do. The fact that the employee intentionally committed a tort, was doing something he had been prohibited from doing or committed a tort while on a frolic of his own are relevant factors in considering whether a servant was acting within the course of his employment. They are not, however, conclusive against the imposition of vicarious liability.

21.5 As a general rule an employer will not be liable for the acts of his independent contractors. However, in recent years the courts have held that an employer will be liable where he owes the plaintiff a non-delegable duty. The circumstances in which non-delegable duties have been found to exist are many and various.

21.6 Where two or more tortfeasors cause the same damage to a plaintiff, the plaintiff may sue any or all of them to recover his loss. In such a case the tortfeasors will either be joint tortfeasors (where they act in pursuance of a common design to cause the same damage) or several concurrent tortfeasors (where they act separately to cause the same damage). Where two or more tortfeasors act separately to cause different damage they are separate and independent tortfeasors and must be sued separately.

21.7 Joint and several concurrent tortfeasors may recover contribution from the other tortfeasors. The rules on contribution are contained in the Civil Liability (Contribution) Act 1978.

Exercises

21.1 In what circumstances will a employer be liable for his employees?

21.2 Is the principle of vicarious liability justifiable?

21.3 If a employer is liable for the torts of his employee why should he not be liable for the torts of his independent contractors?

21.4 A Ltd own a number of nightclubs. B Co hire out 'bouncers' for nightclub work. A Ltd hire Kevin, who is on B Co's books, for six months. B Co pay their 'bouncers' a nominal £25 per week when they are not employed by another company. Under the terms of the agreement between A Ltd and B Co, A Ltd agree to pay B Co £50 per week for Kevin's services. It is also agreed that A Ltd can dismiss Kevin for 'misconduct' and that A Ltd will pay Kevin £200 per week in cash (to avoid any tax problems). Kevin's contract with A Ltd describes him as self-employed.

A Ltd tell Kevin that under no circumstances must he drink on duty or strike a customer unless he is attacked first.

One night Kevin gets drunk in the club with a 'friend' of his, C. C, who is very drunk, starts to cause trouble. The manager of the club tells Kevin to eject C. Kevin tries to persuade C to leave. C starts to leave but on his way out he turns around and calls Kevin a coward. Kevin chases after C and catches him. Kevin stabs C with a knife he carries for 'protection'. C is seriously injured.

Advise the parties as to their rights and liabilities in tort.

21.5 What is meant by the control test? Is it a satisfactory determinant of the question whether an employer–employee relationship exists?

21.6 Should an employer ever be liable where an employee does something that the employer has expressly forbidden him to do?

21.7 Why should an employer not be liable in respect of torts committed by an employee on the way to work?

21.8 Is there any coherent principle underlying the cases where the courts have held that an employer owes a non-delegable duty?

22 Remedies

In this chapter we consider the remedies available to the victim of a tort. We concentrate in particular on the formal rules governing the recovery of damages for personal injuries and death. In addition, we examine the rules governing the recovery of damages for loss of or damage to property and the circumstances in which an injunction may be granted in a tort action.

22.1 The Indemnity Principle

In contrast to the law of contract, where the purpose of an award of damages is to put the injured party in the position he would have been in had the contract been performed, the purpose of an award of damages in tort is to put the person who has suffered the loss in the position he would have been in had no tort occurred. As Lord Scarman said in *Lim Poh Choo* v. *Camden and Islington Area Health Authority* [1980] AC 174, 187, 'the principle of the law is that compensation should as nearly as possible put the party who has suffered in the same position as he would have been in if he had not sustained the wrong.' Thus, the overriding principle of the law of damages is that the person who has suffered the loss should be fully *compensated* for the loss he has suffered. Damages are, therefore, generally awarded to compensate the plaintiff and not to punish the defendant.

22.2 Kinds of Damages

Although damages are ordinarily awarded in order to compensate the plaintiff for his injury, that need not be the case. Awards of damages may be made which are non-compensatory in intent. Within this category are (a) contemptuous damages, (b) nominal damages, (c) exemplary damages and (d) restitutionary damages. A court may also award 'aggravated' damages which, although often difficult in practice to distinguish from exemplary damages, are in fact compensatory in intent.

Contemptuous Damages

Although the plaintiff may succeed in his action, the court may indicate that it has formed a low opinion of the merits of the plaintiff's claim or of the plaintiff's conduct by awarding a derisory amount. Such damages are contemptuous and the amount awarded is usually 'the smallest coin' in the realm. An award of contemptuous damages may imperil the plaintiff's chances of recovering his costs. The reason for this is that while costs usually 'follow the event' (i.e. are borne by the losing party), the award of costs is at the judge's discretion. Thus, although the award of contemptuous damages does not necessarily lead to the conclusion that costs will not be awarded to the successful plaintiff, the fact that the court awarded contemptuous damages only is a material factor for the court to take into account in exercising its discretion. Contemptuous damages are most commonly awarded in the context of libel actions.

Nominal Damages

Nominal damages are awarded where a person's legal rights have been infringed but he has suffered no actual loss. Where, for example, a person succeeds in an action for assault (which is actionable *per se*) but cannot prove that he has suffered any injury or loss, the damages awarded are likely to be nominal only. The function of nominal damages is, therefore, to mark the fact that the plaintiff's rights have been vindicated albeit that he has suffered no damage. The award of nominal damages does not involve any finding that the plaintiff was guilty of any misconduct nor does it reflect on the merits of the plaintiff's case. However, as is the case with contemptuous damages, the fact that the court made an award of nominal damages is a material factor for the judge to consider in exercising his discretion in awarding costs.

Exemplary Damages

In *Rookes* v. *Barnard* [1964] AC 1129, the House of Lords referred to damages intended to punish, deter and convey disapproval as 'exemplary'. This terminology has become commonplace so that damages awarded with a punitive intent are now generally known as 'exemplary' damages. In *Rookes* v. *Barnard* Lord Devlin, with whom the other members of the House of Lords concurred, expressed the opinion that the availability of an exemplary award of damages in a civil action was anomalous because the punitive considerations that it reflects properly belong to the criminal law. However, because of the weight of authority supporting exemplary damages and the fact that they could, in rare circumstances, vindicate the strength of the law he preferred to restrict their availability rather than abolish them outright.

Since *Rookes* v. *Barnard*, a claim for exemplary damages can succeed only when it falls within one of three categories. These are (a) oppressive, arbitrary or unconstitutional action by servants of the government, (b) wrongful conduct by the defendant which has been calculated by him to make a profit for himself that may well exceed the compensation payable to the plaintiff, and (c) any case where such an award is authorised by statute. In addition to the requirement that a claim must fall within one of Lord Devlin's categories, the Court of Appeal in *A.B.* v. *South West Water Services Ltd* [1993] QB 507 held that the plaintiff must prove that the cause of action (i.e. tort) upon which his claim is based is one in respect of which exemplary damages had been awarded prior to *Rookes* v.

Barnard (the 'cause of action' test). Even if these two preconditions for the award of exemplary damages are satisfied, a court is not *compelled* to award them. As was made clear by the House of Lords in *Cassell & Co* v. *Broome* [1972] AC 1027, a court retains a discretion to refuse a plaintiff's claim; exemplary damages are discretionary, not mandatory. These preconditions for the award of exemplary damages will be considered in turn.

Lord Devlin's Categories

The first category was derived from a series of eighteenth-century cases that sought to protect the liberties of the subject from the power of the state. Although limited to oppressive *governmental* action, the House of Lords in *Cassell & Co* v. *Broome* made clear that 'servants of the government' should not be narrowly interpreted. Thus, it has been held to include not only crown servants, but also others who exercise government functions, such as police officers and local government officials. It does not, however, encompass the misuse of powers by businesses and other powerful non-governmental bodies despite the fact that the former may exercise considerably more economic power than a local authority and may also perform similar functions. What is relevant, according to the House of Lords in *Cassell & Co* v. *Broome*, is the nature of the functions or powers being exercised. Thus, in *A.B.* v. *South West Water Services Ltd*, a nationalised body set up under statute for a commercial purpose, namely the supply of water, was regarded by the Court of Appeal as outside the first category because in conducting commercial operations it was not engaged in performing governmental functions.

Lord Devlin's second category covers cases where the defendant's conduct has been calculated by him to make a profit for himself which may well exceed the compensation payable to the plaintiff. Once again it is clear that a broad interpretation should be given to these words. The aim of the category is, to use the words of Lord Hailsham in *Cassell & Co* v. *Broome*, 'to teach the wrongdoer that tort does not pay'. Thus, it is not essential that the defendant should be seeking to profit in *monetary* terms. It is enough that the defendant was, for example, seeking to gain some property at the plaintiff's expense. Defamation cases provide many examples of awards in this category. In *Cassell & Co* v. *Broome*, where the defendant published a book containing grave imputations on the plaintiff's conduct, an award of £25 000 exemplary damages was upheld by a majority of the House of Lords. The book was published only after the publishers had been warned as to the defamatory material it contained. Further, there was, according to their Lordships, enough evidence for the jury to have reached the decision they did that the defendant had made a cynical calculation that the damages they might have to pay would not exceed the profit they would make. That is not to say, however, that all defamatory material printed in a newspaper with a view to increasing the publication's circulation will necessarily be redressed by an award of exemplary damages. In addition, it will have to be shown that the defendant made a decision to proceed knowing that it was wrong, or was reckless as to whether or not it was wrong, because he had calculated that the financial benefits outweighed any risks involved. In practice it may be extremely difficult to show that a decision was taken to publish in order to boost a publication's circulation.

Lord Devlin's third category recognises the obvious fact that exemplary damages may be awarded whenever a statute allows such an award to be made. There are, however, few modern statutes that expressly authorise the award of exemplary damages. Further, it is not clear that those statutes that appear to allow the award of exemplary damages do in fact do so. The Law Commission in its recent consultation paper on exemplary damages (Law Commission, 1993, para. 3.52) commented that 'it is possible that both of the statutes (s. 13(2) of the Reserve and Auxiliary Forces (Protection of Civil Interests) Act 1951 and ss. 97(2) and 229(3) of the Copyright, Designs and Patents Act 1988) which are often cited as falling within this category are actually examples of statutes which permit aggravated damages as opposed to exemplary awards.' In any event, little use has been made of this justification in practice.

The 'Cause of Action' Test

It is now clear, following the decision of the Court of Appeal in *A.B.* v. *South West Water Services Ltd*, that in addition to bringing his claim for exemplary damages within one of Lord Devlin's categories, the plaintiff must also prove that the cause of action on which his case is based was one for which exemplary damages were available prior to *Rookes* v. *Barnard*. While it has been pointed out that precedent did not dictate this conclusion (see Burrows, 1993), two practical effects of the decision are to prevent any further extension of exemplary damages to wrongs for which they have not previously been awarded and also to end the award of exemplary damages in discrimination cases. Causes of action that do satisfy the 'cause of action' test include defamation, trespass (both to the person (*Thompson* v. *Comr of Police of the Metropolis* [1997] 2 All ER 762) and to land and chattels) and malicious prosecution. Although the question was left open by the court in *A.B.* v. *South West Water Services Ltd*, exemplary damages are probably also available in an action for private nuisance. Wrongs that clearly fail the 'cause of action' test include negligence, public nuisance, deceit and the statutory torts created by the Sex Discrimination Act 1975 and the Race Relations Act 1976. Whatever one's view as to the merits of exemplary damages, the decision in *A.B.* v. *South West Water Services Ltd* is unsatisfactory. The effect of the decision is that the availability of exemplary damages depends on a decision actually having been made prior to *Rookes* v. *Barnard*, and, therefore, on the accidents of litigation, and not on any principled view of the underlying justification for such damages.

Overriding Discretion and Assessment

Even when both preconditions for the award of exemplary damages are satisfied it is still open to a court or jury to decide not to award them. The award of exemplary damages is discretionary and a court or jury may decide in its exercise of discretion that the case is not a proper one for the award of exemplary damages. In considering whether to exercise the discretion particular regard will be had to the conduct of plaintiff and defendant, whether or not the defendant has already been subject to a criminal penalty for his actions and, since *A.B.* v. *South West Water Services Ltd*, whether there is a *class* of plaintiffs. In *A.B.* v. *South West Water Services Ltd*, the Court of Appeal viewed the large number of plaintiffs affected by the nuisance as an aspect of the case which made it peculiarly unsuitable for the award of exemplary damages.

Where a court or jury decides that the case is an appropriate one for the award of exemplary damages, the amount to be awarded must be decided. As the purpose of an exemplary award is to punish, deter or condemn the defendant's conduct, the damages awardable should, in theory, be measured by 'the gravity of the defendant's conduct, by whatever sum is sufficient to deter it, or by a sum which represents an appropriate symbolic indemnification'. (Law Commission, 1993, para. 3.87) Such considerations are of course very difficult to put a value on. However, a number of principles relevant to the assessment of exemplary damages have been developed by the courts. Thus, awards should be 'moderate' and take account of the wealth of the defendant. Account must also be taken of any award of compensatory damages made. Only where that sum is inadequate to 'punish' the defendant for his outrageous behaviour can an award of exemplary damages be made. Where a plaintiff sues more than one defendant, the principle of proportionality in punishment means that the sum awarded should be the lowest which the conduct of *any* of the defendants deserves. In the case of multiple plaintiffs, the jury should determine a single global sum for 'punishment' and this should then be divided among the plaintiffs.

The assessment of exemplary damages has been the subject of considerable criticism. This is, in part, due to the fact that such awards are often made by juries which are notoriously unpredictable in their awards and, until the passing of s. 8 of the Courts and Legal Services Act 1990 and Rules of the Supreme Court, Order 59, r. 11(4), virtually uncontrollable. However, there is also some evidence that judges have difficulty in assessing these awards. It may be that the s. 8 of the 1990 Act, which empowers the Court of Appeal to substitute its own award for that made by the jury where the damages are excessive, will enable that court to give more guidance than has heretofore been the case and will generate a body of awards to which reference can be made in subsequent cases. In two recent cases (*Thompson* v. *Comr of Police of the Metropolis*; *John* v. *MGN Ltd* [1996] 2 All ER 35) the Court of Appeal has made clear that 'excessive' awards will not be upheld and in both cases maximum amounts for trespass to the person and defamation respectively were indicated.

There are arguments both in favour and against exemplary damages. At the root of the arguments in favour is the claim that, while compensation may be the predominant aim of a civil award of damages, 'the pursuit of retributory, deterrent and condemnatory aims is in certain instances and under certain conditions a legitimate function of the law of civil wrongs.' (Law Commission, 1993, para. 5.13) The award of exemplary damages may also lead to a better protection of rights, as well as vindicating the strength of the law and individual rights. By way of example, serious interferences with interests of personality that give rise to such 'intangible' harms as insult, humiliation or degradation are difficult to assess in compensatory terms. Such wrongs may be more effectively remedied by a punitive model. The main arguments against their award are that they confuse the purposes of the civil and criminal law, import 'criminal'-type punishments into the civil law without any of the corresponding protections, provide the plaintiff with an undeserved windfall, and are difficult to assess and invariably excessive. Further, the opponents argue that since non-pecuniary harm is now freely compensable, exemplary damages are no longer necessary.

In its recent Consultation Paper on exemplary damages (Law Commission, 1993), the Law Commission provisionally concluded in favour of the civil law continuing to recognise the punitive principle in some form. It was particularly impressed by the argument that such damages had an important role to play in the protection of personality rights. However, it was also of the opinion that the current law relating to exemplary damages was unprincipled and needed to be changed. Two possible models were suggested for the rationalisation of exemplary damages. The first would involve legislation providing for the general recognition of such damages, leaving the courts to develop the law by traditional common law methods. The second, which was provisionally favoured by the Commission, would define the circumstances in which an award of exemplary damages might be made and the conditions that would govern the process.

Aggravated Damages

Aggravated damages are typically awarded where the *manner* in which the tort was committed was such as to injure the plaintiff's proper feelings of pride and dignity, or gave rise to humiliation, insult or other distress. In theory, such damages are compensatory only. They are not, as are exemplary damages, awarded to punish the defendant but instead to compensate the plaintiff for any additional injury resulting from the high-handed way in which the defendant has behaved. The defendant's conduct is relevant only to cast light upon the plaintiff's injury and not to punish, condemn or otherwise deter the defendant. In order for an award of aggravated damages to be made, two elements must be satisfied. First, the defendant's conduct must be 'exceptional', i.e. particularly offensive or accompanied by malevolence or spite. Examples of such conduct would include the wrongful eviction of a tenant where that is accompanied by abuse or other forms of harassment, police misconduct, a particularly humiliating and vicious sexual assault, and malicious libel. Such conduct must, however, be exceptional and, therefore, aggravated damages are not available for negligence even where the negligence is particularly serious. Conduct subsequent to the wrong may be sufficient to give rise to aggravated damages. In *Sutcliffe* v. *Pressdram Ltd* [1991] 1 QB 153, 184, in the context of a defamation action, the Court of Appeal viewed as aggravating, 'a failure to make any sufficient apology and withdrawal; a repetition of the libel; conduct calculated to deter the plaintiff from proceeding; persistence, by way of a prolonged and hostile cross-examination of the plaintiff or in turgid speeches to the jury, of a plea of justification which is bound to fail; the general conduct either of the preliminaries or of the trial itself in a manner calculated to attract further wide publicity; and persecution of the plaintiff.'

The second requirement is of an injury to a personality interest. This requirement means that a company, which has no feelings, and a person who is unaware of the defendant's motives, should not be able to recover aggravated damages. In *Cassell & Co* v. *Broome* the House of Lords thought that mental distress, injury to feelings, insult, indignity, humiliation, and a heightened sense of injury or grievance were sufficient to give rise to an award of aggravated damages. More doubtful, however, is whether aggravated damages are available in respect of feelings of anger and indignation excited by the defendant's conduct. A claim purporting to rely on such feelings was struck out by the Court of Appeal in *A.B.* v. *South West Water Services Ltd.* In the court's view, feelings of anger and indignation were not a proper subject for compensation. However, this view would appear to conflict with previous law (*Cassell & Co* v. *Broome*) and the better view is that feelings of anger and indignation may be compensable.

In terms of their availability, aggravated damages are both wider and narrower than exemplary damages. They are wider in the sense that they do not need to satisfy the 'cause of action' test set out in *A.B.* v. *South West Water Services Ltd*, nor need they be brought within one of Lord Devlin's three categories. They are, however, narrower in the sense that damages are available only where the plaintiff suffers a 'personality' injury and the exceptional conduct requirement is satisfied. Notwithstanding these differences, distinguishing between the two in practice is unlikely to be easy. In theory, as we have seen, aggravated damages are compensatory only while exemplary damages are awarded to punish the defendant or deter future conduct. But the way in which aggravated damages are actually awarded lead the Law Commission (1993, paras. 3.28–3.31) to conclude that they are often used to punish, deter or condemn the defendant's conduct, rather than 'to cast light upon the plaintiff's injury'. In the light of this, the Commission provisionally concluded that the exceptional conduct requirement, which the Commission felt made it difficult to see the awards as wholly compensatory, should be abandoned. Injury to feelings and the like could then be approached from a purely compensatory perspective in which, 'the court would simply ask whether the plaintiff had actually been caused intangible loss by the defendant's wrongful conduct' (para. 6.48).

Restitutionary Damages

The branch of law concerned with 'unjust enrichment' is commonly called 'restitution'. As we have seen, the governing concern of this area of law is the restitution of benefits that the defendant received at the expense of the plaintiff. While some benefit-based remedies are generated by 'restitutionary' claims that are clearly independent of any tort, breach of contract or equitable wrong, there has been an increasing awareness that restitutionary claims may overlap with over types of claim. Of course, in the majority of tort claims there will be no such overlap. In a typical personal injuries action, the defendant acquires no benefit at the expense of the plaintiff; 'there is no gain, only a loss' (Rogers, 1994, p. 642). However, that need not be the case. Restitutionary claims are particularly likely to overlap with tort claims where the defendant has benefited by the wrongful use of the plaintiff's property. This may commonly arise in what have been called the proprietory torts: trespass to land and chattels, conversion and the infringement of intellectual property rights. If, for example, the defendant wrongfully made use of the plaintiff's property he may be liable for trespass to land. In such a case, the defendant may also have, by the use of the land, wrongfully benefited at the plaintiff's expense. In a number of cases involving the wrongful acquisition of a benefit by the defendant at the expense of the plaintiff, courts have awarded damages that fit much more easily into a restitutionary rather than a compensatory model. In *Strand Electric & Engineering Co Ltd* v. *Brisford Entertainments Ltd* [1952] 2 QB 246, for example, damages were awarded in respect of theatre equipment wrongfully used by the defendant. The Court of Appeal assessed damages by reference to a reasonable hiring charge for the equipment even though there was no market for such property and the plaintiff could not, therefore, have hired it out. Such a result is defensible only on the basis that it prevents unjust enrichment and may deter the wrongful use of another's goods.

There is much to be said, from the point of view of policy, for allowing restitutionary awards to be made in tort claims in certain limited circumstances. The restitutionary approach prevents the defendant benefiting from his own wrong in the sense that he will be forced to hand over any benefit he gained at the plaintiff's expense. It also provides a method of deterring the deliberate exploitation of wrongdoing and provides a valuable means of vindicating the plaintiff's rights (especially property rights). Against that it might be argued that the plaintiff gets an undeserved windfall and such awards may, in certain circumstances, inhibit enterprise and discourage economic activity (see Law Commission, 1993, para. 7.18). In its recent Consultation Paper on restitutionary damages (Law Commission, 1993), the Law Commission provisionally concluded that restitutionary awards are prima facie justified provided certain conditions are satisfied. First, there must have been either interference with a proprietory or analogous right or deliberate wrong-doing that could have been restrained by injunction. Second, the gains made by the defendant must be attributable to the interest infringed' (para. 7.19–20).

22.3 Damages Recoverable Once Only

The damages that the plaintiff is entitled to recover from the defendant can be recovered once only. This rule has two aspects to it. First, the plaintiff cannot bring a second action on the same facts simply because the initial loss turned out to be more serious than was thought when judgment was given in the first action. This rule was laid down in *Fetter* v. *Beal* (1701) 1 Ld Raym 339. The plaintiff recovered damages from the defendant in respect of a trespass to the person. After the judgment had been given 'part of [the plaintiff's] skull came out of his head.' The plaintiff sought to bring a second action in respect of the deterioration in his condition. The court held that the recovery in the first action for trespass barred the second action in respect of the subsequent loss.

The second aspect of the rule is that damages are awarded on a once-and-for-all basis and paid in the form of a single lump sum. This requires that the court make an assessment not only of what the plaintiff has lost between the accident and the trial but also of what he will lose in the future as a result of the accident. Future contingencies must therefore be translated into a present value. In the case of property damage this rarely gives rise to much difficulty in that future losses can usually be estimated with some accuracy. However, where personal injury has been suffered the difficulty of predicting whether the plaintiff will recover, and if so when and to what extent, has caused problems for the courts. There has, as a result, been a great deal of debate as to whether the system of once and for all payments should be retained or whether some form of periodic payments should replace it; see the Pearson 1978, Report (Pearson, 1978, paras. 555–71).

Proponents of the existing system argue that it leads to finality in litigation; the defendant (usually an insurance company) can close its files and the plaintiff can concentrate on getting better free of any 'compensation neurosis'. Further, the plaintiff is given a free hand in spending the money. Opponents argue, however, that these advantages, to the extent that they are advantages, are outweighed by the disadvantages of the existing system. First, as Lord Scarman acknowledged in the *Lim Poh Choo* v. *Camden and Islington AHA* [1980] AC 174, assessment of future losses is replete with problems:

'[K]nowledge of the future being denied to mankind, so much of the award as is attributed to future loss and suffering . . . will almost surely be wrong. There is only one certainty: the future will prove the award to be either too high or too low.'

Second, there is a danger that if the plaintiff fritters away his award the state will have to maintain him when the award runs out. Periodic payments would to a large extent solve these problems.

Although the general rule remains that the award must be made in a lump sum there exist three exceptions. Two of these arise from legislation while the third, and potentially the most important, depends on the parties reaching an agreed settlement. The first is the award of provisional damages. Where there is a chance that at some definite or indefinite time in the future 'the injured person will, as a result of the act or omission which gave rise to the cause of action, develop some serious disease or suffer some serious deterioration in his physical or mental condition' (s. 32A(1), Supreme Court Act 1981), then a court may, by virtue of s. 32A(2) of the 1981 Act, award '(a) damages assessed on the assumption that the injured person will not develop the disease or suffer the deterioration in his condition; and (b) further damages at a future date if he develops the disease or suffers the deterioration in his condition.' The effect of this provision is that a court has the power to compensate a plaintiff whose condition deteriorates after the trial. In order to recover, the plaintiff must establish a 'chance' of developing some '*serious* disease' or suffering some '*serious* deterioration'. The legislation does not define the words 'chance' or 'serious', however, some guidance on their meaning can be gained from the decision of Scott Baker J in *Willson* v. *Ministry of Defence* [1991] 1 All ER 638. The judge held that in order to qualify as a chance it must be 'measureable and not fanciful' (p. 642). However, in the judge's view a 'slim' chance was a measureable one. As to 'serious deterioration', Scott Baker J held that something 'beyond ordinary deterioration' was required. This was ultimately a question of fact but what was envisaged by the legislation was a severable risk rather than a gradual deterioration. Thus, on the facts of that case, the judge held that the possibility of developing arthritis was insufficiently serious because it was not a severable risk.

Second, where certain preconditions are satisfied a court may make an award of interim damages. Part II of Or. 29, r. 11 of the Rules of Supreme Court provides that:

'If . . . the court is satisfied – (a) that the defendant against whom the order is sought . . . has admitted liability for the plaintiff's damages, or (b) that the plaintiff has obtained judgment against the respondent for damages to be assessed, or (c) that, if the action proceeded to trial, the plaintiff would obtain judgment for substantial damages against the respondent . . . the court may, if it thinks fit . . ., order the respondent to make an interim payment . . .'.

Such an award can only be made against an insured person, a public authority or a person whose means and resources are such as to enable him to meet any interim payment. As to the amount to be awarded, this is at the discretion of the court but must not exceed a 'reasonable' proportion of the damages which are likely to be recovered by the plaintiff at trial. In practice, courts have limited such payments to sums for which need is shown and have assessed the amount of an interim payment against the plaintiff's pecuniary losses rather than on account of general damages (Law Commission, 1994, para. 4.2). This practice was justified on the ground that it protects against the danger of large interim awards being made that might exceed the final damages award, thereby requiring the plaintiff to repay the difference. Such an approach was, however, criticised by the Court of Appeal in *Stringman* v. *McArdle* [1994] PIQR 230, which thought that the court's overriding discretion was adequate to control any excesses. Stuart-Smith LJ summarised the view of the court by stating, 'It should be noted that the plaintiff does not have to demonstrate any particular need over and above the general need that a plaintiff has to be paid his or her damages as soon as may reasonably be done. It will generally be appropriate and just to make an order where there will be some delay until the final disposal of the case.' Therefore, what the court is concerned with in fixing the quantum is that it does not exceed a reasonable proportion of the damages which in the opinion of the court are likely to be recovered.

Finally, there is the possibility of the parties, where the defendant has liability insurance, agreeing to a structured settlement. A structured settlement is:

> 'an agreement settling a claim or action for damages for personal injury on terms whereby – (a) the damages are to consist wholly or partly of periodical payments; and (b) the person to whom the payments are to be made is to receive them as the annuitant under one or more annuities purchased for him by the person against whom the claim or action is brought or, if he is insured against the claim, by his insurer.' (s. 5, Damages Act 1996)

Such a concept was, until relatively recently, virtually unknown in the UK because it offered few advantages over the traditional lump sum payment. However, an agreement in mid-1987 between the Association of British Insurers and the Inland Revenue to the effect that certain forms of structured settlement are not liable to income tax boosted the use of such settlements. Structured settlements were given statutory recognition by the Damages Act 1996. Importantly, however, the Act does not give a court the power to order a structured settlement. The main purpose of the provisions was simply to 'rationalise and build on the existing vountary system'. Thus, the Act does not represent a new start but rather an attempt to regularise the existing system and make it easier and less complicated to administer.

In practice, a structured settlement will usually consist of two parts: a lump sum to cover the past losses and existing needs of the plaintiff at the date of settlement, and a series of further instalments of the damages for which the defendant is liable.The parties agree how much the claim would have been worth according to conventional principles. Some discount on this figure, currently around 10 per cent, is likely to be agreed between the parties (Law Commission, 1994, para. 3.125) because of the fiscal advantages to the plaintiff of accepting a structured settlement. Part of the agreed sum will then be allocated to meet any existing needs and to compensate the plaintiff for past pain and suffering and cost and expenses already accrued, leaving the balance to be structured. As to the periodic payments, the defendant insurer will fund its liability by purchasing a life annuity from a life insurer (Damages Act 1996, s. 5(1)). The Inland Revenue has given advance clearance in principle to structured settlements provided they incorporate one of four standard form periodic payment schedules (Law Commission, 1994, para. 3.4). Any variations require individual clearance.

The structured settlement has substantial advantages to both the defendant insurer and the plaintiff. So far as the insurer is concerned the main attraction is that, because the income from the annuity is not taxable in the hands of the plaintiff, it will be able to negotiate a discount to be made from the sum to be invested in the annuity. Although the Law Commission expressed some concern that the discounts typically negotiated may sometimes exceed the amount of tax that would be payable in respect of the income from an ordinary annuity (Law Commission, 1994, para. 3.125), it was satisfied that there was at least some evidence to suggest that plaintiffs also benefited from the favourable tax status (Law Commission, 1994, para. 3.126). In addition to the tax advantage, the main advantages cited for the plaintiffs are certainty and flexibility. So far as certainty is concerned, the plaintiff is relieved of the burden of having to manage a large sum of money, something of which he may have had little previous experience, and is protected from the possible dissipation of funds. Structured settlements also offer considerable flexibility. A settlement can be structured such that payments in some years are greater than others (s. 5(3)), or so as to take account of inflation (s. 5(3)(b)), and it can be linked to the life of the plaintiff so that the money does not run out before the plaintiff dies. It is also possible for a guarantee to be built into the structure whereby periodic payments are made for the lifetime of the plaintiff or for a guarantee period whichever is the longer (s. 5(2)). By this method, provision can be made for the plaintiff's dependants to benefit, rather than the insurance company, in the event of the plaintiff's premature death.

While the structured settlement does have considerable advantages over the traditional lump sum award, it also has its limitations. First, it does not avoid the need for forecasting. In fact, the process of assessing the future requirements of the plaintiff may place 'an undesirable emphasis on forward planning which is avoided where lump sums are used' (Law Commission, 1994, para. 3.20). In order to decide how to structure the periodic payments, a complex 'budget for life' will have to be prepared by the plaintiff's experts. Where damages are paid in a single lump sum, payments will be made by the plaintiff to meet his needs as required. The whole process of advance planning is thus avoided. Second, structured settlements do not completely remove the risk that the monies will be adequate to meet the plaintiff's needs. Once the settlement has been agreed, changes cannot be made if the plaintiff's prognosis changes. Further, the plaintiff is still able to squander his periodic payments; there is nothing to guarantee that he will spend them on what he was supposed to. Finally, there is the possibility that the plaintiff will, despite the advantages of the structured settlement, want his damages paid in a single lump sum. As has already been mentioned, the structured settlement is a 'creature of negotiation': the Act makes no change to the existing practice that if no structure is agreed voluntarily a court cannot order one.

22.4 Special and General Damages

When a court makes an award of damages the amount awarded will be divided between special and general damages. The distinction between the two is a matter of pleading. General damages are awarded in respect of loss which is *presumed* to flow from the wrong and which therefore does not have to be specially pleaded. Special damages are those damages beyond general damages that arise from the particular facts of the plaintiff's case. If the plaintiff wishes to claim special damages he must specifically plead them. Examples of general damages would include loss of amenities, pain and suffering and loss of future earnings. Expenses incurred in travelling to and from hospital, the cost of an operation which the plaintiff has had done privately and pre-trial loss of earnings would, however, be classified as special damage. The distinction is important not only for pleading purposes but also for the calculation of interest. It is, however, of little importance so far as the substantive law of damages is concerned.

22.5 Damages for Personal Injuries

Before examining the formal rules on the recovery of damages for personal injury something must be said by way of general introduction. It might be thought that for most people who have been injured as a result of an accident their most important consideration is how much can they get for their injury. Readers of newspapers cannot have failed to notice that awards of damages in excess of £1 million are becoming more common. Is this, therefore, the sort of award that a person who has been injured in an accident can expect? The answer to this is 'No'. First, studies have shown that only a small proportion of accident victims succeed in recovering any damages at all. Most people simply give no thought to attempting to recover any damages: they are concerned solely with physically recovering from their injuries. A survey done in 1976 by the Oxford Centre for Socio-Legal Studies (the 'Oxford Survey') showed that only one in seven accident victims reached the stage of consulting a lawyer and, of these, one out of seven failed to get any damages (Harris *et al.*, 1984). Thus in the vast majority of accidents the victim will recover nothing at all.

Second, most claims are settled out of court as a result of negotiations between the parties' representatives. In the 'Oxford Survey', for example, only 2 per cent of those who received some award of damages received these after a contested trial. In some ways this is a good thing. Parties to litigation should be encouraged to settle their differences quickly and as cheaply as possible. Staying out of court means that the lawyer's costs will be lower and the plaintiff's claim should be dealt with more expeditiously. Further, if all personal injury actions were actually litigated then the courts would be totally overwhelmed with work and the already unacceptably long time it takes to complete a personal injury action would be lengthened.

It must be borne in mind, however, that there are serious disadvantages to the settlement process. As Harris (1988) pointed out, the parties to a typical personal injury action are unlikely to have the same bargaining strength. The advantage almost invariably lies with the defendant, which is usually an insurance company. For the plaintiff this is a one-off action that he cannot afford to lose. He is often without a job as a result of the accident and has no other source of income. He may have little or no recollection of the accident and will almost inevitably want to get the whole thing over as quickly as possible. Further, he may well have gone to his local solicitor, who may not have had much experience of personal injury litigation. For the defendant, however, this is likely to be one of many actions in which it is involved. The insurance company is interested not so much in the result of an individual case as with the aggregated results of all its cases (it is a 'repeat player'). It is also likely to be represented by personal injury specialists. Further, while an insurance company will have to pay a plaintiff who is awarded damages interest for the time he was kept out of the award, this rate of interest is likely to be less than the rate the company can get by investing (or lending) the money itself. The longer it delays paying out to the plaintiff, the better. The pressures on a plaintiff to settle and to settle for less than a court may award are, therefore, very real. Only looking at sums awarded in contested trials distorts the picture and ignores the fact that the vast majority of cases are settled out of court for considerably less than the awards made in court.

Finally, even where cases do reach a court and are contested it is only in the most serious cases of disabling injury or death, and sometimes not even then, that a plaintiff is awarded a sum in excess of £1 million. Most actions for personal injury or death are for much smaller amounts, as a quick glance at *The Quantum of Damages* by Kemp and Kemp, (1985) will show (see also, Law Commission, 1994b).

With this background in mind, we now turn to examine the way in which the courts assess damages for personal injury or death.

22.6 The Assessment of an Award of Damages

As we have seen, the purpose of an award of damages in tort is to put the injured person into the position he would have been in had no tort occurred. In order to see how this principle is put into effect in practice let us consider the following hypothetical accident:

Arnold and his daughter Jane are injured in a car accident for which Simon admits full responsibility. At the trial on the amount of damages recoverable the following facts are established.

Arnold is a 35-year-old bricklayer working for a major building company. Prior to the accident he was earning £18 000 per annum gross. Out of his gross income he paid £4500 in income tax and £1500 per annum in national insurance contributions. Arnold is a very good bricklayer and it is highly probable that he would have continued to be employed to the normal retirement age. Prior to the accident Arnold was a keen footballer, playing each weekend for a local side.

In the accident Arnold suffered a broken back, which resulted in paralysis from the waist down and fractured ribs. He also suffered an injury to his lungs when he inhaled poisonous fumes given off as a result of the fire caused by the accident. The injury to his lungs is so serious that his life expectancy has been reduced to 10 years. He was in hospital for 12 weeks after the accident during which time he had three operations to try to remedy the paralysis. This time in hospital was spent in a private hospital because Arnold's employer pays for him to be a member of a private health care scheme.

Despite the operations Arnold will not be able to work as a brick layer again. He is also unable to find any alternative work and there is a very high probability that he will never work again. Arnold also requires round the clock nursing supervision. During the day this is provided by his wife, Gina, who is 29. Gina finds it impossible to provide the round the clock care that Arnold requires and so a nurse is hired at a cost of £10 000 per annum to provide the necessary night cover.

Arnold's friends are very upset about his accident and decide to launch an appeal for him. They manage to raise £15 000. In addition to this sum Arnold receives a state mobility allowance of £15 per week and a £50 per week pension from his employer.

Jane is a 7-year-old school girl who was, by all accounts, doing well at school. As a result of the accident she was rendered permanently unconscious, a state from which she will never recover. Her life expectancy is, however, unchanged. She now requires round-the-clock-care which is provided in a National Health Service hospital.

22.7 **Non-Pecuniary Loss**

As we have already seen, non-pecuniary losses are those losses that are not readily quantifiable in monetary terms. Despite this, English law does seek to put a value on such losses. The problem arises, however, of how such losses are to be valued. What is the loss of a leg or arm worth? How much money would compensate for the loss of the ability to play football or to dance? Undoubtedly any award made for such losses is likely to be perceived as arbitrary. Yet this is the task facing the court. While accepting that any award is likely to seem too much to some people and yet inadequate to others the courts do at least seek to treat like cases alike. The trial judge will have previous awards cited to him and, taking these into account, will award a sum that is fair and reasonable in all the circumstances. Since 1992 judges, and practitioners who deal with personal injury cases, have also been able to refer to the Judicial Studies Board's *Guidelines for the Assessment of General Damages in Personal Injury Cases*. The *Guidelines*, a revised edition of which was published in 1994, 'suggest, on the basis of previous cases and the working party's own collective experience, the appropriate bracket of non-pecuniary award for particular types of injury' (Law Commission, 1995a, para. 1.5). They represent the first attempt to provide official guidance to the courts in respect of the assessment of non-pecuniary loss and are now widely used by both judges and practitioners. An appeal court will only interfere with the trial judge's assessment if the judge has misdirected himself as to the law, misapprehended the facts, or for some other reason made an award that is wholly erroneous.

Pain and Suffering

Under this head the court will award damages to reflect the pain and suffering felt as a consequence of the accident. In so far as 'pain' and 'suffering' can be separated, the Law Commission (1995a, para. 2.10) thought that 'pain' meant 'physical hurt or discomfort attributable to the injury itself or consequent upon it', while 'suffering' referred to 'the mental or emotional distress which the plaintiff may feel as a consequence of the injury . . .'. Courts do not, however, usually distinguish between the two elements. In our example, Arnold would be able to recover a sum to compensate him for the pain he suffers that is attributable to his injuries (in other words the pain of his fractured ribs and damaged lungs). He would also be entitled to recover for any pain or suffering attributable to medical treatment he receives. Prior to the Administration of Justice Act 1982, Arnold would also have had a separate claim for the shortening of his life expectancy and would have received a conventional sum in respect of this. Such a claim was a separate and independent head of non-pecuniary loss, quite apart from that in respect of any suffering caused to the plaintiff as a result of knowing that his life expectancy was reduced. Loss of expectation of life was abolished as a separate head of damages by s. 1(1)(a) of the 1982 Act. However, loss of life expectancy may still be relevant when assessing damages for pain and suffering. Where *knowledge* that his life expectancy is reduced causes the plaintiff mental suffering or anguish, this may increase the damages awardable under the head of pain and suffering. The court is no longer restricted to awarding a conventional sum but should instead award an amount based on the plaintiff's particular circumstances and attitude to the fact that his life expectancy has been reduced.

Where the plaintiff is rendered permanently unconscious as a result of the accident, he will not be able to recover damages under this head. The courts have held, and this was confirmed by the House of Lords in *Lim*

Poh Choo, that damages will not be awarded for pain and suffering where the plaintiff is unconscious or otherwise incapable of experiencing pain. As the Law Commission pointed out, pain and suffering is an 'inherently subjective head of non pecuniary loss' (Law Commission, 1995a, para. 2.12), and as such recovery under this head depends upon the plaintiff's awareness of it. In our example, therefore, Jane will not be able to recover any damages under this head.

Loss of Amenities

An injury may deprive a plaintiff of his ability to do things that before the accident he could do. Thus, a plaintiff who is rendered deaf or blind by the accident can obviously no longer enjoy the sensations associated with those senses. The law allows damages to be recovered for losses of this type under the head 'loss of amenities of life'. Damages are recoverable under this head both for the loss of faculties or amenities which are inherent in the injury itself and also loss of any special amenities peculiar to the plaintiff. In our example, Arnold can no longer walk. He is entitled, therefore, to be compensated for the loss of that faculty. However, prior to the accident he was a keen footballer and the accident prevents him from playing. This loss of a special amenity, the ability to play football, would increase the amount recoverable under this head. In addition to the loss of capacity associated with loss of, or damage to, limbs or the body and loss of any of the senses, damages are also awardable under this head for, *inter alia*, loss of marriage prospects, loss of sexual function and even loss of pleasure in one's work.

Whether an unconscious plaintiff (like Jane in our example), who is unable to appreciate that she has lost any of the normal 'amenities of life', should be able to recover damages under this head has been the subject of considerable debate. This question raises two separate issues. First, what is the purpose of an award of damages for non-pecuniary loss? Is it to put a value on what the plaintiff has lost – the 'diminution of value' approach? Or, is it to provide a plaintiff with sufficient damages to enable him to purchase substitute sources of satisfaction – the 'functional' approach? If it is the latter, then an unconscious plaintiff should not be compensated for loss of amenity because he will not be able to benefit in any way from the damages awarded. Although the Pearson Commission thought that English law should adopt the 'functional approach' and damages should not be awarded to an unconscious plaintiff where they can serve no useful purpose (Pearson, 1978, vol. 1, paras. 393–8), this is not the approach which the courts have adopted. In *H. West & Son* v. *Shephard*, the majority of the House of Lords held that damages for loss of amenities were awarded for the fact of their deprivation. The court rejected the view that the appropriate method of assessing such damages was to ask what could the plaintiff 'buy' to provide solace for the loss. Instead, the court should seek to put a value on what the plaintiff had lost.

Second, even if one takes the view that in assessing damages for non-pecuniary loss a court should seek to put a value on what the plaintiff has lost, that does not necessarily mean that an *unconscious* plaintiff should be able to recover damages for loss of the amenities of life. The question still arises whether such a loss should be assessed subjectively (through the plaintiff's awareness of it) or objectively (irrespective of the plaintiff's awareness of it). The current approach taken by English law is to assess the loss of amenities of life objectively. The House of Lords in *H. West & Son* v. *Shephard* viewed the loss of amenities of life as a grave deprivation for which the plaintiff was entitled to be compensated regardless of whether he was aware of the loss or not. As Lord Morris put it in that case, 'the fact of unconsciousness does not, however, eliminate the actuality of deprivations of the ordinary experiences and amenities of life which may be the inevitable result of some physical injury' (p. 349).

This approach was criticised by the Law Commission in its recent Consultation Paper on non-pecuniary loss (Law Commisssion, 1995a). The Law Commission was 'attracted' to the view that non-pecuniary loss should be rationalised 'in terms of the mental suffering and loss of happiness caused to the plaintiff' (para. 4.14) and that it should be assessed subjectively and not objectively. The Commission felt that in the case of a seriously injured plaintiff who is incapable of suffering, it was at least strongly arguable that the plaintiff should be regarded as having suffered no non-pecuniary loss. Where a plaintiff is incapable of suffering he is, in a very real sense, in almost the same position as a person who is killed instantly in an accident. If no damages for non-pecuniary loss are awardable in the latter case, nor should they be awardable in the former. Further, applying a subjective as opposed to objective method of assessment should not make much difference in the majority of cases. It would only make a difference where the plaintiff was incapable of suffering because, for example, he was rendered temporarily or permanently unconscious. While there is much to be said for the provisional recommendations of the Law Commission, care will have to be exercised, if the subjective assessment approach is adopted, to avoid 'a premium [being] put on protestations of misery' in order to increase the award for non-pecuniary damages.

The Injury Itself

The injury itself is also a proper subject of a claim in a personal injury action. This claim is in addition to any amount that may be awarded for pain and suffering and loss of amenities. However, while in principle the claims are separate, it will be a rare case in which 'the plaintiff is compensated for the injury as distinct from its consequences (be they pain, suffering or loss of amenity)' (Law Commission, 1995a, para. 2.20).

22.8 Pecuniary Loss

Although the amount awarded for non-pecuniary loss in a serious accident may be substantial, damages for pecuniary loss will usually make up the greater part of the plaintiff's claim. As we have seen, the usual practice is that damages are awarded on a once-and-for-all basis and paid in a single lump sum. In assessing the plaintiff's pecuniary loss the court must, therefore, award a sum to take account of both the plaintiff's actual pre-trial loss and also any future pecuniary losses he will suffer.

Where a seriously injured person is in employment, the majority of any damages awarded for pecuniary loss is likely to be for loss of earnings. However, this is not the only head of damages awarded under pecuniary loss. Damages, as we shall see, can also be awarded for other expenses reasonably incurred, both before and after the trial.

Loss of Earnings

Damages for loss of earnings can conveniently be divided into two categories, pre-trial and post-trial. The assessment of pre-trial loss of earnings is relatively straightforward. The court will simply seek to ascertain the sum of money which the plaintiff would have been paid had he not been injured. If we assume, using our hypothetical accident, that Arnold's case comes to trial exactly three years after the accident and that his wages had not altered during that period of time, his pre-trial loss of earnings would be calculated in the following way. First, his net annual loss would be established. This would be arrived at by deducting from his gross annual income the amount he would pay in tax (*British Transport Commission* v. *Gourley* [1956] AC 185) and national insurance contributions (*Cooper* v. *Firth Brown Ltd* [1963] 1 WLR 418). In earning his annual income Arnold would have to pay tax and national insurance and thus, to avoid over-compensating him, these must both be deducted from his gross income. After tax and national insurance Arnold would have earned £12 000 per annum. This is then multiplied by the number of years between the accident and the trial and yields a sum of £36 000 (plus interest) for his pre-trial loss of earnings.

The calculation of post-trial or future loss of earnings is more complicated. As damages are payable at the time of the trial in a lump sum, it is necessary for a court to convert the plaintiff's future loss of earnings into a lump sum that reflects that future loss. The method adopted is the 'multiplier method' (see below). Calculation of the plaintiff's future loss is, however, an exercise fraught with difficulty. To take some examples, how long would the plaintiff have lived if he had not had the accident? Would he have remained in the same job? Would he have been promoted or made redundant? What will the rates of wage and price inflation be? Will the tax or national insurance rates change? Some or all of these problems are likely to arise in all claims for future loss of earnings. In the light of this, it might be thought that the courts would enlist the help of experts such as actuaries or economists to assist them. However, for many years the practice was to take no account of such evidence. Indeed in one case, Oliver LJ said '. . .the predictions of an actuary can be only a little more likely to be accurate (and will almost certainly be less entertaining) than those of an astrologer.' (*Auty* v. *NCB* [1985] 1 WLR 793, 800)

The publication by the Government Actuary's Department of *Actuarial Tables with Explanatory Notes for use in Personal Injury and Fatal Accident Cases* (the 'Ogden Tables') appears to have done much to change the practice. The purpose of the Ogden Tables is to provide those involved in personal injury litigation with tables specifically geared to the assessment of damages in personal injury actions. In addition to taking account of the various contingencies that may befall individuals, the Ogden Tables take account of potential changes in inflation by assuming that the damages will be invested in Index-Linked Government Securities (ILGS). These provide a virtually risk-free and inflation proof investment. Initially the Ogden Tables were not regarded as acceptable evidence, but it would appear from comments made by the House of Lords in *Hunt* v. *Severs* [1994] 2 AC 350 that greater use is now being made of them. Lord Bridge commented (p. 365), 'We are told by counsel that the practice has changed in recent years and that actuarial tables tend to figure more prominently in the evidence on which courts rely.' Although Bingham LJ in the Court of Appeal ([1993] QB 815) had thought that the practice had much to commend it, the House of Lords was rather more circumspect;

'The assessment of damages is not and never can be an exact science. There are too many imponderables . . . [B]efore a judge's assessment of the appropriate multiplier for future loss, which he has arrived at by the conventional method of assessment and which is not attacked as wrong in principle, can properly be adjusted by an appellate court by reference to actuarial calculations, it is essential, in my judgment, that the particular calculation relied on should be precisely in point and should be seen as demonstrably giving a more accurate assessment than the figure used by the judge' (per Lord Bridge, p. 365).

The Law Commission recommended in its final report on *Structured Settlements and Interim and Provisional Damages* (Law Commission, 1994, para. 2.15) that actuarial evidence, in the form of the Ogden Tables, should be admissible in evidence in any action for damages for personal injury in order to help establish the capital value of any future pecuniary loss to which the claim relates. The Commission recognised the courts' fears of loss of flexibility but commented that the Tables did not prevent individual characteristics being taken into account. Further, the added certainty and consistency that would be achieved by the use of the Tables had much to commend it. Most importantly, the Commission commented that use of the Tables should 'reduce delay and take some of the guesswork out of the present process' (para. 2.15).

With the above in mind, how, then, do the courts assess future loss of earnings? What the court is seeking to achieve is to award a sum of money that, when invested, will produce annually out of income and capital, for as long as that loss is expected to last, a sum equivalent to the plaintiff's loss. The method of assessment used to achieve this is the 'multiplier method'. The starting point is to work out the multiplicand. This is, in essence, the net annual loss of income that the plaintiff suffers as a result of the accident, in other words the plaintiff's gross income less tax and national insurance. This sum is then multiplied by a 'multiplier' to reflect the fact that the plaintiff's annual loss will continue for some years.

How do the courts decide upon the appropriate multiplier? To return to our example, at the time of his accident Arnold is 35 years old. If it is assumed that he would have worked until the usual retirement age he would have another 30 years of potential earnings. Should the courts, therefore, simply set the multiplier at 30? The courts have answered this question in the negative. In determining the multiplier, the courts make certain deductions to avoid over-compensating the plaintiff. First, a deduction of between 5 per cent and 10 per cent is made to allow for 'the general vicissitudes of life'. The plaintiff might, independently of the defendant's tort, have contracted some fatal illness or lost his job This must be taken into account. Second, and more importantly, some reduction in the multiplier must be made to take account of the fact that the plaintiff is getting his money early. The payment of £1000 today is worth more than the payment of the same sum in a year's time. In the former case, the money can be invested and will be worth, at an interest rate of (say) 10 per cent, about £1100 in a year's time. In our example paying Arnold 30 times £12 000 would considerably over-compensate him. Invested prudently, the lump sum would probably be sufficient to enable Arnold to maintain himself wholly out of his investment income and he would be left at the end of 30 years with the entire capital sum intact. Therefore, the court choses a multiplier to ensure that the plaintiff receives a sum of money which, when invested, will produce annually out of capital and investment income a sum equivalent to the total earnings that the plaintiff has lost. The effect of this is that the multiplier awarded in Arnold's case will be considerably less than 30 and will in fact be likely to be around 16. In practice, the highest multiplier applied by the courts is 18. Multipliers awarded to plaintiffs in their thirties will generally be less than 18, and the older the injured plaintiff is the lower the multiplier will be.

Assessing loss of earnings claims made by children give rise to a number of difficulties. In principle, there should be no reason why, in our original example, Jane should not recover damages for loss of earnings. The accident means that she will not be able to work and she ought to be compensated for that loss. The difficulty lies in assessing her loss. First, how should the multiplicand be assessed? As she has never worked it is obviously impossible to assess the multiplicand in the ordinary way. As a result the courts have awarded infant children the national average earnings as the multiplicand (see, as an example, *Croke* v. *Wiseman* [1982] 1 WLR 71). One exception to this approach is where the infant is a child prodigy. In such a case the court will make an assessment of the lost earnings on the basis of what has actually been lost and what the child was likely to earn in the future.

As to the multipliers awarded to children, these have generally been comparatively low The reasons for this are two-fold. First, the uncertainties in such cases are greater than in cases of working adults. The child might never have reached the age of majority. The child might never have worked or might only have been able to get very low paid work. The imponderables are many and justify the award of a lower multiplier. Second, where a child is very young there will be several years before he would have been able to work. As a result a lump sum awarded to a young child can be invested for a considerable period before the loss is deemed to accrue. Less capital will, therefore, be needed to compensate fully the child for the loss of future earnings.

The most obvious problem with the multiplier/ multiplicand approach is that it seems to ignore the effect of inflation. The last 20 or 30 years have demonstrated that both wage and price inflation are facts of life in a modern economic society. Price inflation has the effect of eroding the value of money so that £1000 today will be worth more (in the sense that you can buy more with it) than £1000 in a year's time. Obviously, the longer the likely duration of the plaintiff's loss the greater the effect inflation will have on the real value of the award. Do the courts take inflation into account when assessing the multiplier? The answer to this question, rather confusingly, is yes and no. The House of Lords, in a number of cases, have made clear that no adjustment to the multiplier is to be made to take account of future inflation. Inflation is to be ignored and money treated as retaining the value it had at the time of the trial. One reason that is often given for this is the real difficulty of anticipating what the rate of inflation will be. As Lord Scarman said in *Lim Poh Choo*, 'it is pure speculation whether inflation will continue at present, or higher rates, or even disappear. The only sure comment one can make upon any inflation prediction is that it is as likely to be falsified as borne out by the event.' However, the real reason why no adjustment is necessary to the multiplier to take account of inflation is that existing multipliers already take account of future inflation. The multipliers applied by the courts assume that the plaintiff invests the lump sum he gets and receives a *real* rate of return (i.e. the rate of return after taking out the effect of inflation) on that investment of between 4 per cent and 5 per cent. For example, it is assumed by the courts that when inflation is running at 4 per cent per annum the plaintiff, through the use of a prudent investment policy, can find a safe investment returning 8 per cent to 9 per cent per annum. Thus, the calculation of the present-day value of any future loss involves, at least in theory, the application of a discount rate (the real rate of return which the courts assume is achievable by a plaintiff if he invests his damages prudently) to the total loss that the plaintiff will sustain over the expected period of the loss. The multipliers used by the court reflect the discount rate applied. Thus, the higher the discount rate the lower the multiplier.

Is the assumption of a 4 per cent to 5 per cent real rate of return realistic? While it is true that it is possible to achieve through prudent and safe investments a real rate of return on investment of between 4 per cent and 5 per cent this may involve a level of investment sophistication that is simply not possessed by the average person. For example during the mid-1980s investing in safe 'blue chip' shares would have yielded a return of at least 4 per cent to 5 per cent per annum. However, anybody invested in shares during 1987 (the year in which shares fell over 20 per cent in one day) would have found it extremely difficult to make any return. Similarly, for much of the early 1980s government bonds offered a rate of return of at least 4 per cent to 5 per cent. However, during the late 1970s the *real* return on such investments was negative. Is it realistic to expect the average plaintiff to show the necessary level of sophistication to cope with the difficulties inherent in obtaining a 4 per cent to 5 per cent real rate of return? In its report on *Structured Settlements and Interim and Provisional Damages* (Law Commission No.224 (1995a), at 2.24-2.35) the Law Commission recognised that the average plaintiff was faced with real difficulties in choosing an investment 'guaranteed' to yield a real rate of return of 4 to 5 per cent per annum. It concluded that the real rate of return achievable by investing in Index-Linked Government Securities (ILGS) constituted 'the best evidence of the real return on any investment where the risk element is minimal, because they take account of inflation, rather than attempt to predict it as conventional investments do' (para. 2.28). The Commission, therefore, recommended that the courts ought, when determining the return to be expected from investment of the sum awarded in damages, to assume that the plaintiff invested his damages in ILGS (see also Kemp, 1985). Thus, the discount rate applied by the court should reflect the real rate of return achievable by investing in ILGS. If the multipliers used by the courts were to be based on the rate of return achievable by investing in ILGS, a substantial increase in multipliers would result. As was mentioned above, the higher the discount rate the lower the multiplier and vice versa. As the real rate of return typically achievable by investing in ILGS is between 2 per cent and 2½ per cent per annum, the effect of applying this as the discount rate, as compared with the current 4 per cent to 5 per cent, would be a large increase in multipliers and therefore an increase in the amount of damages payable. The Law Commission took the view that this increase was justified. Its empirical survey (Law Commisssion, 1994b) had revealed that nearly two in five recipients of damages thought that they did not receive sufficient damages to compensate all their losses (Law Commission, 1994b, esp. Ch. 11). This was an unjustified shortfall which was appropriately remedied by an increase in the multiplier applied. Section 1 of the Damages Act 1996 responds to this criticism by requiring a court to take into account when assessing damages any rate of return set out in an order made by the Lord Chancellor. No such order has been made at the time of writing.

Notwithstanding the compelling arguments marshalled by the Law Commission, the Court of Appeal, in three appeals that were heard together (*Wells* v. *Wells* [1997] 1 All ER 673), has reversed judgments at first instance where the discount rate was based on the rates of return on ILGS. The court said that the correct test to apply was what would be the rate of return achieved on the investments that a prudent investor would make. This the court thought was likely to be 4.5 per cent because a prudent investor would not invest all of a large fund in ILGS but would also invest in higher-returning equities.

The rate chosen as the *real* rate of return achievable by the plaintiff on his investment is the rate achievable *after* tax. Do the courts take some account of the fact that if the lump sum awarded is large enough the plaintiff will become liable to pay tax at a higher rate? Despite initially taking the view that some increase in the multiplier should be made where the plaintiff will be liable to pay tax at a higher rate, the House of Lords decided in *Hodgson* v. *Trapp* [1989] AC 807 that no addition, save in exceptional circumstances, should be made to the multiplier in respect of a liability to pay higher rate tax. Two main reasons were given in the speech of Lord Oliver. First, '[F]uture taxation . . . is as much as an imponderable as future inflation': the courts should not guess as to the likely direction of tax rates. Second, as with inflation, taxation is already taken into account in the existing multiplier. Any addition to the multiplier would simply overcompensate the plaintiff.

The 'Lost Years'

In our hypothetical example, Arnold suffered such a serious injury to his lungs that his life expectancy was reduced to 10 years. As we have seen, damages are no longer available for loss of expectation of life as a separate head, though a plaintiff may recover a sum under pain and suffering for the knowledge that he is going to die early. However, the problem we are concerned with here is whether Arnold can claim for the earnings he will lose in the 'lost years' (in other words those years which, but for the accident, he would have expected to be alive and working) or whether he can only claim in respect of the years for which he is expected to be alive.

One approach to this problem might be to say that, because 'Nothing is of value except to a man who is there to save or spend it', damages ought not to be awarded for lost earnings in the lost years. In other words, assessed *subjectively*, the plaintiff has lost nothing. Why award him damages to make up for lost earnings in respect of the lost years when he will not need them? The House of Lords, however, rejected this view in *Pickett* v. *British Rail Engineering Ltd* [1980] AC 136 and held that where an injury reduces the plaintiff's normal life expectancy, the *pre-accident* life expectancy should still be used in order to assess the appropriate multiplier. Even though the plaintiff will not be around to 'enjoy' the fruits of his earnings, he has still objectively suffered a loss and is entitled to be compensated. Further, the court commented that the effect of not allowing a claim in respect of the 'lost' years would mean that the plaintiff's dependants would lose out. Because the plaintiff's claim would have been settled or he would have obtained judgment before his death no claim could be made under the Fatal Accidents Act 1976. Therefore, the effect of denying a claim in respect of the lost years would mean that the plaintiff's dependents would be uncompensated. Two responses might be made to this latter point. First, such an argument assumes that the plaintiff has dependents. If he does not its validity disappears. Second, if the damages are intended to benefit the dependants, then why not award them to the dependants? Such a result could be achieved either by allowing, dependants to bring an action under the Fatal Accidents Act 1976 notwithstanding the fact that the plaintiff's claim for damages for personal injury had been settled or he had obtained judgment before his death, or allowing dependants a cause of action for pecuniary loss where the person on whom they are dependant is injured as well as where he has been killed (see Burrows, 1994, pp. 201–2).

Two further points need to be made. First, a deduction is made from the earnings that the plaintiff would have been paid in the 'lost years' to take account of his living expenses. In the 'lost years' the plaintiff would have had to pay 'living expenses' out of his earnings. As he will have no living expenses in the 'lost years' a deduction is made from his earnings to take account of that. In *Harris* v. *Empress Motors Ltd* [1984] 1 WLR 212 the Court of Appeal held that the plaintiff's living expenses included not only what the plaintiff would have spent in maintaining himself but also a pro-rata amount of any family living expenses. This should be contrasted with the position under the Fatal Accidents Act 1976 (see below) where only the amount that the plaintiff would have spent exclusively on himself is deducted when assessing the loss of dependency. The reason for the difference is that lost years' damages are intended to compensate the plaintiff for his own loss while damages under the Fatal Accidents Act 1976 are intended to compensate the dependants for their loss. The latter includes the deceased's contributions to joint living expenses; the former does not.

Second, the courts have generally refused to allow a child to recover for lost earnings in the 'lost years' (see, for example, *Connolly* v. *Camden and Islington Area Health Authority* [1981] 3 All ER 250). The reason given by the courts is that the valuation of a child's lost earnings in the 'lost years' simply involves too much speculation. In addition to the uncertainty that surrounds the assessment of what the child would have earned as an adult, there is also the problem of assessing what the child's living expenses would have been in the 'lost years'. While claims by infant plaintiffs for lost earnings in the lost years have generally been denied, the courts have left open the possibility of such a claim by a child prodigy or in a case where the infant plaintiff is the heir to a large estate.

Future Prospects

In our example Arnold was likely to have remained a bricklayer for the rest of his working life. Would the damages he would receive be any different if, for example, he had just completed a part-time degree in law and wanted to become a solicitor? As a solicitor he would probably earn more than as a bricklayer. The courts take account of prospective pay increases like this by increasing the multiplicand for the plaintiff. Conversely, if the plaintiff was likely to have lost his job or was in work that was inherently dangerous the multiplicand or the multiplier may be reduced.

As well as making this adjustment in the multiplicand to take account of the plaintiff's future prospects, the courts have also awarded damages for 'loss of earning capacity'. Under this head of damages a court may compensate the plaintiff for the possibility that if he loses his existing job he may, as a result of the injury, find it more difficult to get another job. Damages have also been awarded to children under this head where a child's future employment prospects have been reduced because of the injury. Assessment of damages under this head is inevitably somewhat speculative. However, the courts have required that there is a 'real' or 'substantial' risk that the plaintiff will suffer this disadvantage before the end of his working life. Once the court has decided that there is a real risk, the chance of the risk eventuating must be valued.

Medical, Hospital and Other Nursing Expenses

The plaintiff is entitled to recover for all medical, hospital and other rehabilitation expenses that he has reasonably incurred, or will reasonably incur, as a result of the accident. Whether a particular expense is reasonable is a question of fact and will depend on such matters as whether the course of treatment claimed for has been recommended by the plaintiff's doctor, any scientific proof relating to the efficacy of the treatment proposed and whether the charges of the treatment provider chosen are in line with charges of other providers of the same services. Thus, in our example, Arnold would be able to recover the cost of the operation and the cost of his hospital stay unless the defendant could show that these expenses were not reasonably incurred.

In the example, it will be noted that Arnold had the operations in a private hospital. Should he be allowed to claim for that cost notwithstanding the fact that he could have availed himself of the services of the National Health Service (NHS) and avoided the cost altogether? Controversially, a plaintiff in Arnold's position is entitled to claim for the cost of private medical care even where those services are available on the NHS. Section 2(4) of the Law Reform (Personal Injuries) Act 1948 provides that: 'In an action for damages for personal injuries . . . there shall be disregarded, in determining the reasonableness of any expenses the possibility of avoiding these expenses or part of them by taking advantage of facilities available under the National Health Service.' Courts have interpreted this provision to mean that when an injured plaintiff incurs expenses that are reasonable, the fact that he could have taken advantage of the services provided by the NHS and avoided the expenses altogether, is to be ignored (see, for example, Slade J in *Harris* v. *Brights Asphalt Contractors Ltd* [1953] 1 QB 617, 635). The fundamental argument in favour of the current position is that it would be inconsistent with the 'freedom of the individual to take private treatment', to prevent the plaintiff from claiming the cost of it from the defendants. Yet, even conceding the general right of the individual to choose, it might be objected that, given the existence of universal national health care, the *public* (through the cost of insurance) should not have to subsidise those who want private treatment (Cane, 1993, p. 182). If the *defendant* actually paid for the plaintiff's stay in a private hospital, the award might be justified But *defendants* don't pay damages; their insurance company, which collects premiums from you and us, pays. Effectively therefore it is the *public* that pays and it is not right to fix us with the cost of private health care. While it is suggested that there is much in the arguments (see Law Commission, 1996, paras. 3.7–3.17) of those opposed to the principle enshrined in s. 2(4), the Law Commission in its recent Consultation Paper (Law Commission, 1996) provisionally recommended that s. 2(4) should not be repealed or reformed (para. 3.18). The objection discussed above was dismissed as a 'non-argument';

> '[A]s the central tort principle that the victim is entitled to be fully compensated by the tortfeasor means that damages should cover reasonably incurred private health costs, it is simply a non-argument to point to who ultimately may share the burden of those costs.' (at 3.17)

Where a plaintiff is treated by the NHS, and does not incur any medical or hospital expenses, he cannot make any claim in respect of the cost of such treatment. So far as the plaintiff is concerned that is sensible: he has suffered no loss and therefore needs no compensation. But where he has made use of NHS services, it has incurred expenses. Currently, the NHS is unable to recover any of its loss. However, the Law Commission has provisionally recommended that the NHS should, where its services are used by an injured plaintiff, have a right of recourse against the tortfeasor for the costs of NHS services resulting from the tort (Law Commission, 1996, para. 3.42). If introduced, and it is likely to be a politically popular suggestion given the Law Commission's estimate that as much as £120 million might be recoverable each year, the rights of the NHS would be broadly similar to those of private care providers.

Before we consider the question of the recovery of nursing care, reference must be made to a potential problem of duplication between loss of earnings and cost of care. In our example Jane is, after her accident, being nursed 24 hours a day in an NHS hospital. As we have seen, she is entitled to be compensated for the loss of earnings she would have made when old enough to work. If, however, she is allowed to claim her full loss of earnings she will be over-compensated because, as she will still be fully maintained by the state, she will not have to apply any of her earnings to living expenses as she would otherwise have had to do. To guard against this danger, the ordinary living expenses saved are deducted from the cost of staying in a private hospital, and by s. 5 of the Administration of Justice Act 1982 any saving to the injured person that is attributable to his being maintained at public expense in a hospital, nursing home or other institution must be set off against any lost earnings. An analogous problem arises in respect of private medical care: if the plaintiff recovers damages for the cost of residential accomodation at a private hospital as well as full damages for loss of earnings he will be over-compensated. To prevent this, the courts now deduct the 'hotel' element from damages for the cost of private medical care (*Lim Poh Choo* v. *Camden and Islington AHA*).

Finally, consideration must be given to the question of home nursing. In our example Arnold was being nursed partly by his wife and partly by a professional nurse. Provided the professional nursing expenses are reasonably incurred there will be no problem in the cost being recovered. It is also clearly established that the plaintiff can claim for the nursing services rendered by his spouse (or for that matter anyone else) even though they are rendered gratuitously. The latter claim requires some explanation. If the plaintiff's partner provides the nursing services gratuitously why should the plaintiff receive any compensation? Surely he has suffered no loss? If anyone has suffered any loss it is the person who gratuitously provides the nursing services. In *Donnelly* v. *Joyce* [1974] QB 454 Megaw LJ sought to reconcile the award with normal compensatory principles by treating the plaintiff's loss as the existence of the need for care rather than as the incurring of the nursing expenses. However, this view was rejected as unconvincing by the House of Lords in *Hunt* v. *Severs* [1994] 2 AC 350. The underlying rationale of awarding damages to plaintiffs in this type of case 'is to enable the voluntary carer to receive proper recompense for his or her services'. Where, therefore, the plaintiff needs nursing care and that care is provided gratuitously by another, the damages awarded are to be held on trust for the benefit of the provider of the services.

The facts of *Hunt* v. *Severs* involved a relatively common twist on the above situation. The plaintiff in that case suffered serious injuries in a motorcycle accident where she was a pillion passenger on a motorcycle driven by the defendant. The defendant, whom the plaintiff later married, admitted he was negligent but disputed the plaintiff's claim in respect of the caring services which had been and would continue to be provided by the *tortfeasor* (of course, the action was defended by an insurer; the 'real' defendant was rooting for the plaintiff). The House of Lords agreed with the defendant and refused to allow the claim. Once it was established that a plaintiff in receipt of 'gratuitous care' could recover damages but should hold them on trust for the carer, it followed logically that where the carer was the defendant no damages should be awarded because they would be recovered from and held on trust for the same person. Where, therefore, it is the tortfeasor who provides the gratuitous services, no damages will be paid to the plaintiff at all.

It is suggested that the decision, and in particular the use of the trust concept, is unsatisfactory (see Matthews and Lunney, 1995, for a particularly trenchant, and justified, criticism of the case). Not only does the House of Lords fail to tell us what kind of trust is established and what its characteristics are, but the consequences of imposing a trust are simply not examined (see Matthews and Lunney, pp. 400–4). What, for example, is the position if the plaintiff dies before the 'carer' damages are consumed? Are those damages to be returned to the tortfeasor on a resulting trust or is the carer to have the money on the basis that he was the intended beneficiary and he is ready and willing to provide the services? Further, the result itself can justly be criticised. What if, in a *Hunt* v. *Severs* type case, the plaintiff and defendant separated, or the defendant simply found it impossible to continue to provide the necessary nursing services? The plaintiff is, in such a case, likely to be left without any means of paying for the services and will either, therefore, have to rely on the state or go short. Neither result is satisfactory and the only person who benefits is the tortfeasor, or, more likely, the tortfeasor's insurance company.

In the light of the above, and other, criticisms, it is hardly surprising that the Law Commission in its recent Consultation Paper (Law Commission, 1996) considered whether *Hunt* v. *Severs* should be reversed. It provisionally concluded, in cases where the services are gratuitously provided by a person other than the defendant, in favour of the result reached by the House of Lords, but dissented from the reasoning adopted by the court. As to the appropriate mechanism for renumerating the carer, the Commission suggested either (a) the plaintiff should hold the damages awarded on trust (suitably clarified) for the providers of past and future care, or (b) a personal obligation should be imposed on the plaintiff to account to the past and future providers for those damages (para. 3.55). Where, however, the caring services are gratuitously provided by the *defendant*, the Law Commission recommended that there should be a legislative provision reversing *Hunt* v. *Severs* and laying down that the defendant carer's liability to pay damages for the plaintiff's nursing (or other care) should be unaffected by the plaintiff's liability to recompense the defendant as the person who provided the care (para. 3.68). There is much to be said for the provisional recommendations of the Law Commission and it is to be hoped that Parliament acts swiftly to remedy the currently unsatisfactory situation.

Other Expenses

Any other expenses that the plaintiff can show he has reasonably had to incur as a result of the accident are recoverable. So, in our example, if Arnold had to travel to and from hospital for a number of appointments, his travel expenses would be recoverable. He would also be able to recover, to be held on trust for her (*Hunt* v. *Severs*), the expenses of his wife if she visited him in hospital. If the plaintiff's expenses are unreasonable they will either be disallowed in full or reduced to a level the court considers reasonable.

If the plaintiff's house has to be adapted to provide easier access for him in his injured state the cost of the conversion will be recoverable. Where, however, the plaintiff's existing house is unsuitable for adaptation to suit his injured state, the plaintiff may have to move to more suitable accommodation. Where there is no difference in capital value between the two houses no problem arises, but if the new house is worth more, should the plaintiff be able to recover as damages the difference between the two? The courts have refused to award the full difference because to do so would overcompensate the plaintiff: on the plaintiff's death the extra capital value remains intact and therefore his estate gets a windfall. The solution adopted by the Court of Appeal in *Roberts* v. *Johnstone* [1989]

QB 878, the leading case in the area, was to treat the loss to the plaintiff not as a capital loss but as a loss of an annual sum representing the loss of the income on the capital expended. Thus, an interest rate (of 2 per cent) is applied to the extra capital value to turn it into an annual sum and then a multiplier is applied.

22.9 **Interest**

In our example, Arnold had to wait three years for his case to come to court. His right to damages for the injuries he suffered accrued at the moment he was injured and he has, therefore, been deprived of the damages to which he was entitled for three years. In order to compensate him for the loss of the right to use the money during those three years the court will, and indeed must, make an award of interest. The courts have in a series of cases laid down guidelines for the awarding of interest. First, interest is not payable on damages awarded either for future pecuniary or for non-pecuniary loss. This is logical in that the purpose of an award of interest is to compensate a plaintiff for having been deprived of the use of money he would otherwise have had. At the time of the trial the future loss has not yet been suffered and hence the plaintiff has not been deprived of the use of the money due to him.

Second, in respect of pre-trial loss, the rate of interest payable depends on whether the loss is pecuniary or non-pecuniary. Pecuniary loss attracts a rate approximately equivalent to half the normal short-term rates for the period from the accident to the trial. The rate is halved to take account of the fact that, while interest runs from the date of the accident, the losses have not all been incurred at that time. Non-pecuniary loss attracts a rate of only 2 per cent. The reason for this comparatively low rate is that damages for non-pecuniary loss are calculated at the *date of the trial* and therefore any changes in the value of money from the accident to the trial are already reflected in the award. The 2 per cent simply represents what the plaintiff could have gained over and above inflation by investing his damages. The Law Commission has criticised the 2 per cent interest rate applicable to non-pecunairy loss and suggested adopting the net rate of return on Index-Linked Government Secruities (ILGS) (Law Commission, 1995, para. 4.125). As the Law Commission has pointed out, 'ILGS now constitute the best evidence of the real return on any investment where the risk element is minimal' (para. 4.121) and, unlike the fixed 2 per cent rate, it is a more accurate reflection of the rate that could have been received by a person investing conservatively.'

22.10 **Collateral Benefits**

In our hypothetical example Arnold received a number of 'benefits' as a direct result of his accident. The benevolence of his friends, his prudence in paying his pension premiums and the 'benevolence' of the state in providing him with a mobility allowance all contributed to an improvement in his position after the accident. One might have thought that where the plaintiff's position has been, or will be, improved as a result of the tort these benefits would be taken into account; if they are ignored the plaintiff would be left in a better position than if no tort had been committed. However, the position with regard to collateral benefits is one of some complexity and while some collateral benefits are deducted, many are not. Our concern here is to indicate in outline the rules on deductibility.

The main source of compensation for accident victims is the social security system. Unsurprisingly, the question whether a plaintiff in receipt of social security payments should have to deduct such payments from any damages awarded has been a matter of considerable controversy. The law on the deduction of social security benefits has been radically changed and is now to be found in the Social Security Administration Act 1992, Pt IV, and the Social Security (Recoupment) Regulations 1990.

The main purpose of the provisions is to ensure that, in the case of accidents that occur on, or after, 1 January 1989, the *full* value of specified benefits received or to be received for a period of five years from the date of the accident or, if shorter, from the date of the accident to the settlement of the plaintiff's claim, should be deducted. While at common law (*Gaskill* v. *Preston* [1981] 3 All ER 427) no deduction from damages payable would have been made where the award did not include an amount representing 'loss of earnings or profits' because the plaintiff was not working, the position is different under the Act. In *Hassall* v. *Secretary of State for Social Security* [1995] 3 All ER 909, the Court of Appeal held that benefits received by unemployed plaintiffs should be deducted from the damages awarded even where that award consisted wholly of damages for non-pecuniary loss. The recoupment scheme, which is administered by the Compensation Recovery Unit, applies to most social security benefits and all compensation payments in excess of £2500. Before making any compensation payment, the defendant is required to apply to the Secretary of State for a certificate of total benefit. Once furnished with such a certificate, the defendant should deduct the amount specified from the damages payable and furnish the plaintiff with a certificate of deduction. The defendant should then pay to the Secretary of State an amount equal to that which is required to be deducted. The aim of the provisions is to ensure that the plaintiff is not over-compensated and that the defendant's liability is not reduced simply because the plaintiff is in receipt of state benefits. Thus, in our example, the £15 per week Arnold receives as mobility allowance will have to be deducted for a period of five years (or shorter, if his claim is settled before then).

Although s. 22 has the effect of ending 'double compensation', at least for a maximum of five years, the area of collateral benefits remains one of considerable complexity. For example, the recoupment provisions of s. 22 do not apply to 'exempt payments'. Included among 'exempt payments' are 'small payments', a term applied to payments not exceeding £2500. In respect of small payments, the complicated rules of s. 2(1) of the Law

Reform (Personal Injuries) Act 1948, which previously governed all cases regardless of size, are applied. Under these rules the compensator is entitled to offset half of any specified benefits received or to be received for five years from the date the cause of action accrued. The Secretary of State has no right to 'claw back' any of the sums so deducted.

Where the benefit received is not specified in s. 22, the common law continues to apply. The decisions in this area are often not easy to reconcile. However, it is possible to identify a number of factors that appear to have influenced the courts in reaching their decisions. Where the benefit received is the result of the generosity of others the courts have refused to allow deduction. Thus charitable or *ex gratia* payments are not deducted. The reason behind this appears to be a understandable reluctance to discourage charitable giving. The £15 000 paid to Arnold as a result of the appeal would not, therefore, be deductible.

Where a plaintiff has paid for, or in some sense earned, his 'benefit' the courts have generally refused to deduct the 'benefit' Thus, where a person benefits from a contract of insurance he has taken out or sets up his own pension scheme (even where his employer contributes to the scheme: *Smoker* v. *London Fire and Civil Defence Authorities* [1991] 2 AC 502), this has been held to be non-deductible. By way of contrast, where the benefit is financed by taxation or by the defendant himself the courts have tended to insist on deductiblity. Thus long-term sickness benefits payable under an insurance scheme run by the defendant employers have been held to be deductible as have sick pay and wages.

22.11 Damages for Death

The death of a person can have two effects in the law of torts. First, it may affect existing tortious actions in which the plaintiff is involved. Second, it may give rise to a cause of action in favour of the deceased's dependants. The first part of this section deals with the effect of death on existing causes of action. In the second part, the question of an action for dependency will be considered.

22.12 The Effect of Death on Existing Causes of Action: The Law Reform (Miscellaneous Provisions) Act 1934

At common law any cause of action in which the deceased person was involved, whether as plaintiff or defendant, died with that person. This rule was abolished by the Law Reform (Miscellaneous Provisions) Act 1934. This provides, in s. 1(1), that 'all causes of action subsisting against or vested in [the deceased] shall survive against, or, as the case may be, for the benefit of, his estate'. Thus, if in our hypothetical example Arnold had been killed instantaneously in the accident caused by Simon, Arnold's cause of action would survive for the benefit of his estate. Similarly, if

Simon had also been killed in the accident, Arnold's estate would still have an action against Simon's estate.

The Act sets out a number of qualifications in respect of the right of the plaintiff to sue or claim damages. First, by virtue of s. 1(2)(a)(ii), no claim can be made in respect of loss of income for the period after the person's death. This is to prevent the defendant's double liability both to the dependants (under the Fatal Accidents Act 1976) and to the estate (suing in respect of the deceased's 'lost years'). In the case of instantaneous death, therefore, as there will be no non-pecuniary loss, all the estate will be able to recover are the funeral expenses (s. 1(2)(c)). If, however, the victim died some time after the accident but before the trial of any action against the tortfeasor, his estate will be able to recover damages for the earnings lost up to the date of death and also a sum of money in respect of any non-pecuniary losses suffered in that period. Where death is almost, but not quite, instantaneous, it appears from the case of *Hicks* v. *Chief Constable of the South Yorkshire Police* [1992] 2 All ER 65 that no damages for either pecuniary or non-pecuniary loss can be recovered. In *Hicks*, one of the several cases arising out of the Hillsborough football disaster, the House of Lords held that the plaintiff's estate had no claim under the 1943 Act in respect of either the fear of impending death or any pain and suffering they experienced in the moments before they died from traumatic asphyxia. Second, s. 1(2)(c) provides that the damages recovered for the benefit of the estate are to be calculated without reference to any loss or gain to the estate consequent on the death of the deceased. Thus if, to use our example, Arnold had taken out an insurance policy that accrued to the benefit of his estate on his death, this would not be taken into account in calculating the damages payable under the Act. Finally, any action for defamation dies with the deceased.

22.13 Claims by the Deceased's Dependants: The Fatal Accidents Act 1976

The original Fatal Accidents Act was passed in 1846, a time when, as a result of the Industrial Revolution, the number of industrial accidents was on the increase and an increasing numbers of close dependants were being left uncompensated for the loss of the family breadwinner. The purpose of the original Act was to remedy the perceived unfairness of the rule in *Baker* v. *Bolton* (1808) 1 Camp 493. This rule denied the existence of any claim on the part of dependants of a deceased person. In its original form the Act gave actions to the widow and children only; however, subsequent Acts have widened the class of those entitled to bring an action for the loss of dependency.

The Act of 1976, which was a consolidating statute, gives 'dependants' an action for the loss of their dependency provided certain criteria are met. The first requirement is that the death must have been caused by 'any wrongful act, neglect or default which is such as would (if death had not ensued) have entitled the person injured to maintain an action and recover damages in respect thereof . . .' (s. 1(1)). If the deceased would have had no action, neither will his dependants. Thus, if A went for a joyride in B's light aircraft knowing that B was extremely drunk and the aircraft crashed killing A, A's action would be likely to fail on the ground that he had voluntarily assumed the risk (see 11.3). In such a case, A's dependants would also be barred.

The second requirement is that the person claiming must be within the class of dependants set out in the Act. Since the Fatal Accidents Act of 1846, the class of persons categorised as dependants has been widened considerably. Section 1(3) of the Act provides that not only are husband, wife, former husbands and wives and legitimate children of the deceased within the class of dependants, but so too are: natural ascendants and descendants; any person *treated* by the deceased as his parent or child; adopted, illegitimate and step-children; brothers, sisters, and uncles and aunts and their issue; and any person who has been living as husband or wife of the deceased in the same household for at least two years prior to the death. Further, by s. 1(5), '(a) any relationship by affinity shall be treated as a relationship of consanguinity, any relationship of the half blood as a relationship of the whole blood, and the stepchild of any person as his child, and (b) an illegitimate person shall be treated as the legitimate child of his mother and reputed father.' While the coverage may seem broad, there are some notable exceptions. Most obviously, same-sex partners of the deceased are not within the class of dependants. The current system, under which Parliament adds to the existing list of dependants as and when it wakes up to changes in society's view of the 'acceptable' family, is unsatisfactory. Surely the better approach is to allow anyone who can show that he was 'factually' dependant on the deceased, other than as a business associate, to bring an action.

To claim under the Act not only must the plaintiff show that he is within the class of dependants, but also, that he was in fact *financially* dependant on the deceased. No damages are awarded to dependants under this head for their own mental distress (they may, of course, have their own cause of action against the defendant for negligently causing them 'psychiatric injury') or for the loss of society of the deceased. A fairly broad approach has, however, been taken to what is a financial dependency. If we were to assume in our example that Arnold had been killed as a result of the accident, both Gina, his wife, and Jane, his daughter, could recover for the loss of any financial support they suffered as a result of Arnold's death. As well as this, Gina may be entitled to claim for the loss of her husband's services, as she may have to incur the cost of hiring a gardener or general handyman to do the jobs which Arnold did before his death. Similarly, Arnold would be able to claim for the loss of his wife's services if she had been killed. Jane would also be entitled to recover for the loss of Arnold's services as her father.

As well as a dependant being able to claim for the loss of an *actual* dependency, claims for loss of a *potential future* dependency are allowed. Thus, in *Taff Vale Railway* v. *Jenkins* [1913] AC 1, the House of Lords allowed parents to recover for the loss of support their daughter, who was at the time of her death training to be a dressmaker, would have provided when she finished her training. Despite the *Taff Vale Railway* case it seems unlikely, if Jane had been killed in our example, that Arnold and Gina would have any claim in respect of any potential future support they might have received. The House of Lords stressed the requirement of a reasonable expectation of pecuniary benefits. In the case of very young children the possibility of future pecuniary benefit is too speculative to be recoverable.

In order to be able to recover for the loss of a dependency, not only must the loss be a financial one, but the pecuniary advantage that has been lost must also stem from a familial relationship. In *Burgess* v. *Florence Nightingale Hospital for Gentlewomen* [1955] 1 QB 349 the deceased and her husband were professional dancing partners. The husband sought to recover for the loss of his wife's services as a dancing partner. The court held that no damages were available to compensate the husband for this loss as the lost benefit arose out of their business partnership rather than the family relationship.

The Act also recognises two further claims. First, a claim may be made for damages for 'bereavement' under s. 1A of the Act. This provision allows for the payment of a fixed sum of £7500 to the wife or husband of the deceased and, where the deceased was a minor, to the parents of a legitimate child and the mother of an illegitimate child. It is not necessary to prove any actual mental suffering: this is presumed by law. Second, a claim may be made in respect of funeral expenses.

22.14 Assessment of Damages for Loss of Dependency

Once the plaintiff has established that he falls within the category of dependants and that he has suffered a loss of dependency that arose solely from the familial relationship the court will consider what is the appropriate measure of damages. The purpose of an award of damages in a fatal accidents claim is, in the words of Lord Diplock in *Mallet* v. *McMonagle* [1970] AC 166:

'to provide the widow and other dependants of the deceased with a capital sum, which, with prudent management, will be sufficient to supply them with material benefits of the same standards and duration as would have been provided for them out of the earnings of the deceased had he not been killed by the tortious act of the defendant.'

As in a personal injuries claim, damages are assessed by using the multiplier method.

In assessing the multiplicand, the starting point for the calculation is the deceased's net earnings (the deceased's earnings after tax and national insurance have been deducted). From this must be deducted the amount the deceased would have spent exclusively on himself. The deceased's share of the joint expenses, such as rent or mortgage payments, the cost of running a car and other general household bills are not deducted. The sum left after deducting the plaintiff's personal expenditure from his net earnings is what is left for the dependants. In practice, unless there is compelling evidence to the contrary, the courts simply deduct a conventional percentage from the net earnings to represent the plaintiff's personal expenditure. Where the family consists of husband and wife, a deduction of one third is made to represent the plaintiff's personal expenditure. Where there are children the deduction for personal expenditure is reduced to one quarter.

Once the multiplicand has been calculated the court proceeds to assess the appropriate multiplier. The multiplier will be set at a figure which, when multiplied by the multiplicand, provides the dependants with a sum of money that will compensate them for the loss of the material benefits that the deceased was likely to provide them over the estimated period of the dependency. However, unlike a personal injuries action where the multiplier is assessed as at the date of the trial, the multiplier in a Fatal Accidents Act action is generally assessed as at the date of death. The reason for this was explained by Lord Fraser in *Cookson* v. *Knowles* [1979] AC 556, where he said:

'[I]n a personal injury case, if the injured person has survived until the date of trial, that is a known fact and the multiplier appropriate to the length of his future working life has to be ascertained as at the date of trial. But in a fatal accident case the multiplier must be selected once and for all as at the date of death, because everything that might have happened to the deceased after that date remains uncertain.'

It will be recalled that the multiplier in an ordinary personal injury action is assessed at the date of trial. Why should the date generally chosen for assessment of the multiplier in actions under the Fatal Accidents Act be any different? Assessing damages is, as has been remarked, an inexact science. Knowledge of the future being denied to them, the courts have to make the best guess that they can based on such information as is available. In an ordinary personal injury action, the court does at least know what has happened to the plaintiff between accident and trial. Thus, the multiplier is assessed as from the date of trial. In an action brought under the Fatal Accidents Act, however, everything that might have happened, had the deceased not died, after the date of the death is uncertain. Nothing is gained in terms of certainty, therefore, by postponing the time of assesment of the *multiplier* until the time of trial. Thus, the multiplier is assessed from the date of death. Where, however, there is a substantial delay between the date of death and the trial, some adjustment to the multiplier may be appropriate to take account of the fact that one element of a dependency calculation is now less speculative (i.e. the continued survival of the dependant – see *Corbett* v. *Barking, Havering and Brentwood Area Health Authority* [1991] 2 QB 408).

In assessing what multiplier should be awarded in the case of a fatal accident there are, as Purchas LJ pointed out in *Corbett* v. *Barking Havering and Brentwood Health Authority*, at least five essential elements that must be considered: first, the likelihood of the provider of the support continuing to live; second, the likelihood of the dependants being alive to benefit from that support; third, the possibility of the providing capacity of the provider being affected by the changes and chances of life either in a positive or in a negative manner; fourth, the possibility of the needs of the dependant being altered by the changes and chances of life, again in a positive or negative way; finally, the discount necessary to take account of (a) the immediate receipt of compensatory damages in advance of the date when the loss would actually have been incurred, and (b) the requirement that the capital should be exhausted at the end of the period of the dependency.

To illustrate the application of this we must return to our original hypothetical. If we assume that Arnold has been killed immediately as a result of Simon's tortious act and, for the present, that his wife, Gina, is his only dependant, then in assessing the multiplier account must be taken of Arnold's and Gina's life expectancy. In ordinary circumstances a wife will be presumed to outlive her husband and thus the starting point for the calculation will be Arnold's life expectancy. This figure is then adjusted to take account of the vicissitudes of life, for example that Arnold or Gina may have died at a particularly young age due to illness or an accident or that Arnold may have lost his job or retired early. This figure is then adjusted to take account of the fact that Gina will receive the sum awarded before she suffers the actual loss and that the capital must be exhausted at the end of the period of dependency. As in a personal injuries action, the multiplier awarded is unlikely to be close to the deceased's estimated life expectancy. In our example Arnold's estimated life expectancy would be about 37 years. However, the multiplier awarded would be no more than 16.

Once the multiplier has been assessed the sum awarded is divided into special damages and general damages. Special damages are awarded for the pre-trial loss and attract interest at the same rate as pre-trial damages for pecuniary loss in a personal injuries action. General damages are awarded for the loss thereafter and do not attract interest.

So far we have dealt with the general approach taken by the courts in assessing the sums awardable in a fatal accident case. Some comments must now be made as to particular difficulties that arise in fatal accident claims. First, by virtue of s. 3(3) of the 1976 Act, the benefits accruing to a wife as a result of the prospects or fact of remarriage are not to be taken into account when considering a wife's claim in respect of her husband's death. This provision has, in relation to actual remarriage, been the subject of some criticism. The point has been made that where, after the death of her husband, a woman remarries a richer man it is somewhat unsatisfactory to compensate her on the basis that she suffered a loss as a result of her husband's death. To the contrary, she may be said to have gained from his death; she is now financially better off than she was before. While there is force in this objection, the provision can be justified on the basis that it accords with the general principle expressed in s. 4 of the Act that 'benefits which . . . accrue to any person from the deceased's estate *or otherwise as a result of his death* shall be disregarded' (emphasis added).

Second, claims by children of the deceased, although assessed using the same general approach as above, raise a number of different issues. In most cases the child's dependency will be presumed to end after he has completed his secondary education. Where a child is likely to proceed to tertiary education or, alternatively, to leave school at 16, the multiplier ·will be adjusted accordingly. Thus, in relation to a claim by a child, the issues identified by Purchas LJ in *Corbett* v. *Barking, Havering and Brentwood Area Health Authority* in the second, third and fifth criteria would be relevant.

More problematic is the assessment of the multiplicand in respect of a child's claim. If we return to and adapt our original example and assume that Gina had been killed in the accident and Jane had been uninjured, how would the court assess the multiplicand? Clearly Jane has been deprived of the services (physical, educational and moral) of her mother. These services have a value. How do the courts value such a loss? If, Gina was not employed but was instead looking after Jane full-time, the approach taken is usually to value the loss as the cost of a full-time nanny. Further, the Court of Appeal held in *Corbett* that the award of an additional sum to be added to the cost of hiring a nanny to take account of the fact that a parent does not work set hours and is in constant attendance may be justified. However, where the mother is in full-time employment and could only care for the children on a 'part-time' basis a discount may be made to the multiplicand.

22.15 Apportionment Between Dependants

Section 2(3) of the Fatal Accidents Act 1976 provides that '[n]ot more than one action shall lie for and in respect of the same subject matter of complaint.' Thus an action under the Act must be brought by the executor or administrator of the deceased's estate in the name of the dependants. As to the apportionment of any award, ss. 3(1) and 3(2) of the Act provide that such damages may be awarded as are proportioned to the injury resulting from the death to the dependants respectively and shall be divided among the dependants in such shares as may be directed. In practice the compensation paid to the spouse of the deceased will be the larger amount; the children, if any, will receive smaller shares. This may be justified on the basis that the spouse will maintain the children so long as they are dependants. Sums paid to a younger child will usually be greater than those paid to an older child on the basis that the expected dependency was longer.

22.16 Deductions in Dependency Cases

By s. 4(1) of the Act 'the benefits which have accrued or will or may accrue to any person from [the deceased's] estate or otherwise as a result of his death shall be disregarded'. Unlike the case of a living plaintiff, the general position in respect of a claim by dependants is, therefore, that no deductions will be made in respect of 'collateral benefits' accruing either to the estate or to dependants directly. Thus not only will no deduction be made where there would be no deduction in the case of a living plaintiff but there will also be no deduction even in the case of benefits that are deductible in the case of a living plaintiff. In the light of this difference in approach, it must be asked why it should be that dependants are more favourably treated than living plaintiffs? If the answer is that no reason exists, then which is the correct approach as a matter of policy: general deductibility of benefits or non-deductibility?

In *Stanley* v. *Saddique* [1992] 1 QB 1 the Court of Appeal held that s. 4 applied to all forms of material benefit and was not just confined to direct pecuniary benefits. In *Stanley* v. *Saddique* the infant plaintiff's mother was killed. The court held that the benefits, in terms of a more stable family situation, accruing to the infant plaintiff as a result of his father's remarriage were, by virtue of s. 4, to be disregarded. Thus, it would appear to be the case that if the plaintiff's wife is killed and he remarries a much richer woman, this should not be taken into account in assessing his loss of dependency. If the 'benefit' is provided by the defendant, however, it is arguable that the position is different. In *Hayden* v. *Hayden* [1992] 1 WLR 986, the Court of Appeal held that, where a father (who was the tortfeasor in respect of a road accident in which his wife was killed) had given up work to look after their infant child, his services were not a benefit that accrued as a result of the death: his daughter acquired nothing new as a result of the death.

22.17 Property Damage and Economic Loss

The basic principle for the assessment of damages is that the plaintiff should be put in the same position as if the tort had not occurred and this principle applies to the recovery of damages for loss of, or damage to, property and the recovery of damages for pure economic loss, as well as to the recovery of damages for personal injury.

Where, as a result of the defendant's tort, the plaintiff's property has been lost or damaged, the plaintiff is entitled to compensation for the loss of its value to him. The usual measure where there is total loss or destruction is the market value of the lost property assessed at the time and place of the loss. So, for example, if owing to the defendant's negligence the plaintiff's car was damaged beyond repair, the plaintiff would be entitled to recover in damages an amount that would enable him to replace his lost car valued as at the time the loss occurred.

Where the plaintiff obtains a brand new replacement for his damaged property, must he give credit for its 'betterment'? No clear answer can be given. In *Harbutt's Plasticine Ltd* v. *Wayne Tank and Pump Co* [1970] 1 QB 447 it was held that no credit should be given because to insist on this would be to insist that the plaintiff improve his property. However, where the plaintiff's property is very old and would have needed replacement in the near future it is likely that the courts would insist that credit be given and that the damages would be reduced accordingly.

Where the plaintiff's property is merely damaged and can be repaired, damages may be assessed by reference either to the diminution in value of the property or to the cost of cure. Diminution in value is usually assessed by taking the difference between the market price for damaged and undamaged property; the cost of cure is assessed by reference to the cost of repair or reinstatement. Useful guidance on the choice between the two measures in the context of damage to real property can be found in Donaldson LJ's judgment in *Dodd Properties* v. *Canterbury City Council* [1980] 1 All ER 928. After identifying the two measures he said:

> 'Which is appropriate will depend on a number of factors, such as the plaintiff's future intentions as to the use of the property and the reasonableness of those intentions. If he reasonably intends to sell the property in its damaged state, clearly the diminution in capital value is the true measure of damages. If he reasonably intends to continue to occupy it and to repair the damage, clearly the cost of repairs is the true measure. And there may be in-between situations.' (p. 938)

Where a claim is made in relation to damage to real property there is no invariable practice as to which measure is used. Each case depends upon its own facts. However, courts have awarded damages on the basis of the cost of cure notwithstanding that the amount claimed was considerably in excess of any diminution in the value of the property. Such an approach is understandable, particularly in relation to domestic property, where the plaintiff will often want to repair the damage caused by the tort in order that he can go on living there. Where a claim is made in respect of damage to goods, the almost invariable basis of assessment of such loss will be cost of cure. This reflects the general practice that goods are usually owned for use rather than sale. However, if it could shown that the damaged goods were owned for sale rather than use and the repair costs were considerably in excess of any diminution in their market value, then the diminution in the market price should be the appropriate measure.

In the case of both loss of and damage to property, damages for consequential loss may be recoverable. Thus, where as a result of the tort the plaintiff is forced to hire a substitute chattel while his is repaired, the cost of hiring the substitute would be recoverable. Where the chattel is profit-earning, damages are also recoverable for any profits lost while it is repaired.

As we have seen, the English law of torts only rarely allows a plaintiff to recover in respect of a pure economic loss. As with any other type of harm, the basic principle for the assessment of damages in respect of such a loss is that the plaintiff should be put in the same position as if the tort had not occurred. It is beyond the scope of this book to discuss in any detail the issues that may arise in relation to the assessment of damages in relation to such loss but one particular issue of general interest will be mentioned here.

Lay people often seek advice of professionals before entering into particular types of transaction. Thus, a solicitor may be consulted about legal problems likely to arise in relation to the sale of a company and a surveyor is invariably asked to value a house before it is purchased. A difficulty may arise in such cases in ascertaining the extent of the professional's liability if the advice which he gives is negligent. Is the professional in such a case liable for all the foreseeable consequences that flow from the advisee entering into the transaction or just the consequences of the advice being incorrect? By way of example, in *South Australia Asset Management Corporation* v. *York Montague Ltd* [1996] 3 All ER 365 (HL) a valuer, engaged by a lender to value a property on which the lender was considering making a loan, negligently over-valued the property. The lender relying, *inter alia*, on the valuation, lent money to a borrower on the security of the property. Had the lender known the property's true valuation it would not have lent at all. Soon after the loan was made property prices collapsed and the borrower defaulted on the loan; the security proved inadequate to repay the loan. The lender sued the valuer, claiming that had it known the true value of the property it would not have entered into the transaction at all and, therefore, that it was entitled to recover damages for *all* the consequences that flowed from its having entered into the transaction. In other words, the lender was claiming that in a case such as this the valuer would bear the whole risk of a transaction that but for its negligence would not have happened, *including* any loss attributable to the market fall.

The Court of Appeal (reported as *Banque Bruxelles Lambert SA* v. *Eagle Star Insurance Co Ltd* [1995] 2 All ER 769) agreed with the lender. Where the lender would not, absent negligence, have entered into the transaction (a so-called 'no transaction' case) the valuer should bear the whole risk of any transaction going wrong. However, if, absent negligence, the lender would have gone ahead but would have lent less or on different terms (the 'successful transaction' cases), the lender could recover as damages only the difference between what he actually lost and what he would have lost if he had lent the lesser amount. In the House of Lords, Lord Hoffman held that the Court of Appeal had started at the wrong point. As his Lordship pointed out, 'Before one can consider the principle on which one should calculate the damages to which the plaintiff is entitled as compensation for the loss, it is necessary to decide for what kind of loss he is entitled to compensation.' A duty of care, as we have seen, does not exist in the abstract. Not only must the plaintiff establish that a duty was owed to him but also that it was a duty in respect of the kind of loss that was suffered. Until the scope of the duty was established, damages could not be assessed because a defendant is liable only for the consequences of his breach of duty. What then was the scope of the defendant's duty in this case? It was, according to Lord Hoffman, to provide information to the lenders to help them to decide whether to lend money on the property or not. It was not a case where the adviser undertook a duty to advise the plaintiff whether to enter into a particular transaction or not. The valuation was simply one of the factors to be considered by the plaintiff in deciding whether to lend money on the property. Thus, the extent of the valuer's liability was limited to the consequences of the advice given being wrong. The consequences of the valuer's advice being wrong was that the lender had less security than it thought it had. The consequences did not, however, include the market fall: that would have happened regardless of the valuer's negligence.

The case is by no means an easy one, but it is suggested that the principles on which it is based are correct. Prior to any assessment of damages, the scope of the defendant's duty must be established in order to ascertain whether the defendant undertook merely to *supply information* or whether he undertook to give the plaintiff advice as to whether to enter into a transaction or not. If the duty was only to *supply information* the professional must take reasonable care to ensure that the information is correct but if he is negligent he is liable *only* for the consequences of that information being incorrect. He is not responsible for all the consequences that flowed from the lender entering into the transaction. Again, where the adviser's duty was to give the advisee advice as to whether to enter into a transaction, the adviser is liable for all the consequences of his advice being incorrect. In this case, however, a foreseeable consequence of the defendant's negligence would be that the plaintiff entered into a transaction that he would not otherwise have entered into. The plaintiff would, therefore, be entitled to compensation for all the consequences of that.

22.18 Injunctions

Instead of, or sometimes in addition to, the award of damages a court may grant the plaintiff an injunction. An injunction is an order of the court restraining the commission of some wrongful act or ordering the defendant to take some positive steps to rectify a wrongful act. Originally an injunction could only be granted by the Court of Chancery; today, however, any division of the High Court may grant one. As an injunction is an equitable remedy it is never available 'as of right'. Instead the issue of an injunction lies within the discretion of the court. In this section we look briefly at four different types of injunction. These are: prohibitory, mandatory, interlocutory and *quia timet* injunctions.

A prohibitory injunction is, as its name suggests, an order of the court that restrains the defendant from committing or continuing a wrong. Injunctions are commonly sought to prevent or stop a nuisance or in cases of continuing or repeated trespasses. However, there seems to be no reason why an injunction should not be granted to prevent the commission or continuation of other torts. Where liability has been established and where there is a likelihood of recurrence or continuation the plaintiff will nearly always be granted this type of injunction. In rare cases (considered below) damages may be awarded in substitution for an injunction.

A mandatory injunction differs from a prohibitory injunction in that, instead of preventing or restraining the defendant from doing a wrongful act, it orders the defendant to take positive steps to rectify that which he has already done. In *Redland Bricks Ltd* v. *Morris* [1969] 2 All ER 576 the House of Lords held that a mandatory injunction would only be awarded where three criteria are satisfied. These are: (a) damages are not a sufficient or adequate remedy; (b) the defendant has acted wantonly or unreasonably in relation to his neighbour; (c) the terms of the injunction can be stated clearly such that the defendant can know what it is he has to do.

An interlocutory injunction is a provisional and temporary injunction that is designed to restrain the commission or continuance of an activity pending the final settlement of the plaintiff's claim. In *American Cyanamid Co* v. *Ethicon Ltd* [1975] AC 396 the House of Lords held that for an interlocutory injunction to be granted there must be a serious question to be tried. If there is, then the court must decide whether, on the balance of convenience, to award an injunction. In considering whether the balance of convenience lies in favour or against interlocutory relief the court should take into account whether damages would be an adequate remedy for the plaintiff, whether the plaintiff's undertaking in damages gives the defendant adequate protection if the plaintiff loses at trial and whether the preservation of the status quo is important enough to demand an injunction. Where, after considering these factors, the court is of the opinion that the balance of convenience is 'even' the court may consider the relative merits of the two parties' cases.

Usually an injunction will only be awarded where a tort has already been committed. However, where, to use the language of Lord Upjohn in *Redland Bricks Ltd* v. *Morris*, 'the plaintiff shows a very strong probability on the facts that grave damage will accrue to him in the future' a *quia timet* injunction may issue. *Quia timet* actions are, therefore, ordered to prevent threatened torts. Lord Upjohn, however, made clear that a *quia timet* injunction would only be awarded where the threatened or intended damage was imminent and where damages would be an inadequate remedy.

Lord Cairns' Act (now Supreme Court Act 1981, s. 50) allows damages to be awarded 'in addition to, or in substitution for, an injunction'. However, as we have seen, the general rule is that where a plaintiff can show that his legal rights will be violated by the defendant he will be entitled to the grant of an injunction. Section 50 of the Act was not intended to alter that by licensing 'judicial expropriation' of the plaintiff's property. But it must not be forgotten that the award of an injunction is, like any equitable remedy, discretionary. In many cases an injunction will be granted almost as 'of course', but one will never be granted if this would cause 'injustice' or 'be oppressive' (see the judgments of Millet LJ and Sir Thomas Bingham MR in *Jaggard* v. *Sawyer* [1995] 2 All ER 189). It is in such cases that the award of damages in substitution of an injunction may be appropriate. The court in *Jaggard* v. *Sawyer* accepted that the well-known passage from the judgment of Smith LJ in *Shelfer* v. *City of London Electric Lighting Company* [1895] 1 Ch. 287, pp. 322–3 provided a good working rule to the exercise of the discretion. In *Shelfer*

Smith LJ said: '(1) If the injury to the plaintiff's legal rights is small, (2) And is one capable of bing estimated in money, (3) And is one which can be adequately compensated by a small money payment, (4) And the case is one in which it would be oppressive to the defendant to grant an injunction: – then damages in substitution for an injunction may be given.'

Summary

22.1 The purpose of an award of damages in tort is to put the injured person in the position he would have been in had no tort occurred. The overriding principle of the law is to compensate the plaintiff fully for his loss.

22.2 In certain circumstances the purpose of an award of damages may not be to compensate the victim. Awards of contemptuous, nominal or exemplary damages are made for purposes other than to compensate the plaintiff. Aggravated damages are, however, intended to be compensatory.

22.3 Damages are recoverable once only. This rule has two aspects. First, the plaintiff cannot bring a second action on the same facts simply because his injury turned out to be worse than he had originally thought. Second, damages are payable in a lump sum once and for all. There exist three exceptions to this: an award of interim damages; an award of provisional damages; and structured settlements.

22.4 Where a court makes an award of damages the amount will be divided between special and general damages.

22.5 Newspapers often report the conclusion of litigation involving a very large award of damages. Excessive concentration on these reports obscures the fact that most people who are injured as a result of a tort do not pursue legal action and of those who do the vast majority of their claims are settled out of court for comparatively small sums of money. The formal rules of damages must be set against that background.

22.6 Damages may be awarded for both pecuniary and non-pecuniary losses.

22.7 Non-pecuniary losses are those that are not readily quantifiable in money terms. Pain and suffering, loss of amenities and the injury itself are examples of non-pecuniary loss. An award of damages for loss of amenities is made for the fact of their deprivation, while an award of damages for pain and suffering is made only when the plaintiff actually experiences the pain and suffering. Although it is obviously difficult to put a figure on these non-pecuniary losses, the courts assess damages by having regard to previous cases.

22.8 Pecuniary loss is the financial loss the plaintiff suffers consequent upon his injury. The main item of pecuniary loss is likely to be loss of earnings but also recoverable are medical and other expenses. Damages for loss of earnings are divided into pre-trial and post-trial loss. For post-trial losses the court seeks to award a sum of money that when invested will produce annually out of capital and investment income a sum equivalent to the total earnings that the plaintiff has lost. This is assessed by the multiplier method.

22.9 Interest is payable on all pre-trial losses. The rate of interest payable depends upon the type of loss suffered. No interest is payable on post-trial losses.

22.10 Charitable payments and payments under an insurance policy are not to be taken into account in assessing the damages payable to the plaintiff. Virtually all other benefits that accrue to the plaintiff as a result of the tort must be taken into account in some way. The deduction of social security benefits is governed largely by statute.

22.11   The death of a person can have two effects in the law of torts. It may affect existing causes of action in which the plaintiff is involved and it may give rise to a cause of action in favour of the deceased's dependants.

22.12   Section 1(1) of the Law Reform (Miscellaneous Provisions) Act 1934 provides that any cause of action subsisting against or vested in the deceased survives for the benefit of, or against, the deceased's estate. No damages are payable under the Act in respect of loss of income for the period after the deceased's death.

22.13   The Fatal Accidents Act 1976 gives a cause of action to 'dependants' (defined in s. 1(3)) for loss of a dependency. In order to recover a dependant must show that he was financially dependent on the deceased and that that dependency arose from a familial relationship. A more limited class of persons can recover damages for bereavement (s. 1A). Funeral expenses are also recoverable under the Act.

22.14   The purpose of an award under the Fatal Accidents Act 1976 is to provide the dependant with a capital sum that will be sufficient to supply him with material benefits of the same standard and duration as would have been provided for him out of the earnings of the deceased had he not been killed. The method of assessment is again the multiplier method, appropriately modified.

22.15   An action under the Fatal Accidents Act 1976 is usually commenced, on behalf of the dependants, by the deceased's executor or administrator. Each dependant recovers such damages as are proportioned to the loss suffered as a result of the death.

22.16   By virtue of s. 4 of the Act, any benefit accruing to a person as a result of the deceased's death is not to be taken into account when assessing damages. The courts have held that s. 4 is not just confined to direct pecuniary benefit but instead applies to all forms of material benefit.

22.17   Where property has been totally lost, the usual measure of damages is the market value of the lost property assessed at the time and place of the loss (i.e. the replacement value). Where the plaintiff's property is only damaged, a court may award damages based on either diminution in value or cost of cure. Damages may be recovered for any consequential loss.

22.18   Where a tort is threatened or likely to be repeated or continued, a court may grant an injunction. An injunction is an order of the court restraining the commission of some wrongful act or ordering the defendant to take some positive steps to rectify a wrong. The injunction is an equitable remedy and is never available as of right. Four types of injunction are considered in the text. These are: prohibitory, mandatory, interlocutory and *quia timet*. Damages may sometimes be awarded in addition to or, rarely, in substitution for, an injunction.

Exercises

22.1   What is the purpose of an award of damages in tort? How does it differ from the purpose of an award of damages in contract?

22.2   When are exemplary damages available in a tortious action? Is the existing English law satisfactory (see Law Commission, 1993)? Should the victim of a tort be able to recover exemplary damages?

22.3   When are aggravated damages awarded? Are they truly compensatory? Should damages be recoverable in respect of such intangible injuries as injury to feelings, injury to dignity or indignation?

22.4   What is a structured settlement? Why has it been described as 'the greatest advance in personal injury law of recent times' (Lewis, 1988)? Should a court have the power to order a structured settlement?

22.5 Why should an unconscious plaintiff be able to recover damages for loss of amenities? Should the courts continue to award damages for non-pecuniary loss?

22.6 How do the courts assess loss of future earnings? Why is the multiplier rarely equal to the number of years of work the plaintiff would have been likely to do? Why are the courts still wary of actuarial evidence? Should the assessment of multipliers be based on an assumed *real* rate of return of 4 per cent to 5 per cent as currently?

22.7 Should a plaintiff be able to recover damages for the 'lost years'?

22.8 Why are the multipliers awarded in cases of personal injury to young children comparatively low? Why can a child not recover for the 'lost years'?

22.9 A's wife gives up her job as a partner in a City solicitor's office to nurse him. She was earning £100 000 per annum. Can A recover this amount in respect of cost of nursing? Should A have to hold the damages awarded on trust for his wife? What alternatives exist to this approach?

22.10 Why should the cost of private medical care be recoverable?

22.11 Why are benefits generally taken into account when considering an action for personal injuries when they are not taken into account when assessing damages in respect of death? Is there an underlying rationale for the different treatment of different benefits in a personal injuries action?

22.12 Why are no damages recoverable under the Law Reform (Miscellaneous Provisions) Act 1934 in respect of loss of income in the period after the deceased's death?

22.13 Is the current list of 'dependants' in the Fatal Accidents Act 1976 satisfactory? How do the courts assess damages under the Act of 1976? Should the fact of remarriage be taken into account when assessing damages for loss of a dependency?

22.14 What are: prohibitory injunctions, mandatory injunctions, *quia timet* injunctions and interlocutory injunctions? When will damages be awarded in lieu of an injunction?

22.15 A car crash leaves a number of people dead or injured. Liability for the accident was not disputed. Advise the following parties on the damages they may recover.

   (i) Alpesh, aged 4, is left unconscious in a coma from which it is feared that he will never recover. His life expectancy is 47 years. He is sustained in a private hospital. All the costs of the private care are covered by a health insurance policy.

   (ii) Bettina, a 32-year-old bus driver and keen fun-runner, loses a leg in the accident. Before the accident she was earning £10 000 per annum. Afterwards, she is unemployed for two years while she recovers and then is able to take a clerical job earning £8000 per annum. For the first 18 months of her recovery Bettina's lover, Cynthia, is given unpaid leave from her job at a bank where she was earning £50 000 per annum, to nurse Bettina back to health. A year after the accident, the Department of Social Security agree to pay Bettina £20 per week in severe disablement allowance. Her case on quantum is heard 4 years after the accident.

   (iii) Deborah is killed immediately in the accident. She is survived by Edward, her boyfriend of the last several years, and their two young children. As a result of an argument Deborah and Edward had lived apart for the four months preceeding the accident; however, hopes of a reconciliation were high. Deborah was 36 at the time of the accident and earned £50 000 per annum as a partner in a major solicitor's firm. Edward, also a solicitor, had left work to bring up the children, but expects to return to work after a couple of years. Just before the trial on quantum, Edward marries Fiona, who has just inherited £2 million. Fiona wants to stay at home and look after the children full-time.

How would your advice have been different if Deborah and Edward had been married?

345

Bibliography

Alexander (1972) 'The Law of Tort and Non-Physical Loss: Insurance Aspects', 12 *JSPTL* 119.
Allen *et al.* (1979) *Accident Compensation after Pearson* (Sweet & Maxwell).
Anderson (1994) in Markesinas & Deakin, *Tort Law*.
Atiyah (1967) *Vicarious Liability in the Law of Torts* (Sweet & Maxwell).
Atiyah (1972) 'Res Ipsa Loquitur in England and Australia', 35 *MLR* 337.
Atiyah (1989) *An Introduction to the Law of Contract*, 4th edn (Oxford University Press).
Baker (1990) *An Introduction to English Legal History*, 3rd edn (Butterworths).
Baker and Milsom (1986) *Sources of English Legal History* (Butterworths).
Bell (1983) *Policy Arguments in Judicial Decisions* (Oxford University Press).
Beyleveld and Brownsword (1991) 'Privity, Transivity and Rationality', 54 *MLR* 48.
Birks (1985) *An Introduction to the Law of Restitution* (Oxford University Press).
Birks (1991), 'Civil Wrongs: A New World', *Butterworths Lectures 1990–91*.
Bishop (1980) 'Negligent Misrepresentation through Economists' Eyes', 96 *LQR* 360.
Bishop (1982) 'Economic Loss in Tort', 2 *OJLS* 1.
Bowman and Bailey (1986) 'The Policy Operational Dichotomy – A Cuckoo in the Nest', 45 *CLJ* 430.
Buckley (1996) *The Law of Nuisance*, 2nd edn (Butterworths).
Burrows (1994) *Remedies for Torts and Breach of Contract*, 2nd edn (Butterworths)
Burrows (1993), 'The Scope of Exemplary Damages', 109 *LQR* 358.
Calabresi (1970) *The Costs of Accidents* (New Haven, CT).
Calcutt (1990) *Report on Privacy and Related Matters* (HMSO), Cmnd 1102.
Calcutt (1993) *Review of Press Self-Regulation* (HMSO), Cm 2135.
Cane (1989) 'Economic Loss in Tort: Is the Pendulum out of Control', 52 *MLR* 200.
Cane (1996) *Tort Law and Economic Interests*, 2nd edn (Oxford University Press).
Cane (1993) *Atiyah's Accidents, Compensation and the Law*, 5th edn (Butterworths).
Clerk and Lindsell (1995) *Torts*, 17th edn, ed. M. Brazier (Sweet & Maxwell).
Cornish and Clark (1989) *Law and Society in England 1750–1950* (Sweet & Maxwell).
Craig (1994) *Administrative Law*, 3rd edn (Sweet & Maxwell).
Dewees and Trebilcock (1992), 'The Efficiency of the Tort System and its Alternatives: A Review of the Empirical Evidence', 30 *Osgoode Hall LJ* 57.
Dias (1967) 'Trouble on Oiled Waters: Problems of the Wagon Mound (No. 2)' [1967] *CLJ* 62.
Dworkin (1986) *Law's Empire* (Fontana).
Fleming (1988) *The American Tort Process* (Oxford University Press).
Fleming (1989a) 'Probabilistic Causation in Tort Law', 68 *Can Bar Rev* 661.
Fleming (1989b) 'Property Damage–Economic Loss: A Comparative View', 105 *LQR* 508.
Fleming (1990) 'Requiem for Anns', 106 *LQR* 525.

Fleming (1992) *The Law of Torts*, 8th edn (The Law Book Co.).

Furmston (ed.) (1986) *The Law of Tort: Policies and Trends in Liability for Damage to Property and Economic Loss* (Duckworth).

Gearty (1989) 'The Place of Private Nuisance in the Modern Law of Torts', 48 *CLJ* 214.

Gilmore (1974) *The Death of Contract* (Ohio State University Press).

Givelber (1982) 'The Right to Minimum Social Decency and the Limits of Evenhandedness: Intentional Infliction of Emotional Distress by Outrageous Conduct', 82 *Columbia Law Review* 42

Goodhart (1966) Note, 82 *LQR* 444

Government Actuaries Department *Actuarial Tables with Explanatory Notes for Use in Personal Injury and Fatal Accident Cases* (The 'Ogden' Tables).

Green (1989) *Land Law* (Macmillan).

Grubb and Mullis (1991) 'An Unfair Law for Dangerous Products: The Fall of Anns' [1991] *Conv* 225.

Grubb and Pearl (1990) *Blood Testing, Aids and DNA Profiling: Law and Policy* (Jordan).

Harris (1988) *Remedies in Contract and Tort* (Weidenfeld & Nicolson).

Harris, Maclean, Genn, Lloyd Bostock, Fenn, Corfield and Brittan (1984) *Compensation and Support for Illness and Injury* (Oxford University Press).

Harris and Veljanovski (1986) 'Liability for Economic Loss in Tort', in Furmston (1986), 45.

Hart and Honoré (1985) *Causation in the Law*, 2nd edn (Oxford University Press).

Hedley (1995), 'Negligence – Pure Economic Loss – Goodbye Privity, Hello Contorts' [1995] *CLJ* 27.

Hepple and Matthews (1991) *Tort: Cases and Materials*, 4th edn (Butterworths).

Hitcham (1986) 'Some Insurance Aspects', in Furmston (1986), 191.

Holmes (1881) *The Common Law* (London).

Honoré (1983) 'Causation and Remoteness of Damage', *Int Enc Comp L*, XI, *Torts*, Ch. 7.

Huber (1988) *Liability: The Legal Revolution and its Consequences* (Basic Books).

Jaffey (1985) 'Volenti Non Fit Injuria', 44 *CLJ* 87.

Jolowicz (1987) 'Product Liability – Directive and Bill', 46 *CLJ* 16.

Judicial Studies Board (1994) *Guidelines for the Assessment of General Damages in Personal Injury Cases*.

Kemp (1984) 3 *CJQ* 120.

Kemp (1985) 101 *LQR* 556

Kemp and Kemp (1985) *The Quantum of Damages*, 4th edn.

Kennedy & Grubb (1994) *Medical Law*, 2nd edn (Butterworths).

Kennedy (1995) *Note* 3 *Med LR* 189

Kodilinye (1986) 'Public Nuisance and Particular Damage in Modern Law', 6 *LS* 182.

Kodilinye (1989) 'Standing to Sue in Private Nuisance', 9 *LS* 284.

Law Commission (1969) *The Interpretation of Statutes*, Law Com No 21.

Law Commission (1970a) *Civil Liability for Dangerous Things and Activities*, Law Com No 32, Cmnd 142.

Law Commission (1970b) *Civil Liability of Vendors and Lessors for Defective Premises*, Law Com No 40, Cmnd 184.

Law Commission (1976) *Report on Liability for Damage or Injury to Trespassers and Related Questions of Occupiers' Liability*, Law Com No 75 (HMSO).

Law Commission (1993) *Aggravated, Exemplary and Restitutionary Damages*, Consultation Paper No 132 (HMSO).

Law Commission (1994) *Structured Settlements and Interim and Provisional Damages*, Law Com No 224 (HMSO).

Law Commission (1994b) *How Much is Enough? A Study of Compensation Expereiences of Victims of Personal Injury*, Research Report No 225 (HMSO).

Law Commission (1995), *Liability for Psychiatric Illness: A Consultation Paper*, Consultation Paper No. 137 (HMSO).

Law Commission (1995b) *Damages for Personal Injury: Non-Pecuniary Loss*, Consultation Paper No 140 (HMSO)

Law Commission (1996) *Damages for Personal Injury: Medical, Nursing and Other Expenses*, Consultation Paper No 144 (HMSO).

Lewis (1988) 'Pensions Replace Lump Sum Damages: Are Structured Settlements the Most Important Reform of Tort in Modern Times?', 15 *JLS* 392.

Likierman (Chairman) (1989) *Professional Liability Review* (HMSO).

Lord Chancellors Department (1993) *Infringement of Privacy*.

Lunney (1996–7), 'Chances of Recovery in Tort' 7 *KCLJ* 101

Matthews and Lunney (1995) 'A Tortfeasor's Lot is Not a Happy One?, 58 *MLR* 395

McKendrick (1994) *Contract Law*, 2nd edn (Macmillan).

McKendrick (1990) 'Vicarious Liability and Independent Contractors – A Re-examination', 53 *MLR* 770.

Maitland (1936) *The Forms of Action at Common Law* (Cambridge University Press).

Markesinis (1987) 'An Expanding Tort Law – the Price of a Rigid Contract Law', 103 *LQR* 354.

Markesinis (1989) 'Negligence, Nuisance and Affirmative Duties of Action', 105 *LQR* 104.

Markesinis and Deakin (1992) 'The Random Element of their Lordships' Infallible Judgement: An Economic and Comparative Analysis of the Tort of Negligence from Anns to Murphy', 55 *MLR* 619.

Markesinis and Deakin (1994) *Tort Law*, 3rd edn (Oxford University Press).

Milmo (1996) 146 *NLJ* 222

Mullis (1991) 'Review of Tort Cases', *All England Rev* 396–8.

Mullis (1993) 'Wrongful Conception Unravelled', 1 Med LR 320.

Mullis and Oliphant (1991) Auditors' Liability', 7 *PN* 22.

Mullis (1997) 'Compounding the Abuse? The House of Lords, Childhood Sexual Abuse and Limitation Periods', 5 *Med LR* 22

Newark (1949) 'The Boundaries of Nuisance', 65 *LQR* 480.

Newark (1961) 'Non-Natural User and *Rylands* v. *Fletcher*', 24 *MLR* 557.

Newdick (1985) 'Strict Liability for Defective Drugs in the Pharmaceutical Industry', 101 *LQR* 405.

Newdick (1988) 'The Development Risk Defence of the Consumer Protection Act 1987', 47 *CLJ* 455.

North (1972) 'Breach of Confidence: Is There a New Tort?', 12 *JSPTL* 149.

O'Dair (1991) '*Murphy* v. *Brentwood District Council*: A House with Firm Foundations?', 54 *MLR* 561.

Oliphant (1996) 'Tort', 49 *CLP (Part I Annual Review)* 29.

Ogus, Barendt and Wikeley (1995), *The Law of Social Security*, 4th edn (Butterworths).

Pearson, Lord (Chairman) (1978) *Royal Commission on Civil Liability and Compensation for Personal Injury* (HMSO), Cmnd 7054.

Posner (1992), *Economic Analysis of Law*, 4th edn (Little, Brown & Co.).

Priest (1987) 'The Current Insurance Crisis and Modern Tort Law', 96 *Yale LJ* 1521.

Prosser (1953), 'Palsgraf Revisited', 52 *Mich L Rev* 1.

Prosser (1955) 'False Imprisonment: Consciousness of Confinement', *55 Columbia Law Review* 847.

Prosser and Keaton (1984) *On Torts*, 5th edn (West Publishing Co.).

Salmond and Heuston (1996) *The Law of Torts*, 21st edn by R. F. V. Heuston and R. A. Buckley (Sweet & Maxwell).

Schlechtriem (1989) 'Presentation of a Product and Products' Liability under the EC Directive', 9 *Tel Aviv Studies in Law* 33.

Shalleck *et al.* (1992) 'Five Approaches to Legal Reasoning in the Classroom: Contrasting Perspectives on *O'Brien* v. *Cunard*', *Missouri LR* 351.

Skegg (1988) *Law, Ethics and Medicine* (Clarendon Press).

Smith and Burns (1983) *'Donoghue* v. *Stevenson* – the Not So Golden Anniversary', 46 *MLR* 147.

Spencer (1987) 'Flooding, Fault and Private Nuisance', 46 *CLJ* 205.

Spencer (1989) 'Public Nuisance – A Critical Examination', 48 *CLJ* 55.

Stanton (1986) *Breach of Statutory Duty* (Sweet & Maxwell).

Stapleton (1986a) *Disease and the Compensation Debate* (Oxford University Press).

Stapleton (1986b) 'Products' Liability Reform – Real or Illusory?', 6 *OJLS* 392.

Stapleton (1988a) 'The Gist of Negligence: Part I (Minimum Actionable Damage)', 104 *LQR* 213.

Stapleton (1988b) 'The Gist of Negligence: Part II (The Relationship between Damage and Causation)', 104 *LQR* 389.

Stapleton (1991) 'Duty of Care and Economic Loss: A Wider Agenda', 107 *LQR* 249.

Stapleton (1994) *Product Liability* (Butterworths).

Stapleton (1995) 'Duty of Care: Peripheral Parties and Alternative Opportunities for Deterrence', 111 *LQR* 301.

Stapleton (1997) 'Negligent Valuers and Falls in the Property Market', 113 *LQR* 1.

Stevens (1964) *'Hedley Byrne* v. *Heller*: Judicial Creativity and Doctrinal Possibility', 27 *MLR* 121.

Sutherland (1992) 'Fair Comment by the House of Lords?', 55 *MLR* 278.

Tan (1981) 'A Misconceived Issue in the Tort of False Imprisonment', *MLR* 166

Tunc (1983) 'Introduction', *Int Enc Comp L*, XI, *Torts*, Ch. 1.

Warren and Brandeis (1890) 'The Right to Privacy', 4 *Harvard Law Review* 193

Wedderburn (1978) 'Natural Nuisances Again', 41 *MLR* 589.

Weinrib (1975) 'A Step Forward in Factual Causation', 38 *MLR* 518.

Weinrib (1995), *The Idea of Private Law* (Harvard University Press).

Weir (1989) 'Government Liability' [1989] *PL* 40.

Weir (1990) 'Statutory Auditor not Liable to Purchaser of Shares', 49 *CLJ* 212.

Weir (1991) 'Fixing the Foundations', 50 *CLJ* 24.

Weir (1992) *A Casebook on Tort*, 7th edn (Sweet & Maxwell).

Weir (1996) *A Casebook on Tort*, 8th edn (Sweet & Maxwell).

Weir (1996b) 'Swag for the Injured Burglar', *CLJ* 182

Whittaker (1989) 'European Product Liability and Intellectual Products', 105 *LQR* 125.

Williams (1951) 'The Aims of the Law of Tort', 4 *CLP* 137.

Williams (1960) 'Penal Legislation in the Law of Tort', 23 *MLR* 232.

Williams and Hepple (1984) *Foundations of the Law of Tort*, 2nd edn (Butterworths).

Winfield and Jolowicz (1994) *Tort*, 14th edn, ed. W. V. H. Rogers (Sweet & Maxwell).

Wright (1985) 'Causation in Tort Law', 73 *Cal L Rev* 1737.

Index